Eric G. Berger

Microprocessors

Principles,
Programming,
and Interfacing

Microprocessors

Principles, Programming, and Interfacing

Kenneth Muchow
Bill R. Deem

San Jose City College

Reston Publishing Company, Inc.
A Prentice-Hall Company
Reston, Virginia

Library of Congress Cataloging in Publication Data

Muchow, Kenneth.
  Microprocessors: principles, programming, and
interfacing.

  1. Microprocessors.   I. Deem, Bill R.   II. Title.
QA76.5.M76   1983   001.64   82–22990
ISBN 0–8359–4383–6

10 9 8 7 6 5 4 3 2 1

Printed in the United States of America

Contents

Chapter 3   LOGIC AND GATES 43

Chapter 4   FLIP-FLOPS AND REGISTERS 83

Chapter 5   MICROCOMPUTER CONCEPTS   111

Chapter 6   INTERFACE CIRCUITS   125

Chapter 7   PROGRAMMING CONCEPTS   151

Chapter 8   THE STACK AND INTERRUPTS   177

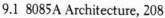

Chapter 11 INTERRUPTS FOR THE 8085A 257

Chapter 12 8085A SPECIAL DEVICES 271

Chapter 13 THE 6502 MICROPROCESSOR 297

Chapter 14 THE 8086 AND 8088 MICROPROCESSORS 313

Preface

The purpose of this text is to provide the computer technology student with the fundamental concepts of logic, logic circuits, microprocessors, and microcomputers. The text will help prepare students for positions in the industry by providing a firm foundation in the basic concepts of logic circuits. This text is written for students in technical schools, junior colleges, and community colleges, and for computer technicians currently employed in the field.

Although there have been rapid technological changes in the computer technology field in the past few years, the basic concepts have not changed. Concepts are covered first in the text, followed by examples and applications. A hypothetical microprocessor, called "LIMP," is introduced for the purpose of teaching concepts basic to all microprocessors. In addition, LIMP is used to introduce the concepts and circuits related to interfacing the processor to various peripherals.

Various 8- and 16-bit microprocessors are presented, with emphasis placed on the 8085A. The presentation of the 8085A includes its architecture, interface hardware, and programming. The instruction set for the 8085A is included in Appendix C. Each instruction is detailed with examples.

Chapter 1 introduces the concept of a computer system. The various number systems needed to understand and work with computer circuits and systems are introduced in Chapter 2, along with binary arithmetic.

Concepts of logic, including logic functions and Boolean algebra, are presented in Chapter 3. Also covered are gates, with particular emphasis on the TTL family. In Chapter 4 flip-flops and registers are discussed.

Chapter 5 introduces microprocessor and programming concepts using LIMP. Interfacing circuit concepts are covered in Chapter 6. Buses and bus concepts are also included.

Chapter 7 introduces the student to the concepts of machine and assembly language programming. Flowcharts, program structure, and the LIMP instruction set are all included in this chapter. Stacks and interrupt control input/output are covered in Chapter 8.

The architecture and bus structure of the 8085A are covered in Chapter 9. Chapter 10 is devoted to the programming of the 8085A. The instruction set, addressing modes, and advanced programming concepts are part of this chapter.

An in-depth study of interrupt input/output for the 8085A is provided in Chapter 11. Special devices for memory, input/output, and timing are presented in Chapter 12.

Chapter 13 is devoted to the 6502 microprocessor. The architecture, addressing modes, interrupt techniques, and interfacing are included.

The 8086 and 8088, 16-bit processors, are covered in Chapter 14. The architecture, bus structure, and addressing modes are presented.

The LSI-11, another 16-bit processor, is introduced in Chapter 15. The bus structure, addressing modes, and the instruction set are discussed.

We would like to express our appreciation to the many companies who were very helpful in making available to us their application notes, data sheets, and instruction sets. Special thanks also go to the other members of the Electronics Department at San Jose City College, and to Tony Zeppa at Evergreen Valley College, for their advice and support.

Chapter

1

Introduction to Computers

What is a computer? Is it a giant brain? Can it think? Can it be trained? Or is it less sophisticated and able only to follow instructions? If the latter is true, what are these instructions? What form do they take? What kinds of things can computers do, and, in general, how do they work?

To the neophyte there are many such questions that need to be answered. In this chapter we will attempt to give the student an overall picture of computers, microcomputers, and microprocessors.

Figure 1-1. A microcomputer system.

PARTS OF THE COMPUTER

Figure 1-2 is a block diagram of a computer system. Only major blocks are shown. Included is a block labeled PROCESSOR. The processor is made up of three major parts: the ALU (Arithmetic Logic Unit), REGISTERS, and a CONTROL UNIT. All arithmetic and logic opera-

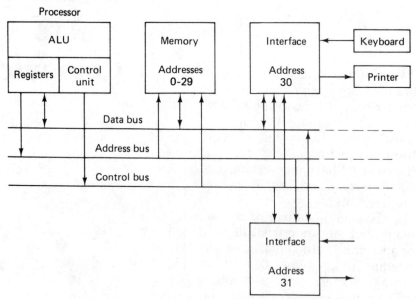

Figure 1-2. Block diagram of a simple computer system.

tions performed by the computer are performed in the ALU. The part labeled REGISTERS represents locations within the processor where information is stored. This information may be data, addresses, or instructions. The third part, the CONTROL UNIT, is the part of the processor that controls the sequence of operations of the system.

A second block is labeled MEMORY. The memory block is made up of many cells that can store binary numbers (1's and 0's). A typical computer would have thousands of these memory blocks. These binary numbers may represent instructions to be executed or data to be processed. Each binary number is stored in a location having a unique address. If a number is to be stored in or retrieved from memory, the address is used to identify the number's location.

There are two blocks labeled INTERFACE. The interface circuits are used to provide the appropriate electrical connections between the peripheral devices (keyboard, printer, etc.) and the rest of the system. The interface circuit at ADDRESS 31 is used to expand the number of peripherals connected to the system.

The processor communicates with other parts of the computer system by means of buses. Usually there are three: one for data, one for addresses, and one for control signals. A *bus* is a conductor or a group of conductors that has connections to all of the system's major blocks.

The number of conductors in the DATA BUS (Figure 1-2) is determined by the number of binary digits the processor is able to handle at a given time. For example, a processor with an eight-binary-digit capability uses eight lines in its data bus. Notice that arrows point in both directions between the data bus and all the major blocks. This is done to show that data can travel in both directions on the bus. Because of this feature, the data bus is referred to as a bidirectional bus. Data or instructions move on the data bus between the processor and memory or between the processor and peripherals (via the interface circuits).

The ADDRESS BUS is a number of conductors used to send addresses to memory and to the interface circuits. The information on this bus identifies where in memory we are going to store new data, or from where we are going to retrieve data previously stored. Information on this bus also provides for the selection of one of the interface circuits to input or output data from a peripheral device. Notice in Figure 1-2 that the arrows indicate that addresses originate in the processor only. The address bus is unidirectional—information moves in one direction only.

The CONTROL BUS is used in this system to tell memory and the interface circuits whether the processor is inputting, or whether it is outputting, data. There are two conductors in the control bus: READ and WRITE. If the processor is retrieving data from memory, or inputting data from a peripheral, it activates the READ line. If the processor is storing data in memory or outputting data to a peripheral, it activates the WRITE line.

The control bus in larger systems may have many more conductors, depending on the complexity of operations to be controlled.

To help understand how a computer works, let's substitute a human being for the processor. We'll call him Sam. In this analogy, Sam does not work as fast as the processor would, but he does follow instructions and he can remember (store) data. Sam's work station is at a mailroom sorting box. Each box, or "pigeon hole," is called an *address*. In our computer, these addresses are in the section called *memory*. Figure 1–3 shows the sorting box with addresses from 0 to 29, a total of 30 addresses.

Cards containing a sequence of instructions are located in boxes starting with the box whose address is 0 and ending with the box at address 9. The boxes contain the following instructions (see Figure 1–4):

Box Number (Address)	Card Contents
0	GET the card at address 20
1	READ the number on the card
2	REPLACE the card
3	GET the card at address 21
4	READ the number on the card
5	REPLACE the card
6	ADD the two numbers
7	WRITE the sum on a card
8	PUT the card in location 25
9	STOP

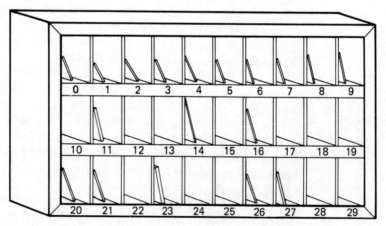

Figure 1–3. Mail sorting box with addresses numbered from 0 through 29.

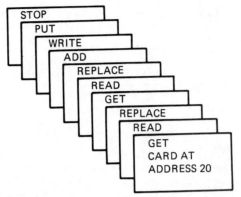

Figure 1-4. Contents of sorting box, addresses 0 through 9.

Sam executes the program in the following manner:

1. He goes to each address in sequence, starting with address 0
2. He removes the card, reads it, and then replaces it
3. He then follows the instruction on the card explicitly

Because the instructions are in plain language, there is no need to explain what the program does. However, notice that the first word of each instruction describes what kind of an operation is to take place, i.e., GET, READ, REPLACE, etc. Let's call this word the *operation code*. The remaining part of some of the instructions describes where a number is located. This part of the instruction is called the *operand address*. An operand is the data on which the operation is performed.

The instruction at address 0 contains two important parts: the first part is the operation word GET and the second part is the operand address—20. The other words in the instruction are redundant. It is understood, in this example, that the boxes contain cards. Furthermore, we do not need to say "address 20," we need only say "20." Therefore, the instruction may be shortened to only two words—GET 20. Carrying the thought one step further, notice that after the execution of the GET instruction, READ and REPLACE instructions always follow. If this is the case, then the three instructions may be combined into one. Therefore, the first three instructions could be represented by the single instruction READ 20. READ is the operation word, and 20 is the operand.

In a similar manner, the next four instructions can be simplified to "ADD 21" because inherent in the ADD instruction is a READ instruction. ADD is the operation code, and 21 is the operand.

WRITE and PUT would always be together, so the instruction WRITE 25 replaces the two.

After all the combining, the program would look like this:

Address	Operand Word	Operand Address
0	READ	20
1	ADD	21
2	WRITE	25
3	HALT	

To execute the program, Sam again goes to each address in sequence and executes the instruction at each address. At address 0, he reads and then replaces the instruction. He interprets that instruction (READ 20) to mean "Go to address 20, get the card at that address, read the number on the card, and then replace the card." Of course, Sam has to remember (store) what the number was!

He interprets ADD 21 to mean "Go to address 21, read the number on the card, replace the card, then add that number to the number previously saved." When Sam reads "WRITE 25," the instruction at address 2, he gets a card, writes the sum on the card, and then places the card at address 25. The instruction at address 3 tells him the job is done.

Now let's use our computer to execute the program. First of all, we can't execute the program until we store it in memory. Just as Sam's instructions were located at addresses 0 through 3, we will place our instructions at addresses 0 through 3 in memory. The format used to enter programs into the computer will be discussed in later chapters. In our system, we would place this program in memory from the keyboard. When we instruct the computer to run the program, the following sequence of events will happen: The processor places the address of the first instruction on the address bus, and then the control unit activates the READ line of the control bus. The combination of these two signals causes the instruction at address 0 (READ 20) to be placed on the data bus. (Actually, READ 20 was stored in memory as a binary number, and it is this binary number that is placed on the data bus, just as the binary number for address 0 was placed on the address bus.) This instruction is sent to the processor where the instruction is *decoded*. That is, the processor interprets the instruction. The instruction directs the processor to read the number stored at address 20.

After the processor decodes the instruction, it activates the READ line again and places address 20 on the address bus. The contents of address 20 is then placed on the data bus where it is sent to the processor and stored in one of the registers. The first instruction has now been executed.

The processor again activates the READ line and places address 1 on the address bus. The contents of address 1 is then placed on the data bus where it is sent to the processor for decoding. ADD 21 causes the READ line to be activated, and address 21 is placed on the address bus. The data at address 21 is placed on the data bus and is stored in a register in the processor. The processor then adds this data to the data stored previously and stores the sum in another of its registers.

Next, address 2 is placed on the address bus, and then the READ line is activated. The contents of address 2 is then placed on the data bus. This instruction (WRITE 25) is then decoded by the processor. The instruction causes the processor to activate the WRITE line and place address 25 on the address bus. The sum that was previously stored in a register in the processor is then placed on the data bus and sent to address 25, where it is stored.

The processor then places address 3 on the address bus, and then causes the READ line to be active. The contents of address 3 are placed on the data bus, the instruction is decoded, and the computer halts.

Of course we have simplified considerably the action of the processor in executing the program. Now that we're beginning to develop some understanding of the relationship between the different parts of the system, let's execute the same program, except that this time we will add two numbers that are entered from the keyboard. We will also examine the actions of the processor in more detail. Here is program 2:

Address	OpCode	Operand
0	IN	30
1	WRITE	20
2	IN	30
3	WRITE	21
4	READ	20
5	ADD	21
6	WRITE	25
7	OUT	30
8	HALT	

This program incorporates two more instructions—IN and OUT. These instructions allow us to input data from a keyboard and output data to a printer. Address 30 is used for the keyboard and printer. Let's consider how our computer might execute this program.

There are two phases related to the execution of each instruction. The first has to do with reading the instruction itself. It is called the *instruction phase*. The second deals with executing the instruction and is called the *execution phase*. Let's deal with the instruction phase first.

This phase is controlled by the control unit and is identical for all instructions. Its purpose is to read the instruction and to decode it. Depending on the opcode (operation code), new information is then passed to the control unit, which controls the system during the execution phase. One of the registers in the processor is called the Program Counter (PC). It contains the address of the instruction to be executed. First, the processor places this address (address 0) on the address bus. This causes the particular address in memory to be selected. Next, the control signal READ is issued by the control unit. This causes the memory to respond by placing the contents of the selected address on the data bus. The processor then takes the data and places it in another register called the Instruction Register (IR). Remember, the data that is now contained in the IR is the code for the instruction IN 30. The processor decodes this instruction and enters the execution phase.

In the execution phase, the processor places address 30 (operand address) on the address bus; this causes the interface circuit to be selected instead of memory. Then the control unit issues the READ signal again, causing the data from the keyboard to be placed on the data bus. The processor takes this data and saves it in one of its registers. The execution of the first instruction is complete.

One important point that must be clarified is that as soon as the address in the PC is used, the PC is incremented (1 is added to its contents) so that the PC contains the address of the next instruction. This occurs during the instruction phase.

The instruction phase for the second instruction is the same as for the first except that the address is now 1 instead of 0. After the instruction is read and decoded, the processor enters the execution phase. The processor accomplishes this by the following sequence: placing the operand address on the address bus (address 20), placing the data previously inputted on the data bus, and issuing a WRITE signal on the control bus. Memory responds by taking the data and storing it at the selected memory address (20). The second instruction has been executed.

The third instruction is exactly the same as the first instruction. When this instruction has been completed, a second number is in one of the registers in the processor. The fourth instruction is the same as the second except that the operand address is 21 instead of 20. We have saved the first number at address 20 and the second number at address 21.

The READ instruction is executed in the same manner as the IN instruction except that memory is being read instead of the keyboard. This instruction causes the contents of address 20 to be placed in a register in the processor.

When the instruction ADD 21 is decoded, address 21 is placed on the address bus and the READ line of the control bus is activated, causing the contents of address 21 to be placed on the data bus. The processor takes this data and adds it to the data previously read in the fifth instruction.

Next, the WRITE instruction causes the sum to be stored at address

25. In addition, the OUT instruction causes the sum to be printed. The OUT instruction is executed just like the WRITE instruction except that a peripheral is addressed instead of a memory location. Finally, HALT stops the processor.

If you have been wondering if the IN and OUT instructions are redundant, you are right. READ and WRITE could be used in their place. Because the interface circuits have unique addresses, the processor addresses them just like they were memory locations. IN and OUT were used in this example to differentiate between memory read and write operations and peripheral input and output operations.

The preceding example is intended to convey the basic concepts that are fundamental to all computers. Of course, large computers are much more complex. However, the basic concepts are the same. This is true for minicomputers as well as microcomputers.

What is the difference between large computers, minicomputers, and microcomputers? Well, except for the obvious, large computers have the ability to process larger numbers at a time, perhaps thirty-two binary digits or more! They also have many more circuits, allowing more than one operation to be executed at a time. All of this means that large computers can do more work in a given period of time.

Minicomputers are smaller; most process sixteen binary digits at a time. Operations tend to be executed one at a time, contributing to a slower *throughput* (computerese for the amount of work done in a given period of time).

Large computers and minicomputers have been constructed using small scale (SSI) or medium scale (MSI) integrated circuits (ICs). Each of these circuits uses less than 10,000 components (transistors, etc.). This means that a large number of ICs are required. Today's microtechnology has advanced to a point where it is possible to have tens of thousands of devices and components on a one-quarter-inch chip of silicon. This is known as LSI—Large Scale Integration.

Processors fabricated with this new technology are called microprocessors. Computers that use microprocessors are called microcomputers.

Some smaller microcomputers are entirely fabricated on a single chip. These chips contain the processor, memory, and the interface circuits. Typical applications for this kind of microcomputer are in consumer products such as microwave ovens, dryers, refrigerators, automobile ignition systems, and TV games.

Applications for the microprocessor are limited only by the ingenuity of the application designer. It has been said that "a microprocessor is a solution in search of a problem."

Questions

1. How are peripheral devices connected to the buses?
2. What is a bus?
3. Which of the buses is/are bidirectional?
4. Which of the buses is/are unidirectional?
5. What does the instruction IN 40 mean in our computer? Which part of the instruction is the op-code? Which part is the operand?
6. What does the instruction WRITE 15 mean in our computer? Which part of the instruction is the opcode? Which part is the operand?
7. During the instruction phase of an instruction, which control line is activated?
8. During the execution phase of an instruction, which control line is activated?
9. When the instruction ADD 21 was executed, where did the addition take place?
10. Where, in the processor, was the sum stored?
11. What is the register called that contains the address of the next instruction?
12. During which part of the instruction is the PC incremented?
13. What did IN 30 mean in program 2?
14. Which instructions caused the WRITE line to be activated?
15. What is the purpose of the Instruction Register?

Data
and
Number Systems

The basic tools for understanding computers are an understanding of the number systems used and an understanding of basic logic functions. Number systems are covered in this chapter. Logic functions are discussed in Chapter 3.

We all know and understand the decimal number system; this is the number system we use daily. In the computer world, the binary number system is the system used. All data is stored and manipulated inside the computer in binary. That is, within the computer all data is reduced to 1's and 0's. These 1's and 0's are stored in logic circuits called *registers*, or they are stored in *memory*. The size of a register or memory location varies according to the kind of computer used. Today's microcomputers will store either 8 or 16 binary digits in each location. Large computers may store as many as 125 binary digits in each location.

We normally enter data into the computer in some number system other than binary because entering data in binary is too time-consuming and too prone to error—too many 1's and 0's. Data is entered into the computer using the decimal, octal, or hexadecimal number systems. Octal and hexadecimal are used most often because they are more closely related to binary than is the decimal system.

It is important to our understanding of these number systems that we know how they are related one to another.

2.1   BINARY NUMBER SYSTEM

In the binary number system, there are two digits: 0 and 1. The binary system is used for internal computer operations because only two signal levels are required—as opposed to decimal where ten signal levels would be necessary. Because a digit in the units position has a value of 0 or 1, numbers greater than 1 cause a carry to the next position. Each position represents the base raised to a power. In base 10, the units position has a power of 10^0, the next position 10^1, and so on. Thus, a digit in any position other than the units position has a weight (value) depending on its position in the number. A 4, for example, has a weight of 4 in the units position, 40 in the 10's position, 400 in the 100's position and so on.

In binary, or base 2, the same reasoning applies. The units position has a power of 2^0, the next position 2^1, and so on, as illustrated in Figure 2-1. A binary digit in any position other than the units position has weight depending on its position in the number. A 1 has a weight of 1 in the units position, 2 in the 2's position, 4 in the 4's position and so on. Binary digits are called *bits* (a contraction of "binary digits"). Therefore, the digit in the units position is called the *least significant bit* (LSB), and so on until we reach the *most significant bit* (MSB).

MSB	4SB	3SB	2SB	LSB
2^4	2^3	2^2	2^1	2^0
16	8	4	2	1

Figure 2-1. Positional value of the first eight positions for the binary number system.

2.1.1   Binary–Decimal Conversions

Converting from base 2 to base 10 is quite easy. We convert the bit in each position to its decimal equivalent. These individual decimal numbers are then added together to get the decimal equivalent. If a 1 is present in a given position, the weight of that bit is added. If a 0 is present, the weight of that bit is not added. Consider the number 11010 in Example 2.1. The decimal equivalent is 26.

Example 2.1. $11010_2 = (?)_{10}$

Solution: $(1 \times 2^4) + (1 \times 2^3) + (0 \times 2^2) + (1 \times 2^1) + (0 \times 2^0) =$
$16 \quad + \quad 8 \quad + \quad 0 \quad + \quad 2 \quad + \quad 0 \quad = 26$

Because there are only 1's and 0's in binary, each bit position equals either the weight of that digit position, or it equals 0. In this example, the decimal values of the bit positions are added to get the decimal equivalent. In the 2^4, or 16's position, there is a 1. Therefore that bit position converts to 16. In the 2^3, or 8's position, there is a 1. That bit position converts to 8. In the 2^2, or 4's position, there is a 0. That bit converts to 0. In the 2's (2^1) position there is a 1. That bit position converts to 2. There is a 0 in the units position (2^0). Adding the numbers together, we get decimal 26.

Whenever converting from binary to decimal, find the value or weight of the MSB. Work down to the LSB, adding the weight of that position if a 1 is present, or a 0 if a 0 is present. Table 2–1 is a conversion table for all the computer number systems.

Example 2.2.   Change the following binary numbers to decimal numbers:
  (a) 1100   (b) 10001   (c) 101011   (d) 111101

Solutions:

(a) $1100_2 = (1 \times 2^3) + (1 \times 2^2) + (0 \times 2^1) + (0 \times 2^0) =$
  $\qquad\quad 8 \quad + \quad 4 \quad + \quad 0 \quad + \quad 0 \quad = 12$

(b) $10001_2 = (1 \times 2^4) + (0 \times 2^3) + (0 \times 2^2) + (0 \times 2^1) + (1 \times 2^0) =$
  $\qquad\quad\; 16 \quad + \quad 0 \quad + \quad 0 \quad + \quad 0 \quad + \quad 1 \quad = 17$

(c) $101011_2 = (1 \times 2^5) + (0 \times 2^4) + (1 \times 2^3) + (0 \times 2^2) + (1 \times 2^1) +$
  $\qquad\quad\; 32 \quad + \quad 0 \quad + \quad 8 \quad + \quad 0 \quad + \quad 2$
  $\qquad\quad (1 \times 2^0) =$
  $\qquad\qquad 1 \quad = 43$

(d) $111101_2 = (1 \times 2^5) + (1 \times 2^4) + (1 \times 2^3) + (1 \times 2^2) + (0 \times 2^1) +$
  $\qquad\quad\; 32 \quad + \quad 16 \quad + \quad 8 \quad + \quad 4 \quad + \quad 0$
  $\qquad\quad (1 \times 2^0) = \quad 1 \quad = 61$

Let's turn the process around and find the binary equivalent of a decimal number.

Example 2.3.   Convert 13_{10} to binary

Solution: Step 1. $\dfrac{13}{2} = 5 + 1$

  Step 2. $\dfrac{5}{2} = 2 + 1$

  $\qquad\qquad\qquad\qquad\qquad\qquad\qquad$ LSB

  Step 3. $\dfrac{2}{2} = 1 + 0$

  Step 4. $\dfrac{1}{2} = 0 + 1$ —MSB— 1   0   1   1

Because we are converting to base 2, we first divide the decimal number by 2 (step 1). The answer is 5 with a remainder of 1. This remainder is the LSB in the answer. The whole number left after this initial division (5) is again divided by 2 (step 2). The answer is 2 with a remainder of 1. This 1 is the bit in the 2^1 position. The whole number left (2) is divided by 2 (step 3). The result is 1 and a remainder of 0. This 0 is the bit in the 2^2 position. Step 4 is the final step because no further divisions are possible. The remainder in the final step is the MSB.

A second method of converting from decimal to binary is shown in the following example.

Example 2.4 Convert 167 to binary.

Solution: We start by looking for the highest multiple of 2 in 167, which is 128 (2^7). Therefore, we start assembling the binary number by placing a 1 in the MSB position, which has a weight of decimal 128. Because this bit has a weight of 2^7 in binary, it is referred to as bit 7. It is also called the 128-bit when referring to decimal system. The binary number then must be 1XXXXXXX, where "X" is either 1 or 0 depending on the conversion of the remainder of the number. Next, the remainder is determined by subtracting 128 from 167, which is 39.

Bit position 6 (2^6) has a weight of 64. Since 64 is greater than 39, a 0 is placed in this position. The remainder is still 39.

Bit position 5 (2^5) has a weight of 32. Because the remainder is greater than 32, a 1 is placed in this position and 32 is subtracted from the remainder. The new remainder is 7. This procedure is followed for each bit position. Can we use a 16? No, a 16 is too much. Put a 0 in the 16's (2^4) position. Now we have 1010XXXX. Can we use an 8? No, so put a 0 in the 2^3 position. Now we have 10100XXX. Can we use a 4? Yes. Our number is now 101001XX. Do we need a 2? Yes. Our number is now 1010011X. Do we need a 1 or 0 in the LSB position? We need a 1. Our binary number is 10100111. Any decimal number can be converted to binary in this manner. With practice, this method is faster than the method shown previously. The process is detailed in Figure 2–2.

Example 2.5. Convert the following decimal numbers to binary numbers:
(a) 7 (b) 34 (c) 89 (d) 203

Solutions: (a) 111 (b) 100010 (c) 1011001 (d) 11001011

2.2 OCTAL NUMBER SYSTEM

Octal, or base 8, is an important computer number system. Because there are eight digits in octal (0, 1, 2, 3, 4, 5, 6, 7), the digit of greatest value is 7—which is 1 less than the base. In counting, the sequence is 0 to 7. On the

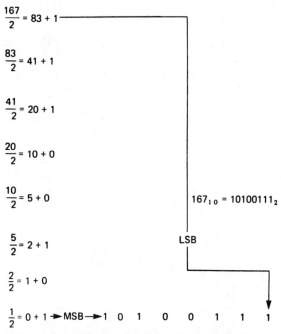

$$\frac{167}{2} = 83 + 1$$

$$\frac{83}{2} = 41 + 1$$

$$\frac{41}{2} = 20 + 1$$

$$\frac{20}{2} = 10 + 0$$

$$\frac{10}{2} = 5 + 0$$

$167_{10} = 10100111_2$

$$\frac{5}{2} = 2 + 1$$

LSB

$$\frac{2}{2} = 1 + 0$$

$\frac{1}{2} = 0 + 1 \rightarrow$ MSB $\rightarrow$ 1   0   1   0   0   1   1   1

Figure 2-2. Routine for converting 167_{10} to binary.

next count, we return to 0 in the units position (just as we do when we reach 9 in decimal) and a carry is generated. The resulting number is 10 and is read "one-zero". "One-zero" is equal to decimal 8 because the carry is equal to 8. This process continues—the sequence goes from 0 to 7 and back to 0 again. Each time a count greater than 7 is reached, a carry is generated.

In the octal number system, digits in the units position have the indicated value 8^0. Digits in the next position have *place value*. That is, digits in this position indicate the number of 8's present. This, then, is the 8's (8^1) position. The next position indicates the number of 64's (8^2) present, and so on, as shown in Figure 2.3. This concept of place value must be understood so that we can work in any base. Recall that in the number 56_{10} the 5 has a value of 50. The 5 is in the 10's position, so we have five 10's, or 50. There are six 1's, or 6. In the number 56_8, the 5 has a value of 40. The 5 is in the 8's position: therefore, we have five 8's, or 40. There are six 1's, or 6, as before.

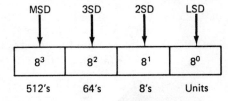

MSD	3SD	2SD	LSD
8^3	8^2	8^1	8^0
512's	64's	8's	Units

Figure 2-3. Positional value of the first four positions for the octal number system.

2.2.1   Octal–Decimal Conversions

Let's examine the number 1025 in octal. We normally think in decimal and decimal is the number system we use most; therefore, let's convert the number 1025_8 to base 10. There is a 1 in the 512's position, plus a 0 in the 64's position, plus a 2 in the 8's position, plus a 5 in the units position.

$$1025_8 = (1 \times 8^3) + (0 \times 8^2) + (2 \times 8^1) + (5 \times 8^0) =$$
$$512 \quad + \quad 0 \quad + \quad 16 \quad + \quad 5 \quad = 533_{10}$$

Example 2.6.   Change the following octal numbers to decimal:

   (a) 73_8 (b) 432_8 (c) 600_8 (d) 1234_8

Solutions: (a) 59_{10} (b) 282_{10} (c) 384_{10} (d) 668_{10}

Let's reverse the process. In Example 2.7. the number 189 is converted from decimal to octal.

Example 2.7.   Convert decimal 189 to octal

Solution: Step 1. $\dfrac{189}{8}$ = 23 + 5

Step 2. $\dfrac{23}{8}$ = 2 + 7

Step 3. $\dfrac{2}{8}$ = 0 + 2 —MSB—2   7   5 $189_{10} = 275_8$

Because we are converting to base 8, we first divide the decimal number by 8 (step 1). The answer is 23 with a remainder of 5. This remainder is the LSD (Least Significant Digit) of our base 8 number. The whole number left after this initial division (23) is again divided by 8 to determine the value of the digit in the next (8^1) position. This division leaves a remainder of 7, which becomes the digit in the 8's position. The whole number resulting from this division (2) is again divided by 8, and the remainder (2) is the digit in the 8^2 position. This digit is the MSD (Most Significant Digit) because no further division is possible.

Example 2.8.   Convert the following decimal numbers to octal numbers:

   (a) 78   (b) 376   (c) 1463

Solutions: (a) 116_8 (b) 570_8 (c) 2667_8

2.3 HEXADECIMAL NUMBER SYSTEM

Another important computer number system is the hexadecimal system (base 16). How many digits exist in hexadecimal? Sixteen because the base is 16. What is the value of the largest digit in hexadecimal? Fifteen, one less than the base. However, 15 is a decimal number and requires *two digits* (15). In the hexadecimal number system, sixteen *different* symbols must be used. Zero through 9 are used for the first ten, and A through F are used for the remaining six, as shown in Table 2–1. Figure 2–4 indicates positional value of the first four positions of the hexadecimal number system.

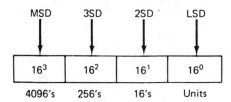

Figure 2–4. Positional value of a four-digit hexadecimal number.

2.3.1 Hexadecimal–Decimal Conversions

The hexadecimal number 3AC2 may be converted to base 10 as follows:

$$
\begin{array}{lr}
\text{Three 4096's, which equal} & 12288 \\
+ \text{ ten 256's, which equal} & 2560 \\
+ \text{ twelve 16's, which equal} & 192 \\
+ \text{ two 1's, which equal} & 2 \\
\text{SUM} & 15042_{10}
\end{array}
$$

or:

$$(3 \times 16^3) + (10 \times 16^2) + (12 \times 16^1) + (2 \times 16^0) = 15042_{10}$$

Example 2.9.   Convert the following hexadecimal numbers to decimal numbers:

(a) 72   (b) C29   (c) 12AB   (d) 1A2A

Solutions: (a) 114_{10} (b) 3113_{10} (c) 4779_{10} (d) 6698_{10}

The conversion of decimal numbers to hexadecimal is identical to conversion using other bases. In Example 2.10, the number 1324 is converted from hexadecimal to decimal. Because the hexadecimal number

Table 2-1. Computer Numbering Systems

Numbering system	Decimal		Binary						Octal		Hexa-decimal	
Base	10		2						8		16	
Position weight — Power	10^1	10^0	2^5	2^4	2^3	2^2	2^1	2^0	8^1	8^0	16^1	16^0
Position weight — Value	10	1	32	16	8	4	2	1	8	1	16	1
										(LSD)		(LSD)
	0	0	0	0	0	0	0	0	0	0	0	0
		1	0	0	0	0	0	1		1		1
		2	0	0	0	0	1	0		2		2
		3	0	0	0	0	1	1		3		3
		4	0	0	0	1	0	0		4		4
		5	0	0	0	1	0	1		5		5
		6	0	0	0	1	1	0		6		6
		7	0	0	0	1	1	1		7		7
		8	0	0	1	0	0	0	1	0		8
		9	0	0	1	0	0	1	1	1		9
	1	0	0	0	1	0	1	0	1	2		A
	1	1	0	0	1	0	1	1	1	3		B
	1	2	0	0	1	1	0	0	1	4		C
	1	3	0	0	1	1	0	1	1	5		D
	1	4	0	0	1	1	1	0	1	6		E
	1	5	0	0	1	1	1	1	1	7		F
	1	6	0	1	0	0	0	0	2	0	1	0
	1	7	0	1	0	0	0	1	2	1	1	1
	1	8	0	1	0	0	1	0	2	2	1	2
	1	9	0	1	0	0	1	1	2	3	1	3
	2	0	0	1	0	1	0	0	2	4	1	4
	2	1	0	1	0	1	0	1	2	5	1	5
	2	2	0	1	0	1	1	0	2	6	1	6
	2	3	0	1	0	1	1	1	2	7	1	7
	2	4	0	1	1	0	0	0	3	0	1	8
	2	5	0	1	1	0	0	1	3	1	1	9
	2	6	0	1	1	0	1	0	3	2	1	A
	2	7	0	1	1	0	1	1	3	3	1	B
	2	8	0	1	1	1	0	0	3	4	1	C
	2	9	0	1	1	1	0	1	3	5	1	D
	3	0	0	1	1	1	1	0	3	6	1	E
	3	1	0	1	1	1	1	1	3	7	1	F
	3	2	1	0	0	0	0	0	4	0	2	0

Example: $1_{(10)} = 1_{(2)} = 1_{(8)} = 1_{(16)}$

Example: $10_{(10)} = 1010_{(2)} = 12_{(8)} = 0A_{(16)}$

Example: $25_{(10)} = 11001_{(2)} = 31_{(8)} = 19_{(16)}$

system has a base of 16, division is by 16. In working with remainders greater than 9, we substitute the characters A, B, C, D, E, and F as required.

Example 2.10.   Change 1324_{10} to hexadecimal.

Solution: Step 1. $\dfrac{1324}{16} = 82 + 12$ ──────────────┐

                                               LSB

           Step 2. $\dfrac{82}{16} = 5 + 2$ ──────────┘

           Step 3. $\dfrac{5}{16} = 0 + 5$ —MSD—5 2 C $1324_{10} = 52C_{16}$

Example 2.11.   Convert the following decimal numbers to hexadecimal numbers.

        (a) 672   (b) 1763   (c) 12760

Solutions: (a) $2A0_{16}$ (b) $6E3_{16}$ (c) $31D8_{16}$

2.4   BINARY–OCTAL–HEXADECIMAL CONVERSIONS

2.4.1   Binary to Octal Conversions

Many 1's and 0's are required using binary numbers to represent large quantities. If we convert from binary to octal, the number of digits required is reduced by a factor of 3 because one octal digit equals three bits. That is, all octal digits, 0 through 7, can be represented by three bits.

$$0 = 000 \qquad 4 = 100$$
$$1 = 001 \qquad 5 = 101$$
$$2 = 010 \qquad 6 = 110$$
$$3 = 011 \qquad 7 = 111$$

For example, the binary number 110111100001 can be converted to octal by separating the bits into groups of three and substituting octal digits for each group of three bits. To separate the binary numbers into three-bit groups, the count begins with the LSB.

Example 2.12.   Convert 110111100001_2 to octal.

Solution: 110   111   100   001   (binary number divided into groups of three)

           6   7   4   1   (octal representation)

Example 2.13.   Convert 11101001_2 to octal.

Solution: 011   101   001
                    3   5   1

Remember, the three-bit groups start with the LSD. A zero was added to the leftmost group of bits to remind us that three bits represent one octal digit.

The procedure may be reversed in order to convert from octal to binary.

Example 2.14.   Convert 417_8 to binary.

Solution: 4   1   7
                 100   001   111 $417_8 = 100001111_2$

Example 2.15.   Convert 362_8 to binary.

Solution: 3   6   2
                 011   110   010 $362_8 = 11110010_2$

In each example, three bits are substituted for each octal digit. Of course, a zero in the leftmost bit position has no meaning and need not be written in the answer.

2.4.2 Binary to Hexadecimal Conversions

If we convert from binary to hexadecimal, the number of digits required is reduced by a factor of 4 because one hexadecimal digit equals four bits. That is, all hexadecimal digits (0 through F) can be represented by four bits.

0 = 0000	8 = 1000
1 = 0001	9 = 1001
2 = 0010	A = 1010
3 = 0011	B = 1011
4 = 0100	C = 1100
5 = 0101	D = 1101
6 = 0110	E = 1110
7 = 0111	F = 1111

For example, the binary number 110110011011 can be converted to hexadecimal by separating the bits into groups of four and substituting hexadecimal digits for each group of four bits. To separate the binary number into four-bit groups, the count begins with the LSB.

Example 2.16.   Convert 110110011011_2 to hexadecimal.

Solution: 1101   1001   1011   (binary number divided into four-bit groups)

              D   9   B   (hexadecimal substitution for each four-bit group)

Example 2.17.   Convert 11000111001_2 to hexadecimal.

Solution: 0110   0011   1001

          6   3   9 $11000111001_2 = 639_{16}$

Remember, the four-bit groups start with the LSD. A zero was added to the leftmost group of bits to remind us that four bits represent one hexadecimal digit.

The procedure may be reversed in order to convert from hexadecimal to binary.

Example 2.18.   Convert $3A8_{16}$ to binary.

Solution: 3   A   8

       0011   1010   1000 $3A8_{16} = 1110101000_2$

Example 2.19.   Convert $A0B5_{16}$ to binary.

Solution: A   0   B   5

       1010   0000   1011   0101 $A0B5_{16} = 1010000010110101_2$

2.5   ADDITION

2.5.1   Adding Decimal Numbers

Add the numbers 23 and 45. When numbers are added, they are added in columns—one number is placed below the other. Either number may be placed first. In Example 2.20 the numbers 23 and 45 are placed in the position for addition. The digits are separated to emphasize positional differences. Eight is in the units position (3 + 5), and 6 is in the tens position (2 + 4). The answer is 68. (Six 10's and eight 1's.)

Example 2.20.   Add 23 and 45.

Solution:
```
          2  3
     (+)  4  5
          ────
          6  8
```

Example 2.21.   Add the (decimal) numbers 64 and 87.

Solution: carry   1   1
```
                              6     4
                              8     7
                         ───────────────
                         1   (15)  (11)
(subtract value of carry)     10    10
                         ───────────────
                         1    5     1    (remainders taken as decimal sum)
```

In Example 2.21, there is an 11 in the units position. This number is greater than 9, which tells us there must be a carry (10). The digit remaining in the units position will be the difference of 10 and 11, or 1. The 10's position now contains 6 + 8 + a carry of 1, or 15. Again, the number is greater than 9, so a carry is indicated. Subtracting 10 from 15, we get 5 with a carry of 1. The third position contains only the carry. Of course, we have been adding for years in decimal so our experience allows us to perform these operations automatically. We have taken time to discuss the arithmetic steps because this is the addition process in all bases.

2.5.2   Adding Octal Numbers

Example 2.22.   Add the octal numbers 736 and 215.

Solution: carry   1   1
```
                                  7   3   6
                                  2   1   5
                              ─────────────────
(decimal sum)                 1  (9)  5  (11)
                                  8       8      $736 + 215 = 1153_8$
                              ─────────────────
                              1   1   5   3
```

Again, the LSD, or units position, is added first. The sum of 6 and 5 is 11. The number is greater than 7 (7 is the largest digit in base 8), which tells us there must be a carry. Subtracting 8 (the value of the carry) leaves 3 with a carry of 1. The 8^1 position now contains $3 + 1 +$ a carry of 1, or 5. Because 5 is less than 7, no carry exists. In the 8^2 position, $7 + 2$ is 9. The number is greater than 7, so a carry is generated. Subtracting the carry (8) yields a remainder of 1 with a carry of 1. The 8^3 position contains only the carry, so the answer is 1153_8.

Example 2.23.   Add the following octal numbers:

$$
\begin{array}{ccc}
\text{(a)} \ 243 & \text{(b)} \ 764 & \text{(c)} \ 604 \\
172 & 414 & 777 \\
\end{array}
$$

Solutions: (a) 435_8 (b) 1400_8 (c) 1603_8

2.5.3   Adding Hexadecimal Numbers

Example 2.24.   Add the hexadecimal numbers 7AF and 579.

Solution: carry

$$
\begin{array}{lcccl}
 & 1 & 1 & & \\
 & 7 & A & F & \\
 & 5 & 7 & 9 & \\
\hline
\text{(decimal sum)} & (13) & (18) & (24) & \\
\text{(Subtract value of carry)} & & 16 & 16 & \\
\hline
 & D & 2 & 8 & = D28_{16} \\
\end{array}
$$

Adding the units position yields 24. Twenty-four is greater than the largest digit (F), which is equal to decimal 15. This indicates that a carry should exist. Subtracting the value of a carry (16) leaves a remainder of 8 with a carry of 1. In the 16^1 position, the sum of A (decimal 10) $+ 7 +$ a carry of 1 is 18. Again, a carry is generated leaving a remainder of 2 with a carry of 1. In the 16^2 position, the carry $+ 7 + 5$ equals decimal 13. In hexadecimal, 13 is D, so the answer is $D28_{16}$.

Example 2.25.   Add the following hexadecimal numbers:

$$
\begin{array}{ccc}
\text{(a)} \ 4D3 & \text{(b)} \ 789 & \text{(c)} \ F347 \\
818 & C47 & E006 \\
\end{array}
$$

Solutions: (a) CEB_{16} (b) $13D0_{16}$ (c) $1D34D_{16}$

2.5.4   Adding Binary Numbers

Example 2.26.   Add the binary numbers 1101 and 1001.

Solution:

```
                 1        1
              1  1  0  1
              1  0  0  1
              _____
(decimal sum)   (2) 1  1 (2)
(subtract value of carry)  2        2
              _____
              1  0  1  1  0  = 10110₂
```

The method of addition is the same as that used with other bases. Notice that $1 + 1$ equals decimal 2. Because 2 is invalid in base 2, a carry is generated into the next position. We see from the example that a carry is generated whenever a sum greater than 1 results from the addition of numbers in a column.

Example 2.27.   Add the following binary numbers.

| | (a) 10 | (b) 111 | (c) 1001 | (d) 11100 |
| | 11 | 101 | 1010 | 01010 |

Solutions: (a) 101_2 (b) 1100_2 (c) 10011_2 (d) 100110_2

From working with these and other examples of binary addition, we see that:

1. $0 + 0$ always equals 0
2. $0 + 1$ always equals 1
3. $1 + 1$ always equals 0 and a carry
4. $1 + 1 +$ a carry always equals 1 and a carry

2.6   SUBTRACTION

2.6.1   One's Complement

The one's complement of a binary number is found by subtracting the binary number to be complemented from a binary number made up of all ones. In the following example, the one's complement of 10110010 is found.

Example 2.28.   Find the one's complement of 10110010.

Solution:
```
  1  1  1  1  1  1  1  1
- 1  0  1  1  0  0  1  0
―――――――――――――――――――――――――
  0  1  0  0  1  1  0  1   (one's complement of 10110010)
```

Careful inspection reveals that the one's complement of a binary number may be produced by changing all of the ones in the number to zeros and changing all of the zeros to ones.

```
  1  0  1  1  0  0  1  0   (change each bit to get
  0  1  0  0  1  1  0  1    one's complement)
```

The computer is able to perform this operation very simply with a circuit called an *inverter*. Notice that carries or borrows are not involved in this operation.

In order to subtract using the one's complement method, the one's complement of the subtrahend is added to the minuend. The carry out of the highest bit position is then added to the *lowest bit position* (LSB). This is called *end-around carry*.

Example 2.29.   Find the difference between 10110011 and 01101101.

Solution:

(Minuend)	10110011	10110011	
(Subtrahend)	01101101	10010010	(one's complement)
	1	01000101	
		1	(end-around carry)
		01000110	(difference)

Example 2.30.   Find the difference between 11011000 and 10110011 using the one's complement method.

Solution:

(Minuend)	11011000	11011000	
(Subtrahend)	10110011	01001100	(one's complement)
	1	00100100	
		1	(end-around carry)
		00100101	(difference)

2.6.2   Two's Complement

Perhaps the most popular method of subtraction used by computers is the two's complement method. The two's complement of a number may be found by adding 1 to the one's complement. Let's find the two's complement of 10011101. First, change all 0's to 1's and all 1's to 0's (one's complement). Then add 1 as follows:

$$10011101 \qquad \begin{array}{r} 01100010 \quad \text{(one's complement)} \\ (+) \qquad\quad 1 \\ \hline 01100011 \quad \text{(two's complement)} \end{array}$$

In order to subtract, we obtain the two's complement of the subtrahend and then add to the minuend.

Example 2.31.   Subtract 01001010 from 01100111.

Solution:

$$\begin{array}{lll} \text{(Minuend)} & 01100111 & 01100111 \\ \text{(Subtrahend)} \ (-) & \underline{01001010} \quad (+) & \underline{10110110} \quad \text{(two's comp)} \\ & & \cancel{1}\ \ 00011101 \quad \text{(answer)} \end{array}$$

(this carry is ignored)

The carry resulting from the most significant bit position is ignored. There is no end-around carry as there is with the one's complement method. The computer obtains the one's complement by using an inverter. The two's complement is then obtained by starting the addition process with a carry.

The number of bit positions in the subtrahend must agree with the number of bit positions in the minuend. This is usually accomplished by providing a fixed number of storage cells in the computer. In the preceding examples there were eight bit positions used; therefore, eight storage cells were used to store the numbers. Eight cells were also used to store the difference, causing the carry out of the most significant bit position to be dropped because there was no place to store it. Each of the above eight-cell combinations is called a register. Example 2.32 illustrates the concept of registers with fixed numbers of bit positions.

Example 2.32.   Subtract 00001100 from 01001010 (Figure 2–5).

Solution: The minuend is placed in the Y register; the one's complement of the subtrahend is placed in the X register. The LSB is in the rightmost bit position. A 1 is placed in the LSB position of the carry register. All the other positions of the carry register store a zero at the start. If a carry is produced with the addition of a column, a 1 is stored in the next bit position of the carry register. Because the output register is limited to eight bit positions, the carry out of the MSB (most significant bit) position is dropped.

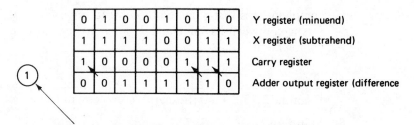

0	1	0	0	1	0	1	0	Y register (minuend)
1	1	1	1	0	0	1	1	X register (subtrahend)
1	0	0	0	0	1	1	1	Carry register
0	0	1	1	1	1	1	0	Adder output register (difference

(carry out is dropped because there is nowhere to store it)

Figure 2–5. Concept of registers with fixed numbers of bit positions.

2.6.3 Sixteen's Complement

When large signed binary numbers are added or subtracted, it is convenient to use the sixteen's complement method. The sixteen's complement of a number is obtained by taking the fifteen's complement and adding one. The fifteen's complement is obtained by substituting each digit with the difference between its value and 15. For example, the fifteen's complement of A is 5.

Because microprocessors are typically 8-bit or 16-bit machines, in our examples we will consider only 8- or 16-bit numbers. This means 2- or 4-digit hexadecimal numbers. For example, let's find the sixteen's complement of various 2- and 4-digit numbers.

Example 2.33. Find the sixteen's complement of: (a) 7A   (b) C209

Solutions:

	(a)			(b)	
	F F			F F F F	
(−)	7 A		(−)	C 2 0 9	
	8 5	(15's comp)		3 D F 6	(15's comp)
(+)	1		(+)	1	
	8 6	(16's comp)		3 D F 7	(16's comp)

Another way to find the 16's complement of a number is to simply subtract the LSD from 10_{16} rather than F. This has the same effect as subtracting the LSD from F and then adding one.

Example 2.34. Find the sixteen's complement of: (a) 7A   (b) C209

Solutions:

	(a)			(b)	
	F (10)			F F F (10)	
(−)	7 A		(−)	C 2 0 9	
	8 6	(16's comp)		3 D F 7	(16's comp)

2.6.4 Eight's Complement

In many systems, octal is used to represent large binary numbers. Therefore, it is convenient to use the eight's complement method for performing signed binary number additions and subtractions. The seven's complement is first obtained by substituting each octal digit with the difference between its value and 7. Then 1 is added to produce the eight's complement.

Example 2.35.   Find the eight's complement of 136_8.

Solution:

$$
\begin{array}{r}
7\ 7\ 7 \\
(-)\ \underline{1\ 3\ 6} \\
6\ 4\ 1 \quad \text{(15's comp)} \\
(+)\ \underline{1} \\
6\ 4\ 2 \quad \text{(16's comp)}
\end{array}
$$

Another way to find the 8's complement of a number is to simply subtract the LSD from 10_8 rather than 7. This has the same effect as subtracting the LSD from 7 and then adding one.

Example 2.36.   Find the eight's complement of 136_8.

Solution:

$$
\begin{array}{r}
7\ \ 7\ (10) \\
(-)\ \underline{1\ \ 3\ \ \ 6} \\
6\ \ 4\ \ \ 2 \quad \text{(8's comp)}
\end{array}
$$

There is one major difference though, compared to the 16's complement method, when dealing with 8-bit or 16-bit machines. With base sixteen, we worked with 8- or 16-bit numbers and the maximum hexadecimal number was FF (8-bit) or FFFF (16-bit). With base 8, these 8- or 16-bit numbers result in maximum octal numbers of 377 (8-bit) or 177777 (16-bit).

| 11 111 111 | 1 111 111 111 111 111 | (binary numbers) |
| 3 7 7 | 1 7 7 7 7 7 | (octal equivalents) |

This means that our MSD is not 7 but is either 3 or 1, depending on whether we are dealing with an 8-bit or a 16-bit number. The following examples illustrate this restriction.

Example 2.37.   Find the eight's complement of the following octal numbers:

(a) 274   (b) 37. Consider both 8-bit and 16-bit registers.

Solutions: If the numbers are to be stored in an 8-bit register:

          (a) 3 7 (10) (use method discussed in Example 2.36)

          (−) 2 7   4

               1 0   4 (8's comp)

          (b) 3 7 (10)

          (−) 0 3   7 (must be a 3-digit number because 8 bits are stored)

               3 4   1 (8's comp)

If the numbers are to be stored in a 16-bit register:

    (a)   1 7 7 7 7 (10)

        (−) 0 0 0 2 7   4   (must be a 6-digit number)

            1 7 7 5 0   4   (8's comp)

    (b)   1 7 7 7 7 (10)

        (−) 0 0 0 0 3   7

            1 7 7 7 4   1   (8's comp)

The following subtraction is performed in an 8-bit machine by using the two's complement method:

       11001011   11001011

  (−) 10011000   01101000   (2's comp)

                  $\cancel{1}$ 00110011   (answer)

(carry is dropped because there is no place to store it)

The same problem may be solved by using the 16's complement method.

    $11001011_2 = CB_{16}$ $10011000_2 = 98_{16}$

     C B   C B

  (−) 9 8   (+) 6 8   (subtrahend in 16's comp form)

            $\cancel{1}$ 3 3   (answer)

          (carry is dropped)

To solve the problem in octal:

    $11001011_2 = 313_8$ $10011000_2 = 230_8$

     3 1 3   3 1 3

  (−) 2 3 0   (+) 1 5 0   (subtrahend in 8's comp form)

            $\cancel{1}$ 0 6 3   (answer)

          (carry is dropped)

Remember, we are dealing with an 8-bit number or a maximum octal number of 3 in the MSD position. The addition yielded 3 + 1 in the MSD position, which results in a sum of 0 + a carry. Of course in positions other than the MSD position a carry results when the sum is greater than 7.

2.7   FRACTIONAL NUMBERS

How are numbers with values of less than 1 represented in binary? As in decimal, a point is used to separate the whole number from the fraction. This binary point is not stored but is assumed to appear ahead of the register containing the fraction. The MSB of this register represents the first bit position to the right of the binary point. This bit represents the decimal fraction 0.5 (2^{-1}); the second bit to the right represents 0.5 divided by 2, or 0.25 (2^{-2}); the third, 0.25 divided by 2 or 0.125 (2^{-3}); and so on. Figure 2-6 is a table of powers of 2 from 2^{16} to 2^{-16}.

Power	Value	Power	Value
2^0	1	2	
2^1	2	2^{-1}	0.5
2^2	4	2^{-2}	0.25
2^3	8	2^{-3}	0.125
2^4	16	2^{-4}	0.062 5
2^5	32	2^{-5}	0.031 25
2^6	64	2^{-6}	0.015 625
2^7	128	2^{-7}	0.007 812 5
2^8	256	2^{-8}	0.003 906 25
2^9	512	2^{-9}	0.001 953 125
2^{10}	1024	2^{-10}	0.000 976 562 5
2^{11}	2048	2^{-11}	0.000 488 281 25
2^{12}	4096	2^{-12}	0.000 244 140 625
2^{13}	8192	2^{-13}	0.000 122 070 312 5
2^{14}	16,384	2^{-14}	0.000 061 035 156 25
2^{15}	32,768	2^{-15}	0.000 030 517 578 125
2^{16}	65,536	2^{-16}	0.000 015 258 789 062 5

Figure 2-6. Table of powers of 2.

The decimal number 0.1875 would be represented in binary as 0.0011. In the same manner, decimal 56.375 is represented in binary as 111000.011. Because we are usually dealing with 8-bit or 16-bit machines, the binary representation of decimal numbers will be limited to 8 or 16 bits. If we limit the binary numbers in this manner, we may sacrifice some resolution (accuracy). In converting from decimal to binary, the binary number is usualy *truncated* rather than rounded. That is, the ninth bit is simply not considered.

Example 2.38. Convert the following decimal numbers to binary:
(a) 0.0235   (b) 3.475   (c) 8.005

Solutions: (a) $.00000110_2$ (b) 11.01111001_2 (c) 1000.00000001_2

Fractional binary numbers may be converted to hexadecimal just as they were before. However, the bits are separated, beginning with the point, into groups of four.

Example 2.39. Convert the following binary numbers to hexadecimal:
(a) .00111010   (b) 01010011.11001001

Solutions: (a) .0011   1010
　　　　　　.   3   A $.00111010_2 = 0.3A_{16}$
(b) 0101 0011 . 1100 1001
　　　5   3 . C   9 $01010011.11001001_2 = 53.C9_{16}$

Fractional binary numbers may be converted to octal just as they were before. However, the bits are separated into groups of three beginning with the point.

Example 2.40. Convert the following binary numbers to octal:
(a) .00111010   (b) 01010011.11001001

Solutions: (a) .001   110   10
　　　　　　. 1   6   2 $.00111010_2 = 0.162_8$
(b) 01 010 011 . 110 010 01
　　　1 2   3 . 6   2   1 $01010011.11001001_2 = 123.621_8$

Quite often, two registers are used to store binary numbers. The first register stores the whole number, and the second stores the fraction. For example, if the binary number 1110101.1011001 were stored in two 16-bit registers it would be stored like this:

1st Register　　　　　2nd Register
0000000001110101　　1011001000000000

The hexadecimal notation for the above binary number would be $75.B2_{16}$
The octal notation for this binary number would be 165.544_8

A fixed number of bits, like those in the above example, is called a *word*. The length of the word depends on the computer and the way data is handled in the computer. For example, in the Motorola 6800 microprocessor, each word is eight bits in length. Intel's 8086 microprocessor uses 16-bit words.

2.8   CODES

2.8.1   BCD Codes

Substituting binary bits for characters in other number systems is called *encoding*. When three bits are substituted for an octal character, Binary-Coded Octal (BCO) is produced. Substituting four bits for a hexadecimal character produces Binary-Coded Hexadecimal (BCH). BCO and BCH are straight binary numbers.

What about encoding decimal? Substituting four binary bits for a decimal character produces a code called Binary-Coded Decimal (BCD). Because ten decimal characters exist, at least four bits are required. Figure 2-7 shows the most common form of BCD. Because of the natural binary number system used, this code is sometimes referred to as NBCD.

There are sixteen possible combinations of four bits (0000–1111). This means that six combinations must be deleted for BCD. For natural BCD, the last six combinations are not used (1010 through 1111). For exam-

DECIMAL	BCD
0	0000
1	0001
2	0010
3	0011
4	0100
5	0101
6	0110
7	0111
8	1000
9	1001

Figure 2-7. Binary coded decimal (BCD).

ple, 1001 is the code for decimal 9 but what does 1010 represent? In straight binary, it has a value of 10; but in decimal, there is no single character for 10. Two characters are required, a one and a zero (10). Ten in BCD would appear as follows:

$$0001 \quad 0000$$

The six combinations that have been deleted are invalid because they do not represent one of the ten decimal characters. The procedure for converting from decimal to BCD (encoding) is the same as that used for converting from hexadecimal or octal to binary (as discussed earlier).

Example 2.41.   Convert 563_{10} to BCD.

Solution: 5   6   3
                0101   0110   0011 $563_{10} = 010101100011_{BCD}$

One must remember that this BCD number is *not* a binary number, and 563_{10} does not equal 010101100011_2! The decimal number 563 equals 1000110011 in binary.

Example 2.42.   Convert: (a) 1769_{10} to BCD;   (b) 63.7608_{10} to BCD.

Solutions: (a)   1   7   6   9
                    0001 0111 0110 1001 $1769_{10} = 0001011101101001_{BCD}$
               (b)   6   3   .   7   6   0   8
                    0110 0011 . 0111 0110 0000 1000
                    $63.7608_{10} = 01100011.0111011000001000_{BCD}$

You may ask, "Why not use BCD in the computer?" Some computers do use BCD. However, the trend is toward straight binary for two important reasons. First, more data can be stored in a given number of memory cells when binary is used. This is because for every four bits of memory, only ten decimal digits can be stored; whereas four bits of memory can store sixteen digits of hexadecimal. Remember, six of the sixteen possible combinations of bits are invalid for BCD. Second, BCD complicates the arithmetic process.

The computer must first find the binary sum of the BCD digits and then decide if this sum is valid. If the sum is invalid, 0110 must be added. You may have guessed that another advantage of using straight binary is that less time is required.

Where is BCD used? BCD is used as a binary code to represent decimal digits. Whenever decimal information is required, such as in digital voltmeters and electronic calculators, BCD is used. The process of encoding BCD from decimal is simple, whereas changing from decimal to binary (or vice versa) is complex and requires a great deal of circuitry. Thus, calculators use BCD because the input data (keyboard) as well as the output data (display) is decimal. As a result, calculators have rather complex arithmetic circuitry and are considerably slower than computers.

2.8.2 ASCII

The computer also uses alphabetic data as well as special characters such as punctuation marks and mathematic symbols. Data that is transmitted between peripherals and the CPU or over telephone lines is usually in the form of a character-oriented code such as ASCII. Although other codes exist and are used, we will confine our discussion of codes to ASCII.

In an attempt to standardize an alphanumeric code, an association of manufacturers and users has published the American Standard Code for Information Interchange (ASCII). This code appears in graphic form in Figure 2–8. Notice that this is a 7-bit code. The three most significant bits are the zone bits; the remaining four are the digit bits. For example, zone 011 contains all of the numeric characters as well as six special characters. The numeral four is represented as 011 0100; numeral nine as 011 1001; a question mark (?) as 011 1111; etc. The letter A is represented as 100 0001; J is 100 1010, etc. Control characters are also included in this code.

Example 2.43.   Write the expression GO TO 36. using the ASCII code.

Solution: G   O   b   T   O   b   3   6
47   4F   20   54   4F   20   33   36   2E   (b is blank)

2.9 SIGNED NUMBERS

Within any numbering system, positive and negative values can exist. Numbers that are preceded by a plus (+) or a minus (–) sign are called *signed numbers.* When binary numbers are stored in a computer, the MSB position of a register is reserved for the *sign bit,* which is used to indicate the sign of the number stored in that register. If the MSB is a 0, the number stored has a positive value. If the MSB is a 1, the number has a negative value. Figure 2–9 demonstrates how the number 23 would be stored in an 8-bit position register. Negative 23 could be stored in binary as in Figure 2–10.

	000	001	010	011	100	101	110	111
0000	NULL	(1) DC$_0$	b	0	@	P		
0001	SOM	DC$_1$	!	1	A	Q		
0010	EOA	DC$_2$	''	2	B	R		
0011	EOM	DC$_3$	#	3	C	S		
0100	EOT	DC$_4$ (stop)	$	4	D	T		
0101	WRU	ERR	%	5	E	U		
0110	RU	SYNC	&	6	F	V		
0111	BELL	LEM	'	7	G	W		Unassigned
1000	FE$_0$	S$_0$	(	8	H	X		
1001	HT / SK	S$_1$	)	9	I	Y		
1010	LF	S$_2$	*	:	J	Z		
1011	V$_{TAB}$	S$_3$	+	;	K	[		
1100	FF	S$_4$	(comma) ,	<	L	\		ACK
1101	CR	S$_5$	−	=	M	]		(2)
1110	SO	S$_6$	.	>	N	↑		ESC
1111	SI	S$_7$	/	?	O	←		DEL

Example: | 100 | 0001 | = A

b$_7$ ———————b$_1$

The abbreviations used in the figure mean:

NULL	Null Idle	CR	Carriage return
SOM	Start of message	SO	Shift out
EOA	End of address	SI	Shift in
EOM	End of message	DC$_0$	Device control (1)
			Reserved for data
			Link escape
EOT	End of transmission	DC$_1$ - DC$_3$	Device control
WRU	"Who are you?"	ERR	Error
RU	"Are you . . . . ?"	SYNC	Synchronous idle
BELL	Audible signal	LEM	Logical end of media
FE	Format effector	SO$_0$ - SO$_7$	Separator (information)
HT	Horizontal tabulation		Word separator (blank, normally non-printing)
SK	Skip (punched card)	ACK	Acknowledge
LF	Line feed	(2)	Unassigned control
V/TAB	Vertical tabulation	ESC	Escape
FF	Form feed	DEL	Delete Idle

Figure 2–8. American Standard Code for Information Interchange (ASCII).

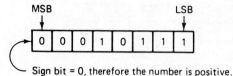

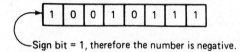

Figure 2–9. The number 23 stored in an 8-bit position register.

Figure 2–10. The number –23 stored in an 8-bit position register.

The negative number in the above example is said to be stored in *true form*. However, most computers store negative numbers in either the one's or two's complement form. Negative 23 in the one's complement form would be stored as shown in Figure 2–11. The inversion process used to produce the one's complement automatically produces the 1 indicating a minus number.

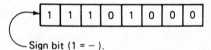

Figure 2–11. Storing –23 in one's complement form.

Figure 2–12 demonstrates how negative 23 is stored in the two's complement form.

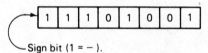

Figure 2–12. Storing –23 in two's complement form.

In the above examples, one bit position is used to store the sign bit, leaving only seven bit positions for the absolute value of the number. Eight-bit registers are used in this chapter to provide ease of reading. Most computers use registers longer than eight bits. However, the MSB position is used for the sign bit regardless of the length of the register.

2.10 ADDING AND SUBTRACTING SIGNED NUMBERS

The rules for adding or subtracting signed binary numbers are the same as those employed with signed decimal numbers:

1. To add numbers having like signs, give the sum the same sign; that is, two positive numbers produce a positive sum, and two negative numbers produce a negative sum.

2. To add numbers having different signs, find the difference and give it the sign of the larger number.

3. To subtract signed numbers, change the sign of the subtrahend and add the subtrahend to the minuend according to the preceding rules.

Most large computers store negative numbers in the two's complement form. The following examples demonstrate the advantage of the two's complement form. Let's find the sum of positive 6 and positive 8.

```
      + 6    00000110    (positive numbers are stored in true form)
(+)   + 8    00001000
      ----   --------
      + 14   00001110    (sum is positive and in true form)
```

Now let's find the sum of negative 6 and negative 8.

```
      - 6    11111010    (negative numbers are stored in the two's
(+)   - 8    11111000                          complement form)
      ----   --------
      - 14   11110010    (sum is negative and in two's complement
                                                            form)
```

Remember, the MSB is the sign bit! This sum is negative and the computer stores it in the two's complement form. There is no need to recomplement this number unless it is to be printed out.

Now let's add negative 6 and positive 8.

```
      - 6    11111010    (two's complement of 6)
(+)   + 8    00001000    (true form of 8)
      ----   --------
      + 2    00000010    (true form of positive 2)
```

OK! Let's add positive 6 and negative 8.

```
      + 6    00000110    (true form of 6)
(+)   - 8    11111000    (two's complement of 8)
      ----   --------
      - 2    11111110    (two's complement of 2)
```

Again, the sign bit reveals a negative number (– 2) in the two's complement form.

Now let's try subtracting positive 6 from positive 8.

```
      + 8    00001000    00001000    (true form of 8)
(-)   + 6    00000110    11111010    (two's complement of 6)
      ----   --------    --------
      + 2                00000010    (true form of 2)
```

To subtract, the subtrahend is complemented and added.

Subtract positive 8 from positive 6.

```
      + 6    00000110    00000110    (true form of 6)
(-)   + 8    00001000    11111000    (two's complement of 8)
      ----   --------    --------
      - 2                11111110    (two's complement of 2)
```

In this case, the difference is negative and appears in the two's complement form. Remember, the computer stores negative numbers in the two's complement form. Now let's subtract negative 8 from positive 6.

	+ 6	00000110	00000110	(true form of 6)
(−)	− 8	11111000	00001000	(true form of 8)
	+ 14		00001110	(true form of 14)

To subtract, the subtrahend is complemented and added.

In the last example, because 8 was a negative number, it was stored in the two's complement form. Then, in order to subtract, it was recomplemented before adding.

The final example demonstates subtracting a positive number from a negative number.

	− 8	11111000	11111000	(two's complement of 8)
(−)	+ 6	00000110	11111010	(two's complement of 6)
	− 14		11110010	(two's complement of 14)

When performing addition and subtraction using the two's complement method, the computer needs *only* circuitry to perform the add operation and the two's complementation. Multiplication and division are performed by routines of repeated addition and subtraction.

2.11   OVERFLOW

The largest positive number that can be stored in a 8-bit register is 01111111 (+127). The largest negative number is 10000000 (−128). If the result of an arithmetic operation exceeds these numbers, the effect will be an *overflow*. All such overflows are erroneous and can be detected if:

1. There is a carry into the sign bit position with no carry out of it or,

2. There is no carry into the sign bit position with a carry out of it.

A computer that uses 8-bit registers can manipulate 8 bits at a time. However, larger numbers can be handled by successive operations of the processor. For example, a 32-bit number can be processed by four successive operations.

Problem Set 2–1

Convert the following numbers to decimal numbers.

1.	111_2	2.	110_2
3.	1101_2	4.	1000_2
5.	100110_2	6.	110011_2

7. 1100101_2 8. 1000111_2

9. 11110000_2 10. 10101010_2

11. 14_8 12. 27_8

13. 77_8 14. 100_8

15. 276_8 16. 667_8

17. 4176_8 18. 1171_8

19. $1A_{16}$ 20. $A1_{16}$

21. $4C_{16}$ 22. $1B_{16}$

23. 200_{16} 24. 400_{16}

25. $11AA_{16}$ 26. $FACE_{16}$

Problem Set 2–2

Convert the following decimal numbers to (a) binary, (b) octal, (c) hexadecimal numbers.

1. 5   2. 7

3. 12   4. 14

5. 77   6. 63

7. 100   8. 200

9. 130   10. 150

11. 256   12. 512

13. 300   14. 400

15. 673   16. 735

Convert the following binary numbers to (a) octal and (b) hexadecimal.

17. 100110   18. 110101

19. 11100010   20. 10110101

21. 10001000   22. 11000011

23. 1011100100111110   24. 0110111110111100

25. 1111110000001011   26. 1110001101111011

Perform the following conversions.

27. $275_8 = $ _____$_2 = $ _____$_{10} = $ _____$_{16}$

28. $103_8 = $ _____$_2 = $ _____$_{10} = $ _____$_{16}$

29. $2A_{16} = $ _____$_2 = $ _____$_8 = $ _____$_{10}$

30. $B3_{16} = $ _____$_2 = $ _____$_8 = $ _____$_{10}$

31. $3F20_{16} = $ _____ $_2 = $ _____ $_8 = $ _____ $_{10}$

32. $7A0C_{16} = $ _____ $_2 = $ _____ $_8 = $ _____ $_{10}$

Consider that binary numbers are stored in 8-bit registers in the following problems.

33. $73.14_8 = $ _____ $_2 = $ _____ $_{16}$

34. $27.36_8 = $ _____ $_2 = $ _____ $_{16}$

35. $2A.0C_{16} = $ _____ $_2 = $ _____ $_8$

36. $A5.5A_{16} = $ _____ $_2 = $ _____ $_8$

37. $43.25_{10} = $ _____ $_2$

38. $73.147_{10} = $ _____ $_2$

39. $10110101.00110101_2 = $ _____ $_8 = $ _____ $_{16}$

40. $10010110.11010011_2 = $ _____ $_8 = $ _____ $_{16}$

Problem Set 2–3

Add the following octal numbers. Give answers in both octal and decimal.

1. (a) 763   (b) 277   (c) 763
       214   641   367

2. (a) 273   (b) 444   (c) 637
       171   367   214

Add the following hexadecimal numbers. Give answers in both hexadecimal and decimal.

3. (a) 4A3   (b) ABCD   (c) 109A
       D13   EF01   2D1C

4. (a) A14   (b) B29C   (c) FACE
       3D7   ED4F   BADE

Add the following binary numbers. Give answers in both binary and decimal.

5. (a) 101   (b) 1011   (c) 110011
       110   1101   100011

6. (a) 1111   (b) 10011   (c) 101111
       1111   11011   110011

Subtract the following octal numbers.

7. (a)   73   (b)   376   (c)   2133
       (−) 56   (−) 277   (−) 1574

8. (a)   72   (b)   673   (c)   6014
         (−) 15   (−) 176   (−) 3247

Subtract the following hexadecimal numbers.

9. (a)   A17   (b)   7A29   (c)   FADE
         (−) 26B   (−) 100F   (−) 2C3F

10. (a)   B27   (b)   4A9B   (c)   FACE
         (−) 6A4   (−) 2BC9   (−) AB3F

Subtract the following binary numbers. Give answers in both binary and decimal.

11. (a)   1010   (b)   110010   (c)   1100110
         (−) 0101   (−) 100111   (−) 1011001

12. (a)   1100   (b)   10110   (c)   100111
         (−) 0110   (−) 01101   (−) 001101

Problem Set 2-4

Perform the indicated operations in binary. (Assume the binary numbers are stored in 8-bit registers.) Give answers in both binary and decimal.

1. (a)   −9   (b)   13   (c)   9   (d)   −13   (e)   −6
         (+) 6   (−) −5   (+) −4   (+) 8   (−) −9

2. (a)   −8   (b)   16   (c)   7   (d)   −17   (e)   −8
         (+) 3   (−) −7   (+) −3   (−) 6   (−) −8

Convert the following decimal numbers to BCD.

3. 17

4. 38

5. 83.47

6. 73.56

Logic is an organized method of reasoning. Therefore, logic must be used when making decisions, or when calculating or processing data. One logical methodology used in the design of all digital computers is called Boolean Algebra. It was developed by Englishman George Boole around 1847. In 1938, Claude E. Shannon, a research assistant at M.I.T., published a paper describing how Boolean algebra could be used to represent two-state, or binary, circuits used in today's modern digital computers.

Boolean algebra uses three basic operators: logical multiplication, called the AND function; logical addition, called the OR function; and logical complementation, called the NOT function. The variables in Boolean algebra are binary. That is, the resulting variable of an operation or a set of operations can have only one of two values: 1 or 0. Variables may also be interpreted as being true or false, or yes or no.

Gates and *inverters* are circuits that are used to implement the basic logic functions. An inverter is a logic circuit that has one input and one output. A gate is a logic circuit that has at least two inputs and one output. These gates and inverters are made up of transistors, diodes, and resistors. In the present technology, they are always packaged as integrated circuits, and there are anywhere from two to many thousand gates and/or inverters in a single chip. All the flip-flops, registers, counters, adders, and other logic circuits in a computer are made up of these basic circuits.

Chapter

3

Logic and Gates

To develop an understanding of how gates and inverters are used in a computer, we must first develop an understanding of the logic functions they can perform. All input and output variables can have only one of two possible states—true or false. Because this is true, Boolean algebra becomes a valuable tool to the designer and to the technician because we can utilize the laws and theorems of Boolean algebra to simplify complex circuits and to help us understand existing circuits and systems.

In this chapter we will cover Boolean algebra, logic functions, logic gates, and logic circuits. The concepts developed in this chapter will be used throughout the book whenever a logic circuit is to be built or discussed.

3.1 LOGIC VARIABLES

Boolean algebra is used in manipulating logic variables. A variable is either completely true or completely false; partly true or partly false values are not allowed. When a variable is not true, by implication it must be false. Conversely, if the variable is not false, it must be true. Because of this characteristic, Boolean algebra is ideally suited to variables that have two states, or values, such as YES and NO, or for a number system that has two values, 1 and 0 (i.e., the binary number system).

A variable is a quantity represented by a symbol. For example, B (the variable) could represent the presence of Bob. B has two values: if Bob is present, B equals "true"; if Bob is absent, B equals "false." Note that Bob is not the variable; B is the variable that represents the presence of Bob.

A switch is ideally suited to represent the value of any two-state variable because it can only be "off" or "on." Consider the SPST switch in Figure 3-1. When the switch is in the closed position, it indicates that Bob is present (B = true). When it is in the open position, it then represents that Bob is absent (B = false).

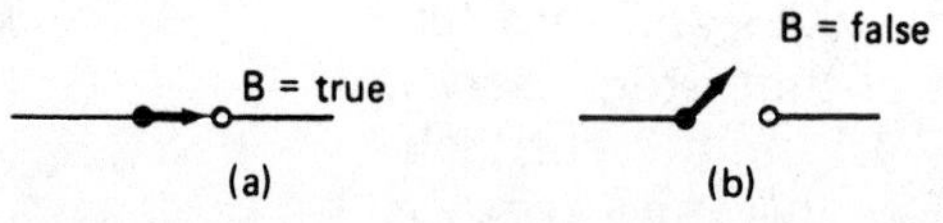

Figure 3-1. SPST switch: (a) closed, (b) open.

It should be obvious that a closed switch could also represent values such as true, yes, one (1), HIGH (H), go, etc.; and the opened switch, false, no, zero (0), LOW (L), no go, etc.

3.2 LOGIC OPERATIONS

There are only three basic logic operations:

1. The conjunction (logical product) commonly called AND, symbolized by (·).

2. The disjunction (logical sum) commonly called OR, symbolized by (+).

3. The negation commonly called NOT, symbolized by (') or (−).

These operations are performed by logic circuits. All functions within a computer can be performed by combinations of these three basic logic operations.

3.3 THE AND FUNCTION

The AND function can be illustrated by the following analogy. The members of group A are Bob, Charley, and Dick. Note that the names in this group are combined by the conjunction "and." That means group A equals the presence of Bob and Charley and Dick. This may be symbolized as

$$A = B \cdot C \cdot D$$

A is true (group A is present) when B is true (Bob is present); AND C is true (Charley is present); AND D is true (Dick is present). A is not true if any one (or more) of the members are absent.

The circuit in Figure 3–2 can be used to produce the AND function of the above example. The light indicates that group A is present only when all members of the group are present. A logic circuit producing the AND function is called an AND gate and is symbolized in Figure 3–3.

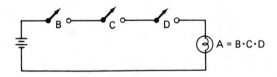

Figure 3–2. Switches connected in series to produce the AND function.

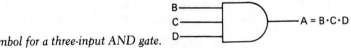

Figure 3–3. Logic symbol for a three-input AND gate.

Figure 3–4(a) shows the logic symbol for a 2-input AND gate. The function (A · B) is produced when A is true AND B is true. In order to show all of the conditions that may exist at the input and output of a logic gate, truth tables are used. Because there are two inputs and each input has two possible states (true and false), the number of possible conditions at the input would be 2 raised to the second power (2^2), or 4. The truth table for a 2-input AND gate is shown in Figure 3–4(b). Note that condition 4 is the only one in which all of the inputs are true so that the AND function is produced and a true output appears.

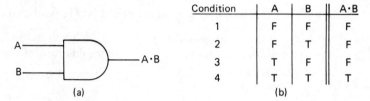

Condition	A	B	A·B
1	F	F	F
2	F	T	F
3	T	F	F
4	T	T	T

(a)   (b)

Figure 3–4. Two-input AND gate: (a) logic symbol, (b) truth table.

AND gates may have two or more inputs. Figure 3–5 shows a 3-input AND gate and its truth table. Ones (1) and zeros (0) are used for the values of the variables. Because three variables are used, eight possible conditions exist ($2^3 = 8$). Condition 8 is the only one that will produce a true output (1) because all of the input variables are true (equal to 1).

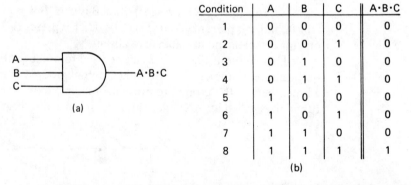

Condition	A	B	C	A·B·C
1	0	0	0	0
2	0	0	1	0
3	0	1	0	0
4	0	1	1	0
5	1	0	0	0
6	1	0	1	0
7	1	1	0	0
8	1	1	1	1

(b)

Figure 3–5. Three-input AND gate: (a) logic symbol, (b) truth table.

At this point, it should be stated that the (·) symbol used in the expression A · B · C is the AND operator and indicates logical multiplication. For example, condition 8 in Figure 3–5 can be interpreted as $1 \times 1 \times 1 = 1$; whereas condition 7 can be interpreted as $1 \times 1 \times 0 = 0$.

Using the same approach, we find that all other conditions (1 through 6) also produce a zero. It is important to remember that in the binary system, a 2 cannot exist—only 1's and 0's. As with ordinary algebra, the operator symbol (·) can be omitted; thus, $A \cdot B \cdot C = ABC$ and is read "A AND B AND C."

3.4 THE OR FUNCTION

The OR function is exemplified by the following analogy. The members of group A are Bob, Charley, and Dick. A representative of this group could be Bob or Charley or Dick, or any combination of them. This expression may be symbolized as

$$R = B + C + D$$

Where R is a representative of group A, R is true (a representative of group A is present) when B is true (that is, when Bob is present); OR C is true (Charley is present); OR D is true (Dick is present). Only one of the members must be present in order that group A be represented. However, group A is also represented when more than one member is present. Group A will not be represented when all members are absent.

The circuit in Figure 3–6 can be used to produce the OR function of the above example. The light (R) indicates that a representative of group A is present when one OR more members are present. A circuit producing the OR function is called an OR gate; it is symbolized in Figure 3–7.

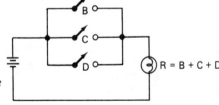

Figure 3–6. Switches connected in parallel to produce the OR function.

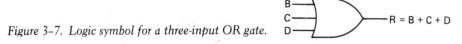

Figure 3–7. Logic symbol for a three-input OR gate.

Figure 3–8(a) shows the logic symbol for a 2-input OR gate. The function (A + B) is produced when A is true OR B is true. The OR function described here is inclusive; that is, it allows for the possibility that a true output is produced when both inputs are true.

A truth table for the 2-input OR gate appears in Figure 3–8(b). Because there are two input variables, a total of four conditions are possible ($2^2 = 4$). Note that conditions 2, 3, and 4 produce a true output because at least one of the input variables is true. Condition 1 produces a false output because neither one of the input variables is true.

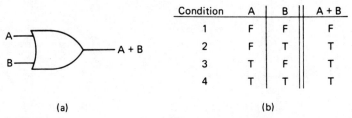

Condition	A	B	A + B
1	F	F	F
2	F	T	T
3	T	F	T
4	T	T	T

(a)   (b)

Figure 3-8. Two-input OR gate: (a) logic symbol, (b) truth table.

OR gates may have two or more inputs. Figure 3-9 shows a 3-input OR gate and its truth table. Ones (1) and zeros (0) are used for the values of the variables. Because three variables are used, eight possible conditions occur ($2^3 = 8$). Conditions 2 through 8 produce a true (1) output because at least one of the input variables is true (1). Condition 1 is the only one that does not produce a true output.

It should be pointed out at this time that the " + " symbol used in the expression A + B + C is the OR operator and indicates logical addition. In logical addition, $1 + 0 = 1$ and $1 + 1 = 1$. One OR one does not equal two! Condition 8 in Figure 3-9 may be interpreted as $1 + 0 + 0 = 1$. Condition 1 produces a zero (0) output because $0 + 0 + 0 = 0$.

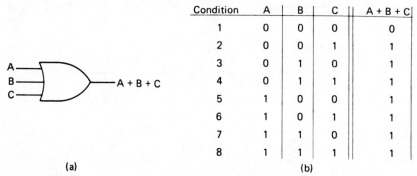

Condition	A	B	C	A + B + C
1	0	0	0	0
2	0	0	1	1
3	0	1	0	1
4	0	1	1	1
5	1	0	0	1
6	1	0	1	1
7	1	1	0	1
8	1	1	1	1

(a)   (b)

Figure 3-9. Three-input OR gate: (a) logic symbol, (b) truth table.

3.5 THE NOT FUNCTION

The NOT function is produced by the inverting operation. The concept can be illustrated by the circuit in Figure 3-10. The switch is normally closed; therefore, the indicator lamp will light (true). Activating the switch (turning it off), however, will break the circuit, and the lamp will go out (not true). We may then say that the lamp is on (true) only when the switch is not activated. This condition can be expressed as

$$L = \bar{A}$$

This condition is verbalized as "L equals NOT A."

A logic circuit producing the NOT function is called an inverter; its symbol appears in Figure 3-11. An inverter converts the state or value of a variable to its complement. Thus, if variable A appears at the input, $\overline{A}$ is produced at the output; conversely, when $\overline{A}$ appears at the input, A is produced at the output. When performing the NOT function, a 1 will be changed to a 0 and vice versa, as shown in the truth table in Figure 3-11(b).

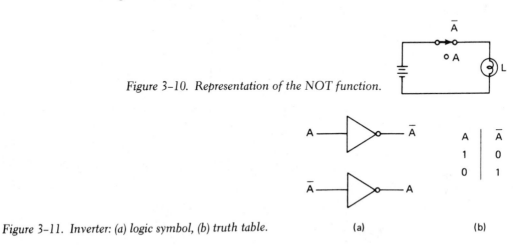

Figure 3-10. Representation of the NOT function.

Figure 3-11. Inverter: (a) logic symbol, (b) truth table.   (a)   (b)

A	$\overline{A}$
1	0
0	1

3.6 BOOLEAN EXPRESSIONS

The three basic logic functions discussed—AND, OR, and NOT—either individually or in various combinations, are the basic building blocks for all computer logic circuits. A few of these combinations will be illustrated by our group "A" analogy consisting of the presence of Bob (B), Charley (C), and Dick (D). Suppose we wish to describe a situation where the group (A) is represented by the presence of Bob (B) and Charley (C), but not Dick (D). This situation could be expressed as $X = BC\overline{D}$, which states that Bob and Charley are present, but Dick is NOT present; it is illustrated in Figure 3-12. Note the use of the inverter.

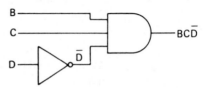

Figure 3-12. Logic circuit used to represent the expression
$A = BC\overline{D}$.

How would you describe a condition whereby the group (A) is represented by at least two members—in other words, a majority? This situation could be expressed in Boolean algebra as

$$X = BC + BD + CD$$

and is symbolized in Figure 3-13.

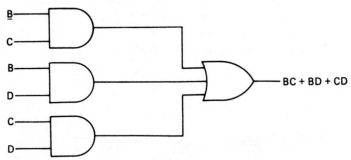

Figure 3-13. Logic circuit used to represent the expression
BC + BD + CD.

How could the group be represented by the presence of Charley (C) and the absence of both Bob (B) and Dick (D)? One possible method would be

$$A = \overline{B} C \overline{D}$$

It is shown in Figure 3-14.

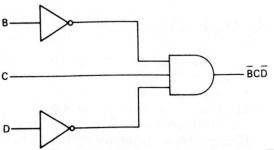

Figure 3-14. Logic circuit used to represent the expression $\overline{B}C\overline{D}$.

Suppose we wish to express the situation whereby the *entire group* is NOT present—in other words, one or more members are absent. The Boolean expression would be

$$A = \overline{B \; C \; D}$$

It is illustrated in Figure 3-15. Note that the entire group is affected by the inverter.

Figure 3-15. Logic circuit used to represent the expression $\overline{BCD}$.

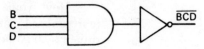

Finally, how would you express a situation where the group is represented by either Bob and Charley or by Dick alone? One possible method is shown in Figure 3-16.

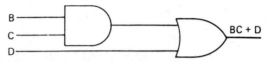

Figure 3-16. Logic circuit used to represent the expression BC + D.

Logic diagrams are drawn in order to symbolize logic expressions. When the student interprets the diagrams, he should be able to verbalize the expression. For example, let's interpret the diagram in Figure 3-17. In order to get a true output, Charley must be present (C), AND the other input to the AND gate must also be true. This input may be interpreted as true when B OR D are not present ($\overline{B+D}$). Therefore, a true output is indicated when Charley (but not Bob and Dick) is present $C(\overline{B+D})$. The student must understand that both Bob and Dick must be absent for there to be a true output.

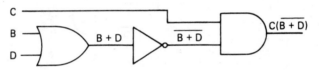

Figure 3-17. Logic circuit used to represent the expression $C(\overline{B+D})$.

3.7   THE EXCLUSIVE-OR FUNCTION

The EXCLUSIVE-OR function is an extension of the AND, OR, and NOT functions. The function may be illustrated by the following analogy. Suppose we wanted group A to be represented by the presence of either Bob or Charley, but not both. The expression may be symbolized as

$$R = B \oplus C$$

where R is a representative of group A and is true only when B is true or C is true, and is false when B and C (B·C) are true. The EXCLUSIVE-OR operator symbol is $\oplus$, an encircled plus sign.

The logic symbol for the EXCLUSIVE-OR gate appears in Figure 3-18(a); its truth table is shown in Figure 3-18(b). Notice that this truth table is identical to the truth table for the OR gate in Figure 3-8(b) with the exception of the last condition where an F appears instead of a T. The only difference between an EXCLUSIVE-OR and the OR is that for the EXCLUSIVE-OR, when both inputs are true, the output is false.

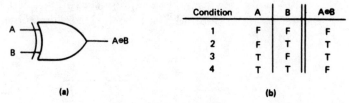

Condition	A	B	A⊕B
1	F	F	F
2	F	T	T
3	T	F	T
4	T	T	F

(a)   (b)

Figure 3-18. Two-input EXCLUSIVE-OR gate: (a) logic symbol, (b) truth table.

As previously mentioned, the AND, OR, and NOT functions are basic logic building blocks. These may be used to produce the EXCLUSIVE-OR function. One Boolean expression for the EXCLUSIVE-OR function is $B\overline{C} + \overline{B}C$. The logic diagram for this expression is shown in Figure 3-19(a).

Another expression is $(A + B)\overline{A\,B}$ The logic diagram for this expression appears in Figure 3-19(b).

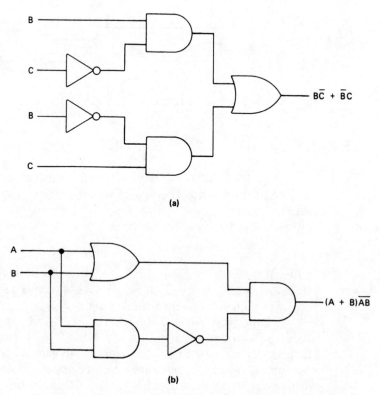

Figure 3-19. Logic diagrams for the EXCLUSIVE-OR function.

3.8 BOOLEAN POSTULATES AND THEOREMS

The following postulates, laws, and theorems are important in the simplification and manipulation of logic expressions. The student is encouraged to become familiar with these because they will be used throughout this chapter. Note that each postulate, law, or theorem is described in two parts. These are duals of each other; that is, the dual of the OR operator is the AND, while the dual of a given variable is its complement.

POSTULATES	
1a. $A = 1$ (if $A \neq 0$)	1b. $A = 0$ (if $A \neq 1$)
2a. $0 \cdot 0 = 0$	2b. $0 + 0 = 0$
3a. $1 \cdot 1 = 1$	3b. $1 + 1 = 1$
4a. $1 \cdot 0 = 0$	4b. $1 + 0 = 1$
5a. $\bar{1} = 0$	5b. $\bar{0} = 1$

Postulates are self-evident truths. Consider postulates 1a and 1b. A variable is either true (1) or false (0). Postulates 2a, 3a, and 4a represent the conjunctive (AND) form and define the function of the AND operator, as shown in Figure 3–20. Postulates 2b, 3b, and 4b represent the disjunction (OR) form and define the function of the OR operator, as shown in Figure 3–21. Postulates 5a and 5b define the function of the NOT operator, as illustrated in Figure 3–22.

Figure 3–20. *Logic symbolization of postulates 2a, 3a, and 4a.*

Figure 3–21. *Logic symbolization of postulates 2b, 3b, and 4b.*

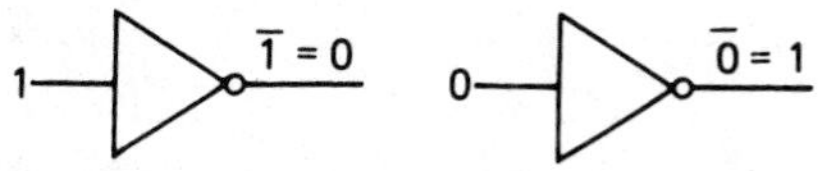

Figure 3–22. *Logic symbolization of postulates 5a and 5b.*

The following are properties of ordinary algebra that also apply to Boolean algebra. Remember, Boolean expressions contain variables having only two possible values.

ALGEBRAIC PROPERTIES

Commutative

    6a. $AB = BA$ 6b. $A + B = B + A$

Associative

    7a. $A(BC) = AB(C)$ 7b. $A + (B + C) = (A + B) + C$

Distributive

    8a. $A(B + C) = AB + AC$ 8b. $A + BC = (A + B)(A + C)$

The commutative property simply means that the circuit is not affected by the order or sequence of the variables. This is illustrated in Figure 3–23.

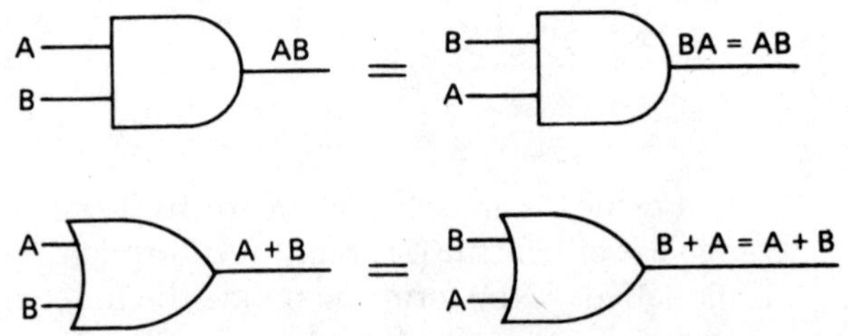

Figure 3-23. Logic symbols used to demonstrate commutative property.

The associative property pertains to the parentheses. It shows that a sequence exclusively of AND functions (property 7a) or a sequence exclusively of OR functions (property 7b) is not affected by the placement of the parentheses as indicated in Figure 3–24.

The distributive property for 8a and 8b may be proven by performing the algebraic multiplication or by factoring. Figure 3–25 shows that the application of the distributive property produces two forms of an expression, and thus, two circuits may be realized for each.

The following theorems define the application of the operators to variables:

THEOREMS

9a. $A \cdot 0 = 0$	9b. $A + 0 = A$
10a. $A \cdot 1 = A$	10b. $A + 1 = 1$
11a. $A \cdot A = A$	11b. $A + A = A$
12a. $A \cdot \overline{A} = 0$	12b. $A + \overline{A} = 1$
13a. $\overline{\overline{A}} = A$	13b. $A = \overline{\overline{A}}$

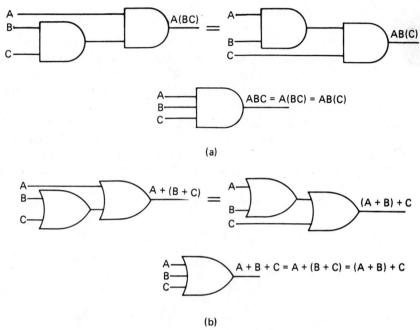

(a)

(b)

Figure 3-24. Logic symbols and circuits used to demonstrate the associative property: (a) logic circuit to demonstrate AND, (b) logic circuit to demonstrate OR.

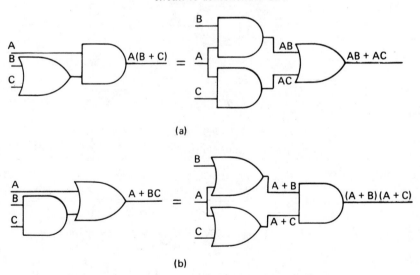

(a)

(b)

Figure 3-25. Logic symbols and circuits used to demonstrate distributive property: (a) logic circuit to demonstrate A(B + C) = AB + AC; (b) logic circuit to demonstrate A + BC = (A + B)(A + C).

Theorems 9a, 10a, 11a, and 12a pertain to the AND function. These are symbolized in Figure 3–26. For theorem 9a, one of the variables is always a zero. Therefore, the output will be a zero regardless of the value of A. Theorem 10a tells us the output will be determined by the input variable A. If A = 1, then $1 \cdot 1 = 1$. If A = 0, then $1 \cdot 0 = 0$. For 11a, if the input variable A = 1, the output will be $1 \cdot 1 = 1$. If the input variable A = 0, the output will be $0 \cdot 0 = 0$.

For theorem 12a, the output will always be 0 because when the input variable A = 1, the other input variable will be 0 ($\overline{A}$), causing the output to be $1 \cdot 0 = 0$. The same output will be produced when the values of the input variables are reversed. Theorem 12a is called a self-contradiction.

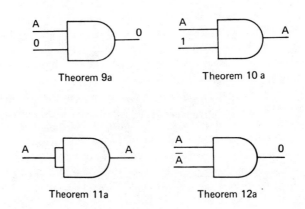

Figure 3–26. Logic symbolization of the AND function.

Theorem 13a expresses double negation. An expression that has been inverted twice equals its original value, as shown in Figure 3–27.

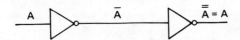

Figure 3–27. Logic symbolization of double negation.

Theorems 9b, 10b, 11b, and 12b pertain to the OR function and are illustrated in Figure 3–28. For the OR function, one or more of the input variables must be true in order that a true output be present. For theorems 9b and 11b, the output is determined by the input variable A. For 10b and

12b, the output will be a 1 regardless of the value of A. For theorem 12b, either A or $\overline{A}$ must always equal 1.

DeMorgan's Theorem

14a. $\overline{A}\,\overline{B}\,\overline{C} = \overline{A + B + C}$ 14b. $\overline{A} + \overline{B} + \overline{C} = \overline{A\,B\,C}$

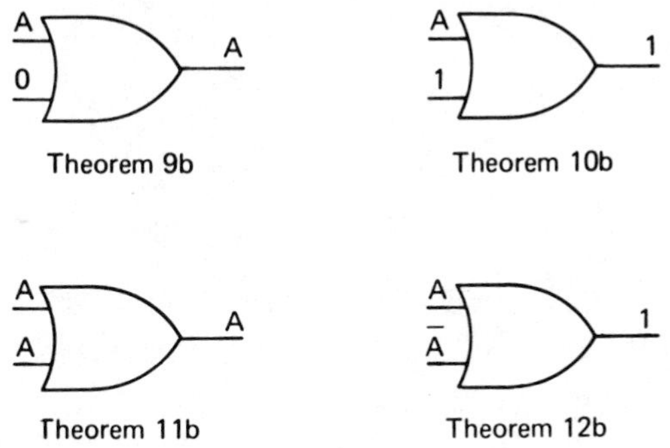

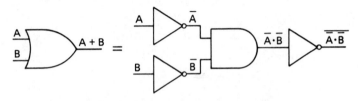

Figure 3–28. *Logic symbolization of the OR function.*

The equivalent of the Boolean expression can be found by using DeMorgan's theorem. Three steps are required: First, replace all of the OR operator symbols (+) with AND operator symbols (·) and all of the AND operator symbols with OR operator symbols; second, replace all variables with their complements; third, complement the entire expression. For example, determine DeMorgan's equivalent of the expression A + B.

Step 1. Replace the OR operator with the AND operator $A \cdot B$

Step 2. Complement each variable $\overline{A} \cdot \overline{B}$

Step 3. Complement the entire expression $\overline{\overline{A} \cdot \overline{B}}$

Therefore, $A + B = \overline{\overline{A} \cdot \overline{B}}$ and is symbolized in Figure 3–29.

Figure 3–29. *Logic symbolization demonstrating that* $A + B = \overline{\overline{A} \cdot \overline{B}}.$

Determine DeMorgan's equivalent of the expression AB.

Step 1. Replace the AND operator with the OR operator A + B

Step 2. Complement each variable $\overline{A} + \overline{B}$

Step 3. Complement the entire expression $\overline{\overline{A} + \overline{B}}$

Therefore, AB = $\overline{\overline{A} + \overline{B}}$ and is symbolized in Figure 3-30.

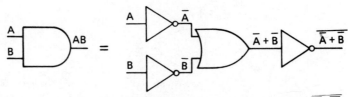

Figure 3-30. Logic symbolization demonstrating that AB = $\overline{\overline{A} + \overline{B}}$.

Let's find the DeMorgan's equivalent of the expression in theorem 14a, $\overline{A} \cdot \overline{B} \cdot \overline{C}$.

Step 1. $\overline{A} + \overline{B} + \overline{C}$

Step 2. $\overline{\overline{A}} + \overline{\overline{B}} + \overline{\overline{C}} = A + B + C$

Step 3. $\overline{A + B + C}$

Therefore $\overline{A}\ \overline{B}\ \overline{C} = \overline{A + B + C}$

The symbols for the equivalent expressions above are given in Figure 3-31.

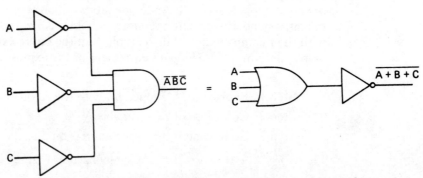

Figure 3-31. Logic symbolization of the DeMorgan's equivalency
$$\overline{A}\ \overline{B}\ \overline{C} = \overline{A + B + C}.$$

Now let's try finding DeMorgan's equivalent of the expression in theorem 14b, $\overline{A} + \overline{B} + \overline{C}$.

Step 1. $\overline{A} \cdot \overline{B} \cdot \overline{C}$

Step 2. $\overline{\overline{A}} \cdot \overline{\overline{B}} \cdot \overline{\overline{C}} = A \cdot B \cdot C$

Step 3. $\overline{A \quad B \quad C}$

Therefore $\overline{A} + \overline{B} + \overline{C} = \overline{A}\ \overline{B}\ \overline{C}$.
The logic symbols for these expressions are given in Figure 3-32.

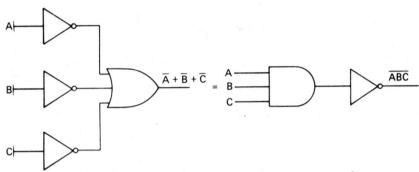

Figure 3-32. Logic symbolization of the DeMorgan's equivalency
$\overline{A} + \overline{B} + \overline{C} = \overline{ABC}$.

Sometimes variables appear in a certain pattern that can obviously be simplified. The absorption theorem shows how substitution may be used on some commonly derived patterns.

ABSORPTION THEOREM

15a. $A(A + B) = A$ 15b. $A + AB = A$
16a. $A(\overline{A} + B) = AB$ 16b. $A + \overline{A}B = A + B$

Theorems 15a and 15b show that the value of B is redundant. A true output occurs only when A is true, as shown in Figure 3-33.

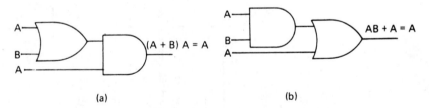

(a) (b)

Figure 3-33. Logic symbolization of: (a) theorem 15a, (b) theorem 15b.

Theorem 16a states that only when A AND B are true, the statement is true, as shown in Figure 3-34. Recall that A and $\overline{A}$ cannot be true simultaneously.

Theorem 16b is the dual of theorem 16a and is shown in Figure 3-35. For the expression to be true, either A must be true or B must be true. ($\overline{A}$ is redundant.)

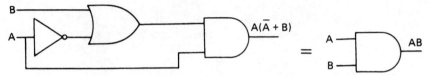

Figure 3-34. Logic symbolization of theorem 16a.

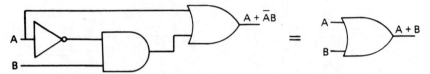

Figure 3-35. Logic symbolization of theorem 16b.

3.9   TRUTH TABLES

Logical expressions can be studied very conveniently by using truth tables. Truth tables present in columnar form all the possible combinations that can exist. The number of possible combinations is a function of the number of variables in question. Since each variable can attain a value of either 1 or 0, the number of possible combinations is equal to 2 raised to the number of variables. For example, if a gate has two variables, A and B, then there exist 2^2, or 4 possible combinations. A three-input gate would have 2^3, or 8 possible combinations, and so forth.

In the construction of a truth table, it is important to keep the correct order of the original statement and not to skip any steps along the way. For example, the truth table that verifies the statement $AB = \overline{\overline{A} + \overline{B}}$ is given in Figure 3-36.

A	B	AB	$\overline{A}$	$\overline{B}$	$\overline{A} + \overline{B}$	$\overline{\overline{A} + \overline{B}}$
0	0	0	1	1	1	0
0	1	0	1	0	1	0
1	0	0	0	1	1	0
1	1	1	0	0	0	1

EQUAL

Figure 3-36. Truth table to verify the statement $AB = \overline{\overline{A} + \overline{B}}$.

Note that the two input variables, A and B, are arranged such that all four possible combinations are represented. The AB column is a result of "ANDing" columns A and B according to postulates previously described. In the next two columns, A and then B are complemented. The $\overline{A} + \overline{B}$ column is a result of "ORing" the $\overline{A}$ and $\overline{B}$ columns. Finally, $(\overline{A} + \overline{B})$ is complemented to produce the $\overline{\overline{A} + \overline{B}}$ column. Note that the contents of column AB and column $\overline{\overline{A} + \overline{B}}$ are identical. Therefore

$$AB = \overline{\overline{A} + \overline{B}} \quad \text{(DeMorgan's theorem)}$$

Consider the expression $A + \overline{A}B = A + B$ (absorption theorem 16b). Because there are two variables, a total of four combinations exist, as shown in Figure 3–37.

The term $A + \overline{A}B$ is broken into three columns, $\overline{A}$, $\overline{A}B$, and $A + \overline{A}B$. Finally, A and B are ORed to form the $A + B$ column. Note that the order of column $A + \overline{A}B$ is the same as that of column $A + B$. Therefore, $A + \overline{A}B = A + B$.

Let us now construct a truth table for DeMorgan's theorem (14a), which states that $\overline{A + B + C} = \overline{A}\ \overline{B}\ \overline{C}$. Because there are three variables,

Input variables		$\overline{A}$	$\overline{A}B$	$A + \overline{A}B$	$A + B$
A	B				
0	0	1	0	0	0
0	1	1	1	1	1
1	0	0	0	1	1
1	1	0	0	1	1

EQUAL

Figure 3–37. Truth table to verify the statement $A + \overline{A}B = A + B$.

2^3, or 8, combinations exist, as shown in Figure 3–38. Note that column $\overline{A + B + C}$ is identical to column $\overline{A}\ \overline{B}\ \overline{C}$. Therefore

$$\overline{A + B + C} = \overline{A}\ \overline{B}\ \overline{C}$$

Input variables			$A + B + C$	$\overline{A + B + C}$	$\overline{A}$	$\overline{B}$	$\overline{C}$	$\overline{A}\overline{B}\overline{C}$
A	B	C						
0	0	0	0	1	1	1	1	1
0	0	1	1	0	1	1	0	0
0	1	0	1	0	1	0	1	0
0	1	1	1	0	1	0	0	0
1	0	0	1	0	0	1	1	0
1	0	1	1	0	0	1	0	0
1	1	0	1	0	0	0	1	0
1	1	1	1	0	0	0	0	0

EQUAL

Figure 3–38. Truth table to verify the statement $\overline{A + B + C} = \overline{A}\ \overline{B}\ \overline{C}$.

The truth table proving the associative property $A + B + C = A + (B + C) = (A + B) + C$ is shown in Figure 3-39.

The process of using truth tables to prove the equality of two expressions is called proof by perfect induction. The student is encouraged to use truth tables to evaluate logic expressions or to prove the results of logic operations. He can also use tables to define the function of various logic circuits.

Input variables							
A	B	C	B + C	A + (B + C)	A + B	(A + B) + C	A + B + C
0	0	0	0	0	0	0	0
0	0	1	1	1	0	1	1
0	1	0	1	1	1	1	1
0	1	1	1	1	1	1	1
1	0	0	0	1	1	1	1
1	0	1	1	1	1	1	1
1	1	0	1	1	1	1	1
1	1	1	1	1	1	1	1

EQUAL

Figure 3-39. Truth table to verify the statement
$A + (B + C) = (A + B) + C$.

3.10   TTL LOGIC GATES

Most microprocessors produced today require and provide signals that are compatible with the TTL (Transistor-Transistor Logic) family of logic circuits. This family is the most widely used family in the industry today.

TTL circuits are classified as current sinking devices; however, most have the ability to source current.

Consider the circuit in Figure 3-40. As in any common emitter configuration, Q_2 is an inverter. In order to activate the function (turn on the transistor), a current must be supplied to the base of the transistor. This may be accomplished by an identical circuit (Q_1) in the off state. A source of current is required to turn on the transistor. When Q_2 is off, its output will supply (source) current to the next circuit. This mode of switching is called current sourcing.

Some circuits use internal components to turn on the transistor, as shown in Figure 3-41. In circuit A, R_1 supplies the required current to turn Q_1 on. Without an input connection, Q_1 is on and its output will be LOW level. This condition causes the input voltage to circuit B to approach 0 volts, virtually shorting out its base current. This shorting path can be

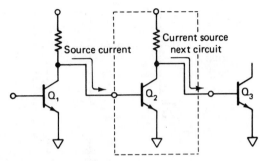

Figure 3–40. Current sourcing.

described as a "sink" for the base current of circuit B. This method of switching is called current sinking.

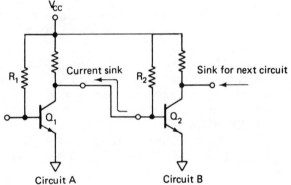

Figure 3–41. Current sinking.

The basic TTL gate uses current sinking and performs the NAND function. Logically, this is the AND function followed by a NOT as shown in Figure 3–42.

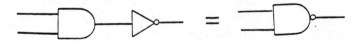

Figure 3–42. Equivalency of the NAND function.

Let's examine the TTL gate in Figure 3–43. Note that Q_2 obtains its base current from the multi-emitter transistor Q_1. If both emitters of Q_1 are HIGH, both emitter-base junctions are reverse-biased. However, the collector-base junction is forward-biased, and the base of Q_2 is "current sourced" through R_1, turning Q_2 on. Q_2 turns on Q_3 and turns off Q_4, producing a LOW level output. The NAND function is realized under these conditions: "If ALL inputs are HIGH, the output will be LOW."

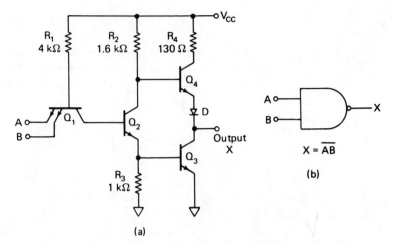

Figure 3-43. Standard TTL 2-input NAND gate: (a) schematic diagram, (b) logic symbol.

The DeMorgan's equivalent function occurs when any one or more of the inputs are LOW level. Any LOW level input provides emitter current for Q_1 and Q_1 saturates turning off Q_2. If Q_2 is off, Q_4 turns on and Q_3 turns off. This results in a HIGH level output—"If one or more inputs are LOW, the output will be HIGH."

Q_3 and Q_4 form a circuit referred to as a totem pole. The advantage of this circuit is that it provides a low-driving source impedance.

3.11 SPECIFICATIONS

In their specification sheets, manufacturers guarantee that a device will operate within specifications over its entire temperature range and supply voltage range. These specs are usually expressed in "worst case" terms: The specifications indicate how the worst-case tests were made. Worst-case testing provides a built-in margin of safety. In the authors' opinion, the most important specifications are:

1.　A definition of logic voltage levels

2.　Loading rules

3.　Noise immunity

4.　Propagation delay

Because transistor-transistor logic (TTL) is currently the most popular logic family, TTL specifications have been selected for discussion. The student should realize that specifications will differ for other logic families.

3.12 LOGIC VOLTAGE LEVELS

Assuming that HIGH level is equal to logical 1 and LOW level is equal to logical 0, note that the following definitions exist:

V_{IL} is the voltage level required for a logical 0 at an input. For the TTL 7400 series, it is a guaranteed maximum of 0.8 volts.

V_{IH} is the voltage level required for a logical 1 at an input. For the TTL 7400 series, it is a guaranteed minimum of 2 volts.

V_{OL} is the voltage level output from an output in the logical 0 state. For the TTL 7400 series, it is a guaranteed maximum of 0.4 volts.

V_{OH} is the voltage level output from an output in the logical 1 state. For the TTL 7400 series, it is a guaranteed minimum of 2.4 volts.

Figure 3–44 lists the voltage level definitions for the standard TTL family of gates.

Spec	Definition	Value
V_{OH}	Min. output voltage in the HIGH state	2.4 V
V_{OL}	Max. output voltage in the LOW state	0.4 V
V_{IH}	Min. voltage level guaranteed to be interpreted as a HIGH at the input	2.0 V
V_{IL}	Max. voltage level guaranteed to be interpreted as a LOW at the input	0.8 V

Figure 3–44. Worst case DC logic levels for the standard TTL gate.

3.13 LOADING RULES

In order to simplify designing with TTL devices, certain rules have been devised. These rules are based on the normalization of input loading and output drive factors. For the TTL 7400 series:

$$1 \text{ Unit Load (U.L.)} = 40 \ \mu A \text{ in the HIGH state}$$
$$1.6 \text{ mA in the LOW state}$$

The driving capabilities of a gate may then be expressed in terms of the number of loads it can drive. Figure 3–45 lists the input and output loading factors for various TTL families of gates. The latest TTL families are the 74S00 (Schottky) series and the 74LS00 (Low power Schottky) series. For example, the 74S00 can drive twelve 7400 loads or fifty 74LS00 loads.

The drive capability of a TTL device reflects its ability to sink current in the output LOW state and to source current in the output HIGH state. Referring to the diagram in Figure 3–46, note that the sinking current (I_{OL}) is defined as the maximum current into the driving gate in the LOW state. This is the sum of the currents from the inputs of the driven gates.

TTL loading factors

	7400	74H00	74L00	74LS00	74S00
7400	10	8	40	20	8
74H00	12	10	50	25	10
74L00	2	1	20	10	1
74LS00	5	4	40	20	4
74S00	12	10	100	50	10

Figure 3-45. Loading factors for various TTL families of gates.

The sinking current required to drive one standard gate to a LOW state is 1.6 mA and is called I_{IL}. The standard gate has a sinking current (I_{OL}) of 16 mA and requires 1.6 mA to drive its input to a LOW state. Therefore, one standard gate has the ability to drive ten standard gate inputs to the LOW state.

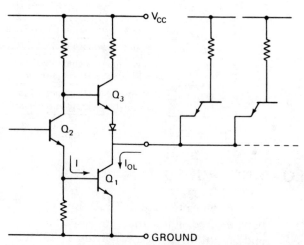

Figure 3-46. TTL output circuit in LOW state. (Courtesy of Fairchild Semiconductor.)

In order to overcome leakage current between the emitter and the base of the input device and stray capacitance, the input must be driven to the HIGH state. This is accomplished by the active pull-up transistor at the output of the driving gate (Q_3 in Figure 3-47); and it assures a fast transition from the LOW to the HIGH state. Each input of a standard gate requires a maximum of 40 μA (I_{IH}) to achieve this transition. The circuit in Figure 3-47 shows a standard gate in the HIGH state.

The active HIGH drive current (I_{OH}) for the standard gate is 800 μA. Therefore, the output of a standard gate has the ability to drive twenty standard inputs. Although the static I_{IH} requirements of most circuits is about 40 μA, about 35 mA is made available at the instant of the LOW to HIGH

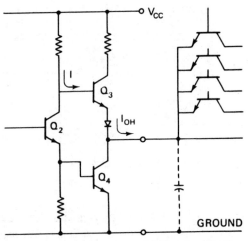

Figure 3-47. TTL output circuit in HIGH state. (Courtesy of Fairchild Semiconductor.)

output transition to charge up the stray capacitances that appear between gates.

Example—Input Load.
1. A 7400 gate, which has a maximum I_{IL} of 1.6 mA and an I_{IH} of 40 μA, is specified as having an input load factor of one U.L. (also called a fan-in of 1).
2. The 93H72, which has a value of I_{IL} = 3.2 mA and an I_{IH} of 80 μA on the CP terminal, is specified as having an input load factor of 3.2 mA/ 1.6 mA or 2 U.L.

Example—Output Drive.
The output of the 7400 will sink 16 mA in the LOW (logic 0) state and source 800 μA in the HIGH (logic 1) state. The normalized output LOW drive factor is (16 mA/1.6 mA) = 10 U.L. and the output HIGH drive factor is (800 μA/40 μA) = 20 U.L.

Limits imposed by the loading rules are based on worst-case conditions. Values for MSI [medium scale integrated (circuit)] devices vary significantly. Consult the appropriate data sheets for actual characteristics.

3.14 NOISE MARGIN

Noise margin is defined in Figure 3-48 as the difference between the worst-case output voltage and the worst-case input voltage. Notice that there is a defined noise margin for the HIGH state (V_{NH}) and another for

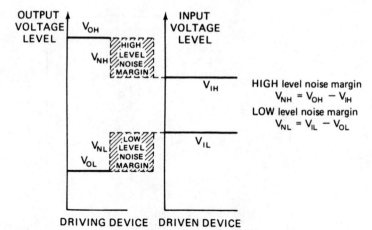

Figure 3–48. *Graph defining noise margin. (Courtesy of Fairchild Semiconductor.)*

the LOW state (V_{NL}). The noise margin allows for variations in logic levels due to switching transients and/or voltage drops on lines that interconnect gates. The voltage transfer characteristics for a standard TTL gate are shown in Figure 3–49. Notice how the noise margin guarantees are obtained.

3.15 UNUSED INPUTS

To minimize noise sensitivity and optimize switching times, unused inputs of all TTL circuits should be held between 2.4 volts and the absolute maximum of 5.5 volts. This eliminates the effect of distributed capacitance, which is associated with the floating input, and ensures that no degradation will occur in the switching times. This may be accomplished by a pull-up resistor for these unused inputs or by tying them to the outputs of unused gates that are in the HIGH state.

3.16 PROPAGATION DELAY

Switching speeds in logic gates are usually expressed in terms of propagation delay times (t_{PD}) rather than rise and fall times. This is because it is important to know how long it takes to produce a function through a gate or series of gates. Two parameters are usually provided in specification sheets: (1) propagation delay time t_{PHL} is the time required for a transition from the HIGH state to the LOW state; and (2) the delay time required for a transition from the LOW state to the HIGH state is called t_{PLH}. These output transitions are measured with respect to an input pulse. The manufac-

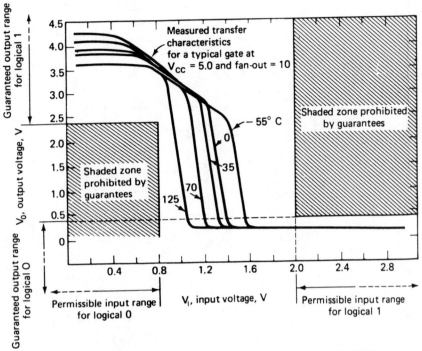

Figure 3-49. Voltage transfer characteristic for a standard TTL 7400 gate. (Courtesy of Texas Instruments, Inc.)

turer also specifies test conditions such as V_{CC}, temperature, loading factors, capacitance, etc. Figure 3-50 shows a test setup used to test the propagation delay of a NAND gate. Average propagation delay (t_{PD}) is the average of t_{PLH} and t_{PHL} and is more generally used because every gate inverts. For example, the propagation delay for the two gates shown in Figure 3-51 is the sum of t_{PHL} and t_{PLH}.

3.17   APPLYING DEMORGAN'S THEOREM TO LOGIC GATES

The NAND gate in Figure 3-52(a) tells the technician, "If both inputs are HIGH level, the output will be LOW level." Although the symbol did not say anything about the other possible conditions, the technician could assume by implication that if either input *or* both inputs are LOW level, the output would be HIGH level. The gate, therefore, could be redrawn as in Figure 3-52(b).

This basic equivalency of gates is expressed by DeMorgan's theorem:

$$\overline{A\,B} = \overline{A} + \overline{B}$$

TEST CIRCUIT

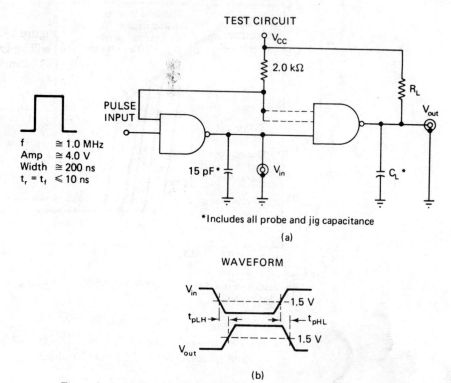

f   ≅ 1.0 MHz
Amp   ≅ 4.0 V
Width ≅ 200 ns
$t_r = t_f$ ≤ 10 ns

*Includes all probe and jig capacitance

(a)

WAVEFORM

(b)

Figure 3-50. *Test circuit used to measure propagation delay: (a) test circuit, (b) waveform. (Courtesy of Fairchild Semiconductor.)*

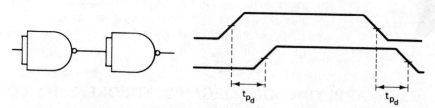

Figure 3-51. *Propagation delay for two TTL gates.*

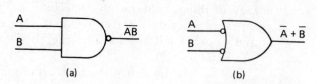

(a)   (b)

Figure 3-52. *(a) NAND gate; (b) DeMorgan's equivalent gate.*

The redrawn version of the NAND gate is called DeMorgan's equivalent gate and may be read as, "If either *or* both inputs are LOW level, the output will be HIGH level."

The technician would read the NOR symbol in Figure 3-53(a) as, "If either input *or* both inputs are HIGH level, the output will be LOW level." The DeMorgan's equivalent gate appears in Figure 3-53(b) and is read, "If both inputs are LOW level, the output will be HIGH level."

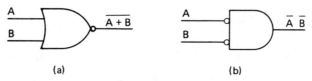

(a)   (b)

Figure 3-53. (a) NOR gate; (b) DeMorgan's equivalent gate.

Again, this basic equivalency of gates is expressed by DeMorgan's theorem:

$$\overline{A + B} = \overline{A} \cdot \overline{B}$$

A very simple rule may be applied to all gates when the DeMorgan's equivalent is desired: The AND and OR symbols may be interchanged if *all* of the level indicators are interchanged. Figure 3-54 shows a number of examples of this rule. For reasons of economy, families of logic are often manufactured so that all functions are performed with one basic circuit. The student should realize that all functions (AND, OR, and NOT) are inherent in every inverting gate.

3.18 INTERPRETING LOGIC DIAGRAMS

Logic diagrams should be drawn so that the reader understands the logic function intended as well as the levels required to activate these functions. Remember that for purposes of this text, high level is associated with "true," "yes," or "one"; and low level is associated with "false," "no," or "zero."

For example, Figure 3-55 demonstrates that the logic symbol for the NOT function can be drawn two ways. The symbol in Figure 3-55(a) should be used to indicate that a high level at its input will produce a low level at its output. In other words, if A is true or equal to 1 at the input, $\overline{A}$ will be false and will be equal to 0 at the output. Figure 3-55(b) should be used to indicate that a low level at the input will produce a high level at the output. In other words if $\overline{A}$ is false or equal to 0 at the input, the output (A) will be true or equal to 1. This distinction is important for the technician because it tells him the level that will exist for the function intended.

| GATES
AND
DEMORGAN'S EQUIVALENTS | | TABLE
OF
COMBINATIONS | | |

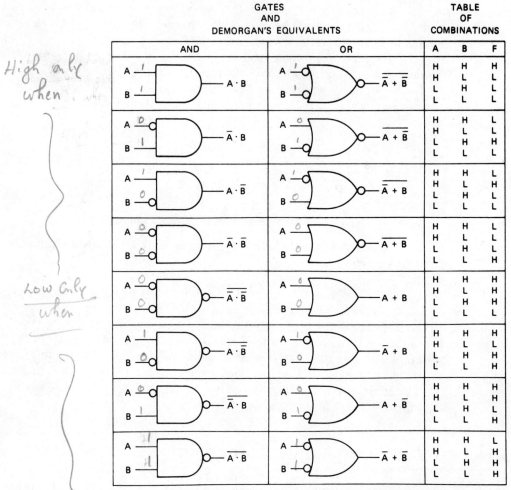

Figure 3-54. Gates and their DeMorgan's equivalents.

There are only two input conditions. The symbol should be drawn to indicate to the technician which condition is significant. The symbol in Figure 3-55(b) tells the technician that the significant input condition is LOW and the significant output condition is HIGH. The symbol in Figure 3-55(a) tells the technician that the significant input condition is HIGH and the significant output condition is LOW.

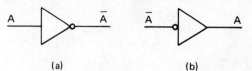

(a)   (b)

Figure 3-55. Inverter with active high level input; (b) inverter with active low level input.

Consider the diagram in Figure 3–56. There are four possible input conditions. Because of the AND function, only one of the four is significant. Only when A is true and $\overline{B}$ is false do we get the indicated output. The diagram tells the technician what the significant input condition is when A is HIGH (no low-level indicator) and $\overline{B}$ is LOW (low-level indicator on input side of the inverter). The technician should know that this condi-

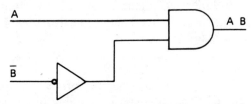

Figure 3–56. Circuit indicating significant input levels.

tion is significant even though he has not yet read all the logic that follows. The diagram also tells him that the significant output condition is high level because there is no low-level indicator at the output.

The logic diagram in Figure 3–57(a) is poorly drawn because it does not indicate clearly the function performed by the circuit. If we apply DeMorgan's theorem to the expression, we simplify it to AB + CD.

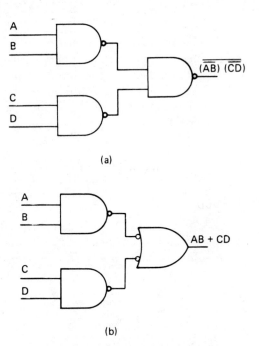

Figure 3–57. (a) Poorly drawn logic diagram; (b) DeMorgan's theorem applied to simplify meaning of logic.

DeMorgan's theorem may also be applied to the diagram itself. The output gate is redrawn so that the AND symbol is changed to OR and the level indicators are all changed. The resulting diagram in Figure 3–57(b) may now be read as

$$\overline{\overline{AB} + \overline{CD}}$$

Logically, whenever a low-level indicator appears at both ends of a line, as they do here, between gates, they may be ignored. The expression then reads

$$AB + CD$$

The technician can interpret this as meaning that whenever A and B are high level or whenever C and D are high level (the two significant input conditions), the output will be high level. Since there is no low-level indicator at the output, the indication is that the significant level is high.

The way that the diagram is drawn can greatly simplify the technician's job of troubleshooting a circuit. Consider this: The logic diagram in Figure 3–57 has a total of sixteen possible input conditions, but the technician need only look for two of the sixteen!

3.19 IMPLEMENTING LOGIC EXPRESSIONS

The process of changing a logic expression into a logic diagram by using a specific family of logic gates is called implementation.

Let's implement the simple expression $A \cdot B$ using NAND gates. (AND gates and OR gates are not as common as NAND gates and NOR gates). Because the NAND gate inverts, an inverter is used as shown in Figure 3–58.

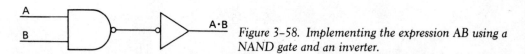

Figure 3–58. Implementing the expression AB using a NAND gate and an inverter.

When using a NAND gate to perform the OR function, the DeMorgan's equivalent symbol is used as in Figure 3–59. Because the NAND gate "ORs" only low levels, two inverters are required at the input.

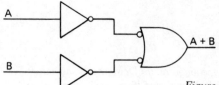

Figure 3–59. Implementing the OR function using a NAND gate.

The AND and OR functions can be accomplished by using NOR gates as shown in Figure 3–60.

The student will note that inverters must be used for each example above. However, gates are usually connected in such a sequence that the inversions tend to cancel themselves.

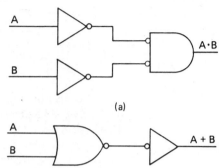

Figure 3-60. (a) Implementing the AND function using a NOR gate and two inverters; (b) implementing the OR function using a NOR gate and one inverter.

The rules given for analyzing logic circuits are also useful for determining how a logic expression may be implemented. In general, a logic expression can be implemented in various ways. The implementation selected depends on considerations such as the number of gates, type of gates, signal levels available, and signal levels required.

When implementing a logic expression, a systematic approach should be followed. First, simplify the expression as much as possible using Boolean algebra. Second, draw a first-level logic diagram. Third, replace gates in drawings with gates available from the family you have selected. Finally, make modifications as required. For example, if we were to implement the expression AB + CD + AB using NAND gates, our first step would be to use Boolean algebra to simplify the expression to

$$AB + CD \qquad (AB + AB = AB)$$

At this time, such a simplification may seem obvious. However, it may not have been so at the time the problem was first expressed. Next, the first-level logic diagram is drawn—as in Figure 3–61. The third step is to redraw the diagram using NAND gate symbols as shown in Figure 3–62. The fourth step is not necessary because modifications are not required.

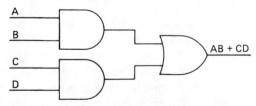

Figure 3-61. First-level logic diagram of the expression AB + CD.

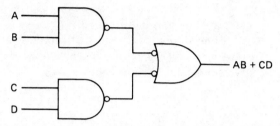

Figure 3-62. Redrawn diagram using symbols from TTL NAND family.

Let us now implement the above expression using NOR gates. Steps 1 and 2 would be the same as above. Step 3 produces the diagram shown in Figure 3-63.

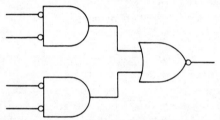

Figure 3-63. Redrawn diagram using NOR gates.

You will note that low-level indicators appear at the inputs and the output. Therefore, modification is required. In order to obtain a true output (high level), an inverter is required as shown in Figure 3-64.

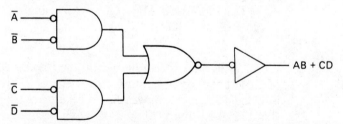

Figure 3-64. Redrawn logic diagram with an inverter at output and appropriate variables at input.

The variables are commonly stored in flip-flops. Therefore, both the variable and its complement are available. Because the inputs to the circuit of Figure 3-64 require the complement form (low level active), care should be used when selecting the appropriate output of the flip-flop.

Let's implement the expression AB + AC using NOR gates. The first step is to simplify the expression, if that is possible, by using Boolean algebra as follows:

1.   AB + AC

2.   A(B + C)   (distributive property)

The second step is to draw the first-level logic diagram as shown in Figure 3-65.

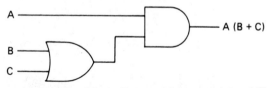

Figure 3-65. First-level logic diagram of the expression A(B + C).

In the third step, the gates in the drawing are replaced by NOR gates as shown in Figure 3-66. Note that the complement of A is required at the input of the equivalent gate. The complement may be obtained by connecting to an active low output or by using an inverter.

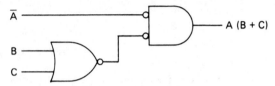

Figure 3-66. Implementation of the expression A(B + C) using NOR gates.

If we implemented the above expression using only NAND gates, the first two steps of the implementation sequence would be the same. The third step is to substitute gate symbols as shown in Figure 3-67. Note that in order to obtain an active high level at the output, an inverter is required. Also, the complements of B and C are required at the input.

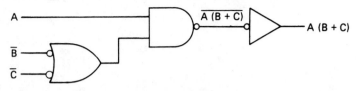

Figure 3-67. Implementation of the expression A(B + C) using NAND gates.

The original expression (AB + AC) may be implemented using TTL NAND gates, as shown in Figure 3-68.

Implementing the expanded form of the expression is sometimes desirable, as in this case, where all inputs and the output are active high level.

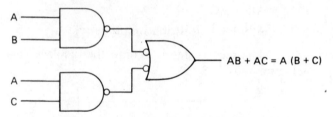

Figure 3-68. *Implementation of the expression AB + AC using NAND gates.*

The student should keep in mind that the input to the next logic function or to a flip-flop may require either a LOW level or a HIGH level to activate it. Therefore, the output level should be modified only if necessary.

It may also be helpful to understand that an expression with a bar extending completely across it relates directly to low level active. For example, if the expression $\overline{AB} + \overline{AB}$ appeared at the input of a logic gate, it should mean that the input is active when it is low level. On the other hand, if the expression $A\overline{B} + \overline{A}B$ appears at the input of a logic gate, that input should be active when it is high level.

Problem Set 3–1

1. What are the three basic logic operations?
2. How many inputs may an AND gate have?
3. How many inputs may an OR gate have?
4. How many inputs may an EXCLUSIVE–OR gate have?
5. Draw the logic symbol for a 4-input AND gate.
6. Draw the logic symbol for a 5-input OR gate.

Construct a truth table for the Boolean statements in problems 7 through 16. (Use 0's and 1's.)

7. $X = BC\overline{D}$
8. $X = BC + BD + CD$
9. $X = \overline{A\,B\,C}$
10. $X = C(\overline{B + D})$
11. $X = A + \overline{A}B$
12. $X = AB + C$
13. $X = A(B + C)$
14. $X = A\overline{B} + \overline{A}B$
15. $X = A\,\overline{BC}$
16. $X = A\,\overline{B} + \overline{C}$

Problem Set 3-2

1.   Write the Boolean expression for the logic diagrams in Figure 3–69.

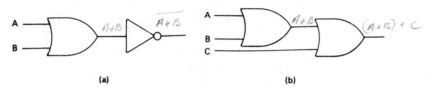

(a)   (b)

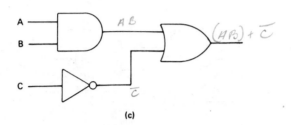

(c)

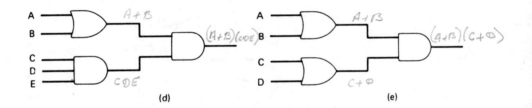

(d)   (e)

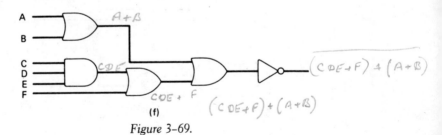

(f)

Figure 3–69.

2.   Write the Boolean expression for the logic diagrams in Figure 3–70.

Draw the logic diagrams that represent the following Boolean expressions:

3. $\overline{A + \overline{B}}$ 8. $\overline{A\,B} + \overline{A}\,C$

4. $A\overline{B} + \overline{A\,C}$ 9. $A\overline{B} + \overline{A}\,B$

5. $ABC + D$ 10. $\overline{B}(C + D)$

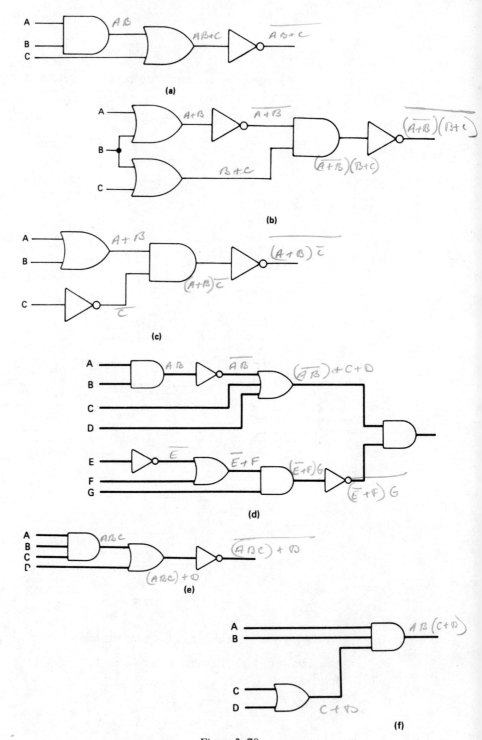

Figure 3-70.

6. $X(\overline{Y + Z})$ 11. $\overline{A\,B} + C + D$

7. $A + B\,\overline{C}$ 12. $B\,C\overline{D} + E$

Problem Set 3–3

1.   In Figure 3–41, when Q_1 is ON, what is the state of the output of Q_2?

2.   Define: (a) fan-out, (b) logical 0, (c) logical 1.

3.   In Figure 3–43, if input A is HIGH level, what is the output level?

4.   Draw the DeMorgan's equivalent circuit and construct the truth table for a 4-input NOR gate.

5.   Draw the DeMorgan's equivalent circuit and construct the truth table for a 4-input NAND gate.

6.   Using the waveforms in Figure 3–71, draw the waveforms for the output of the gate in Figure 3–72.

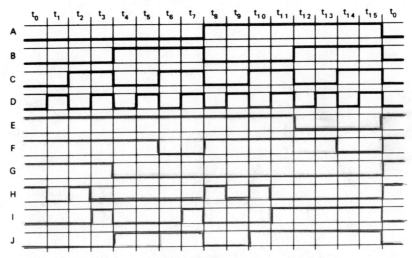

Figure 3–71. Waveforms for problems 6 through 11.

7.   Using the waveforms in Figure 3–71, draw the waveforms for the output of the gate in Figure 3–73.

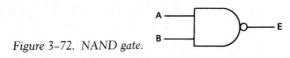

Figure 3–72. NAND gate.

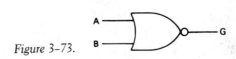

Figure 3–73.

8. Using the waveforms in Figure 3–71, draw the waveforms for the output of the gate in Figure 3–74.

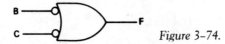

Figure 3–74.

9. Using the waveforms in Figure 3–71, draw the waveforms for the output of the gate in Figure 3–75.

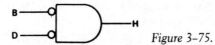

Figure 3–75.

10. Using the waveforms in Figure 3–71, draw the waveforms for the output of the logic circuit in Figure 3–76.

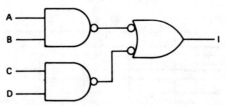

Figure 3–76.

11. Using the waveforms in Figure 3–71, draw the waveforms for the output of the logic circuit in Figure 3–77.

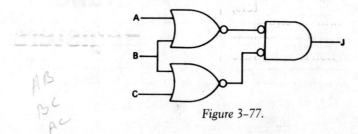

Figure 3–77.

We have learned that the three basic logic functions are AND, OR, and NOT. *All* of the computer's decision-making and arithmetic circuits are made up of these three functions. However, in order to make a decision or perform an arithmetic operation, the computer must have a place to store the input and output information (data). For example, if we are to find the sum of 3 and 6, we must write these numbers down on a piece of paper (store them), or use some of the cells of our brain to remember them. After the sum has been obtained, it is again necessary to store or remember that sum—or its value, 9, will be lost. In computers this very important function of remembering or storing bits of data is performed by various types of *flip-flops*.

Flip-flops are one of the circuits that are made from gates and inverters. A flip-flop has the ability to store one bit of information—a one or a zero. In microcomputers, though, information is stored in 8-bit or 16-bit groups. This requires many flip-flops. When flip-flops are arranged to store multibit information, they are called *registers*. These registers are classified according to the way information is entered and removed. For example, if a register is connected to the data bus in an 8-bit machine, each line of the bus connects to the register. Because the data bus will be an 8-bit bus, there are 8 flip-flops that form the register. When there is information on the data bus, and a particular register is selected to receive data, all the flip-flops will store data

Chapter

4

Flip-Flops and Registers

simultaneously. This kind of register is referred to as a *parallel* register.

When inputting or outputting data, the data is often entered or removed from a register one bit at a time. Where this is the case, the register is called a *serial*, or *shift*, register.

In this chapter we will discuss various kinds of flip-flops and registers.

4.1   THE RS FLIP–FLOP (LATCH)

The simplest flip-flop is called a *latch*. This term was originally used with early electromechanical calculators and computers, which used latching type relays to store data. The basic relay had an armature mechanically connected to various switches that implemented the appropriate logic function. An electromagnet was used to activate the switches by pulling the armature, which was spring loaded. This device did not have the ability to remember anything because when the electromagnet was de-energized, the armature was returned to its original position by the spring action.

Relays that did have the ability to remember (store data) used *two* electromagnets. One electromagnet pulled the armature to activate the function. A mechanical *latch* was used to hold the armature in this position. The second electromagnet, when energized, released the latch allowing the armature to return to its original position. When the armature was in its original or de-energized position, the flip-flop was said to be in the RESET position. When the electromagnet was energized, it was said to be in the SET position. These early day terms SET, RESET, and LATCH are applied to the present day flip-flop shown in Figure 4–1.

The RS flip-flop is bistable; that is, it has two states. When it is storing a 1 bit, it is said to be in the SET state. Conversely, when it is in the RESET state, a 0-bit is stored. Such a flip-flop has two inputs: the SET input (S) and the RESET input (R); and two outputs: the SET output (Q) and the RESET output ($\overline{Q}$). A bit of information may be "erased" by making the R input active. If the flip-flop is SET, the set output (Q) is active. If the flip-flop is RESET, the reset output ($\overline{Q}$) is active. The symbol for the RS flip-flop appears in Figure 4–1(b).

The function of the RS flip-flop may be described by using the first-level logic diagram in Figure 4–1(a). The flip-flop consists of two OR gates and two inverters.

If the S input goes to 1 and the R input remains at 0, the output of gate A will be 1. The output from gate A is fed back through an inverter to gate B, causing both inputs to gate B to be 0 and its output to be 0. The output of gate B is also fed back through an inverter to an input of gate A. This input will be a 1, causing gate A to continue to be active even when the S input returns to 0. With both S and R inputs at 0, the flip-flop will remain in the 1 state (SET).

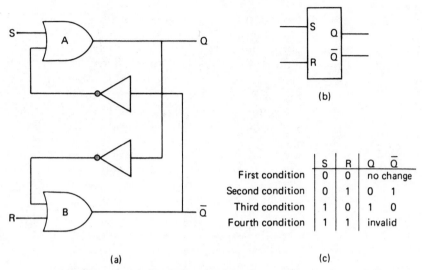

	S	R	Q	$\overline{Q}$
First condition	0	0	no change	
Second condition	0	1	0	1
Third condition	1	0	1	0
Fourth condition	1	1	invalid	

(a) (c)

*Figure 4–1. RS flip-flop: (a) first-level logic diagram, (b) symbol,
(c) truth table.*

In order to reset the flip-flop, the R input is made active by providing it with a 1. Gate B becomes active, and a 1 appears at its output. The output of gate B is fed back through an inverter to the input of gate A, causing gate A to become inactive. A 0 will now appear at the output of gate A, which is inverted, and becomes a 1 at the input of gate B, holding it active. When the R input returns to 0, the flip-flop remains in the RESET, or 0, state.

A truth table may be constructed for the RS flip-flop, like the one in Figure 4–1(c). The two input variables, S and R, appear in the first two columns of the truth table.

The first input condition in the truth table shows both the S and R inputs inactive (both inputs have a 0 present). In this condition, the flip-flop remains in its last state. This state is sometimes called the *remember* state, or the *no change* state.

The second input condition shows the reset input active (a 1 is present). This causes the flip-flop to reset. When the flip-flop is reset, it is in the 0 state. The Q output is inactive (0), and the $\overline{Q}$ output is active (1).

In the third condition, the flip-flop is set because a 1 is present at the set input. When the flip-flop is set, it is in the 1 state. The Q output is active (1), and the $\overline{Q}$ output is inactive (0).

The fourth input condition shown in the truth table should be avoided because we cannot predict the state of the flip-flop if both inputs return to 0 simultaneously. This can be thought of as asking the flip-flop to set and reset at the same time, which is invalid.

A 1 is stored in the flip-flop when the set input is made active momentarily and then returned to 0. A 0 is stored in the flip-flop when the reset input is made active momentarily and then returned to 0. Remember, the primary purpose of the flip-flop is to store a bit of information. Therefore, both inputs are normally 0, causing the flip-flop to remember its last state. If the set input was activated last, the flip-flop will remember that it is in the 1 state so long as both inputs remain in the 0 state, and vice versa.

The RS flip-flop may be implemented with either NOR gates, as shown in Figure 4–2, or NAND gates, as shown in Figure 4–3. Special attention should be directed to the active input and output levels as indicated on the symbols and in the truth tables.

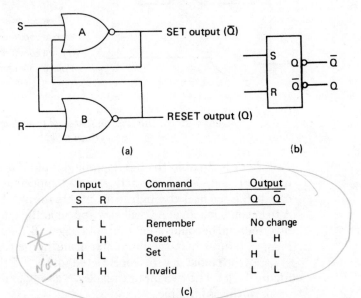

Figure 4–2. RS flip-flop implemented using NOR gates: (a) logic diagram, (b) symbol, (c) truth table.

In Figure 4–4, we have developed a dynamic truth table. That is, we can relate the waveforms labeled A through D to four input variables in a truth table. Because there are four variables, there are sixteen conditions. If we were generating the waveforms, we would relate the sixteen conditions to sixteen time periods. These waveforms could be generated by a logic circuit called a *counter*. In this figure, the count is 0 to 15.

Suppose we connect input C to the set input and D to the reset input of an RS flip-flop implemented using NOR gates as in Figure 4–5. The waveform generated at the set output ($\overline{Q}$) and the reset output (Q) are shown. Notice that whenever the set input is HIGH (C is HIGH), the set output ($\overline{Q}$) is LOW. Whenever the reset input is HIGH (D is HIGH), the reset output (Q) is LOW. When both inputs are HIGH at the same time, both outputs are LOW—the invalid state. Times t_0, t_4, t_8, and t_{12} are left

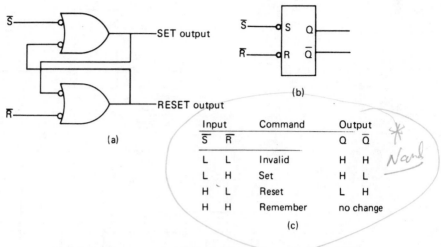

Figure 4–3. RS flip-flop using DeMorgan's equivalent symbols for TTL
7400 NAND gates: (a) logic diagram, (b) symbol, (c) truth table.

blank because the invalid state is followed by a remember state and we cannot predict the state of the flip-flops.

4.2 GATED RS FLIP–FLOP (RST)

When flip-flops are used, it is often desirable to enable or condition
the S and R inputs with their required levels before the flip-flop is to set or
reset. The new state of the flip-flop will now depend on a third input—
possibly a timing pulse. The input information to the flip-flop gives instructions as to *what* to do (set, reset, or remember) and *when* to do it (timing

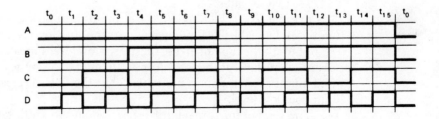

Figure 4–4. Dynamic truth table.

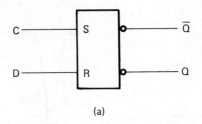

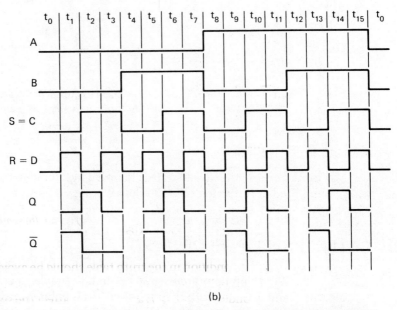

(b)

Figure 4–5. (a) RS flip-flop with variable C connected to the set input and variable D connected to the reset input, (b) input and output waveforms.

pulse). Figure 4–6 shows the logic diagram for a gated RS flip-flop that uses TTL 7402 NOR gates.

In order to set the flip-flop, the $\overline{S}$ input must be low level and the $\overline{R}$ input must be high. The flip-flop will not set until a low level appears at the $\overline{T}$ input. With the flip-flop in the set state, a low level appears at the set output and a high level at the reset output. In order to reset the flip-flop, the R input must be low and the S input high. The flip-flop will reset when the $\overline{T}$ input goes low level.

The symbol for this gated RS flip-flop and its truth table appear in Figures 4–6(b) and (c). Note that the active levels for Figures 4–6(a) and (b) agree.

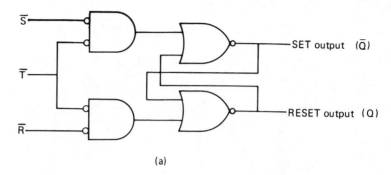

(a)

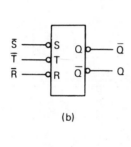

(b)

Input			Command	Output	
$\overline{S}$	$\overline{R}$	$\overline{T}$		Q	$\overline{Q}$
L	L	L	Invalid	L	L
L	L	H		NC	NC
L	H	L	Set	H	L
L	H	H		NC	NC
H	L	L	Reset	L	H
H	L	H		NC	NC
H	H	L	Remember	NC	NC
H	H	H		NC	NC

Nor

(c)

*Figure 4–6. Gated RS flip-flop: (a) logic diagram, (b) symbol, (c) truth
table (NC = no change).*

The first condition in the truth table should be avoided because there
is no way to predict the state of the flip-flop after the $\overline{T}$ input returns to
high level. Conditions 2, 4, 6, 7, and 8 cannot affect the state of the flip-flop
because the $\overline{T}$ or both $\overline{S}$ and $\overline{R}$ inputs are high level. Therefore neither of
the two input gates are enabled. Conditions 3 and 5 will set and reset the
flip-flop, respectively.

The RST flip-flop may also be implemented using NAND gates. The
RST flip-flop in Figure 4–7 uses TTL 7400 NAND gates. The function of
this flip-flop may be described in the same manner as before, except that all
inputs and outputs are active high level. Figures 4–7(b) and (c) show the
symbol and truth table.

Let's look again at our dynamic truth table. In Figure 4–8(a) we again
show our four input variables (A, B, C, D). In addition, we show a clock
pulse, ϕ. Notice that the clock goes high for a short time at the beginning of
each time period. Let's connect our variables and the clock to a flip-flop as
in Figure 4–8(b). The input waveforms at the S, T, and R inputs and the
outputs are shown in Figure 4–8(a). Because the active levels are HIGH,
when S and T are HIGH the flip-flop will set. This happens at the begin-

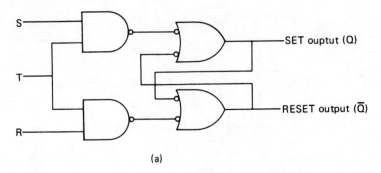

SET ouptut (Q)

RESET output (Q̄)

(a)

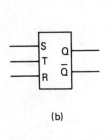

(b)

Input			Command	Output	
S	R	T		Q	Q̄
L	L	L		NC	NC
L	L	H	Remember	NC	NC
L	H	L		NC	NC
L	H	H	Reset	L	H
H	L	L		NC	NC
H	L	H	Set	H	L
H	H	L		NC	NC
H	H	H	Invalid	H	H

(c)

Figure 4–7. Gated RS flip-flop using TTL 7400 NAND gates: (a) logic diagram, (b) symbol, (c) truth table.

ning of t_{11}. (Notice that S is high during t_{10} but T is low and no change takes place.) The flip-flop will reset when R and T are high together. The flip-flop resets, then, at t_5 (we get a reset command at t_7 also, but we are already reset) and t_{13}. All three inputs are high together at t_{15}, causing an invalid state at the beginning of that time period. The rest of t_{15} and all time periods to t_5 are left blank because we cannot predict the state of the flip-flop during these times.

4.3 GATED D FLIP–FLOP

A variation of the RST flip-flop is the gated D flip-flop shown in Figure 4–9. Figure 4–9(a) shows an RST flip-flop and an inverter wired to form a D flip-flop. The use of the inverter allows for only one input (D); therefore there is no invalid state. Whenever the D input is active, the flip-flop will set with an input clock pulse. When the D input is inactive, the flip-flop will reset with a clock pulse. The TTL 7474 Dual D flip-flop is

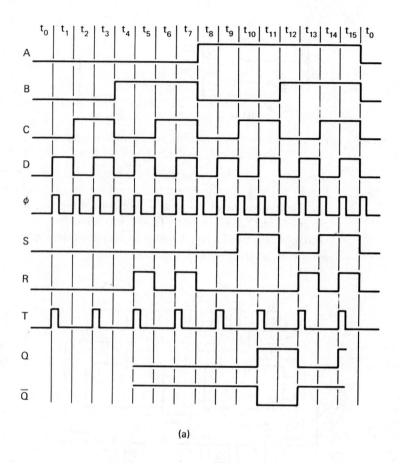

(a)

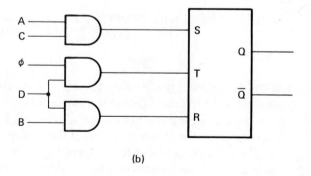

(b)

Figure 4–8. (a) Input and output waveforms; (b) RST flip-flop.

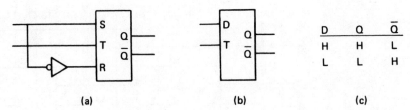

Figure 4-9. Type D flip-flop: (a) RST flip-flop and inverter wired to form a type D flip-flop; (b) prewired type D flip-flop; (c) truth table.

shown in Figure 4-10. Notice the additional inputs labeled $\overline{S_D}$ and $\overline{R_D}$ in Figure 4-10(b). The $\overline{S_D}$ input is a direct set input (sometimes called *preset*) and is active low level. A low at $\overline{S_D}$ will set the flip-flop regardless of the condition of the D and T inputs. The $\overline{R_D}$ input is a direct reset input (also called *clear*) and is active LOW. A low at $\overline{R_D}$ will reset the flip-flop regardless of the conditions at the D and T inputs.

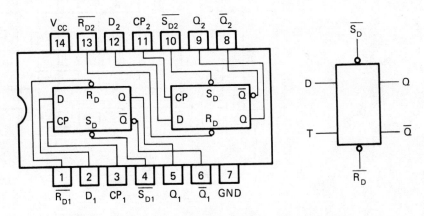

Figure 4-10. TTL 7474 dual D flip-flop: (a) package, (b) symbol showing $\overline{S_D}$ and $\overline{R_D}$ inputs.

The output (Q) will follow the input when the clock is HIGH. When the clock is LOW, the flip-flop is in the remember state.

If the clock input is held in the active state, the flip-flop never latches and the data at the D input appears at the output. When used in this manner, the D flip-flop is said to be operating in the transparent mode. This mode is used to buffer circuits that connect to the address or data bus in microcomputer systems. A buffer provides the necessary current gain to drive the many circuits that are connected to the bus.

A number of D flip-flops may be integrated into one device called a *register*. These registers are the basic building blocks of interface circuits used in microcomputer systems.

4.4 MASTER–SLAVE RST FLIP-FLOP

In many applications the gated RS flip-flop has a serious problem. If the input conditions change at the time the state of the flip-flop is to change, the desired state may not be achieved. This problem is referred to as *race*. This problem may occur when flip-flops are used in counters, shift registers, and other applications.

The race problem is solved by using a master-slave flip-flop. The input variables of this flip-flop are disconnected at the instant the timing or clock pulse first appears. The new state of the flip-flop will then become dependent upon the input levels as they appeared just prior to the clock pulse. This is achieved by using two gated RS flip-flops, as shown in Figure 4-11.

Note that an inverter appears between the T inputs of the two flip-flops. This means that when the T input is high level, the first flip-flop (master) is enabled and will set or reset according to the input (S and R)

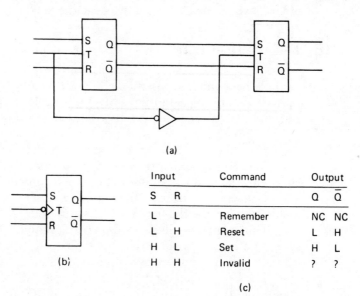

(a)

(b)

Input		Command	Output	
S	R		Q	Q̄
L	L	Remember	NC	NC
L	H	Reset	L	H
H	L	Set	H	L
H	H	Invalid	?	?

(c)

Figure 4-11. Two gated RS flip-flops connected together to form a master-slave flip-flop: (a) logic diagram, (b) symbol, (c) truth table.

levels. When the T input goes low level, the master input is disabled, and the second flip-flop (slave) is enabled and will set or reset in accordance with the state of the master flip-flop.

It should be apparent that after the clock input goes low level, the slave flip-flop cannot be affected by any change of the S and R input levels in the master flip-flop.

The master-slave RST flip-flop is said to be *cocked* when the master sets; it is *triggered* when the slave flip-flop sets. When the slave sets, it will be necessary for the clock pulse to return to high level (cocked) and then to low level (triggered) again before the slave can change state. The symbol for the master-slave RST flip-flop and its truth table appear in Figures 4–11(b) and (c).

The master-slave RST flip-flop can only change state with a low-going transient at the T input (clock pulse). This leaves only the S and R input variables, as is indicated in the truth table of Figure 4–11(c). The output variables, Q and $\overline{Q}$, are shown as they would appear *after* the clock pulse. Notice the > symbol associated with Figure 4–11(b). This indicates an edge-triggered master slave flip-flop. The presence of the bubble tells us that the flip-flop cocks while the clock is high and triggers when the clock goes low. Figure 4–11(b), then, is a negative edge-triggered flip-flop. "No bubble" would indicate a positive edge-triggered flip-flop.

4.5   THE J–K FLIP–FLOP

Perhaps the most useful flip-flop is called the J-K flip-flop. The two most important characteristics of the J-K flip-flop are: (1) it has no invalid input, and (2) it can complement. Its symbol and truth table appear in Figures 4–12(b) and (c).

Since there are two input variables, there are four input conditions. If both J and K are inactive, the flip-flop is instructed to remain in its present state with the next clock pulse. The second condition is where K is active and J is inactive, instructing the flip-flop to reset. The third is if J is active and K inactive, the flip-flop is instructed to set.

The uniqueness of the J-K flip-flop is exemplified by the fourth condition: if both J and K are active, the flip-flop is instructed to change state *(complement)*. It is important to note that all four input conditions are valid!

The J-K flip-flop can be thought of as an RST flip-flop connected to complement, but with two additional gates at the input. When both J and K are high together, these gates allow only one input (set or reset) to be active because the outputs are connected to the gates. Because the outputs are *cross*-connected back to the gates, the result is that the flip-flop will complement with each clock pulse.

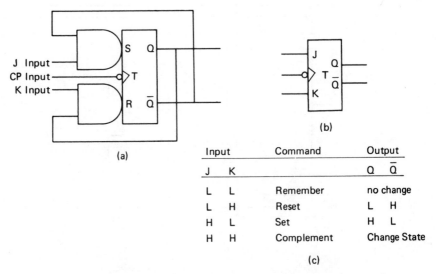

Input		Command	Output	
J	K		Q	$\overline{Q}$
L	L	Remember	no change	
L	H	Reset	L	H
H	L	Set	H	L
H	H	Complement	Change State	

(c)

Figure 4–12. J-K flip-flop: (a) RST flip-flop and two gates connected to form a J-K flip-flop, (b) symbol, (c) truth table.

An understanding of how the J-K flip-flop works can be gained by studying how it is internally wired. The diagram in Figure 4–13 shows a J-K flip-flop wired using NAND gates from the TTL family. Rather than two additional gates at the inputs, the two input gates that are part of the master flip-flop are changed to *three* input gates. The master can set when $\overline{T}$ AND J AND $\overline{Q}$ are HIGH. The master can reset when $\overline{T}$ AND K AND Q are HIGH. Any other combination of inputs causes a remember state for the master. As before, the slave goes to the state of the master when the clock goes low. Notice how the $\overline{S}_D$ and $\overline{R}_D$ inputs are gated into the flip-flops. This allows both master and slave to be directly set or reset, regardless of the other inputs.

Let's examine the $\overline{T}$ input. Gates A and B are enabled when the $\overline{T}$ input is high level, which sets or resets the master flip-flop. When the $\overline{T}$ input goes low level, the J and K inputs are disabled and gates C and D are enabled. This allows the slave to set to the state of the master flip-flop. The timing of these functions is described in Figure 4–14.

Let's consider a J-K flip-flop where the J input is connected to variable B, the K input is connected to C, the clock is $\overline{\phi}$ and $\overline{S}_D$ is $\overline{ABCD}$. Figure 4–15(a) is the circuit; the waveforms are displayed in Figure 4–15(b). The direct set or preset input results from NANDing ABCD causing $\overline{S}_D$ to be low during t_{15}. This causes the flip-flop to set at the beginning of t_{15}. The flip-flop will remain in the set state until a reset command (R is HIGH) and a HIGH clock causes the flip-flop to cock (the master resets). This combina-

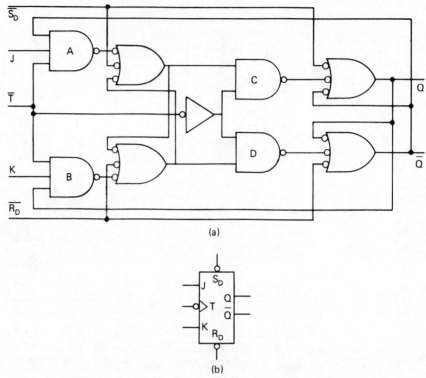

(a)

(b)

Figure 4-13. TTL 7476 NAND gates wired to form a J-K flip-flop:
(a) logic diagram, (b) symbol.

tion occurs during the latter part of t_2. When the clock goes LOW at the beginning of t_3, the flip-flop will trigger. That is, the slave goes to the state of the master. The flip-flop is now in the reset state. Q is LOW and $\overline{Q}$ is HIGH. The flip-flop will remain in this state until the set input and the clock go HIGH together. This condition occurs during the latter part of t_4 (the flip-flop is cocked). When the clock goes LOW at the beginning of t_5, the flip-flop triggers—the slave goes to the state of the master. The flip-flop is now in the set state. Q is HIGH and $\overline{Q}$ is LOW.

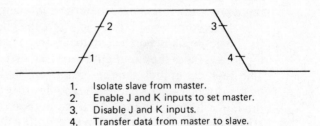

1. Isolate slave from master.
2. Enable J and K inputs to set master.
3. Disable J and K inputs.
4. Transfer data from master to slave.

Figure 4-14. Timing pulse for the T input of the J-K flip-flop.

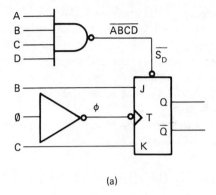

(a)

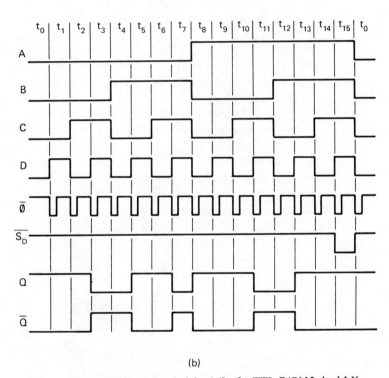

(b)

Figure 4–15. (a) Symbol for 1/2 of a TTL 74S113 dual J-K negative-edge triggered flip-flop and associated input circuits, (b) input and output waveforms.

During t_6, *both* J and K are HIGH. The result is that the flip-flop will cock and then trigger when the clock goes LOW at the beginning of t_7. The flip-flop is now in the reset state. Both J and K are still HIGH during t_7 so when the clock goes HIGH, the flip-flop cocks. At the beginning of t_8 the clock goes LOW and the flip-flop is triggered. The flip-flop is now set. The flip-flop cocks during t_{10} and triggers when the clock goes LOW at the beginning of t_{11}. The flip-flop is now reset. The flip-flop cocks and then is triggered during t_{12} and the beginning of t_{13}. The flip-flop cocks during t_{14} and would trigger at the beginning of t_{15} except that we have a preset command during t_{15} that keeps the flip-flop in the set state. The cycle then repeats itself.

Implementation with other families of logic or other TTL gates may result in different active levels.

4.6 THE EDGE–TRIGGERED D FLIP–FLOP

Operation of the D master-slave flip-flop is similar to the RST master-slave flip-flop and the J-K flip-flop. The symbol for a negative edge-triggered D flip-flop is shown in Figure 4–16. Data present at the D input is stored in the master when the clock is HIGH (cocked) and is transfered to the slave when the clock goes LOW. As with other master-slave flip-flops, the clock must go from HIGH to LOW for the flip-flop to store the data present at the D input.

Figure 4–17 is a TTL 74175 positive edge-triggered quad D flip-flop. There are four negative edge-triggered D flip-flops in the package. The clock and reset lines are common to all flip-flops. Because of the presence of the inverter in the clock line, the clock pulse to the chip must go from LOW to HIGH to trigger the flip-flop.

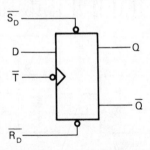

Figure 4–16. Symbol for a negative-edge triggered D flip-flop.

The edge-triggered flip-flop is a master slave type. In order to store data, the data must first be gated into the master (cocked) while the clock input is inactive. Then, when the clock input goes active, the data is transferred to the slave (triggered). Notice that the data at the output becomes

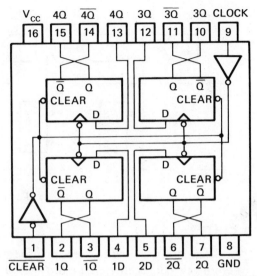

Figure 4–17. TTL 74175 positive-edge triggered quad D flip-flop.

valid when the clock input active transition occurs, hence the name edge-triggered.

The advantage of edge triggering is that the master remembers the state that the flip-flop will take when it is triggered. The state of the slave (output) can only change when the clock transition from inactive to active occurs.

The gated D flip-flop, on the other hand, uses a simple latch and gates at its input. Data is gated into the latch when the clock input is activated. It has the advantage of speed because the output can change whenever the clock is in the active state. Gated D flip-flops are preferred for microcomputer interface circuits because of their speed. However, it is necessary for the processor to provide the appropriate clock pulses.

4.7 REGISTERS

4.7.1 Parallel Entry

Figure 4–18 shows a 4-bit register using parallel entry. The flip-flop may be simply RS flip-flops or latches. Before data may be entered, the contents of the register must be erased. This is done by activating the reset input, which resets all of the flip-flops. To be entered, the data must be present at the inputs of the gates. When the SET input is made active, only those flip-flops which store 1's are set. The stored data is available in parallel form at the output of the flip-flops.

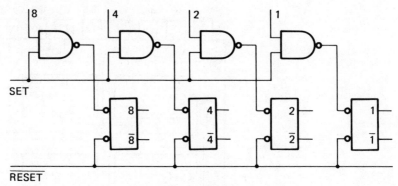

Figure 4–18. Parallel entry.

4.7.2   Jam Entry

Jam entry is used to overcome the necessity of resetting the register before new data is entered. Figure 4–19 shows a 4-bit register with jam entry. The data is gated into the set input of each flip-flop, and the complement of the data is gated into the RESET input of each flip-flop. The result is that new data enters the register whenever an ENTER pulse appears, without first having to reset all of the flip-flops. As before, the data stored is available in parallel form at the outputs of the flip-flops as indicated.

4.7.3   Transfer Function

It is often desirable to tranfer data from one register to another. A simple way to do this is to use jam entry, as shown in Figure 4–20. RST flip-flops are employed so that additional gates are not required. When the

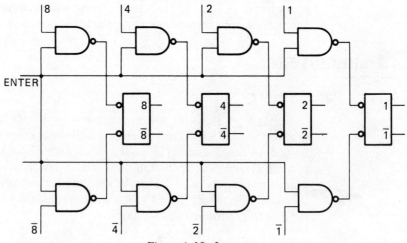

Figure 4–19. Jam entry.

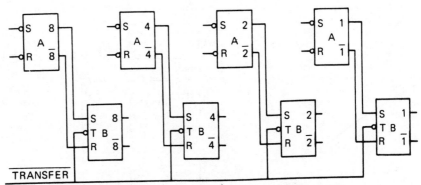

Figure 4-20. The transfer function using jam entry.

$\overline{TRANSFER}$ line is activated, the contents of the A register are duplicated in the B register. Note that each time the $\overline{TRANSFER}$ line is activated, the old contents of the B register are destroyed.

Registers are commonly available in MSI circuits. Refer back to Figure 4-17, the 74175 4-bit latch. Actually, it consists of four type D flip-flops. The inputs D_0, D_1, D_2, and D_3 are for the four bits of data. The data present at the inputs will be jam entered into the register when the clock goes from low to high (positive edge-triggered).

4.7.4 Shift Registers

Occasionally, it will be preferable to handle data in serial. When this is the case, a shift register is used. Figure 4-21 shows a 4-bit shift register that uses J-K flip-flops. With the exception of the first, the input of each flip-flop is conditioned by its preceding flip-flop. The result is that the data appearing in each flip-flop *prior* to a clock pulse is shifted to the next flip-flop *with* the clock pulse. Because there are four flip-flops, four clock pulses are required to shift data through this register. As indicated in the diagram, any number of flip-flops may be used in a shift register. Data appearing at the input and data removed from the output must be synchronized with the clock pulses. Shift registers are available as MSI circuits and in various capacities (bit positions). Figure 4-22 shows a serial-in serial-out 8-bit shift register utilizing TTL circuits.

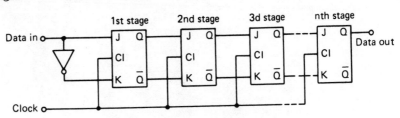

Figure 4-21. Four-bit shift register.

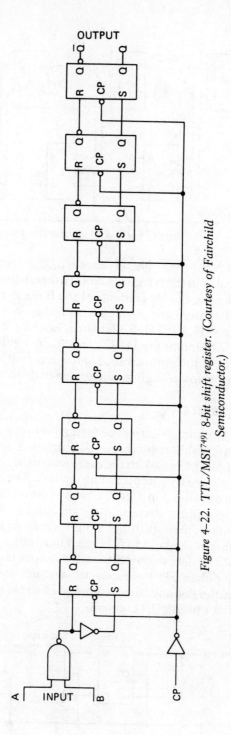

Figure 4-22. TTL/MSI 7491 8-bit shift register. (Courtesy of Fairchild Semiconductor.)

102

In logic diagrams, entire registers are symbolized by a single block symbol. Figure 4–23 shows the symbol for the shift register shown in Figure 4–22. Inputs for such blocks are at either the top or the left side. Outputs appear at the bottom or the right side.

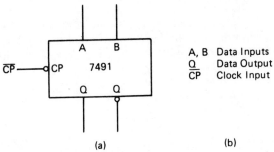

A, B	Data Inputs
Q	Data Output
CP	Clock Input

(a)　　　　　　　　　(b)

Figure 4–23. TTL/MSI[7491] 8-bit shift register: (a) symbol, (b) pin names.

4.7.5 Data Buffering

Data buffering is used between two systems where timing variations exist. For example, in Figure 4–24 a 4-bit gated D type register is connected to a 4-bit data bus. The problem is that data appears on the bus for a very short period of time. A clock pulse occurs while the data is valid on the bus, causing the data to be latched in the register. The data is stored in the register long enough for it to be used by any circuits connected to the outputs of the register. Registers used in this manner are called buffer registers.

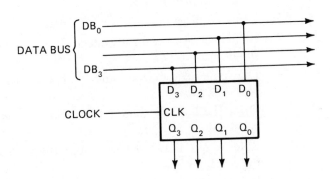

Figure 4–24. Buffer register.

4.7.6   Skew and Deskew

Within a system, data from a common source may arrive at one destination at a different time than it may arrive at a second destination. This phenomenon is due to variations in circuit propagation time, and is called *skew*.

The solution to the problem is to allow time for the data to arrive at the destination before it is gated or triggered into the destination circuit. This additional time is called *deskew*. Figure 4–25 is a diagram showing deskew time.

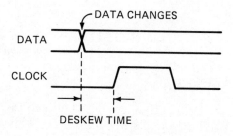

Figure 4–25. *Diagram showing deskew time.*

Problem Set 4–1

1. Using NAND gates, draw the logic diagram for a latch. Draw the logic symbol and truth table.

2. Using NOR gates, draw the logic diagram for a latch.

3. What is the significant advantage of the gated RS flip-flop over the RS flip-flop?

4. Draw the logic diagram and symbol for a gated RS flip-flop using NAND gates.

5. Draw the logic diagram and symbol for a gated RS flip-flop using NOR gates.

6. Refer to question 4. What must be the state of the inputs to set the flip-flop?

7. Refer to question 4. What must be the state of the inputs to reset the flip-flop?

8. Refer to question 5. What must be the state of the inputs to set the flip-flop?

9. Refer to question 5. What must be the state of the inputs to reset the flip-flop?

10. What does race mean when referring to flip-flops?

11. How is the race problem solved?

12. What is the primary advantage of the master-slave flip-flop over the gated RS flip-flop?

13. What do the terms *cocked* and *triggered* mean when applied to the master-slave flip-flop?

14. What is the disadvantage of the master-slave RST flip-flop?

15. What is the advantage of the J-K flip-flop over the master-slave RST flip-flop?

16. Construct a truth table for the J-K flip-flop assuming all inputs and outputs are active HIGH. Include the direct set (S_D) and reset (R_D) inputs.

17. What does the term complement mean when referring to flip-flops?

18. How is the level indicator on the T input of a master-slave flip-flop interpreted?

19. Using the waveforms in Figure 4-26, draw the output waveform (E) for the logic circuit in Figure 4-27. For the times when the results cannot be determined, leave waveform blank. (Refer to flip-flop in Figure 4-3.)

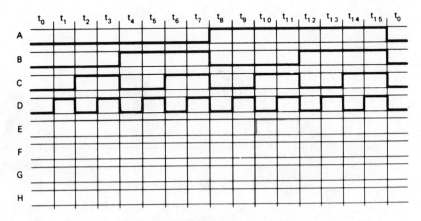

Figure 4-26. Waveforms for problems 19 through 22.

20. Using the waveforms in Figure 4–26, draw the output waveform (F) for the logic circuit in Figure 4–28. For the times when the results cannot be determined, leave waveform blank. (Refer to Figure 4–6.)

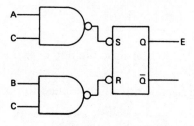

Figure 4–27.

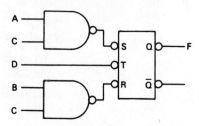

Figure 4–28.

21. Using the waveforms in Figure 4–26, draw the output waveform (G) for the logic circuit in Figure 4–29. For the times when the results cannot be determined, leave waveform blank. (Refer to flip-flop in Figure 4–11.)

22. Using the waveforms in Figure 4–26, draw the output waveform (H) for the logic circuit in Figure 4–30. For the times when the results cannot be determined, leave waveform blank. (Refer to flip-flop in Figure 4–13.)

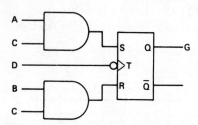

Figure 4–29.

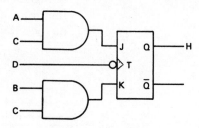

Figure 4–30.

23. Using the waveforms in Figure 4–31, draw the input and output waveforms for the logic diagram in Figure 4–32.

24. Using the waveforms in Figure 4–33, draw the input and output waveforms for the logic diagram in Figure 4–34.

25. Using the waveforms in Figure 4–35, draw the input and output waveforms for the logic diagram in Figure 4–36.

26. Using the waveforms in Figure 4–37, draw the input and output waveforms for the logic diagram in Figure 4–38.

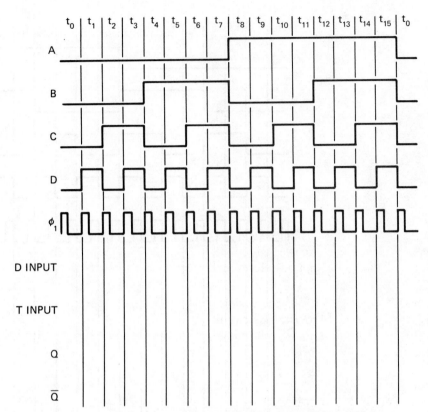

Figure 4–31. Waveforms for the circuit in Figure 4–32.

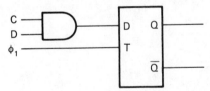

Figure 4–32. Circuit for problem 4–23.

Problem Set 4–2

1. How many bits can a register store?
2. What is the difference between parallel and serial registers?
3. What are buffer registers?
4. If the clock pulses are stopped, how long will the flip-flops in a shift register store the bits of information?
5. When jam entry is used, when may new data be entered?
6. How are the flip-flops in a jam entry register reset?

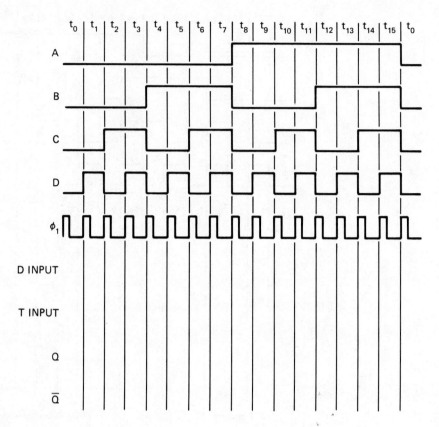

Figure 4-33. Waveforms for the circuit in Figure 4-34.

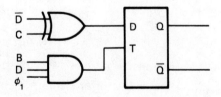

Figure 4-34. Circuit for problem 4-24.

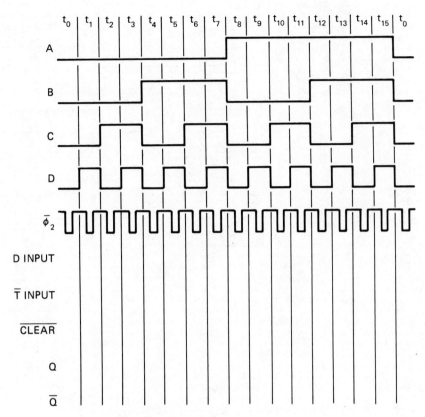

Figure 4–35. *Waveforms for the circuit in Figure 4–36.*

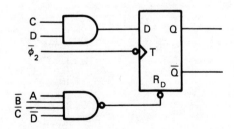

Figure 4–36. *Circuit for problem 4–25.*

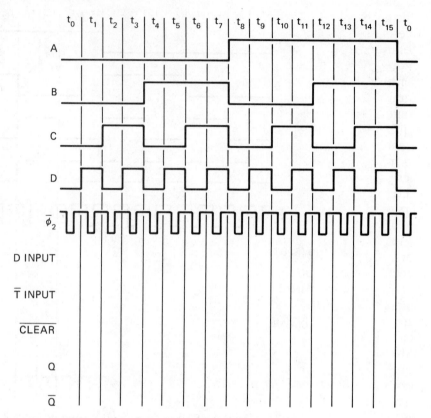

Figure 4-37. Waveforms for Figure 4-38.

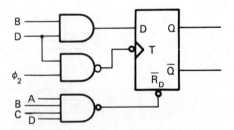

Figure 4-38. Circuit for problem 4-26.

In previous chapters we covered logic gates, flip-flops, and registers. These are Small Scale (SSI) or Medium Scale (MSI) Integrated Circuits (ICs). In Chapter 1 we mentioned the use of large scale integrated circuits (LSIs). As you can imagine, developing an LSI circuit requires a great deal of engineering research and development. There are many possible applications for these circuits. To develop an IC for each of these applications would be very costly. A much better idea is to use an IC that can be *programmed* to fit the needs of many applications. Such an IC was first developed by Intel Corporation. It is the microprocessor. Since then, integrated circuit technology has advanced to the point where it is possible to place an entire computer on a single chip. This phenomenon has caused a marriage between computer technology and integrated circuit technology. As a result, the technician and engineer no longer look at the computer as many individual circuits. Rather, they look at the computer as one, or possibly a few, components. This means that the technician must now be concerned with how to relate these circuits to their applications and how to program.

In this chapter, we are going to introduce a hypothetical microprocessor. It is simple, with few features, and easy to learn. It is called LIMP (LIttle MicroProcessor). LIMP is the vehicle we will use to learn concepts common to most microprocessors. The concepts covered in the next four chapters are common to *all* computers.

Chapter
5

Microcomputer Concepts

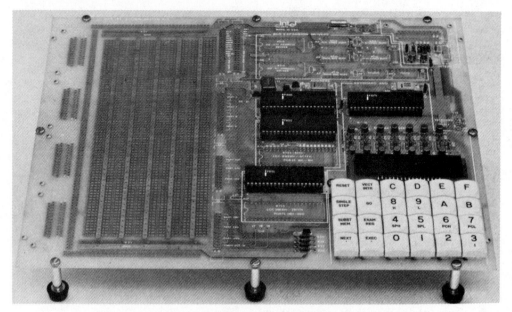

Figure 5-1. SDK-85 design kit that can be used for microprocessor trainer.

5.1   THE LIMP MICROPROCESSOR

Figure 5-2 is a block symbol of LIMP. There are three buses: the address bus, the data bus, and the control bus. Recall that a bus is a line or a set of lines used to exchange data or signals between two or more circuits.

The *data bus* has eight lines, D_0 through D_7. The data bus is used to exchange data between LIMP and memory, or between LIMP and the input and output circuits. This bus is bidirectional, which means that data may pass *from* LIMP or *to* LIMP through the same lines.

The *address bus* also has 8 lines, A_0 through A_7, which carry 8 bits of address information for a total of 256 possible addresses. These addresses will be used to select locations of data or instructions in memory or to select input and output circuits.

Together, the READ and WRITE lines make up the *control bus*. They control the direction of the flow of data between LIMP and memory, or LIMP and the input/output circuits.

5.2   THE MICROCOMPUTER

Figure 5-3 shows the buses connecting LIMP to memory and to two blocks labeled "input port" and "output port." *Ports* are circuits used to in-

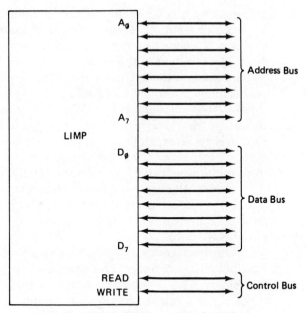

Figure 5-2. Block symbol of LIMP.

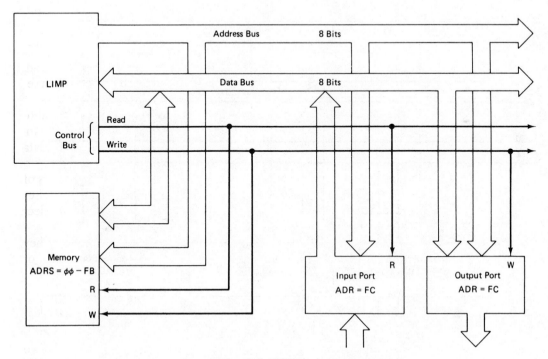

Figure 5-3. LIMP microcomputer system.

113

put or output data between LIMP and peripheral devices such as a terminal keyboard or a printer. These ports are the interface circuits discussed in Chapter 1. Notice that the buses also extend out to the right side of the page. This was done to show that it is possible to add more memory or ports to the buses to expand the system. All electrical connections to the buses are common. Therefore, more memory or ports can easily be added (up to a total of 256). Consider the READ line. It is connected to memory and to the input port. However, it could be connected to additional input ports if the system is to be expanded. The same is true for the WRITE line, which could be connected to additional output ports, as well as the data and address buses, which could be connected to both.

Our LIMP microcomputer is complete with the expansion shown in Figure 5-4. By definition, a microcomputer is a complete system. It must contain a processor (LIMP), memory, input/output ports, and some peripheral devices.

Our microcomputer has 252 memory addresses (00–FB). Addresses FC through FF are reserved for ports. Both instructions and data are stored in memory. This is not very much memory, but will suffice for our purposes. Typical microprocessors can address 65,536 locations and have a 16-bit address bus. Let's limp along with LIMP!

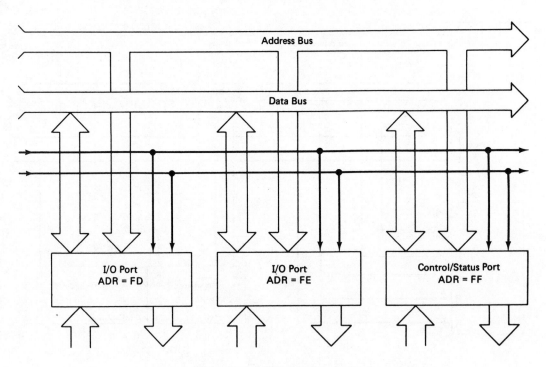

Figure 5-4. LIMP microcomputer expanded.

5.3 FUNCTIONAL ARCHITECTURE OF LIMP

Figure 5–5 is a block diagram showing the major functional parts of LIMP. You will notice that there are seven registers. A register is a circuit used to temporarily store data. Each of these registers can store an 8-bit word—one *byte*. In an 8-bit machine, byte and word have the same meaning.

The A register (Reg) is the accumulator. When the processor executes an arithmetic or logic operation, the results of that operation appear in the A register. Exceptions are the increment and decrement instructions, which can affect any register except the PC. The B, C, D, and E registers are general purpose registers (GPRs). They may be used to store data or addresses.

The P register is also a GPR. In addition, it has a special function. The P Reg can be used to point to data in memory. When used as a pointer, it contains a memory address. The letter M is used to designate the location of this address.

The program counter (PC) is used to point to the instructions stored in memory. At any given time, the PC points to the next instruction to be executed. As soon as an instruction has been executed, the processor will fetch the next instruction and immediately increment the PC. However, if a branch instruction is encountered, the contents of the PC is replaced with a new address. In any case, the PC contains the address of the next instruction to be executed.

The block labeled ALU (Arithmetic Logic Unit) represents the circuits used to execute all arithmetic and logic operations.

The block labeled CONTROL represents the circuits that control all operations within the system. The decoding of the instruction words and timing of all events take place here.

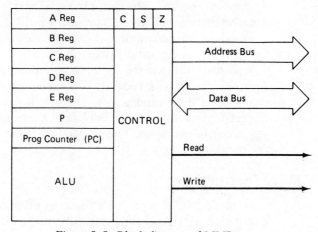

Figure 5–5. Block diagram of LIMP.

The remaining blocks are labeled C, S, and Z. These are the condition flags. A *flag* indicates the value of a condition—true (1) or false (0)—and is used with the branch instructions to make decisions. If the results of an arithmetic or logic operation is zero, the zero flag (Z) is set (Z = 1). If the result is not zero, the Z flag is cleared (Z = 0).

If the result of an operation causes the MSB to equal 1, the sign flag (S) is set (S = 1). If not, the sign flag is cleared (S = 0).

If the results of an arithmetic operation causes an overflow in the A register, the CARRY flag (C) is set (C = 1). If no carry occurs, the carry flag is cleared.

5.4   INSTRUCTION SET

Now that we have discussed some of the hardware, we need to define the operations that LIMP can execute. An *instruction set* is a list of instructions that a particular processor can execute. LIMP has instructions that perform move, arithmetic, logic, rotate, load, store, and branch operations. As discussed in Chapter 1, an instruction has two parts: the operation code (opcode) and the operand. The opcode designates the operation to be performed by the processor. The operand is the data that will be somehow affected by the operation. Usually, however, rather than containing the operand itself, the instruction contains information that allows the processor to find the operand. For example, in the instruction ADD B, ADD is the opcode and B indicates a register that contains the operand. This instruction causes the processor to add the contents of the B register to the contents of the A register (the accumulator). Actually this instruction contains two operands, the source operand and the destination operand. The B register contains the source operand and the A register contains the destination operand. The use of the A register is implied in this instruction because there is only one accumulator in LIMP. Although there are two operands in this instruction, it can be called a single operand instruction because only one register is specified.

Instructions written by the programmer are written in a shorthand form called *mnemonic* codes. INC (increment) and COM (complement) are examples of these mnemonics. The machine, however, can use only machine language instructions. For LIMP, these instructions are contained in either one or two bytes. The second byte is used for addresses or program constants.

5.4.1   Move Instructions

Move (MOV) is probably the most often used instruction in LIMP's instruction set. Processing data always involves moving data between registers or between registers and memory or input/output devices. The move instruction is a double operand instruction. It is necessary to specify both the source and destination operands. For example, MOV A,B moves the contents of the A register into the B register. For all moves, the destination operand becomes a copy of the source operand and the source operand is unchanged. For the above example, A specifies the source operand and B specifies the destination operand.

5.4.2 Arithmetic Instructions

LIMP can execute three arithmetic operations. These are add (ADD), increment (INC), and decrement (DEC). The ADD instruction causes LIMP to add the contents of the designated register or memory location to the contents of the A register. The result always appears in the A register. The ADD instruction affects all three flags, depending on the results in the A register. If the result of an ADD is greater than FF, the C flag is set. If the result is equal to FF or less, the C flag is cleared.

If the result of an ADD is zero, regardless of the C, the Z flag is set; otherwise it is cleared. If the result of an ADD causes the MSB (most significant bit) of the A register to equal one, the S flag is set; otherwise it is cleared.

The INC and DEC instructions cause the designated register or memory location to be incremented or decremented. Z is the only flag affected by these two instructions. Incrementing a register when it contains FF changes its contents to 00 and sets the Z flag. Decrementing a register when its contents are 00 changes the contents to FF and clears the Z flag. The S and C flags are not affected.

5.4.3 Logic Instructions

LIMP is able to execute four logic operations: and (AND), inclusive or (OR), exclusive or (XOR), and complement (COM). Suppose the logic operation AND is performed between the contents of the A register and the contents of some other designated register or memory location. The result always appears in the A register. The logic operation is performed on bits of the same weight in each register. For example, suppose we are going to perform the AND operation between the A register and the C register. The contents of the registers are shown in Figure 5-6(a). The bits are ANDed according to weight. That is, the MSBs are ANDed: 1 AND 1 equals 1. The next significant bits are ANDed: 0 AND 1 equals 0. The next significant bits are ANDed; 0 AND 0 equals 0. And so on. All bits are ANDed simultaneously. The result is shown in Figure 5-6(b).

If the result of the AND operation causes all bits in the A register to be zero, the Z flag is set. Otherwise the Z flag is cleared. If the result causes the MSB in the A register to equal 1, the S flag is set. Otherwise it is cleared. The C flag is not affected.

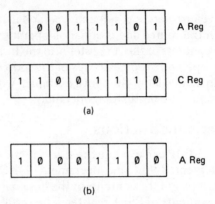

(a)

(b)

Figure 5-6. ANDing the A and C regs: (a) contents of A and C before instruction, (b) contents of A reg after the AND C instruction.

If the logic operation is OR or XOR, the bits are ORed or XORed according to weight, as with the AND operation. As with the AND operation, the Z and S flags are the only flags affected.

The complement instruction (COM) is used to produce the one's complement of the contents of the A register. This instruction will always clear the C flag. If the result of COM causes the MSB of the A register to equal 1, the S flag will be set. The Z flag will be set if the result equals zero.

5.4.4   Rotate Instructions

Two rotate instructions are included in LIMP. These instructions will rotate the contents of the A register either left (ROL) or right (ROR). Each rotate instruction causes all bits to shift one bit position. The diagram in Figure 5-7(a) indicates that the ROL instruction causes the MSB to move to the C flag and the old contents of the C flag to move to the LSB position.

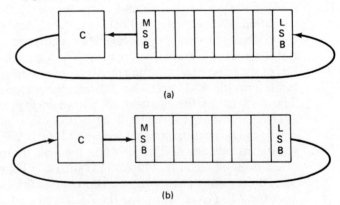

(a)

(b)

Figure 5-7. Rotate instructions: (a) ROL instruction, (b) ROR instruction.

The diagram in Figure 5–7(b) shows that the ROR instruction shifts all bits one bit position right. In both instructions, the C flag is treated as a ninth bit position and all rotates are through the C flag. It would require nine rotate instructions to rotate a bit completely back to its original position. Rotate instructions are used in arithmetic routines such as multiply and divide. They are also used in decoding control words where each bit may have a different purpose. Each bit of the control word can be rotated to the C where it can be tested.

5.4.5   Load and Store Instructions

Instructions that are used to move data to a register are called *load* instructions. For example, LIMP has an instruction that loads the A register from memory (LDA). This is a two-byte instruction. The second byte contains the address of the data to be loaded.

Instructions that are used to move data to memory are called *store* instructions. LIMP has an instruction that is used to move data from the A register to memory (STA). This is also a two-byte instruction. The second byte contains the memory address.

Another method of loading and storing data is to use a *memory pointer*. LIMP's P reg is used for this purpose. The P register must be initialized with a memory address. A MOV M,r (r = any GPR) instruction moves the contents of a memory location into the specified GPR. The address of the memory location must be contained in the P register. This technique is useful when data is stored in consecutive locations in memory because the P register can be easily incremented to the next address. In LIMP, this also allows data to be loaded into registers other than the accumulator. It also allows data to be stored from registers other than the accumulator.

5.4.6   Immediate Data

Sometimes it is necessary for the program itself to contain data. For example, it may be necessary to initialize the P register to a particular address such as the beginning of a table. Suppose the beginning address is 40. The instruction MOV # 40,P will cause the contents of the P register to be 40. The number 40 is immediate data. That is, it is a byte in the program immediately following the byte containing the opcode. Therefore, instructions with immediate data are always two-byte instructions.

Another example of immediate data are constants in the program that control loops. A register can be initialized with a number. Each time a loop is executed, the number is decremented. When the number equals 0, the loop is exited. Therefore, the number to which the register is initialized is the number of times the loop will be executed.

5.5 THE INSTRUCTION WORD

The processor responds to *machine language* code. This code is in binary. All instructions and data internal to the computer are stored as binary numbers. However, we don't normally program in machine language because it is extremely difficult for people. The language we use to program LIMP is called *assembly language*. For each machine language instruction word, there is an assembly language counterpart. When we write a program we must have some way of changing our assembly language program into machine language. The process is called *assembling*.

For LIMP, registers are defined within an instruction word with three bits. Therefore, eight registers can be defined. Because three bits are used, it is convenient to use octal. For the following discussion we will use octal numbers unless otherwise stated. Figure 5–8 is a list of LIMP's registers and the octal code representing them. Notice that "M" is included in the list. It is represented by the octal code 5. M is not a register but a location in memory. As discussed previously, its address is specified by the contents of the P register. The processor deals with this memory location as though it were a register, so it is included in the list.

REG	OCTAL CODE	
A	Ø	ACCUMULATOR
B	1	GPR
C	2	GPR
D	3	GPR
E	4	GPR (SP)
M	5	MEMORY LOCATION
P	6	MEMORY POINTER
PC	7	PROGRAM COUNTER

Figure 5–8. LIMP registers and their octal code.

Figure 5–9 is a list of LIMP's opcodes. The opcodes are represented by three bits of the instruction word so we again use octal numbers. Notice that the octal code 0 has no opcode in this list. When the octal code 0 is encountered, the processor is directed to a second list called unary opcodes (Figure 5–10). Unary opcodes are used for instructions that have no operand designations (exceptions are LDA and STA). An example of a unary operation is COM. Because only the A register can be complemented, an operand designator is not needed in the instruction word.

5.5.1 Assembling Move Instructions

Now let's see what a complete instruction word will look like. Figure 5–11 is a diagram showing how the different parts of the word are as-

OP-CODES

MNEMONIC	CODE	OPERATION
	0	UNARY OPERATION
ADD	1	ADD SRC REG TO A REG
INC	2	INCREMENT REG
DEC	3	DECREMENT REG
AND	4	AND SRC TO A REG
OR	5	OR SRC TO A REG
XOR	6	EXCLUSIVE OR SRC TO A REG
Bxx	7	BRANCH INSTRUCTION

Figure 5-9. LIMP opcodes and their octal codes.

UNARY OP-CODES

MNEMONIC	CODE	OPERATION
NOP	0	NO OPERATION
COM	1	COMPLEMENT THE ACCUMULATOR
ROR	2	ROTATE A REG RIGHT
ROL	3	ROTATE A REG LEFT
LDA	4	LOAD A REG
STA	5	STORE A REG
RET	6	RETURN FROM SUBROUTINE
HLT	7	HALT PROCESSOR

Figure 5-10. Unary opcodes.

INSTRUCTION WORD

BIT 7 = 1 FOR THE IMMEDIATE MODE

BIT 6 = 1 FOR A MOV INSTRUCTION (DOUBLE OPERAND)

BITS 5, 4, 3 = CODE FOR DESTINATION FIELD OR LOGIC FIELD

BITS 2, 1, 0 = CODE FOR SOURCE FIELD, BR TEST FIELD, OR UNARY OPERATION.

BITS:

7	6	5	4	3	2	1	0
IMM	MOV	DST FIELD OR OP-CODE			SRC FIELD OR BR TEST FIELD OR UNARY OP-CODE		

Figure 5-11. Diagram for assembling the instruction word.

sembled. If bit 7 equals 1, the instruction word is two bytes. The second byte is required for immediate data or an address.

If bit 6 equals 1, the instruction is a move instruction. This is the only instruction of LIMP's set that designates two operands (double operand instruction). For the MOV instructions, bits 0, 1, and 2 (source field) designate the source operand, and bits 3, 4, and 5 designate the destination operand. So, if we were to assemble the instruction MOV A,B, then bit 7 would equal 0 because no immediate data or address is required. Bit 6 would equal 1 because it is a move instruction. Bits 2, 1, and 0 would all equal 0 (octal 0) because the A reg contains the source operand. Bits 5, 4, and 3 would equal 001 (octal 1) because the B reg contains the destination operand. The entire word when assembled is 110 (01001000 in binary).

In the same manner, the instruction MOV E,P (when assembled) would equal 164 (01110100 in binary). The instruction MOV # 05,B would be assembled as 310 005 (11001000 00000101 in binary). In this instruction, the first byte contains the instruction. Bit 7 equals 1, indicating a second byte for immediate data. Bit 6 equals 1 because it's a move instruction. Bits 5, 4, and 3 equal 001 (octal 1) because the B reg is the destination register. Bits 2, 1, and 0 equal 0 because no information is required in this field. Rather, the information is contained in the second byte, which is the data.

5.5.2 Assembling Arithmetic and Logical Instructions

All arithmetic and logical instructions are one-byte instructions. Each designates one operand. The opcode appears in bits 5, 4, and 3. The source is designated by bits 2, 1, and 0. The destination for these instructions is always the A register and is not designated. Therefore, the instruction ADD B is assembled as 011 (00001001 in binary). Bits 7 and 6 both equal 0 because there is no immediate data or an address and it is not a move instruction. Bits 5, 4, and 3 equal octal 1, indicating the B register. Bits 5, 4, and 3 indicate the opcode for all instructions except move instructions.

The instruction COM is assembled as 001. Bits 5, 4, and 3 equal 0 because this is a unary operation. Bits 2, 1, and 0 equal 1 as found in the unary op-code table in Figure 5–10.

Two more examples are the instruction DEC D, which is assembled as 033; and ROL, which is assembled as 003.

5.5.3 Assembling Load and Store Instructions

Load (LDA) and store (STA) are two-byte instructions. The first byte contains the opcode, and the second byte contains the address of the operand. LDA 05 assembles as 204 005 (10000100 00000101 in binary). Bit 7 of the first byte equals 1, indicating to the processor that this is a two-byte instruction. Bit 6 equals 0 because this is not a move instruction. Bits 5, 4, and 3 equal 0 indicating that the unary op-code table is used. Bits 2, 1, and 0 equal 4 because the instruction is LDA. STA is assembled in the same manner.

5.5.4   Assembling Branch Instructions

Branch instructions are also two-byte instructions. The first byte contains the opcode and the second byte contains the address of the next instruction to be executed. When assembling a branch instruction, bit 7 always equals 1 and bit 6 always equals 0. Bits 5, 4, and 3 equal 7, indicating a branch instruction. Bits 2, 1, and 0 indicate the particular test condition, as shown in Figure 5–12. For example, if bits 2, 1, and 0 equal 1 (BM), the branch will be executed if the sign flag equals 1; otherwise the branch will not be executed.

The instruction BC 07 (branch on carry to address 07) is assembled as 273 007. All other branch instructions are assembled in a like manner. The CALL instruction is assembled as 277.

The complete instruction set appears in Chapter 7 in Figure 7–5. Both octal and hexadecimal codes are given.

MNEMONIC	CODE	CONDITION
BR	0	UNCONDITIONAL
BM	1	IF SIGN FLAG = 1
BP	2	IF SIGN FLAG = 2
BC	3	IF CARRY FLAG = 1
BNC	4	IF CARRY FLAG = 0
BZ	5	IF ZERO FLAG = 1
BNZ	6	IF ZERO FLAG = 0
CALL	7	CALL TO SUBROUTINE

Figure 5–12. Branch test field opcodes.

Questions and Problems

1. What is the purpose of the PC?
2. How many general purpose registers does LIMP have?
3. How many ports can LIMP address?
4. How much memory does LIMP have?
5. What are the GPRs used for?
6. What is a bus?
7. How many lines are there in the address bus? Data bus? Control bus?
8. What is a port?
9. After an arithmetic operation, the A register contains 10011001. What is the condition of the Z flag? What is the condition of the S flag?

10. What is the source operand in the instruction MOV B,C? What is the destination operand?

11. At some point in a program, the contents of the A register are 10110100 and CY = 1. The next instruction is ROR. After the ROR instruction, what is the content of the A register? What are the conditions of the flags?

12. At some point in a program, the contents of the A register are 10101101 and CY = 0. The next instruction is ROL. After the ROL instruction, what are the contents of the A reg? What are the conditions of the flags?

13. What is the instruction word for MOV M,B in binary, octal, and hexadecimal?

14. What is the instruction word for ADD B in binary, octal, and hexadecimal?

15. MOV #BYTE,B is a two-byte instruction. Let BYTE = 28_{10}. List the bytes in binary, octal, and hexadecimal.

16. STA 40 is a two-byte instruction. List the bytes in binary, octal, and hexadecimal.

17. An instruction word in binary is 01101000. What is the source? What is the destination? What operation is to be performed?

18. An instruction word in binary is 10111101 01100000. What operation is to be performed?

19. The instruction is XOR E. Will bit 7 of the instruction word equal 1 or 0? Why? Will bit 6 equal 1 or 0? Why?

20. The instruction is LDA 60. What does this mean? What does bit 7 of the instruction word equal?

21. If we want the next instruction in a program to cause a branch to address $A3_{16}$ if the result is zero, what would the instruction word look like in binary, octal, and hexadecimal?

22. If we want the next instruction in a program to cause a branch to address $4B_{16}$ if the result is negative, what would the instruction word look like in binary, octal, and hexadecimal?

Chapter

6

Interface
Circuits

Interface is a word defining the
technique of connecting peripheral equipment to the microcomputer. The circuitry between the
processor and some peripheral
device is called an interface circuit.
Various interface circuits are connected to the processor by means
of common connections called a
bus. These circuits are also called
ports. In this chapter we will study
the concepts of interface circuits.

6.1   BUS CONCEPTS

Because microcomputer systems use buses to transfer data between their various circuits, we will review bus concepts.

What is a bus? A bus is a conductor that is used for transferring signals from any one of a number of sources to one or more destinations. For example, if a signal is to be transferred from device A to device C in Figure 6-1, the source of the signal is device A and the destination is device C. The signal in this case is transferred on a single conductor "bus."

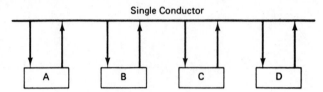

Figure 6-1. Single conductor bus.

If, at another time, a signal is to be transferred from device D (source) to device A (destination), the same conductor can be used because no other transfer operation is being performed. This is true in computers because operations are a sequence of timed events. The bus must be dedicated to a particular source and destination at any given time period (multiplexed). Although there may be more than one destination, there can only be one source.

6.1.1   Open Collector Circuits

Sometimes the outputs of two or more circuits are tied together to perform the AND or OR function. Normally, though, outputs from more than one circuit should not be tied together. If this were done with standard TTL gates, one circuit might try to drive its output HIGH while another circuit might attempt to drive its output LOW. If the two outputs are tied together, a very high current could result (short circuit) and the output level would be unpredictable. To illustrate the problem, a standard TTL circuit schematic is shown in Figure 6-2(a). The outputs of two such circuits are tied together in Figure 6-2(b). For circuit A, in Figure 6-2(b), if Q_3 is ON and Q_4 is OFF, the output should be LOW. However, if Q_4 of circuit B is ON, a high current will flow through Q_4 of circuit B and through Q_3 of circuit A. This current will exceed the rating of the devices, and the output voltage would be neither HIGH nor LOW.

A possible solution to this problem is the use of *open-collector* circuits. In open-collector circuits a pull-up resistor is required to bring the output to a high state. Figure 6-3 shows the outputs of two open-collector circuits tied together with a common pull-up resistor. You will notice that there is

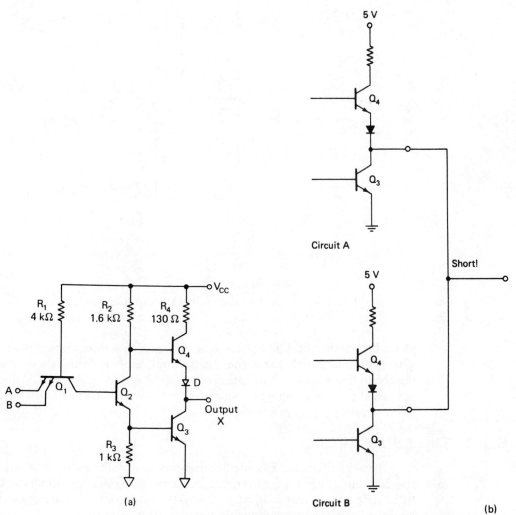

Figure 6–2. (a) Standard TTL 2-input NAND gate; (b) outputs of two
TTL circuits tied together.

no active pull-up in this configuration. Therefore the maximum current
will be limited by the value of the pull-up resistor. The output will be LOW
if either of the two transistors is ON, otherwise, it will be HIGH.

Figure 6–4 shows how open-collector circuits may be used to implement the concept of data transfer in Figure 6–1. For example, if a signal is
to be transferred from device A to device C, $\overline{\text{TRAN A}}$ must be active while
$\overline{\text{TRAN B}}$, $\overline{\text{TRAN C}}$, and $\overline{\text{TRAN D}}$ must remain inactive. This causes
DATA A to appear at the output of gate 1 and its complement to appear
on the bus. Because $\overline{\text{TRAN B}}$, $\overline{\text{TRAN C}}$, and $\overline{\text{TRAN D}}$ are all inactive, Q_2, Q_3, and Q_4 will all be OFF (not connected to the bus). To com-

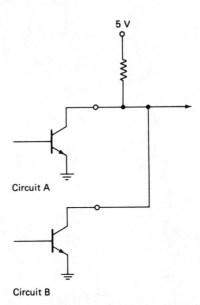

5 V

Circuit A

Circuit B

Figure 6-3. Outputs of open-collector circuits tied together.

plete the transfer, $\overline{\text{RCV C}}$ must also be active. This activates one input of gate 6. The output of gate 6, then, is the complement of the data on the bus. Note that the output of gate 6 equals DATA A. Any other RCV line may also be active resulting in data transfer to more than one destination. However, only one source is allowed.

6.1.2   Three-State Circuits

Three-state circuits provide another means of transferring data onto the data bus. The major difference between open-collector circuits and three-state circuits is that active pull-up is provided for three-state circuits where passive pull-up is used with open-collector circuits.

The "three states" can be defined as: (1) a low impedance to a high potential, (2) a low impedance to a low potential, and (3) a high impedance. In Figure 6-5, if Q_1 is ON and Q_2 is OFF, a low impedance results between the output and V_{CC}, resulting in a HIGH output. If Q_2 is ON and Q_1 is OFF, a low impedance exists between the output and common. If Q_1 and Q_2 are both OFF (third state), a high impedance exists between the output and V_{CC} or common. The third or high impedance state allows the circuit to be electrically disconnected from the bus when it is not used as a source.

A symbol for a three-state inverter is shown in Figure 6-6(a). Note that a second input to the circuit is called disable. When this line is active, the output is in the high impedance state. This line could be called enable, as shown in Figure 6-6(b). However, its active level would be LOW.

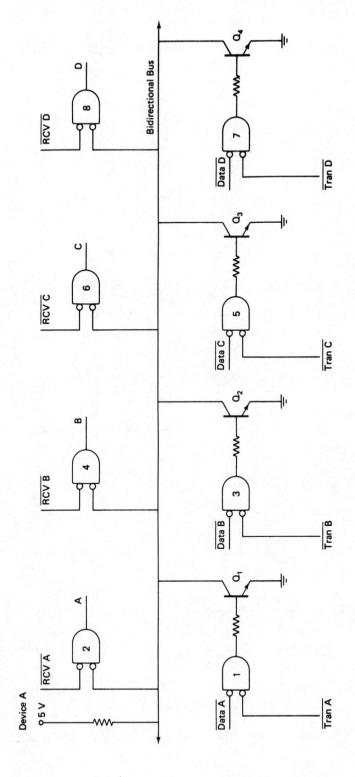

Figure 6–4. Data transfer using open collector circuits.

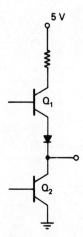

Figure 6–5. *Output of a three-state circuit.*

Three-state circuits are demonstrated in Figure 6–7. Suppose DATA A is to be transferred to device D. $\overline{\text{TRAN A}}$ is made active causing $\overline{\text{DATA A}}$ to appear on the bus. $\overline{\text{RCV D}}$ must be activated to select $\overline{\text{DATA A}}$ to appear at the output of device D. As before, $\overline{\text{TRAN B}}$, $\overline{\text{TRAN C}}$, and $\overline{\text{TRAN D}}$ must remain inactive.

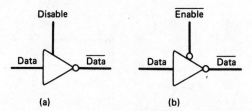

Figure 6–6. *Symbols for three-state inverters.*

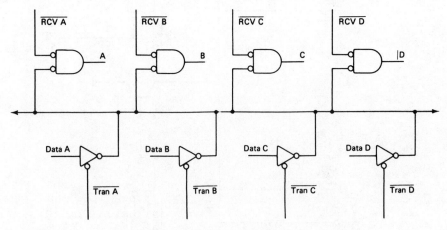

Figure 6–7. *Data transfer using three-state circuits.*

In our discussion we have used only one line of a data bus. If an 8-bit processor is used, eight such lines would be required for the data bus.

6.1.3   Bus Drivers

Microprocessors are usually fabricated as MOS (Metal Oxide Semiconductors) monolithic ICs. Such circuits usually have the ability to drive only a small number of TTL circuits (the output loading factor is low). Because the bus is connected to many circuits, a *buffer-driver* circuit is required between the processor and the bus. *Buffers* have two different functions in digital circuits. The first function is that they can provide *electrical* buffering. Circuits that provide electrical buffering are often referred to as *bus drivers* or buffer-drivers. In this function, signal current gain is provided. Electrical buffering is often required when dealing with address or data buses because most systems require more current than the processor is capable of providing.

The second function is that of *logical* buffering. In this function, the buffer is a latch, usually an 8-bit gated D type latch. This kind of buffering is often required because of timing considerations. Information that would normally be available for a short period of time can be latched into a buffer and retained for as long as is needed.

If the bus is a bidirectional bus, then the buffer-driver must also be bidirectional. Figure 6–8 shows two three-state circuits connected so that only one is enabled at any one time. A control signal is required to enable the appropriate three-state circuit. If the processor is the source of the data, the control signal is HIGH and circuit A is enabled. If the processor is the destination, the control signal is LOW and circuit B is enabled.

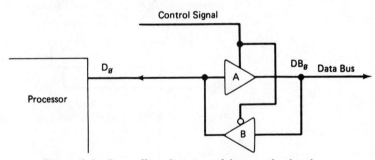

Figure 6–8. Controlling direction of data on the data bus.

Figure 6-9 shows a 4-bit bidirectional bus driver (8216). Two 8216's could be used to implement an 8-bit bidirectional bus. Normally, DI_0 and DO_0 are connected together and to the processor. DI_1 and DO_1; DI_2 and DO_2; DI_3 and DO_3 are connected in a like manner. DB_0 through DB_3 are connected to the bus. When the processor is the destination, "data in

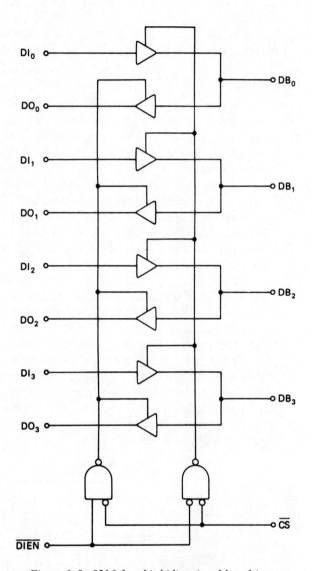

Figure 6–9. 8216 four-bit bidirectional bus driver.

enable" ($\overline{\text{DIEN}}$) is activated. When the processor is the source, $\overline{\text{DIEN}}$ is inactive. A chip select input ($\overline{\text{CS}}$) is provided. If this signal is inactive, then all three-state circuits are disabled and the processor is electrically disconnected from the bus.

6.2 INPUT PORTS

In Figure 6–10, we show 2 lines of an 8-line data bus (DB$_0$ and DB$_7$). Three input ports are implemented (ports 0, 1, and 2). Data to be inputted via port 0 appears on the data lines D$_0$–D$_7$ (D$_1$ through D$_6$ are not shown). Each three-state gate is enabled from a common line, which is the output of gate A. Unless gate A is activated, port 0 is in the high impedance state and is completely disconnected from the bus. In order to input data to the processor, port 0 must be selected ($\overline{PS0}$ is LOW) and a control signal is activated ($\overline{READ}$ is LOW). This causes the data at port 0 to be placed on the data bus. $\overline{READ}$ is common to each port, but only one port is selected. The port select signals are decoded from the processor's address bus. Other ports can also be decoded from the address bus. When the processor reads data from a port, it is assumed that the data is present. However, if the data exists for a very short period of time, it can be latched into a register as shown in Figure 6–11. The peripheral device is responsible for providing a clock pulse to clock the data into the 8-bit latch. The processor can then input the data when it is ready. (The line labeled RESET is discussed in section 6.4.)

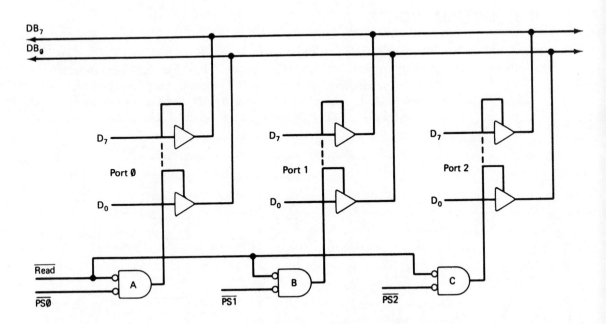

Figure 6–10. Input ports using three-state circuits.

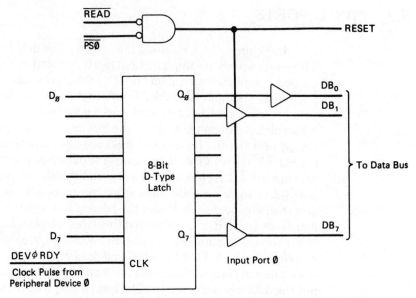

Figure 6–11. Latching type input port using three-state circuits.

6.3   OUTPUT PORTS

Output data should almost always be latched because the control signal is present for such a short period of time. Figure 6–12 shows an 8-bit D-type latch used as an output port. The inputs of the latch connect to the data bus. Data is clocked into the latch by ANDing the write control signal ($\overline{\text{WRITE}}$) and $\overline{\text{PS0}}$. The data for the peripheral device is then available at

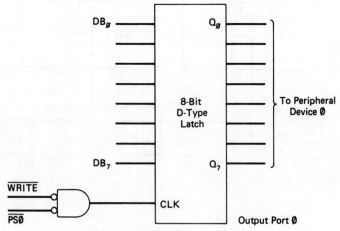

Figure 6–12. Eight-bit output port.

the output of the latch. Notice that three-state circuits are not required because the bus is capable of driving many input circuits. That is, the output port is always a destination, never a source. Also, notice that the same port select signal ($\overline{PS0}$ in our example) can be used to select an input or an output port, depending on the control signals $\overline{READ}$ and $\overline{WRITE}$.

6.4   STATUS PORTS

How does the processor know when data is present to be inputted? How does the processor know when a peripheral is ready to accept data? Consider the process of inputting data. We must let the processor know that the data is available to be processed. This can be accomplished with a *status port* such as the one in Figure 6–13. This circuit uses RS flip-flops that are set by the same clock pulse used to latch data (Figure 6–11). The status information in these flip-flops is inputted by activating the status port select signal ($\overline{PS3}$) and $\overline{READ}$. Even though we implemented four, the circuit may be extended to include as many status signals as required up to a maximum of eight. If more status information is required, another status port could be implemented.

The flip-flops are reset when the data from the selected port is inputted. This is accomplished by connecting the reset input to the signal generated from the read and port select signals (RESET) as shown in Figure 6–11.

The process of inputting data through port 0 can be described as follows:

1. The peripheral provides the data to the input port (D_0–D_7) (Figure 6–11).

2. The peripheral provides a clock pulse that clocks the data into the data latch (Figure 6–11).

3. The clock pulse also sets a latch in the status port causing RDY0 to go HIGH (Figure 6–13).

4. The processor inputs the status information by activating $\overline{READ}$ and $\overline{PS3}$ (Figure 6–13).

5. The processor decodes this information and

6. Inputs data from Port 0 by activating $\overline{READ}$ and $\overline{PS0}$. (The port select signals, $\overline{PS0}$, $\overline{PS1}$, $\overline{PS2}$, and $\overline{PS3}$ are actually decoded from the address bus. The decoder is discussed later in this chapter.)

If we are certain that the peripheral will maintain the status signal long enough for the processor to test it, the signal need not be latched. As shown in Figure 6–13, bits 4, 5, 6, and 7 are not latched but simply inputted through three-state buffers.

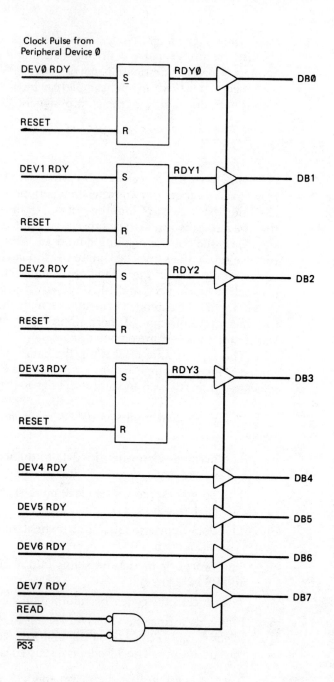

Figure 6–13. Status port.

6.5 CONTROL PORTS

Some peripheral devices require control signals. For example, if data is inputted from a paper tape reader, it is necessary to control the movement of the tape. This is accomplished by outputting a control signal to the tape reader via a control port. The procedure is to output a pulse causing the paper tape to advance to the next frame. Then the processor inputs a status signal to determine if the above has been accomplished. This can be done by using the status port in Figure 6–13.

Figure 6–14 shows an output port which is the same as that in Figure 6–12 except that the signals outputted from this port are used to control up to eight different functions. The control signals in this port are latched, which means that if a particular signal is to be activated, a one-bit must be outputted from the processor. If the signal is to be cleared, a zero must be outputted. Outputting a 1, followed by a 0, results in a pulse being outputted. If a particular function is to be enabled for a given length of time, the processor can output a 1 to that control line, wait the required time, and then output a 0. If multiple functions are to be controlled, all eight bits can be used. The processor would output a complete 8-bit word representing the particular combination of functions.

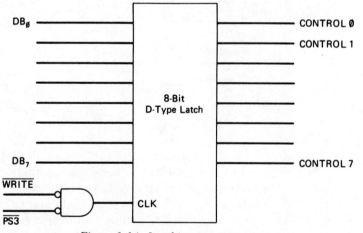

Figure 6–14. Latching type control port.

Many peripheral devices can be controlled by a short pulse, say 1 μsec or less. Figure 6–15 shows a control port that will provide control signals that are pulses. This port does not latch the signals but simply ANDs the particular bit on the data bus with the $\overline{\text{WRITE}}$ and $\overline{\text{PS3}}$ signals. The result is a pulse having the duration of the $\overline{\text{WRITE}}$ signal, which is shorter in duration than the $\overline{\text{PS3}}$ signal, approximately 1 μsec. In this example $\overline{\text{PS3}}$ is

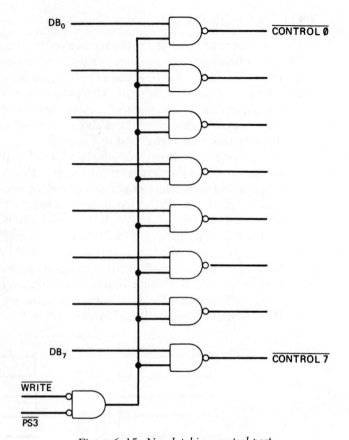

Figure 6–15. Non-latching control port.

used because it is already used as the status port. This is possible because the status port is an input port and the control port is an output port.

The example in Figure 6–16 illustrates how the control port works in conjunction with the status port and data port to input data. The data we have chosen to input is a binary number representing an analog value (voltage) that is an input to an analog-to-digital (A/D) converter. The procedure is as follows:

1.   The processor first outputs a control bit (let's use bit 1 port 3). This causes the control line ($\overline{\text{START}}$) to be active, which in turn starts the analog-to-digital conversion process in the converter. This process may take a considerable amount of time depending on the type of converter. The processor must wait.

2.   The processor inputs the status (READY) bit and tests to see if the conversion is complete. If not, it continues to make this test.

3. When the conversion process is completed, the converter issues the ready signal.

4. The processor detects the ready signal and inputs the data through port 1.

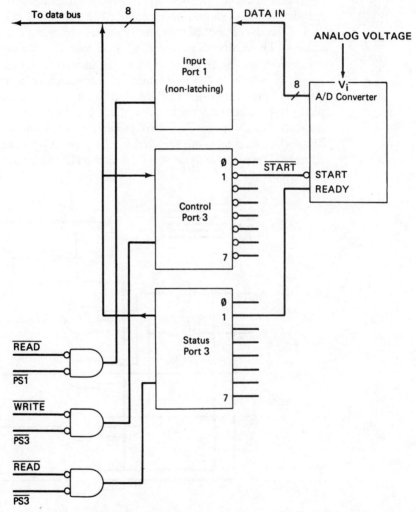

Figure 6–16. Inputting data from a peripheral.

6.6 ADDRESS DECODER

You may recall that LIMP is capable of addressing 252 memory locations (00–FB) and four ports (FC–FF). A decoder is necessary to differentiate between a port and memory location. If it is a port location, it must select one of the four ports. Figure 6–17 is the implemented decoder. Notice that if the six most significant bits all equal 1, a port is addressed. This is the case for all addresses above FB. The 6-input NAND gate develops the port select signal ($\overline{\text{PSEL}}$). The purpose of this line is to select a port and to deactivate memory. In addition, this signal is ANDed with the decoded values of A_0 and A_1 to produce the port select signals $\overline{\text{PS0}}$ through $\overline{\text{PS3}}$. Decoders are used in memory devices to select a particular memory address. These decoders are integrated into the memory chips so that specific addresses can be selected. LIMP uses a limited amount of memory. Larger systems may use more memory than can be placed on a single chip. Different chips are organized into banks (or pages) of memory. For example, a 16-bit microprocessor can address 65,536 (64K) bytes. They may be organized as 256 pages of 256 bytes each. In a system such as this, the addresses within a page are selected by the eight least significant bits of the address. The pages are selected by decoding the eight most significant bits of the address.

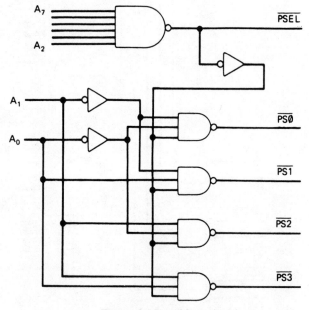

Figure 6–17. Address decoder.

6.7 MEMORY

Memory systems may be placed in two separate categories: random access memories (RAMs) and read-only memories (ROMs). A better name for RAM is "read/write" memory because data is accessed in the same manner for both functions. The term RAM connotes that data may either be written into the memory or read from the memory repeatedly. However, data may be written into the ROM only once. Some ROMs are "programmed" during the manufacturing process.

RAMs are used for main memories; smaller memories associated with arithmetic operations are called *scratch pad* memories; small memories used for input-output operations are called *buffer* memories.

ROMs are used for fixed instructions or data. For example, programs for dedicated applications are usually placed in ROM. This allows the execution of the program to begin immediately when power is applied. There is no need to load the program each time the processor is used.

Figure 6–18 illustrates the memory used by LIMP. It has eight address inputs, A_0–A_7, and eight data lines D_0–D_7. Two memory devices are used. Each device is a 4-bit by 256 static memory device. There are 4 bits at each of 256 addresses. Two devices are required for 8-bits by 256.

If a port address has been decoded, $\overline{\text{PSEL}}$ is LOW. This means that the chip select (CS) input is inactive and memory is not selected. If $\overline{\text{PSEL}}$ is HIGH, CS is HIGH and memory is selected. $\overline{\text{PSEL}}$ will be high level for all addresses below FC.

The address lines A_0–A_7 are used to select a particular memory address; 256 addresses may be selected. Remember, however, that the upper 4 addresses of memory are not used (FC–FF are port addresses). This leaves 252 usable memory locations.

Data lines D_0–D_7 are connected to the data bus. When CS is active and $\overline{\text{WRITE}}$ is not active, a copy of the addressed memory location is placed on the data bus.

If memory is to be read, the memory read cycle is as follows:

1. The processor places the address onto the address bus.
2. The processor does not issue $\overline{\text{PSEL}}$ ($\overline{\text{PSEL}}$ is HIGH and memory is selected).
3. The processor does not issue $\overline{\text{WRITE}}$ ($\overline{\text{WRITE}}$ is HIGH and memory is placed in the read state).
4. The addressed data is placed on the data bus and is transferred to the processor.

The memory write cycle is as follows:

1. The processor places the address on the address bus.
2. The processor does not issue $\overline{\text{PSEL}}$ ($\overline{\text{PSEL}}$ is HIGH and memory is selected).
3. The processor issues $\overline{\text{WRITE}}$ ($\overline{\text{WRITE}}$ is LOW and memory is placed in the write state).
4. The data on the data bus is stored at the addressed memory location.

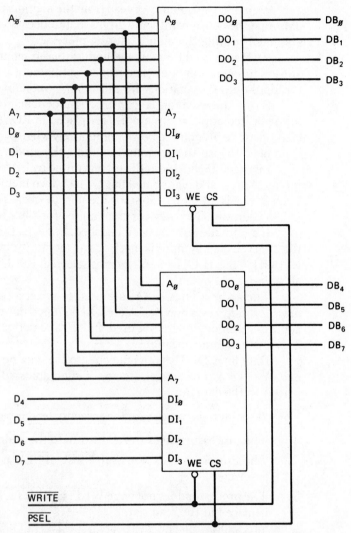

Figure 6–18. Memory for LIMP.

6.8 TIMING DIAGRAMS

When studying the communications between the processor and the I/O ports, it is helpful to use the timing diagrams for the read and write bus cycles. These waveforms show the sequence of events in each bus cycle. A read cycle exists whenever the data bus is used to read data from memory or input data through a port. The write cycle occurs when the bus is used to write data in memory or output data through a port. The duration of bus cycles is the same.

Figure 6–19(a) shows the waveforms for the read cycle. First, let's consider the address lines (A_0–A_7). Only two waveforms are drawn. However, they represent all eight bits of the address bus. No attempt is made to indicate the actual address. Only the time when the information on the bus changes is important. Furthermore, no units of time are used because, after all, LIMP is only a hypothetical processor. You will notice that the information on the address bus changes twice. Prior to the first change, the X indicates that for the read cycle it does not matter what the information is (don't care). After the first change however, the A indicates that a valid address appears on the bus. After the second change the don't care condition occurs again because the cycle is complete.

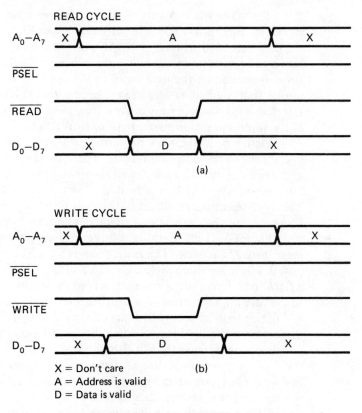

Figure 6–19. Timing diagram for LIMP's read and write cycles:
(a) read; (b) write.

The next waveform shown is $\overline{PSEL}$. You will notice that $\overline{PSEL}$ remains HIGH during the entire bus cycle. This is because the address on the bus is not a port address. Recall that $\overline{PSEL}$ is active only for the four highest addresses that select the four ports.

Notice that the $\overline{\text{READ}}$ waveform shows that it is active for a period of time while the address is valid. During this period, memory asserts data on the data bus. Remember, when reading, memory reacts to the $\overline{\text{READ}}$ control signal by placing the data at the selected address on the data bus. Therefore, you will notice that the waveforms for the data bus (D_0-D_7) indicate valid data only during the time that $\overline{\text{READ}}$ is active. The time between the assertion of the address and the assertion of $\overline{\text{READ}}$ is called *settling time,* or *deskew time.* This time is necessary to allow the memory to decode the appropriate address. The processor will actually take the data toward the end of the assertion of $\overline{\text{READ}}$, allowing time for the data to settle on the bus. The processor maintains the address until the operation is complete.

The write cycle is very similar to the read cycle. Its waveforms are shown in Figure 6–19(b). The differences are that the $\overline{\text{WRITE}}$ control signal is activated instead of $\overline{\text{READ}}$, and the manner in which the data bus is used is different. Because the processor is the source of the data, communication on the data bus is in the opposite direction. You will also notice that valid data is asserted before the $\overline{\text{WRITE}}$ control signal is asserted. This is a necessary deskew time to make certain that data appears at the input circuits of memory prior to $\overline{\text{WRITE}}$.

Figure 6–20(a) shows the timing diagrams for an input bus cycle; 6–20(b) shows the output bus cycle. These two bus cycles are actually read and write cycles. They are drawn separately to show that when inputting and outputting, PSEL is activated. $\overline{\text{PSEL}}$ is used to de-select memory. The port select signals $\overline{\text{PSEL0}}$ through $\overline{\text{PSEL3}}$ are exactly the same as $\overline{\text{PSEL}}$ except that only one of them can be active at a given time.

Figure 6–21 illustrates how bus cycles are placed together for a complete instruction cycle. The instruction is STA FC, which outputs data to port 0. There are three cycles: C1, C2, and C3. The first read cycle is called a *fetch* to differentiate it from other read cycles. In order for the processor to execute an instruction, it must first fetch and decode the opcode. You will notice that C1 is slightly longer than C2 or C3. This is because a little more time is required for decoding. Some instructions have only one byte and do not need to use the bus after the fetch cycle (C1). With these instructions, C1 may even be longer, allowing sufficient time to execute. However, in Figure 6–21, two extra bus cycles are required. All instructions in LIMP require one, two, or three bus cycles.

Let's assume that the instruction is stored in location 20 and that the contents of the A register is AA. The processor first outputs on the address bus the contents of the PC, which is 20 (as shown in the address bus waveforms). The PC is then incremented. Next, the processor asserts $\overline{\text{READ}}$. This causes memory to reply by placing the contents of location 20 on the data bus as shown in the data bus waveforms. The machine language code for STA is 85. While $\overline{\text{READ}}$ is still asserted, the processor

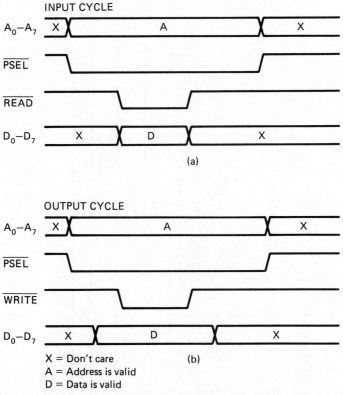

INPUT CYCLE

OUTPUT CYCLE

X = Don't care
A = Address is valid
D = Data is valid

Figure 6–20. Timing diagram for LIMP's input and output bus cycles:
(a) input; (b) output.

takes the information from the data bus and moves it to the instruction register where it is decoded. Because the processor still needs the operand (second byte), another read cycle is executed (C2). This time the operand (FC) is read. Once again, the processor outputs the contents of the PC (21), increments the PC, asserts $\overline{\text{READ}}$, and takes the information on the data bus. The processor saves the operand in a temporary register. The third bus cycle (C3) actually executes the instruction. The processor outputs the address in the temporary register on the address bus. The data in the A register (AA) is then outputted on the data bus. Finally, the processor asserts $\overline{\text{WRITE}}$ causing port 0 to take the data on the data bus. When C3 is complete, the instruction cycle terminates.

6.9 LIMP MICROCOMPUTER SYSTEM

Now that we have discussed the various circuits, let's put together a system. Input and output ports may be combined to form an I/O port. Figure 6–22(a) is the output portion of the port and is like Figure 6–12.

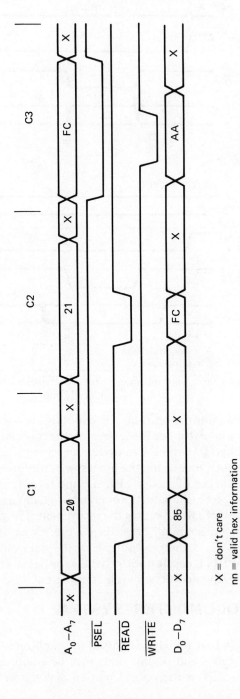

Figure 6-21. Timing diagram for the STA FC instruction.

X = don't care
nn = valid hex information

146

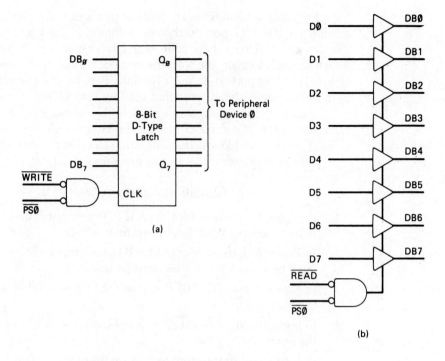

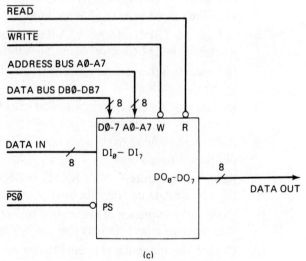

Figure 6–22. LIMP's I/O port: (a) output portion, (b) input portion, (c) symbol of I/O port for LIMP.

Figure 6–22(b) is the input portion of the port and is like Figure 6–10. The symbol for the I/O port is shown in Figure 6–22(c). For purposes of simplification, all lines of the address and data buses are not drawn. A slash drawn through a single line with the number 8 indicates 8 lines exist. Our system uses I/O ports 0, 1, and 2 for data. Port 3 is the control and status port and is exactly the same as that used for data I/O.

Figure 6–23 shows the complete block diagram of the LIMP microcomputer. The decoder block is the same circuit as shown in Figure 6–17. The memory block is the same circuit as that shown in Figure 6–18. This is the system that we will program in Chapter 7.

Questions and Problems

1. In Figure 6–4, to transfer DATA C to the output of gate 8, what lines must be active? What lines must be inactive?

2. In Figure 6–4, to transfer DATA B to the output of gate 4, what lines must be active? What lines must be inactive?

3. In Figure 6–6(a), DISABLE = 0 and DATA = 1. What is the state of the output ($\overline{\text{DATA}}$)?

4. In Figure 6–6(b), $\overline{\text{ENABLE}}$ = 0 and DATA = 1. What is the state of the output?

5. In Figure 6–7, to transfer DATA C to the outputs of devices A and D, what lines must be active? What lines must be inactive?

6. In Figure 6–7, to transfer DATA B to the outputs of devices C and D, what lines must be active? What lines must be inactive?

7. In Figure 6–8 the control signal is HIGH. Is the processor the source or the destination?

8. In Figure 6–9, what conditions must exist for the processor to be the destination for data on the data bus?

9. Referring to Figure 6–10, what lines must be activated in order to input data through port 1?

10. Referring to Figure 6–10, if $\overline{\text{READ}}$ is HIGH, how does Port 2 affect the flow of data on the data bus?

11. Explain the sequence of events that must take place in order to input data through a port such as the one in Figure 6–11.

12. Explain the sequence of events that must take place in order to output data through a port such as the one in Figure 6–12.

13. Refer to Figure 6–16. What conditions must exist for the processor to detect the READY signal?

14. Refer to Figure 6–16. What conditions must exist for the control port to issue a $\overline{\text{START}}$ signal to the peripheral device?

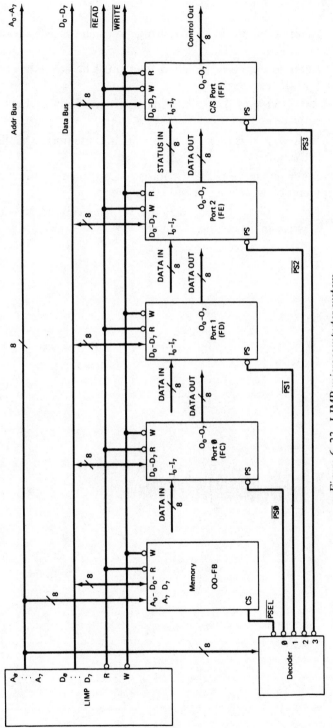

Figure 6-23. LIMP microcomputer system.

149

15.   Refer to Figure 6–17. What lines must be active in order to select Port 2?

16.   Refer to Figure 6–17. What lines must be active in order to select Port 0?

17.   Refer to Figure 6–18. To read data from memory, what lines must be activated?

18.   Refer to Figure 6–18. To write data into memory, what lines must be activated?

19.   Refer to Figure 6–23. If data is to be placed on the data bus from memory, what lines must be activated?

20.   Refer to Figure 6–23. If data is to be placed on the data bus from Port 2, what lines must be activated?

Chapter
7

Programming Concepts

Now that we have studied the instruction set and the architecture of the microprocessor, let's consider programming it. When a programmer writes a program, he is essentially writing a series of instruction words telling the computer what to do. These words are usually stored in sequence. This is because the processor "reads" and "executes" the designated operations in the prescribed order of the program.

Usually, programs are written in blocks of instructions called *routines*. Each routine is a sequence of instructions designed to perform one of the specific tasks of the program. *Subroutines* are routines that exist only in one place in memory but may be used by various parts of the program. Routines and subroutines are discussed in this chapter.

7.1 FLOWCHARTS

A *flowchart,* or *flow diagram,* is one kind of diagram commonly used to assist the programmer. The flowchart is also used by engineers and technicians to provide a bird's-eye view of the logic or solution to a given problem. It is made up of several standardized symbols connected by straight lines. Some of the most commonly used symbols are shown in Figure 7–1.

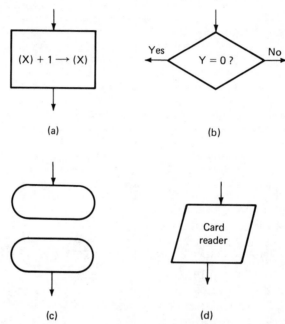

Figure 7–1. Some of the more commonly used flowchart symbols: (a) process operation, (b) decision, (c) terminal, (d) input/output.

The process operation symbol [rectangle in Figure 7–1(a)] tells us that some specific action is to be taken. The action is indicated by a statement inside the rectangle. The statement may be written in plain language, expressed algebraically, or given in some special symbology. For example, the statement $(X) + 1 \rightarrow (X)$, may be interpreted as: "One is added to the contents of the X register, and the sum is placed back into the X register." A line with an arrow between symbols indicates the input and output of the process operation symbol. By convention, the input should be either to the top or left side of the symbol, and the output should be from the bottom or right side. The arrows indicate the direction of logic flow, or the sequence of operations.

The diamond-shaped symbol indicates that a decision of some sort has to be made. This symbol will always have two or three outputs and only one input. For example, the symbol in Figure 7–1(b) asks for a decision: "Are the contents of the Y register equal to zero?" Because the answer can only be YES or NO, two outputs are indicated. In reading the diagram, only one path should be followed, depending on the decision made.

The terminal symbol in Figure 7–1(c) is used to indicate the start and end of a flowchart. Obviously, it is connected with only one line. Other symbols are used to indicate more specific operations, such as the input/output symbol in Figure 7–1(d). The input/output symbol may be used to indicate a typewriter, printer, card reader, or other input/output device.

7.2 PROGRAM STRUCTURE

Figure 7–2 is a flowchart for a linear program. The program is called a linear program because all of the operations in the program are in one sequence and the solution to the problem is concisely diagrammed. The *source program* is shown in Figure 7–3.

The source program is written by the programmer. It contains four columns called fields. The first column is called the *label field*. Labels are reference points in the program. Eventually they will be equated to addresses in the program.

The second column is called the *opcode field*. It contains the mnemonic opcodes. The third column, called the *operand field*, contains the operands. The fourth field is optional. It contains comments about how the instructions are used and what the program is intended to do.

Delimiters are spaces or special characters used to separate the fields. The label field is delimited, or separated, from the opcode field by the use of a colon (:). The comment field is delimited by using a semicolon (;). The opcode and operand fields are separated with spaces.

The student must conform to the format in order to communicate with the *assembler*. The assembler is a program used to produce the machine language code from the programmer's source program. One of the outputs of the assembler is the assembly listing shown in Figure 7–4.

Before we consider how the listing was generated, let's consider what a program listing contains. The first column contains the address of each instruction. The second column is the machine language code. Both columns are listed in hexadecimal. Each machine language instruction is either one or two bytes depending on the instruction. The remaining columns contain the programmer's source program.

Before we discuss the assembly procedure, let's consider what this program does. Its purpose is to add two numbers (numbers stored in locations DATA1 and DATA2) and store their sum in location SUM. Remember, labels represent addresses! The first instruction (MOV # DATA1,P) in-

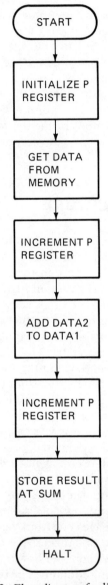

Figure 7–2. Flow diagram for linear program.

itializes the P register so that it contains the address of the first byte of data
(DATA1). The second instruction (MOV M,A) moves the contents of location 48 (DATA1) to the accumulator. The next instruction increments the
pointer to location DATA2. The next instruction (ADD M) adds the contents of location DATA2 to the accumulator. The instruction INC P causes

LABEL	OPCODE	OPERAND	COMMENT
START:	MOV	#DATA1,P	;initialize pointer
	MOV	M,A	;first data to Acc.
	INC	P	;point to DATA2
	ADD	M	;add DATA2 to DATA1
	INC	P	;point to SUM
	MOV	A,M	;store result in SUM
	HALT		;done
DATA1:			;location for DATA1
DATA2:			;location for DATA2
SUM:			;location for SUM

Figure 7-3. Source program for adding DATA1 and DATA2.

the pointer to contain the address of SUM. MOV A,M stores the result in this location. The last instruction causes the processor to halt.

This program is called a *linear program* because each instruction is executed in sequence (without branches or loops) from the first to the last. It is important to note that the values of DATA1 and DATA2 can be changed

ADDR	MACHINE CODE	LABEL	OPCODE	OPERAND	COMMENT
40	F0 48	START:	MOV	#DATA1,P	;initialize pointer
42	45		MOV	M,A	;first data to Acc.
43	26		INC	P	;point to DATA2
44	0D		ADD	M	;add DATA2 to DATA1
45	16		INC	P	;point to SUM
46	68		MOV	A,M	;store result in SUM
47	07		HALT		;done
48		DATA1:			;location for DATA1
49		DATA2:			;location for DATA2
4A		SUM:			;location for SUM

Figure 7-4. Assembly listing.

INSTRUCTION	OPERAND	OCTAL	HEX	INSTRUCTION	OPERAND	OCTAL	HEX	INSTRUCTION	OPERAND	OCTAL	HEX
ADD	A	10	08	XOR	A	60	30	BR	ADR	270	B8
ADD	B	11	09	XOR	B	61	31	BM	ADR	271	B9
ADD	C	12	0A	XOR	C	62	32	BP	ADR	272	BA
ADD	D	13	0B	XOR	D	63	33	BC	ADR	273	BB
ADD	E	14	0C	XOR	E	64	34	BNC	ADR	274	BC
ADD	M	15	0D	XOR	M	65	35	BZ	ADR	275	BD
ADD	P	16	0E	XOR	P	66	36	BNZ	ADR	276	BE
ADD	PC	17	0F	XOR	PC	67	37	CALL	ADR	277	BF
AND	A	40	20	INC	A	20	10	NOP		000	00
AND	B	41	21	INC	B	21	11	COM		001	01
AND	C	42	22	INC	C	22	12	ROR		002	02
AND	D	43	23	INC	D	23	13	ROL		003	03
AND	E	44	24	INC	E	24	14	LDA	ADR	204	84
AND	M	45	25	INC	M	25	15	STA	ADR	205	85
AND	P	46	26	INC	P	26	16	RET		006	06
AND	PC	47	27	INC	PC	27	17	HLT		007	07
OR	A	50	28	DEC	A	30	18	ADD	#BYTE	210	88
OR	B	51	29	DEC	B	31	19	AND	#BYTE	240	A0
OR	C	52	2A	DEC	C	32	1A	OR	#BYTE	250	A8
OR	D	53	2B	DEC	D	33	1B	XOR	#BYTE	260	B0
OR	E	54	2C	DEC	E	34	1C				
OR	M	55	2D	DEC	M	35	1D				
OR	P	56	2E	DEC	P	36	1E				
OR	PC	57	2F	DEC	PC	37	1F				

Figure 7-5. LIMP instruction set coding table. (page 1)

INSTRUCTION	OPERAND	OCTAL	HEX	INSTRUCTION	OPERAND	OCTAL	HEX	INSTRUCTION	OPERAND	OCTAL	HEX
MOV	A,A	100	40	MOV	D,A	103	43	MOV	P,A	106	46
MOV	A,B	110	48	MOV	D,B	113	4B	MOV	P,B	116	4E
MOV	A,C	120	50	MOV	D,C	123	53	MOV	P,C	126	56
MOV	A,D	130	58	MOV	D,D	133	5B	MOV	P,D	136	5E
MOV	A,E	140	60	MOV	D,E	143	63	MOV	P,E	146	66
MOV	A,M	150	68	MOV	D,M	153	6B	MOV	P,M	156	6E
MOV	A,P	160	70	MOV	D,P	163	73	MOV	P,P	166	76
MOV	A,PC	170	78	MOV	D,PC	173	7B	MOV	P,PC	176	7E
MOV	B,A	101	41	MOV	E,A	104	44	MOV	PC,A	107	47
MOV	B,B	111	49	MOV	E,B	114	4C	MOV	PC,B	117	4F
MOV	B,C	121	51	MOV	E,C	124	54	MOV	PC,C	127	57
MOV	B,D	131	59	MOV	E,D	134	5C	MOV	PC,D	137	5F
MOV	B,E	141	61	MOV	E,E	144	64	MOV	PC,E	147	67
MOV	B,M	151	69	MOV	E,M	154	6C	MOV	PC,M	157	6F
MOV	B,P	161	71	MOV	E,P	164	74	MOV	PC,P	167	77
MOV	B,PC	171	79	MOV	E,PC	174	7C	MOV	PC,PC	177	7F
MOV	C,A	102	42	MOV	M,A	105	45	MOV	#BYTE,A	300	C0
MOV	C,B	112	4A	MOV	M,B	115	4D	MOV	#BYTE,B	310	C8
MOV	C,C	122	52	MOV	M,C	125	55	MOV	#BYTE,C	320	D0
MOV	C,D	132	5A	MOV	M,D	135	5D	MOV	#BYTE,D	330	D8
MOV	C,E	142	62	MOV	M,E	145	65	MOV	#BYTE,E	340	E0
MOV	C,M	152	6A	MOV	M,M	155	6D	MOV	#BYTE,M	350	E8
MOV	C,P	162	72	MOV	M,P	165	75	MOV	#BYTE,P	360	F0
MOV	C,PC	172	7A	MOV	M,PC	175	7D	MOV	#BYTE,PC	370	F8

Figure 7–5. *LIMP instruction set coding table. (page 2)*

and the program can be executed again. Further, this program could be a routine within a larger program. Other parts of that program might be used to load the data into locations DATA1 and DATA2 and make use of the data stored at SUM.

7.3   INSTRUCTION SET

Figure 7–5 is the instruction set coding table. When we discussed the instruction set in Chapter 5, we used octal notation for developing the machine code. The coding table lists all of the instructions and all of the possible combinations of instructions so that we may easily code each instruction. You will notice that both octal and hexadecimal notation are used. We prefer hexadecimal notation because only two digits are required. Octal requires two and two-thirds digits and becomes confusing when multiple-byte instruction words or multiple bytes of data (data containing more than 8 bits) are used.

The student is reminded of certain terms that we will use. The opcode refers to the action part of the instruction: MOV, ADD, AND, etc. The operand is the actual data that will be affected by the instruction. The operand field of the instruction word may contain the actual operand but more often designates where the operand may be found. For example, the MOV A,B instruction is a double operand instruction. The first operand (source) appears in the A register and the second operand (destination) appears in the B register. Of course, after execution of this instruction, both operands will be the same. The ADD B instruction is really a double operand instruction. However, it is referred to as a single operand instruction because only one operand is designated. The B register contains the source operand. The destination operand is in the A register and is implied in the instruction.

Sometimes, addresses or constants are contained within an instruction word. For example, the instruction MOV #DATA1,P moves the address of DATA1 into the P register. In this instruction, the address is called *immediate data*. Two bytes of machine language code are required for instructions containing immediate data. The immediate data appears in the second byte of the instruction word.

7.4   ASSEMBLING

Some computer systems, which have an ample amount of memory and file storage capability, can assist the programmer in generating machine language (executable) programs. These systems support programs called *text editors* and *assemblers*.

The programmer first uses the text editor to create the *source program* (Figure 7-3). The source program is then stored on a recording medium such as disk or even paper tape. The text editor can also read old files, allowing the programmer to make changes or additions to his source program.

When the programmer is ready, he runs a program called the assembler. Remember, the purpose of the assembler is to read the programmer's source program and generate the machine language code *(object program)*.

The assembler must be able to read labels and substitute addresses for them. In fact, most assemblers read the entire program, creating what is called a *symbol table*. The table contains the labels and the addresses that they represent. When the table is complete, all of the addresses for the program have been assigned. Next, the assembler reads the program again. This time, machine language code is generated for each instruction. The assembler then creates a new file by writing the object program on the recording medium. The program can be executed at any time by loading it into memory.

Now let's consider the procedure used for assembling the program in Figure 7-3. The process of substituting a machine language word for an assembly language word is called assembling. Instead of using an assembler program, we will perform this task.

The first consideration is where the program is to be located in memory. A number of factors can be involved, but arbitrarily, we have selected location 40. Note that the first instruction has a label (START). Remember, the label START will now mean address 40. This instruction will require two bytes of machine language code. The second byte is immediate data, the source operand. The first byte contains the opcode. When we refer to the coding table, we find listed next to MOV # byte,P, the octal number 360 and the hex number F0. For the remainder of this chapter we will work only with hex numbers.

Referring back to the program in 7-4, you will notice that in the first column we have already placed the number 40 representing the address of the first instruction. In the second column, we place an F0 representing the machine code for the first instruction. Next to it is the second byte or immediate data. The value of this byte (48) may not be known until the assembly procedure is nearly complete. This is because the address of DATA1 needs to be determined. This completes the assembly of the first instruction. The second instruction (MOV M,A) will be located at address 42. Referring to the coding table we get 45. This procedure is continued until the entire program is assembled.

The program in Figure 7-3 may be simplified as shown in Figure 7-6. The program in Figure 7-3 uses indirect addressing, which uses a pointer register (P in LIMP) to contain the address of the data. The P register points to data locations. The program in Figure 7-6 uses direct addressing. With

40	84	49	START:	LDA	DATA1
42	48			MOV	A, B
43	84	4A		LDA	DATA2
45	09			ADD	B
46	85	4B		STA	SUM
48	07			HLT	
49			DATA1:		
4A			DATA2:		
4B			SUM:		

Figure 7-6. Example program using direct addressing.

direct addressing, all addresses are contained within the program itself. Direct addressing is used when only a few references to memory are required, such as in this program. Indirect addressing is more desirable when tables of data are used and when the data appears in sequence. The pound sign (#) in this listing is used to reference the address of the data. If the pound sign is not used, the contents of the address are referenced. For example, #DATA1 refers to the address of DATA1, and DATA1 (no # sign) refers to the contents of the address of DATA1. Therefore, MOV #DATA1,P loads the P reg with the address of DATA1 and LDA DATA1 loads the A reg with the contents of the address of DATA1.

You may wonder about the labels DATA1, DATA2 and SUM. These labels are not required by this routine, but are included so that they may be used by another routine to refer to these values.

7.5 BRANCHING

The programs listed in Figure 7-4 and 7-6 are linear programs. No loops or branches are included. The program in Figure 7-7 makes decisions and has one loop. A flow diagram of the program appears in Figure 7-7(a). The purpose of this program is to initialize a memory buffer to the first 16 counts (0-15) in hexadecimal.

In Figure 7-7(a) the first block after START is labeled INITIALIZE. Relating this block to the program listing in Figure 7-7(b), it represents the first three instructions. The first instruction (MOV #30,P) initializes the pointer to address 30. The instruction MOV #SIZE,C loads the C register with the number of bytes to be stored. For this program, SIZE equals 10 in hexadecimal. Notice that the first line of the program listing contains this information. This line is called an *equate*. It tells the assembler the value of SIZE. The assembler creates a symbol table. This table contains the labels and associated addresses as well as equates and the values they represent.

The third instruction initializes the A register to zero. It is the A register that will contain the number that is to be stored in memory. Any

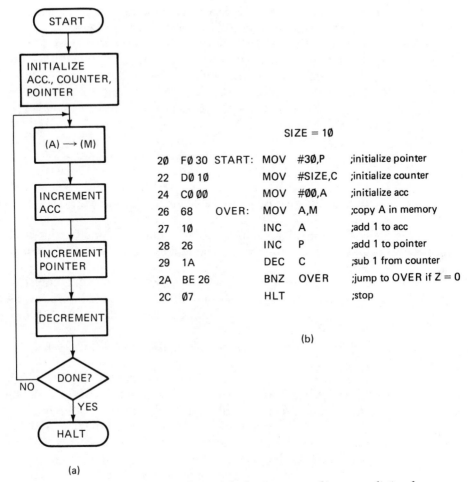

SIZE = 1Ø

2Ø	FØ 30	START:	MOV	#3Ø,P	;initialize pointer
22	DØ 1Ø		MOV	#SIZE,C	;initialize counter
24	CØ ØØ		MOV	#ØØ,A	;initialize acc
26	68	OVER:	MOV	A,M	;copy A in memory
27	1Ø		INC	A	;add 1 to acc
28	26		INC	P	;add 1 to pointer
29	1A		DEC	C	;sub 1 from counter
2A	BE 26		BNZ	OVER	;jump to OVER if Z = 0
2C	Ø7		HLT		;stop

(b)

(a)

Figure 7-7. (a) Flow diagram for loop program, (b) program listing for loop program.

register or memory location that must contain specific information must be initialized because when power is first applied to the processor, all registers and memory locations will contain random numbers from 00 to FF.

The second block in the flow diagram indicates that a byte of data is to be written into memory. The instruction is MOV A,M. Upon completion of this instruction, address 30 contains 00.

The next three blocks in the flow diagram indicate that we are to add one to the contents of the A and P registers and subtract one from the contents of the C register. The A register will now contain 01, the P register will contain 31 and the C register will contain 0F.

The next block asks the question, "Are we done?" The instruction is BNZ OVER. The DEC C instruction affects the zero flag. If DEC C causes the contents of the C reg to equal zero, the zero flag is set (Z = 1), otherwise it is cleared. The BNZ instruction tests the zero flag. If the zero flag is set, the instruction at the next address is executed. If the zero flag is clear, the address contained in the operand is placed in the PC and program execution resumes from that address. The contents of the C reg is not zero. Therefore, the zero flag is clear and the program jumps to the address whose label is OVER, which is address 26. The instruction at this address, MOV A,M, causes 01 to be stored at address 31. We have created a loop through which the program will go until the contents of the C register equals zero, at which time the next instruction after BNZ is executed and the program halts. The loop is executed 16 times. When the program halts, data has been placed in sixteen consecutive memory locations starting with address 30. That is, address 30 contains 00, address 31 contains 01, and so on until address 3F contains 0F. When the program halts, the pointer is pointing to address 40, the A reg contains 10, and C register contains 00. Of course 10 is never stored at address 40 because program execution has stopped.

A flow diagram of another program appears in Figure 7–8. This program, shown in Figure 7–9, makes decisions and has one loop. The purpose of this program is to search through a table of data and find the largest value in the table and its address.

In Figure 7–8 the first block after START is labeled INITIALIZE. Relating this block to the program listing in Figure 7–9, it represents the first three instructions. The first instruction (MOV # TABLE,P) initializes the pointer to TABLE, which is the first address of the data table. The instruction (MOV # SIZE,B) loads the B reg with the number of bytes in the table. For this program, SIZE = 10. Notice that the first line of the program listing contains this information. Whenever the assembler encounters the word SIZE in the program, it will use the value 10 in the assembly.

The third instruction initializes the C reg to zero. This is necessary because the program uses the C reg to save the largest value it has found. The second block in the flow diagram indicates that a byte of data is to be read from memory (TABLE) and is accomplished by the instruction MOV M,A.

The next four instructions make the decision, "Is the data greater than the current contents of the C reg?" To accomplish this, the contents of the A reg are subtracted from the C reg in the following manner: The contents of the A reg is complemented (COM) and incremented (INC A), producing the two's complement. Then the contents of the C reg is added (ADD C) producing the difference in the A reg. More importantly, however, the C flag is appropriately set. If the contents of the A reg was greater than the contents of the C reg, the C flag will be cleared (C = 0). If the contents of the A reg was equal to or less than the contents of the C reg, the C flag will be set (C = 1). The decision is completed with the

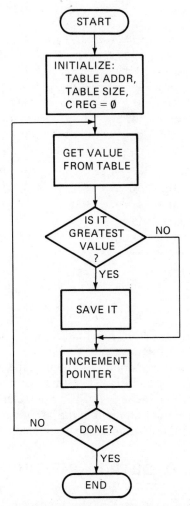

Figure 7–8. Flow diagram of search routine.

branch instruction BC OVER. If the contents of the A reg was greater than the contents of the C reg, the next two instructions (MOV M,C and MOV P,D) will be executed, saving the value in the C reg and its address in the D reg. If, however, the contents of the A reg was less than the C reg, the following two instructions will not be executed. The C reg, then, will always contain the largest value, and the D reg will contain its address.

The next instruction (INC P) causes the P reg to point to the next address in the data table.

The instructions DCR B and BNZ BACK make the decision, "Are we done?" Because the B reg contains the number of bytes in the table and is decremented each time a new byte is read, it will contain 0 when all bytes

SIZE = 10

```
10    F8 23    START:    MOV   #TABLE,P   ;init. pointer to 23
12    C8 10              MOV   #SIZE,B    ;init. B reg to 10
14    D0 00              MOV   #0,C       ;clear C reg
16    45       BACK:     MOV   M,A        ;get next number
17    01                 COM              ;complement A reg
18    10                 INC   A          ;increment A reg
19    0A                 ADD   C          ;add cont. C reg  to A reg
1A    BB 1E              BC    OVER       ;branch if carry
1C    55                 MOV   M,C        ;put number in C reg
1D    5E                 MOV   P,D        ;save address
1E    16       OVER:     INC   P          ;increment pointer
1F    19                 DCR   B          ;decrement counter
20    BE 16              BNZ   BACK       ;loop if not finished
22    07                 HLT              ;finished
23             TABLE:
```

END

Figure 7-9. Program listing of search routine.

have been read. The branch instruction causes the processor to loop back and get the next byte if not done. If done, the processor falls through the branch instruction and executes the next instruction, which is halt (HLT).

The address of TABLE has not been equated. Rather, a label has been placed in the program. The assembler, then, equates TABLE to address 23. The END statement in the last line is used to tell the assembler that this is all of the program to be assembled.

7.6 INPUT AND OUTPUT ROUTINES

In Chapter 6, the process of inputting and outputting data was discussed. Now let's write the necessary routines to accomplish this transfer of data. You may recall that three data ports were implemented: port 0 (address FC), port 1 (FD), and port 2 (FE). Port 3 (FF) is the control and status port.

In Figure 7-10 is a program that will input data via port 0. Port 3, the status port, is also used. The first two lines of the program are the equates for the appropriate addresses (FC and FF). The first instruction inputs the status information. The status information is necessary to determine when the input device is ready. Bit 0 has been assigned as the ready bit for the data to be inputted. The second instruction performs a MASK operation, which causes all bits except bit 0 to be 0. Therefore, if the contents of the A reg after this instruction is zero, then the ready bit is not present and data is

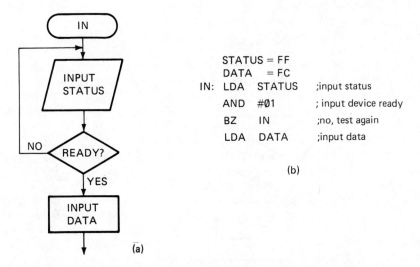

```
              STATUS = FF
              DATA   = FC
         IN:  LDA  STATUS     ;input status
              AND  #Ø1        ; input device ready
              BZ   IN         ;no, test again
              LDA  DATA       ;input data

                                    (b)
```

Figure 7-10. Input routine: (a) flow diagram, (b) source program.

not inputted. Because the contents of the A reg is zero, the zero flag has been set. This condition results in a loop back to the first instruction by the branch instruction BZ IN. The process will remain in this loop until the input device is ready. When the ready bit appears, the AND # 01 instruction will cause the contents of the A reg to equal 01. The zero flag will be cleared, the processor will fall through the BZ IN instruction, and the next instruction will be executed. This instruction (LDA DATA) will load the A reg with the data that is present at port 0. Notice that in the last instruction, the label "DATA" was not preceded with a # sign. If it was, the A reg would have been loaded with FC rather than the contents of address FC. When used in instructions, a label preceded with a # sign means an address or an equated data value. When a label is not preceded with a pound sign, the contents of that address becomes the operand. The last instruction (LDA DATA) should be interpreted as, "Load the A reg with the contents of the address DATA."

In Figure 7-11 is a source program that will output data via port 0. Bit 1 is used as the ready bit for the output device. Therefore, the AND # 02 masks all bits except bit 1. When bit 1 = 1, the output device is ready to accept data. Because the A reg was used to test for the ready bit, the A reg could not contain the data. Therefore, after we fell through the branch instruction, we moved the data to be outputted from its previous location in the C reg to the A reg. In such a routine the C reg is referred to as the transfer register.

Sometimes it is necessary to provide a control signal to the peripheral device. This is accomplished by outputting the appropriate control bit to the control port. Figure 7-12 is an example of a routine that will provide a

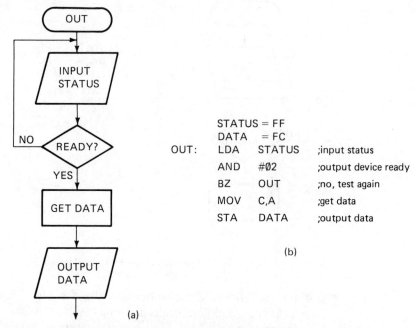

Figure 7–11. Output routine: (a) flow diagram, (b) source program.

control. Bit 7 has been selected as indicated by the "MOV # 80,A" instruction. The following three instructions output the bit as a pulse.

The sequence of these four instructions outputs a 1 followed by a 0, which produces a pulse for the control signal. This sequence is necessary whenever the control port is a latching port.

The student should be aware that all instructions involving memory can be used for I/O purposes because LIMP's ports are accessed as if they were memory. Sometimes this is referred to as memory-mapped I/O.

7.7   SUBROUTINES

Many times, routines are used more than once within a main program. When this is the case, the programmer may find it more efficient to use *subroutines*. A subroutine is just like any other routine except that it does not have to be included within the main program and can be called from the main program as many times as necessary. Another important point is that it may be called from many places in the main program. A call to a subroutine is accomplished with the instruction CALL. The CALL instruction is like the unconditional branch (BR) except that the processor must save the return address. Keep in mind that when a subroutine is called, the processor must have some way of returning to the instruction

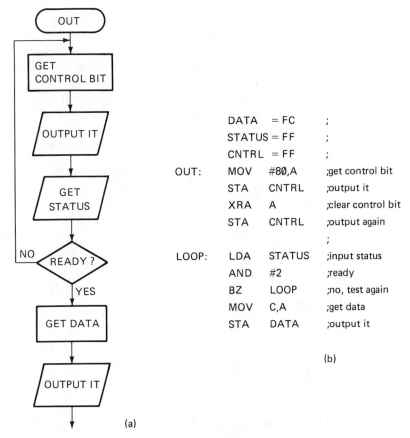

Figure 7–12. *Output routine with control: (a) flow diagram, (b) source program.*

immediately following the CALL instruction after the subroutine has been executed. This means that the return address must be saved. This can be accomplished by saving the contents of the PC in another register. LIMP uses the E register for this special function. The CALL instruction automatically moves the contents of the PC to the E register. Since the PC has already been incremented, the E register contains the address of the next instruction following the CALL instruction (return address). Next, the contents of the PC is replaced with the address of the subroutine, which is the second byte of the CALL instruction.

The subroutine is then executed as if a branch instruction were used. Because the processor must return to the main program after execution of the subroutine, a return (RET) instruction is included as the last instruction of the subroutine. The RET instruction is just like MOV E,PC, causing the contents of the E register to be placed in the PC. The PC now contains the address of the instruction just after the CALL instruction, and the processor continues executing the main program.

Input and output routines are good examples of subroutines. To make the routine in Figure 7–12 a proper subroutine, a RET instruction should be included as its last instruction.

In Figure 7–13 there is a program that will output a message that has been stored in memory. The first location of the characters in the message is called MSG. The ASCII characters appear in order and are terminated with a null byte indicating the end of the message.

22	F8	2F		START:	MOV	#MSG,P	;initialize pointer
24	55			MORE:	MOV	M,C	;move charact. to transfer reg
25	30				XOR	A	;clear A
26	2A				OR	C	;set Z flag if null byte
27	BD	2E			BZ	DONE	;IF Z = 1 THEN done
29	BF	XX			CALL	OUT	;print character
2B	16				INC	P	;increment pointer
2C	B8	24			BR	MORE	;loop for next character
2E	07			DONE:	HLT		;halt
2F	44	4F	20	MSG:			
32	59	4F	55				
35	20	4B	4E				
38	4F	57	20				
3B	54	48	45				
3E	20	57	41				
41	59	20	54				
44	4F	20	53				
47	41	4E	20				
4A	4A	4F	53				
4D	45	3F	00				

Figure 7–13. Program to output message.

The first instruction initializes the pointer to MSG. The next instruction moves an ASCII character to the transfer register (C). Next, the A reg is cleared (XOR A). This is done so that a test can be made to see if the last character has been printed. If the result of OR C sets the Z flag, the null byte has been encountered and the program terminates through the BZ instruction to HLT. If the character is not a null, the CALL instruction is executed. The processor saves the return address in E, places the address of OUT in the PC and executes the subroutine. When the subroutine is complete and the RET is executed, the processor moves the contents of E to the PC. This causes the next instruction in the main program to be executed (INC P). Now P is pointing to the next character. The processor loops back and executes the program again. This continues until a null byte is encountered at address 4F.

7.8   A SAMPLE PROGRAM

Now let's take a look at a practical program that can run on our LIMP. A flow diagram for the program appears in Figure 7–14. This program is called a bubble sort. It sorts a table full of data (bytes) into ascending order without creating a second table, thereby making efficient use of memory. Here is how it works. The first two numbers are compared. If the second number is greater than the first, they are in order and left alone. However, if they are out of order, the two numbers are switched. Then the same is done to the second and third numbers; if they are not in order, they are switched. This process continues until we reach the end of the table. A test is then made to determine if any switches have occurred. If there has been at least one switch, the program is reinitialized and is executed again. This continues until there are no switches and the program halts.

The program listing appears in Figure 7–15. The program is organized in three parts. The first part is the main program. The second and third parts are subroutines that are called by the main program. At the top of the listing are three equates. The first (TABL = 50) establishes address 50 as the starting address of the table. The second (SIZE = 64) establishes the size of the table. Since 64 hexadecimal equals 100 decimal, this program will sort 100 bytes of data. The third equate causes the assembler to assemble the first instruction at address 10. This program can be modified for other use by simply changing the equates and reassembling.

The first three instructions initialize the pointer (P reg), the B reg to the size of the table, and the C reg to zero. The C reg is used as a flag to note whether any switches have taken place. The next instruction CALLs the compare subroutine. The processor returns to the main program with the results of the compare in Z and CY flags. If the two numbers are equal, the Z flag will be set and a branch over the CALL to the switch subroutine is executed. If the CY flag is not set, indicating the numbers are in order, another branch over the CALL is executed. However, if the CY flag is set, the CALL to the switch subroutine will be executed. This causes the position of the two numbers to be switched. In addition, the C reg will be incremented indicating a switch has taken place. Next, the B reg is decremented (DEC B). If this causes the B reg to equal zero, the end of the table has been reached. If not, a branch is executed (BNZ MORE) and the program loops until the end of the table is reached. The next two instructions (XOR A and OR C) test the contents of the C reg. If it is zero, the program is complete and halts. If not, the program is reinitialized and is executed again.

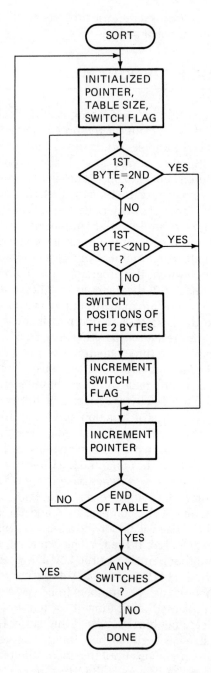

Figure 7-14. Flow diagram for Bubble Sort Program.

```
                        TABL=50
                        SIZE=64

10   E0   10    START:  MOV     #START,E        ;initialize SP
12   F0   50    SORT:   MOV     #TABL,P         ;initialize pointer
14   C8   64            MOV     #SIZE,B         ;initialize table size
16   D0   00            MOV     #0,C            ;clear switch flag
18   BF   28    MORE:   CALL    CMP             ;compare 2nd # with 1st
1A   BD   20            BZ      OVER            ;if equal don't switch
1C   BC   20            BNC     OVER            ;if 1st < 2nd, don't switch
1E   BF   2F            CALL    SWTCH           ;else, switch them
20   19         OVER:   DEC     B               ;bottom of table?
21   BE   18            BNZ     MORE            ;no, sort more
23   B0             XOR     A               ;clear A
24   2A                OR      C               ;switch flag = 0?
25   BE   12            BNZ     SORT            ;no, sort table again
27   07                HLT                     ;done, stop

28   5D         CMP:    MOV     M,D             ;this routine compares·
29   16                INC     P               ;the 1st and 2nd numbers
2A   45                MOV     M,A             ;if the 2nd number is less
2B   01                COM                     ;then CY = 0
2C   10                INC     A               ;if equal, Z = 1
2D   0B                ADD     D               ;
2E   06                RET                     ;return to main program

2F   5D         SWTCH:  MOV     M,D             ;this routine
30   1E                DEC     P               ;switches the
31   45                MOV     M,A             ;1st and 2nd bytes
32   6B                MOV     D,M             ;
33   16                INC     P               ;
34   68                MOV     A,M             ;
35   12                INC     C               ;increment switch flag
36   06                RET                     ;return to main program
                        END
```

Figure 7-15. SORT program listing.

By studying the compare subroutine, you will discover that the second number is subtracted from the first. This is accomplished by complementing (COM) the second number, incrementing it (INC A) and adding it to the first number (ADD D).

The switch subroutine uses the A reg and the D reg to switch the locations of the first and second numbers. Before the RET is executed, the C reg is incremented indicating a switch has taken place.

Questions and Problems

1. What does a diamond-shaped block represent in a flowchart?

2. What does a rectangular-shaped block represent in a flowchart?

3. What information is contained in the second column of a program listing?

4. What is the purpose of the information contained in the label field of the assembly listing?

5. Which field of the listing is optional?

6. Which field of the listing contains the assembly language mnemonic?

7. What is the machine code for MOV C,A?

8. What is the machine code for ADD C?

9. Refer to the program in Figure 7–3. If DATA1 = 2A and DATA2 = B3:

    a) What is the contents of the A register after the MOV M,A instruction has been executed?

    b) What is the contents of the A register after the instruction ADD M has been executed?

    c) What is the contents of the P register after the instruction INC P at address 43 has been executed?

10. Refer to the program in Figure 7–3. If DATA1 = 48 and DATA2 = 9C:

    a) What is the contents of the P register after the instruction MOV #DATA1,P?

    b) What is the contents of the A register after the instruction ADD M?

    c) What is the contents of the P register after the instruction INC P at address 45?

11. Refer to Figure 7–6. If DATA1 = 8A and DATA2 = 3B:

    a) What is the contents of the B register after the instruction MOV A,B?

    b) What is the contents of the B register after the instruction ADD B?

    c) What is the contents of the A register after the instruction ADD B?

    d) What is the contents of the A register after the instruction LDA DATA2?

12. Refer to Figure 7–6. If DATA1 = AB and DATA2 = 30:

    a) What is the contents of the A register after the instruction LDA DATA1?

    b) What is the contents of the B register after the instruction ADD B?

13. Refer to Figure 7–9. Suppose that at some time in the program the contents of the A register is A3, the contents of the B register is 01, the contents of the C register is 4B, and the P register is pointing to address 27. And further, the next instruction to be executed is at address 17(COM):

a) After the COM instruction has been executed, what are the contents of the A, C, and P registers? To what address is the PC pointing?

b) What is the next instruction to be executed after BC OVER?

c) After the instruction ADD C, what are the contents of the A and C registers?

d) What instruction will be executed after BNZ BACK?

14. Refer to Figure 7–15:

a) After the CALL CMP instruction, CY = 1, what is the next instruction that will be executed?

b) The stack pointer (the E register) is initialized to address 10. When the CALL CMP instruction is executed, what is the contents of address 10? What is the contents of address 09?

15. Refer to Figure 7–15. What is the beginning address of the table? What is the last address of the table?

16. What is the difference between a CALL instruction and a BR instruction?

17. Assemble the following source program. Use 60 as the beginning address.

MOV	# NUM1,P
MOV	# 00,A
MOV	M,C
AND	C
STA	NUM1
HLT	
NUM1:	
END	

What does the program do?

18. Assemble the following source program. Use 30 as the beginning address.

MOV	# 42,B
MOV	# DATA1,P
MOV	B,M
INC	P
XOR	A
ADD	B
COM	
INC	A
MOV	A,M
HLT	
DATA1:	
END	

19.   Assemble the following source program. Use address 50 as the beginning address of the main program and address 70 as the beginning address of the subroutine (SUM).

```
                SIZE    = 05
                BEGIN   = 50
                MOV     # BEGIN,C
                MOV     # SIZE,B
                XOR     C
                MOV     # DATA1,P
        MORE:   MOV     M,A
                INC     P
                CALL    SUM
                DEC     B
                BNZ     MORE
                HLT

    DATA1:
    DATA2:
    DATA3:
    DATA4:

    SUM:        ADD     C
                MOV     A,C
                RET
                END
```

What does the program do?

20.   Assemble the following source program. Use address 40 as the beginning address of the main program and A0 as the beginning address of the subroutine (SUB).

```
                RPT     = 5
        START:  XOR     A
                MOV     # 01,A
                ROL
                BNC     OVER
                DEC     D
                BNZ     OVER
                CALL    SUB
                BR      START
```

```
SUB:        MOV        #RPT,D
            ROR
            BNC        SUB
            DEC        D
            BNZ        SUB
            RET
            END
```

What does the program do? What was the purpose of the instruction
XOR A?

The Stack
and
Interrupts

In this chapter we will improve LIMP so that it can handle subroutines and input and output operations more efficiently. Concepts relating to the use of the stack, polling, and interrupt techniques are discussed.

8.1 STACK POINTER AND THE STACK

In Chapter 7, we discussed a technique for saving the return address for a CALL instruction. When the CALL instruction was executed, the return address (the address of the instruction immediately following the CALL instruction) was moved from the PC to the E register. Suppose it is desirable for a subroutine to call another subroutine. Two return addresses must be saved. The first is the return address to the main program, and the second is the return address to the first subroutine. With LIMP as we have described it, this is impossible because only one return address can be saved in the E reg.

Most microprocessors and minicomputers make use of a portion of memory called a *stack* for saving return addresses. The stack we will describe is called a LIFO (last in, first out). The stack can exist anywhere in memory, and the top of the stack (lowest address) is pointed to by the *stack pointer* (SP). Let's modify LIMP so that the E reg becomes the stack pointer. From this point on, the E reg will be referred to as the stack pointer, or SP. This modification of LIMP will cause a certain sequence of events to occur when a CALL instruction is executed.

When a CALL instruction is executed, the stack pointer is first decremented and then the return address is stored in that location. If the subroutine calls another subroutine, the SP is decremented again and the second return address is stored in that location. When the second subroutine is complete, a return instruction (RET) will move the contents of the top of the stack to the PC and then increment the SP. The first subroutine continues until it encounters another CALL or RET. If a RET is encountered, the return address is moved from the top of the stack to the PC, causing a return to the main program, and the SP is then incremented. If a CALL is encountered, the SP is first decremented and then the new return address is stored on top of the stack. By definition, the top of the stack is the lowest address of the stack. This technique allows for nested subroutines (subroutines called by other subroutines). The depth of nesting is limited only by the size of the stack.

Consider this sequence of instructions that starts at address 10.

10	MOV	# F0,SP
12	MOV	# 25,A
14	CALL	SURTN
16	STA	A4

.
.
.

The stack pointer is initialized to address F0. When the instruction CALL SURTN is executed the following occurs: The stack pointer is decremented and now points to address EF; The contents of the PC is saved on the stack; and the address whose label is SURTN is placed in the PC; and program execution continues from that address. We have stored the return address (which is 16, the address of the next instruction) at address EF, which is the top of the stack. When the subroutine is complete, a return instruction (RET) must be executed. The RET instruction will move the contents of the top of the stack to the PC and then increment the SP. The PC now contains 16, the address of the next instruction, and the stack pointer points to address F0.

Another use of the stack and stack pointer is to save the contents of registers. Our modification of LIMP allows for the execution of PUSH and POP instructions in addition to the CALL instruction. A PUSH instruction and a CALL instruction are quite similar. A CALL decrements the SP and then saves the return address on the stack. A PUSH decrements the SP and then saves the contents of a designated register on the stack.

A POP instruction and a RET instruction are quite similar. A RET places the contents of the stack in the PC and then increments the SP. A POP places the contents of the stack into a designated register and then increments the SP.

The stack pointer should be initialized by the main program. The stack is usually created at the very top of memory. The stack then grows downward toward the program. Another technique is to leave room just below the start of the main program. The SP is initialized at the starting address of the program. In this case the stack grows downward and the program upward from the starting address.

To illustrate how the stack works with both CALLs and PUSHes, let's consider the following sequence of instructions:

```
MOV     #F5,SP      ;initialize the stack pointer
MOV     #DATA,P     ;initialize the memory pointer
MOV     #SIZE,C     ;initialize a counter
PUSH    A           ;save registers
PUSH    D           ;
CALL    PRINT       ;call print subroutine
POP     D           ;restore register
POP     A           ;
  •                 ;continue with rest of program
```

The first instruction initializes the stack pointer with the address F5. This address is not part of the stack, but one address higher than the start of the stack. Remember, the stack pointer will decrement *before* anything is stored in the stack. The second instruction initializes the pointer register with an address where some data is stored (DATA). Next, the C register is initialized with the number of bytes of data (SIZE). The CALL PRINT instruction causes the processor to CALL a subroutine that will output the data to a printer. Assume that the subroutine PRINT uses the A and D registers in addition to the C and P registers. Assume also that some information exists in the A and D registers that is vital to the remainder of the program. The contents of the A and D registers are saved by PUSHing them on the stack before the CALL instruction is executed. This frees them for use by the subroutine. The instruction PUSH A will decrement the SP so that it is now pointing to address F4 and save the contents of the A register at this address. The instruction PUSH D will decrement the SP so that it is now pointing to address F3 and save the contents of the D register at this address. When the subroutine is called, the SP is decremented and points to address F2; the return address is saved at this location. If the instruction POP D is at address 6A, then 6A is stored at location F2 because POP D is the next instruction. The result of these three instructions is illustrated in Figure 8–1. Notice that the SP is pointing to the top of the stack which is now address F2.

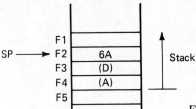

Figure 8–1. Illustration of the use of the stack.

When the subroutine is complete, a RET instruction is executed. This instruction will cause the contents of the address pointed to by the SP (6A) to be placed in the PC and increment the SP. The next instruction to be executed will be the instruction at address 6A, which is POP D. This instruction will place the contents of address F3 into the D register and increment the SP. The next instruction, POP A, will place the contents of address F4 into the A register and increment the SP. The SP is again pointing to address F5. Remember, the stack we have described is called a LIFO. If we were careless and popped A *first*, after execution of the POP instructions, the old contents of the A register would end up in the D register and the old contents of the D register would end up in the A register.

It is possible that, in the example above, the B register also contained vital information. However, because the subroutine did not use the B register, it was not saved.

CALLs, PUSHes and POPs allow for more powerful instruction sets as we shall see in later parts of this chapter and when we study real processors.

8.2   PORTS

8.2.1   Input Port

Figure 8–2 shows the input port that we will use. This port is like the input port discussed in Chapter 6, Figure 6–11, except that an RS flip-flop is added to the circuit. Connecting $\overline{PSEL0}$ to this port indicates that it is

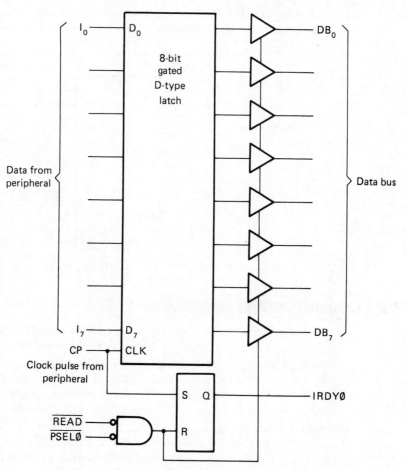

Figure 8–2. New input port 0 for LIMP.

input port 0. Otherwise, input ports 1 and 2 will be exactly the same. These input ports are of the latching type. You will notice that a clock pulse is required from the peripheral. It is the responsibility of the peripheral to assert this pulse *after* it has sent the data signals to the port (asserted data). The pulse causes the data to be latched in the 8-bit latch. Further, notice that an RS flip-flop is also set by this clock pulse. The output of this flip-flop is used as a ready bit, indicating that data is stored in the input port and ready to be input by the processor. The processor reads the port by asserting $\overline{\text{PSEL0}}$ followed by asserting $\overline{\text{READ}}$. This activates the NAND gate, which enables the three-state bus drivers, causing the data to be transmitted on the bus to the processor. At the same time, the ready flip-flop is reset. This is necessary because IRDY0 is sensed by the processor when it goes from LOW to HIGH. Figure 8–3 shows how this port is symbolized for simplification of diagramming.

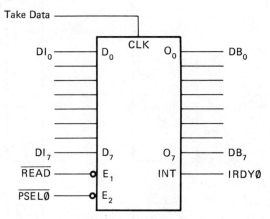

Figure 8–3. Symbol for new input ports 0, 1, and 2.

8.2.2 Output Port

Figure 8–4 shows the output port we will use. This port is identical to the output port discussed in Chapter 6, Figure 6–12. As were other output ports, it is also of the latching type. In order to output data, the processor first asserts data on the data bus. This is followed by asserting $\overline{\text{PSEL0}}$ and then $\overline{\text{WRITE}}$. This causes the data to be latched and available for the peripheral. In addition, a RS latch is reset. The peripheral then takes the data and sets the latch only when it is ready for more data. The peripheral accomplishes this by asserting a clock pulse. The output of this latch is a status signal indicating to the processor that the peripheral is ready. Figure 8–5 shows how this port will be symbolized in further drawings.

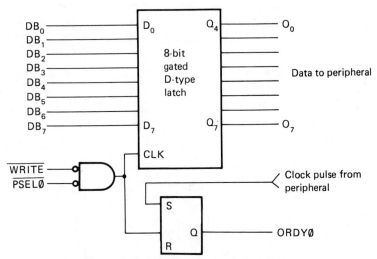

Figure 8-4. New output port 0 for LIMP.

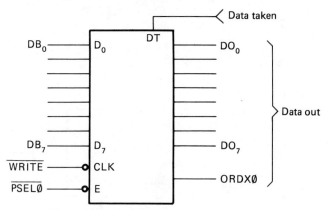

Figure 8-5. Symbol for output ports 0, 1, and 2.

8.2.3   Control and Status Port

Figure 8–6 shows the circuit selected for the status port. Status and control ports and their function were described in Chapter 6. This port is a non-latching input port using three-state circuits. The signals indicated at the inputs are status signals for the three I/O ports. The port in Figure 8–7 is the control port we have selected. It is also non-latching. Therefore, the control signals will be pulses having the duration of $\overline{\text{WRITE}}$. The two control signals, EI and DI will be explained later in the section on Interrupts.

Figure 8–8 shows how we will symbolize the control port and the status port as a single control and status port.

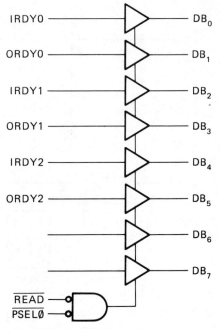

Figure 8-6. Status port.

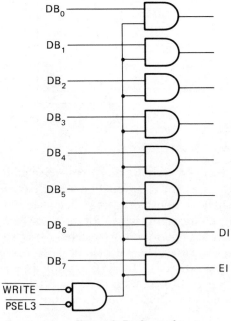

Figure 8-7. Control port.

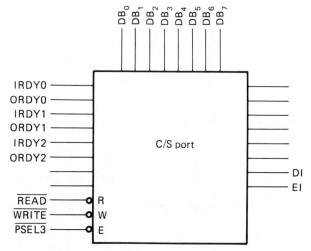

Figure 8-8. LIMP's Control and Status Port.

8.3 PROGRAM CONTROL I/O

Suppose for some reason that we need to have three terminals connected to LIMP simultaneously. Figure 7-10 showed a routine for inputting data from port 0 only. Recall that status information is inputted through the status port, when $\overline{PSEL3}$ and $\overline{RD}$ are active, and then the ready bit is tested. If the ready bit equals 0, this procedure is repeated. However, if the bit equals 1, indicating that data is present, the data is inputted. Using this procedure for inputting (or outputting) data is called *program control I/O* because both the testing and the inputting (or outputting) is initiated by the program itself. The program tests the port to determine if data is present and ready to be inputted. If the port is not ready, the program loops back and tests again. The disadvantage with such a system is that the other two input ports in LIMP would be locked out. This problem can be overcome by a procedure called *polling*. The flow diagram in Figure 8-9 shows how polling works. Notice that when this procedure is used, each port is tested in turn to determine if a ready bit is present. If a ready bit is not found, the procedure is continually repeated. When a ready bit is found, data is inputted through the appropriate port. There must be three separate ready bits because there are three data ports.

An example of a program for polling appears in Figure 8-10. The instruction LDA STATUS inputs the information at the status port (port address FF). This information contains the value of the three ready bits. If you refer to Figure 8-6, the status port, you will see that the ready bits for input (IRDY0, IRDY1, and IRDY2) have been assigned to bits 0, 2, and 4 of the status byte.

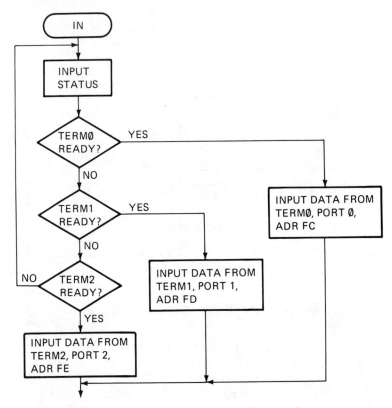

Figure 8-9. Flow diagram for polling routine.

The instruction AND #01 is a mask, stripping all bits (making them all zero) except bit 0, which is the ready bit for port 0. If this bit equals one, the zero flag is cleared and the following branch instruction will be executed. If this bit equals zero, the zero flag is set and the next ready bit is tested. Each ready bit is tested in the same manner. If one of the ready bits equals 1, data is input from that terminal and program execution continues. If no data is present (all ready bits equal 0) the program loops continuously until data is present.

8.4   INTERRUPT I/O

A serious problem exists with program controlled I/O. In the preceding polling example, the processor continued executing the polling routine until data was provided by one of the input terminals. Therefore, if no data was provided, the polling routine kept the processor busy and no other routines could be executed. Because peripherals such as terminals and printers are notoriously slow compared to the speed of the processor,

```
        TERM0  = FC
        TERM1  = FD
        TERM2  = FE
        STATUS = FF
IN:     LDA    STATUS      ;get status
        AND    #01         ;terminal zero ready?
        BNZ    ZERO        ;yes.    input data
        LDA    STATUS      ;get status
        AND    #04         ;terminal one ready?
        BNZ    ONE         ;yes, input data
        LDA    STATUS      ;no, get status
        AND    #10         ;terminal two ready?
        BZ     IN          ;no, start over again
        LDA    TERM2       ;yes, input from port 2
        BR     CONT        ;and continue main program
ONE:    LDA    TERM1       ;input from port 1
        BR     CONT        ;and continue main program
ZERO:   LDA    TERM0       ;input from port 0
CONT:   .                  ;and continue main program
        .
        .
```

Figure 8-10. Program for polling routine.

probably more than 90 percent of the processor's time could be wasted while polling.

A much more efficient procedure for inputting (or outputting) data is called *interrupt I/O*. In order for us to demonstrate this technique using LIMP, LIMP must be modified. Figure 8-11 shows these modifications. Notice a new input to the processor. It is called *interrupt request* (INTR). When activated, INTR causes the processor to be interrupted. INTR can only be activated if the INTE (interrupt enable) flip-flop is set. This flip-flop

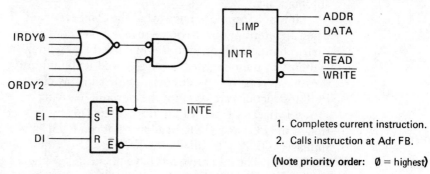

1. Completes current instruction.
2. Calls instruction at Adr FB.

(Note priority order: 0 = highest)

Figure 8-11. LIMP modified for interrupt I/O.

is set by EI (Enable Interrupt). EI is a signal from the control port as shown in Figure 8–7. INTE can be reset by activating DI (disable interrupt), which is another signal from the control port. Because these two signals originate at the control port, INTE may be set or cleared under program control.

If INTE has been set, activating any one of the six ready bits will cause an interrupt. When interrupted, LIMP will:

1. Complete the execution of the instruction that is currently in its instruction register. If it is fetching another instruction, it will terminate that procedure.

2. Execute a CALL to the address located at address FB.

Although it has not fetched a CALL instruction, it will proceed as though it did. In addition, it will take the contents of FB as the destination of the CALL. In other words, it pushes the contents of the PC on the stack and moves the contents of location FB to the PC.

If properly initialized, address FB will contain the address of a subroutine. Because this subroutine is called only when LIMP is interrupted, it is called an *interrupt service routine*.

Before we describe the service routine, let's consider the problems associated with an interrupt. Suppose you are trying to balance your checkbook and you are interrupted at a critical point in that process. What do you do? First, you make a mental note of where in the procedure you were when interrupted. Perhaps you may even write this down. In addition, if you were in the middle of adding up some numbers, you might record a partial sum. In any case, you would attempt to make it possible to return to the job exactly where you left it.

LIMP is faced with the same problem when it is interrupted. First it must save the address of the instruction immediately following the last instruction it executed when it was interrupted. This address is called the *return address*. When interrupted, LIMP CALLed the interrupt service routine. Recall that a CALL instruction pushes the contents of the PC. Therefore, as with subroutine CALLs, the return address is saved automatically.

It is not possible to know what the contents of any of the registers are when an interrupt occurs. Some registers may contain crucial information, such as partial sums or addresses of data. It is absolutely necessary that the contents of these registers are also saved if the interrupt service routine uses these registers. As discussed earlier in this chapter, the PUSH and POP instructions are used for the purpose of saving registers.

LIMP can PUSH or POP the contents of any register with the exception of the PC and the SP. In addition, it can PUSH and POP the *program status word* (PSW). In LIMP, the PSW is a byte containing only the Z, C, and N flags. The other five bits have no meaning. These flags must always be saved because LIMP may be interrupted while it is executing a logical or mathematical routine. Restoring these flags and the registers will allow LIMP to return to the original or main program at the exact point where it was interrupted.

8.5 INTERRUPT SERVICE ROUTINE

Now that we have discussed the concept of interrupts, let's proceed with interrupt service routines. Routines or programs that execute when the processor has been interrupted are called *foreground programs*. The main program that is interrupted is called a *background program*. There may be a number of foreground programs; however, LIMP as it is now implemented can handle only one foreground program.

Now let's use the example of inputting data from the three terminals, but this time we will use interrupt I/O.

Figure 8-12 shows the flow diagram of an interrupt service routine. Keep in mind that a main program is running in the background when the processor is interrupted. Therefore, every precaution must be taken to prevent damage to the background program or its data. This is accomplished by saving the return address, the flags (PSW), and any registers that the foreground program may change. When this is accomplished, the foreground program decides which peripheral was interrupted by polling. It then executes a routine to service that peripheral. When the service is complete, all registers are restored with the data they contained before the interrupt. Next, the flags are restored, the interrupt is enabled, and the processor executes a return to the main program.

Figure 8-13 shows the source listing of the service routine. The first two instructions (MOV # 40,A and STA CNTRL) resets the INTE flip-flop (refer to Figure 8-11). Figure 8-14 shows the organization of the bits in the control and status ports. The signal DI is activated by bit 6 of the control port. This prevents the occurrence of any other interrupt because if another interrupt occurred before all registers are saved, data could be lost. The next six PUSH instructions save the contents of the PSW and all registers. This is followed by the LDA STATUS instruction, which gets the status from the status port. Because three terminals are interfaced, six ready bits are used. Two ready bits, one for input and one for output are required for each port. The next instruction, ROR, causes the LSB of the status byte to appear in the C flag. This instruction is followed by BC IN0, which causes the processor to execute the routine that inputs data from port 0 if the C flag is set. If the C flag is clear, another ROR and BC is executed. This is continued until a ready bit is found.

You will notice that a priority is inherent in this procedure. If two terminals interrupt simultaneously, only one will be serviced. For example, if terminal 1 and terminal 2 should interrupt simultaneously, terminal 1

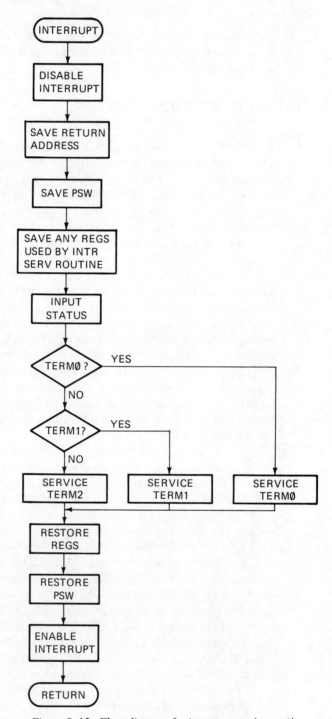

Figure 8–12. Flow diagram for interrupt service routine.

```
                STATUS = FF
                CNTRL  = FF
    INT:    MOV     #40,A       ;disable interrupt
            STA     CNTRL       ;
            PUSH    PSW         ;save flags
            PUSH    A           ;assuming that the
            PUSH    B           ;service routines
            PUSH    C           ;use all registers
            PUSH    D           ;
            PUSH    P           ;
            LDA     STATUS      ;get status
            ROR                 ;input port 0?
            BC      IN0         ;yes, service input port 0
            ROR                 ;output port 0?
            BC      OUT0        ;yes, service output port 0
            ROR                 ;input port 1?
            BC      IN1         ;yes, service input port 1
            ROR                 ;output port 1?
            BC      OUT1        ;yes, service output port 1
            ROR                 ;input port 2?
            BC      IN2         ;yes, service input port 2
            BR      OUT2        ;service output port 2
    RET:    POP     P           ;restore all
            POP     D           ;registers
            POP     C           ;
            POP     B           ;
            POP     A           ;
            POP     PSW         ;and flags
            MOV     #80,A       ;enable interrupt
            STA     CNTRL       ;
            RET                 ;return
```

Figure 8–13. Source listing of the service routine.

would get the service because its ready bit is tested first. However, terminal 2 will receive service as soon as the processor has finished with terminal 1.

An example of one of the routines that service a peripheral is shown in Figure 8–15. This routine inputs data from terminal 0 and stores it in memory. In order to do this, an address is required. The first step is to get this address to the pointer register P. Next, data is inputted by the instruction LDA TERM0. As shown in the program, TERM0 is equated to address FC, which is decoded as $\overline{\text{PSEL0}}$. Notice in Figure 8–2 that when $\overline{\text{READ}}$ and $\overline{\text{PSEL0}}$ are both active, the flip-flop storing the ready bit is

STATUS PORT:

Bit 7   Bit 0

		ORDY2 output	IRDY2 input	ORDY1 output	IRDY1 input	ORDY0 output	IRDY0 input

CONTROL PORT:

Bit 7   Bit 0

EI	DI						

Figure 8-14. Organization of the CONTROL and STATUS bits.

```
        PTR0=60
        TERM0=FC
        IN0:    LDA     PTR0        ;get data pointer from memory
                MOV     A,P         ;put in P register
                LDA     TERM0       ;get data from terminal 0
                MOV     A,M         ;store in memory
                INC     P           ;point to next location
                MOV     P,A         ;store data pointer
                STA     PTR0        ;
                BR      RET         ;back to interrupt routine
```

Figure 8-15. Routine to service terminal 0.

reset. Therefore, LDA TERM0 clears the ready bit (IRDY0). When the data at an input port is read, the ready bit is cleared! This is an important feature because if another peripheral should interrupt, its ready bit will be stored until it receives service. Now (continuing with the program), the data is stored by the instruction MOV A,M. The instruction INC P increments the pointer address so that the next time terminal 0 interrupts, data will be stored in the next memory location. Next, the address is stored back in memory. The location where the address is stored is called a buffer. This is a different location than where data is stored. Using a memory buffer is like having another register, except that it is in memory. This technique of storing addresses in memory is necessary because different addresses are required for each terminal.

The last instruction in this routine (BR RET) causes the processor to execute the remainder of the interrupt service routine. The registers including the PSW are restored by the POP instructions. Remember the nature of the stack. Because P was the last register PUSHed, it must be the first register POPped.

Before returning to the main program, interrupt must be enabled or no further interrupts can occur. This is done with the MOV #80,A and

STA CNTRL instructions. Finally, the RET instruction POPs the return address from the stack and execution of the main program continues from the point where it was interrupted. Suppose an interrupt occurs during the execution of the service routine before the interrupt has been re-enabled? Any interrupt will be ignored until the INTE flip-flop is set, at which time the interrupt sequence starts again.

Interrupts are used when outputting data also. A good example would be outputting data to a printer. Even relatively fast printers are slow when compared to the speed of the processor. Consider a printer with a baud rate of 300. It can print 30 characters (bytes) per second. This means that it can accept data once every 33.3 milliseconds. The procedure is to allow the printer to interrupt the processor each time it is ready for new data. Referring to Figure 8–4, you will notice that the ready flip-flop is set by a pulse from the peripheral (printer). The output of this flip-flop is ORDY0 (output ready 0), which initiates the interrupt. This flip-flop is cleared when $\overline{WRITE}$ and $\overline{PSEL3}$ are active. Writing to the output port clears the ready bit! As a result, the processor can return to the main background program and execute many instructions before it is interrupted again.

LIMP has become much more efficient with interrupt I/O.

8.6 VECTORED AND MASKED INTERRUPTS

The above examples of interrupt input and output must use polling because only one interrupt input to LIMP is provided. Foreground programs should be short and execute rapidly. With polling, much time is used before the routine to service the particular peripheral is executed.

A better interrupt feature is called *vectored interrupt*. This feature allows the processor to access the appropriate service routine directly without going through a polling procedure. Another feature that we will discuss is called *interrupt masks*. Interrupt masks are used to disable particular peripherals and enable only those peripherals that are desired.

In order to implement these features, LIMP must be modified once more! LIMP is becoming more sophisticated and more like some of the current real microprocessors! Figure 8–16 shows LIMP with six interrupt request lines (INTR0 through INTR5). Each line causes a unique address to be called. These addresses are stored in memory at locations automatically addressed by the processor. The locations used by LIMP are F5 through FA. For example, if interrupt request 0 (INTR0) is activated, the processor will call the address located at address F5. Addresses F5 through FA are called *vector addresses* because they store the addresses of the routines to be called. LIMP reads the address at the vector address and then "vectors" to the service routine. The following chart shows each of the interrupting signals and the associated vector address.

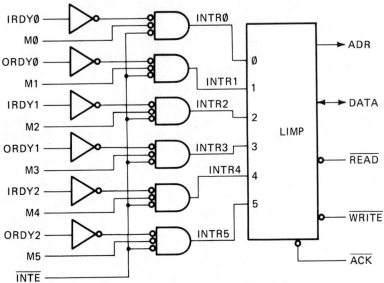

Figure 8–16. LIMP with six interrupt request lines.

INTR0	F5
INTR1	F6
INTR2	F7
INTR3	F8
INTR4	F9
INTR5	FA

It is the responsibility of the programmer to initialize the vector address with the addresses of the service routines. This is usually done in the initialization portion of the main program.

You will also notice that LIMP has a new output. This line is an acknowledge ($\overline{\text{ACK}}$) to an interrupt. Its purpose is to disable interrupts so that a second interrupt will not interfere with the interrupt sequence. Upon receiving an interrupt request, the processor issues an $\overline{\text{ACK}}$ before it vectors to the service routine. This resets the INTE flip-flop.

Referring again to Figure 8–16, notice the six 3-input NOR gates. The first input to each of these gates is the ready bit from the various ports as discussed previously. The second input (M0 through M5) is called a *mask bit*. If the mask bit is HIGH, the respective ready bit cannot cause an interrupt. On the other hand, if the mask bit is LOW and the third input, $\overline{\text{INTE}}$, is LOW, an interrupt will be recognized by the processor. Using the mask bits allows individual control over the enabling or disabling of the various interrupts. When a particular mask bit is HIGH, it is said that the associated interrupt is "masked." That is, the interrupt is hidden from the processor and the processor ignores the interrupt. If the mask bit is

LOW however, the interrupt is "unmasked" and the processor will recognize the interrupt. As before, $\overline{INTE}$ enables or disables all interrupts. Sometimes, the mask bits are referred to as enable bits for the individual peripherals. The only difference would be the context of the discussion and whether a one or a zero activates the function of masking or enabling.

An additional port has been added to LIMP. It is the interrupt control port shown in Figure 8–17. As with our other ports, the interrupt controller port will require a port select line. We'll call this line $\overline{PSEL\,C}$. The addition of another port select line means we need a new decoder. (Our new decoder is drawn in Figure 8–22.) This decoder could be similar to the decoder in Figure 6–17 but with one more output. Of course this additional line requires one more memory address (we'll use FB) so we have now reserved the top *five* memory locations for ports—FB is the interrupt controller port ($\overline{PSEL\,C}$); the three I/O ports still use memory addresses FC, FD, and FE ($\overline{PSEL\,0}$, $\overline{PSEL\,1}$, and $\overline{PSEL\,2}$); and the control and status port is still address FF (renamed $\overline{PSEL\,3}$).

The interrupt controller port has two parts. The first part, which uses bits 0 through 5 (DB_0–DB_5), is the mask register. The six bits that are used to mask various interrupts are stored here. Signals from this register are connected to gates as in Figure 8–16. These three input gates are redrawn and become part of this diagram. The second part is the INTE flip-flop. Information is stored in the mask register and the INTE flip-flop by outputting to the controller at address FB.

Suppose that the following instructions are executed:

```
MOV     #7F
STA     FB
```

All bits in the mask register are set. Therefore, all interrupts are masked. In addition, a 1 was outputted in bit 6 position. This causes the INTE flip-flop to be reset, disabling all interrupts. With the interrupt controller port initialized in this manner, no interrupts can occur. Refer to Figure 8–18, which defines the bit positions in the control port.

Now, let's initialize the interrupt controller to allow an interrupt for inputting data from the terminal at port 0 (address FC). The following instructions will do that job:

```
MOV     #BE,A
STA     FB
```

Close inspection of the control byte (BE) reveals that bit 7 equals 1 and bit 6 equals 0. This enables interrupts. Bits 5, 4, 3, 2, and 1 all equal 1. However, bit 0 equals 0. This bit pattern sets the interrupt enable flip-flop and unmasks the ready bit for input port 0. Keep in mind that outputting data to the interrupt controller can change all of the bits in the mask register. Care

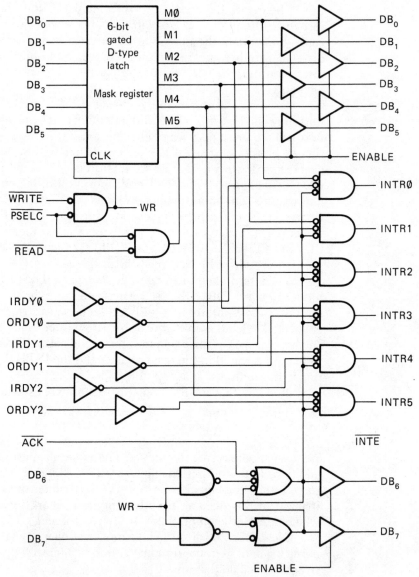

Figure 8-17. Interrupt Controller.

CONTROL PORT:

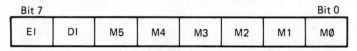

Bit 7							Bit 0
EI	DI	M5	M4	M3	M2	M1	MØ

Figure 8-18. Bit positions in control port for interrupt control.

must be taken that when masking one bit, another bit is not mistakenly masked or unmasked. This problem can be simplified by ORing bits to the controller in the following manner:

```
LDA     FB          ;get current control byte
OR      #01         ;OR in bit 0
STA     FB          ;output to controller
```

The preceding instructions mask only input port 0. All other bits in the controller remain as they were regardless of their previous value. You will notice that when we input from the interrupt controller port we get the current value of the mask pattern as well as bits 6 and 7, which indicate the current value of the INTE flip-flop. In a similar manner, a single bit may be changed to 0 by ANDing. For example:

```
LDA     FB          ;get current control byte
AND     #FE         ;AND to clear bit 0
STA     FB          ;output to controller
```

This series of instructions unmask an interrupt for input port 0 without changing any of the other bits in the control byte. ANDing or ORing bits allows us to change single bits in the control byte without changing any of the other bits!

8.7 INTERRUPT EXAMPLE

A good example of outputting data using interrupts is punching paper tape. Let's imagine a system where the main program has data to be punched. Because the main program has a number of tasks to perform, it is desirable that minimal time is lost while outputting data to such a slow peripheral as a paper tape punch. If the peripheral punches tape at a rate of 100 bytes per second, there is approximately 10 milliseconds between the times that each byte is outputted. With interrupts, the processor may use most of this time for its other tasks.

Figure 8–19 shows part of the main program listing. The first seven instructions initialize the stack pointer, the vector address, and the interrupt controller. The MOV #TERM0,A and STA F5 instructions move the address of the terminal service routine to the vector address (F5) for INTR0 interrupt. This is done so that when an INTR0 interrupt occurs, the interrupt service routine (TERM0) will be executed. The MOV #PUNCH,A and STA FA instructions move the address of the punch interrupt service routine to the vector address for INTR5. This allows the execution of the PUNCH interrupt service routine when INTR5 is activated. Notice that only the input for port 0 has been unmasked by initializing the control byte to BE.

```
MAIN:    MOV    #STK,SP     ;initialize stack pointer
         MOV    #TERM0,A    ;initialize vector address
         STA    F5          ;for terminal 0 (INTR0)
         MOV    #PUNCH,A    ;initialize vector address
         STA    FA          ;for paper tape punch (INTR5)
         MOV    #BE,A       ;unmask port 0 and
         STA    FB          ;enable interrupt
          .
          .
          .
         MOV    #DATA,A     ;address of data to A reg
         STA    DTADR       ;store in intr. service rout.
         LDA    FB          ;get control byte
         AND    #DF         ;unmask punch interrupt
         STA    FB          ;output to controller
          .                 ;continuation of main program
          .
          .
```

Figure 8-19. Part of main program listing.

At some point in the main program when it becomes necessary to output some data to the punch, five more instructions are executed. The first two move the address of the data to the interrupt service routine. DATA is the address, and it is stored at a location called DTADR. The next three instructions unmask the PUNCH interrupt. After these instructions are executed, the interrupt sequence executes automatically.

The first interrupt will probably occur immediately because the punch is ready. The interrupt service routine will output one byte of data to the punch and return to the main program. A number of instructions will be executed in the background before the next interrupt takes place. LIMP is working at microsecond speeds, and the punch is working at millisecond speeds. This continues until all of the data is outputted. At this time the punch interrupt is masked and the sequence is complete.

Figure 8-20 shows the flow diagram for the PUNCH interrupt service routine. Keep in mind that this routine executes each time that a punch interrupt takes place and only one byte is outputted. The interrupt service routine is listed in Figure 8-21. The first three instructions save the PSW, the A register, and the P register. No other registers are used in the routine. Next, the A register is loaded with the address of the data. The address is moved to the P register and the data is moved to the A register. The STA FE instruction outputs the data to the punch through port 2. Next, the address in the P register is incremented so that for the next interrupt, the address will be correct for the next byte of data.

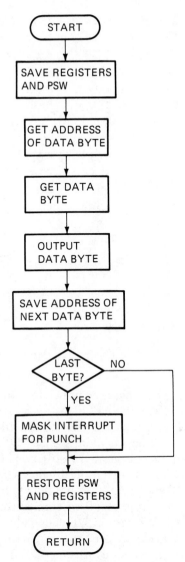

Figure 8-20. Flow diagram for PUNCH interrupt service routine.

The CMP #0 instruction tests to see if the last data byte has been punched. For this example, a null byte is used to terminate the data. This instruction only sets the Z flag if the byte equals 0; otherwise, it is cleared. The next two instructions store the address in memory. These two instructions do not affect the flags; therefore, the Z flag still contains the results of the compare instruction.

Next, a branch is executed if the last byte punched was not equal to 0. However, if the last byte was 0, the following three instructions are exe-

```
PUNCH:    PUSH    PSW        ;save flags
          PUSH    A          ;and registers
          PUSH    P          ;
          LDA     DTADR      ;get address of data
          MOV     A,P        ;move to pointer register
          STA     FE         ;output to port 2
          INC     P          ;increment pointer
          CMP     #0         ;set Z flag if last byte
          MOV     P,A        ;save address
          STA     DTADR      ;of data
          BNZ     MORE       ;branch if not last byte
          LDA     FB         ;get control byte
          OR      #10        ;mask interrupt for punch
          STA     FB         ;output to controller
MORE:     POP     P          ;restore registers
          POP     A          ;and
          POP     PSW        ;flags
          RET                ;and return to main program
DTADR:    0                  ;location for data address
```

Figure 8-21. Punch interrupt service routine.

cuted. They mask the punch interrupt, which terminates the interrupt sequence. The three POP instructions restore the registers with the information they contained prior to the interrupt. Finally, the RET instruction causes the return address to be POPped and the processor continues executing the background instruction.

Figures 8-22(a) and (b) show a block diagram of the entire system. The control and status port has only two status signals indicated. Because the ready bits from port 0 are connected, port 0 may be used for program control I/O or interrupt I/O, depending on how the program is written.

Once more, let's go through the interrupt sequence. Suppose port 1 is connected to some instrument. When this instrument has some data ready to be inputted the following occurs:

1. The peripheral asserts a clock pulse (CP_1) to port 1.

2. Port 1 takes the data and issues IRDY1.

3. The interrupt controller issues INTR2 if it has been unmasked and the INTE flip-flop is set (see Figure 8-17).

4. The processor issues $\overline{ACK}$ and completes execution of the current instruction.

5. The INTE flip-flop is reset.

6. The processor pushes the return address on the stack and places the address at location F7 (vector address) in the PC.

7. The interrupt service routine inputs the data via port 1.

8. Somewhere in the interrupt service routine, instructions are executed which set the INTE flip-flop.

9. When the interrupt service routine is complete, the RET instruction pops the return address to the PC and the background program continues executing.

We have mentioned that LIMP is becoming more like a real microprocessor. Of course, you are aware that the number of address lines that LIMP uses seriously limits its capabilities. Most microprocessors use sixteen address lines. But let's not try to change LIMP again! Rather, let's study some of the real microprocessors that are currently available. How do the various microprocessors differ? The following is a list of some of the things to look for:

1. The number of address lines. Most commonly there are from 12 to 20 lines. The latter addresses up to 1 megabyte locations.

2. The number of data lines. Usually there are 4, 8, or 16 lines, determining the size of the data word to be processed at a single time.

3. Multiplexing. Some microprocessors time share data and address on the same bus. This reduces the number of pin-outs on the processor chip. In addition, it simplifies implementation by reducing the number of lines to the interface circuits.

4. Control lines. The number of lines depend on the various features in a particular system; i.e., input-output techniques.

5. Internal registers. The number of registers depends on the internal architecture of the processor. Some processors make more use of memory for temporary storage, others have more internal registers.

6. The instruction set. Most processors have a more sophisticated instruction set than LIMP. Some have multiply and divide and even floating point instructions. Addressing modes may also cause the instructions to differ.

7. The addressing modes. LIMP uses direct, indirect, and immediate modes. Other processors may also use relative, index, and deferred modes.

8. Input-output. Various types of program control and interrupt techniques are used.

The basic concepts covered while studying LIMP are common to all microprocessors. The following chapters will deal with some of the real microprocessors that are available.

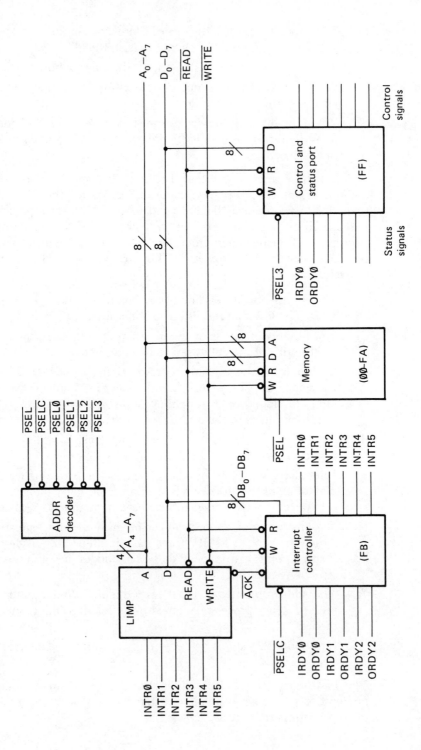

Figure 8-22(a). Block diagram of LIMP microcomputer system.

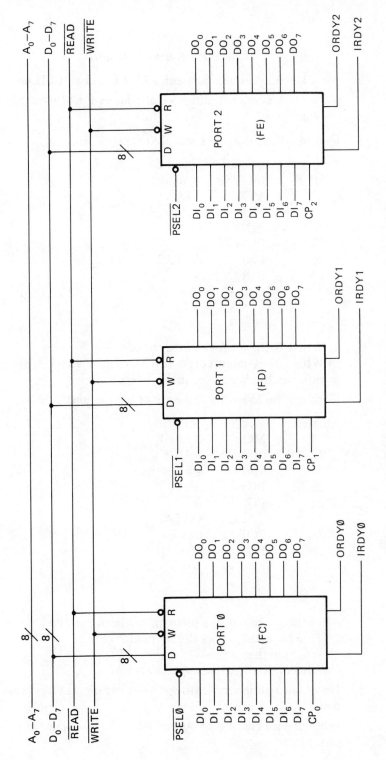

Figure 8–22(b). *Block diagram of LIMP microcomputer system.*

203

Questions and Problems

1. What is the difference between a CALL and a PUSH instruction?

2. If the stack pointer is initialized at address E4, at what address does the stack start?

3. Consider the following sequence of instructions:

Address	opcode	operand
30	MOV	# A0,SP
32	MOV	# 28,A
34	MOV	# 50,D
36	ADD	D
37	PUSH	A
38	CALL	DATA2
3A	POP	A

    •
    •
    •

    a) Where is the return address stored?
    b) What is the contents of address location 9F after this portion of the program has been executed?

4. Consider the following sequence of instructions:

Address	opcode	operand
20	MOV	# FB,SP
22	MOV	# A0,B
24	MOV	# 75,A
26	PUSH	A
27	PUSH	B
28	CALL	DATA1
2A	POP	B
2B	POP	A

    •
    •
    •

    After this portion of the program has been executed:
    a) To what address does the SP point?
    b) What are the contents of address F9?
    c) What are the contents of address FA?

5. How does a peripheral let the processor know that it is ready to input data?

6. When the processor is to output data, what sequence of events must take place?

7. What is the difference between a status port and a control port?

8. What is the main disadvantage of program control I/O as compared to interrupt I/O?

9. What signals must be active before the output port will issue an EI signal?

10. Where does the PC save the return address when it has received an interrupt?

11. Where is the flag and register contents saved during an interrupt?

12. Where does the interrupt enable signal (EI) originate?

13. What is a background program?

14. What is stored at a vector address?

Chapter

9

The 8085A Microprocessor

In Chapters 5 through 8 we studied the architecture and operation of LIMP. In this and in following chapters we will relate the basic concepts learned there to a real microprocessor. The first microprocessor we will discuss is the 8085A, whose block diagram is shown in Figure 9–1. Its pinout diagram is found in Figure 9–2. The 8085A is a third-generation microprocessor manufactured by INTEL. It is an 8-bit general purpose microprocessor that has considerably more capability than LIMP. It is capable of addressing 64 K bytes of memory locations. The 8085A has additional control and status lines, allowing it to control fairly large systems.

9.1   8085A ARCHITECTURE

The 8085A has one accumulator and six 8-bit data registers that can be addressed by the programmer. The accumulator (the A reg) in Figure 9–1 usually stores one of the operands to be manipulated by the CPU. Because the 8085A has only one accumulator, the results of arithmetic or logic operations will be stored in the A register. In general, the A register is involved in the execution of most instructions, as is the case with LIMP.

The B, C, D, E, H, and L registers are general purpose registers (GPRs). They may be used individually as 8-bit registers or in pairs as 16-bit registers. The B and C register pair may contain a 16-bit data word or a 16-bit memory address. The D and E register pair are used in the same manner. The H and L register pair are used in the same way as the P register is used in LIMP. That is, a memory location (M) can be pointed to by the contents of the H and L pair. The stack pointer (SP) is a 16-bit register that allows creation of the stack anywhere in memory. The program counter (PC) contains the address of the next instruction, as in LIMP, except that it is a 16-bit register. Another register included in the 8085A is the Flag register. It contains the carry (CY), zero (Z), and sign (S) flags. In addition, two other flags, auxiliary carry (AC) and parity (P) are used. These flags will be discussed later.

Notice in Figure 9–1 the blocks labeled INSTRUCTION REGISTER and INSTRUCTION DECODER AND MACHINE CYCLE ENCODING. It is in these blocks that the byte of the instruction containing the op-code is decoded and execution of the instruction is directed. Signals are generated by the TIMING AND CONTROL unit as a result of information from the decoded opcode and are synchronized by the clock. The signals labeled $\overline{RD}$, $\overline{WR}$, ALE, S_0, S_1, and IO/$\overline{M}$ are discussed later in the chapter when we talk about the Instruction Cycle. We will briefly describe the remaining signals associated with the Timing and Control block and then expand on them as they are used.

X_1 and X_2:   These inputs are used to establish timing for processor operations. An external source would connect to X_1. A crystal is most commonly used and would connect to X_1 and X_2. The fundamental frequency of the crystal must be 6.25 MHz or less.

CLK OUT: This is a buffered output that is half the frequency of the crystal input signal. Its period equals one machine state.

READY: This is an input signal to the processor and is used to create one or more wait states (T_{WAIT}). This signal can be generated by either memory or an I/O device to lengthen the time of a bus cycle, thus allowing longer access time for slow memory or I/O.

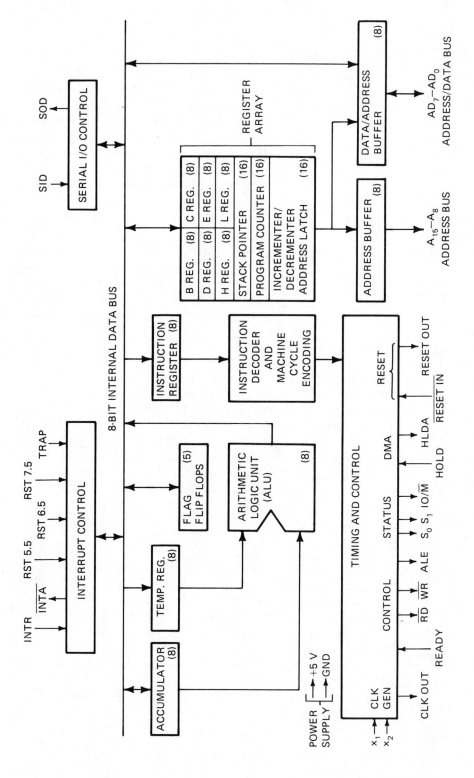

Figure 9–1. 8085A CPU functional block diagram. (Courtesy Intel Corporation)

HOLD and HLDA: These signals are used for Direct Memory Access (DMA) operations. DMA means that I/O devices may access memory without the help of the processor. HOLD is generated by the I/O device. HLDA (Hold Acknowledge) is issued by the processor in response to the HOLD signal. HLDA causes the bus buffers to go to the high Z state, isolating the processor from the bus. HLDA remains active until HOLD is negated.

$\overline{\text{RESET IN}}$
and RESET OUT: $\overline{\text{RESET IN}}$ is usually activated manually and causes the 8085A to execute the instruction at address 0. $\overline{\text{RESET IN}}$ also resets various internal flip-flops including those in the interrupt system. RESET OUT is issued by the processor when $\overline{\text{RESET IN}}$ is activated. RESET OUT resets all peripherals connected to that line.

A temporary register is shown in the block diagram. It is not addressable by the programmer but is used by the processor for manipulating data during execution of some instructions.

The Arithmetic Logic Unit (ALU) is that part of the processor where all arithmetic and logical operations are performed.

At the top of the block diagram is a section labeled INTERRUPT CONTROL. The 8085A has the ability to be interrupted while executing one program, causing it to execute a second program and then returning to the first. The interrupt control capability of the 8085A is a very powerful feature and will be discussed at length in Chapter 11.

The block labeled SERIAL I/O CONTROL allows the 8085A to communicate directly with a serial device such as a teletype or CRT terminal.

The lower right-hand corner of the diagram shows the circuits used to drive the address and address/data buses. An unusual feature of the 8085A is that the address/data bus is a multiplexed bus. This feature reduces the number of pinouts required on the 8085A package. Multiplexing means that the bus is used for more than one function—but at different times. In this case, the bus is first used to output the low byte of the address (AD_0-AD_7) through the address/data buffer. At the same time, the high byte of the address is placed on the bus via the address buffer. At a later time the address/data bus is used for data that is either inputted or outputted by the processor through the address/data buffer. The address/data buffer must be bidirectional because data may be inputted or outputted by the processor.

9.2 INSTRUCTION CYCLE

Events that occur on the bus are synchronized with the 8085A's internal clock. All of the 8085A's control signals are synchronized internally by this signal. As a result, events occurring on the bus are also synchronized. This kind of bus is called a synchronous bus. In synchronous bus systems, signals from the processor control the action of peripheral interface circuits and memory. No response or acknowledgement is required of these circuits. The processor assumes that the circuits will react in the proper manner. Therefore, synchronous buses are also called open loop buses. Although the clock signal is not always required, it is labeled CLK OUT in Figure 9–1. A typical frequency for the 8085A clock is 3 MHz. Therefore, a typical clock period is approximately 330 ns. (The 8085A–2 clock period can be as fast as 200 ns.)

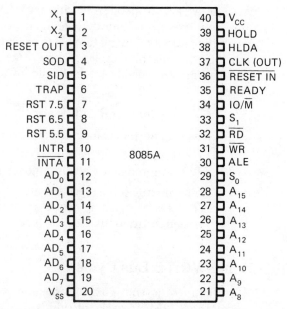

Figure 9–2. 8085A Pinout diagram. (Courtesy Intel Corporation)

As with LIMP, the 8085A has an instruction set that identifies all the various operations the processor is capable of performing. The instruction set is discussed in Chapter 10. At this time we want to discuss, in general, the sequence of events that takes place when an instruction is executed.

Recall that a program consists of a number of instructions. How many, or what they are, depends on the job to be done. Whatever the instruction, however, the time required to complete the instruction is called an *instruction cycle*. All instruction cycles consist of a sequence of READ or

WRITE operations. INTEL refers to each READ and WRITE operation as a machine cycle. In LIMP, and in systems we will discuss in later chapters, we define READ and WRITE operations as bus cycles. Except for two special instructions (DAD and RST) all machine cycles in the 8085A use the bus during T_1, T_2, and T_3. That is, all operations involving the bus occur during these times. Whenever we discuss machine cycles that use the bus, we will call these three states a bus cycle.

The simpler instruction cycles require one machine cycle. More complex instructions require two or more machine cycles, up to a maximum of five. Each machine cycle requires a number of clock periods called T-states.

9.2.1   Opcode Fetch

When an instruction is executed, the first thing that happens is that the instruction opcode is fetched from memory. Therefore, the first machine cycle is an opcode fetch and is a MEMORY READ machine cycle. This opcode fetch machine cycle requires from four to six T-states, depending on the particular instruction being executed. Most instructions require four. All other machine cycles require three T-states.

During the opcode fetch, the following sequence of events takes place:

T_1 The contents of the PC is placed on the address bus.

T_2 $\overline{RD}$ is asserted. Data is asserted on the data bus from memory.

T_3 Contents of the data bus are moved to the instruction register. $\overline{RD}$ is terminated. Data is removed from the data bus.

T_4 The instruction is decoded and is either executed or additional T-states or machine cycles are initiated, depending on the decoded instructions. Address is removed from the address bus.

9.2.2   READ and WRITE Bus Cycles

Figure 9–3(a) shows a timing diagram for a READ bus cycle. The purpose of the READ bus cycle is to input information from memory or a port. Figure 9–3(b) shows a timing diagram for a WRITE bus cycle. The purpose of the WRITE bus cycle is to output information to memory or a port. Timing is similar to that of a READ cycle.

The first waveform in the timing diagrams is the clock. A clock period starts with the negative transition of the CLK signal. Notice that three clock periods are needed (T_1, T_2, and T_3). The slope of the edges of the clock pulses is exaggerated to indicate the existence of rise and fall times.

The second waveform in the diagrams is used to indicate the value of the eight high order bits of the address (A_8–A_{15}). Notice that the high order address is asserted with the first low going transition of CLK. Furthermore,

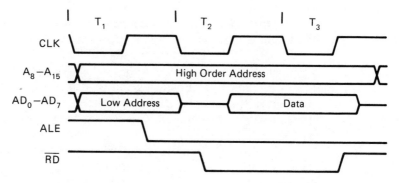

(a) Timing diagram for a READ bus cycle.

Figure 9–3(a). Timing diagram for a READ bus cycle.

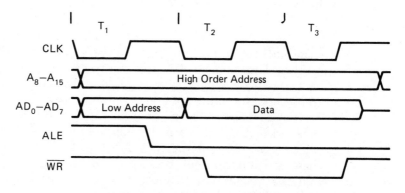

(b) Timing diagram for WRITE bus cycle.

Figure 9–3(b). Timing diagram for WRITE bus cycle.

the high order address remains valid through T_3, the duration of the bus cycle.

The waveform labeled AD_0–AD_7 indicates that the low order byte of the address is asserted at the same time as the high order byte. However, it only remains valid during T_1. If the entire address is to be valid for the entire duration of the cycle, the low order byte must somehow be saved during T_2 and T_3.

ALE is asserted at the beginning of T_1 of each bus cycle and is negated toward the end of that time. ALE is active only during T_1, and is used as a clock pulse to latch the address during T_1.

The waveforms labeled $\overline{RD}$ in Figure 9–3(a) and the waveform labeled $\overline{WR}$ in Figure 9–3(b) are quite similar. $\overline{RD}$ is asserted near the beginning of T_2 and is terminated toward the end of T_3 during READ cycles. For the READ cycle, the low byte of the address is asserted at the beginning of T_1 and terminated at the beginning of T_2. Shortly after, $\overline{RD}$ becomes active causing the port or memory circuits to assert data. Toward the end of T_3, $\overline{RD}$ becomes inactive, causing the port to terminate data.

For the WRITE cycle, immediately after the low byte of the address is terminated, at the beginning of T_2, data is asserted on the Address/Data bus by the processor. Following this, $\overline{WR}$ is activated. $\overline{WR}$ becomes inactive toward the end of T_3. Notice that the processor maintains valid data until after $\overline{WR}$ is terminated. This assures that the memory or port has valid data while $\overline{WR}$ is active.

A close inspection of the figures shows that for the READ bus cycle, data appears on the bus as a result of activating $\overline{RD}$. For the WRITE bus cycle, the time that valid data is on the bus overlaps the time that $\overline{WR}$ is active.

9.3   ELECTRICAL AND DATA BUFFERING

In order to implement the sixteen address lines, both electrical and data buffering are required. First, electrical buffering is required for A_8–A_{15} so that a large number of circuits may be driven by these lines. Second, the information on AD_0–AD_7 during T_1 must be latched so that it is available throughout the entire bus cycle.

An 8-bit gated D-type latch can be used to accomplish both electrical and data buffering. Let's use the 8282 for this purpose. A data sheet for the 8282 can be found in Appendix C; Figure 9–4 shows the circuit. The 8282 has a three-state output. Because this feature is not required, the outputs are always enabled by grounding the output enable input ($\overline{OE}$). To provide electrical buffering for A_8–A_{15}, the gates of the gated D-type flip-flops are enabled by tying STB HIGH. This prevents latching but allows the input signals to pass directly through the latches and appear on the outputs. This is sometimes referred to as the transparent mode of operation. (Note that triggered D-type flip-flops cannot be used in this mode.) The high driving capability of the 8282 provides the necessary current to drive an expanded address bus.

The low order byte of the address appears on the AD_0–AD_7 lines during T_1. Address Latch Enable (ALE) is a signal used to clock the low byte of the address into a second 8282, as shown in Figure 9–4. Notice that ALE goes HIGH (active) at the same time that the low byte of the address is asserted on AD_0–AD_7. When ALE goes back LOW, the low byte of the address is latched into the 8282 making the low byte of the address available through T_3.

The outputs of the two 8282s are labeled BA_0–BA_{15} to indicate the buffered address bus. Connections to address decoders, I/O ports, and memory are made to the buffered address bus.

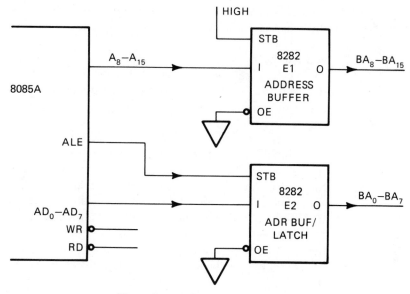

Figure 9–4. 8085A address buffers.

9.3.1 Bidirectional Bus Driver

Because data is inputted and outputted by the processor on the AD_0–AD_7 lines, a bidirectional bus driver is required. The 8286 8-bit bidirectional bus transceiver is made especially for this purpose. A data sheet for the 8286 is shown in Appendix C. A drawing that shows how a single bit is buffered is shown in Figure 9–5. Compare Figure 9–5 to the data sheet; you

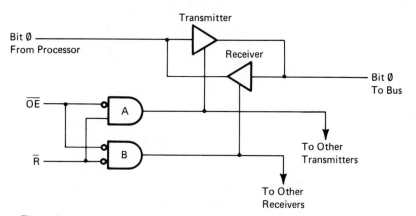

Figure 9–5. Single bit bidirectional bus driver showing direction control for the 8286.

will notice that the gates have been DeMorganized. This helps to interpret the logic as well as indicate proper active levels. Two three-state buffers are used. The first is used to drive the bus and is called the transmitter. The second is used to drive the processor and is called the receiver. Notice that when gate A is active, the transmitter is activated and the bus is driven from the processor. When gate B is active, the receiver is activated and the processor inputs data from the bus. The input signal $\overline{OE}$ must be activated or neither the transmitter nor the receiver will be activated, and because of the three-state circuits, the outputs of the transmitter and receiver will be in the high Z mode. The remaining signal, $\overline{R}$, controls the direction of data. If $\overline{R}$ is active (LOW), then gate B is active and gate A is not active, causing the 8286 to act as a bus receiver. On the other hand, if $\overline{R}$ is HIGH, gate A is active and gate B is not active. This causes the 8286 to act as a bus transmitter. The signal $\overline{R}$, therefore, controls the direction of the data through the 8286 bidirectional bus driver. You may have noticed that we have taken the liberty of redefining the direction control signal, which is labeled T on the data sheet. We have indicated it as being active LOW and have called it $\overline{R}$.

9.3.2 Address and Data Bus Buffering

Figure 9–6 shows how both the address and data buses can be buffered. We are using 8282s for address buffers, just as we did in Figure 9–4. The buffer used for the low byte of the address (E2) has been relabeled ADDRESS DEMULTIPLEXER/BUFFER because demultiplexing takes place here. The Address/Data bus AD_0–AD_7, is a multiplexed bus. Address is asserted on the bus during T_1; data is asserted on the bus during T_2 and T_3. The address is "demultiplexed" by the 8282, and only address is available on the buffered address bus, BA_0–BA_7. This demultiplexing resulted from latching the address into the buffer when ALE went low, as discussed previously. Including the 8286 BIDIRECTIONAL DATA BUS BUFFER completes the buffering of the address and data buses. The output of the 8286 is labeled BD_0–BD_7 to indicate that this is the buffered data bus.

Also shown in Figure 9–6 are the control signals $\overline{RD}$ and $\overline{WR}$. Because these lines are unidirectional, simple electrical buffers may be used if they are required. The 7400 or the 7404, for example, could be used to buffer any of the control signals.

Figure 9–7 shows the timing as it appears on the expanded bus. Comparing these diagrams with those in Figure 9–3, we see that the expanded bus asserts valid address, BA_0–BA_{15}, throughout the entire bus cycle.

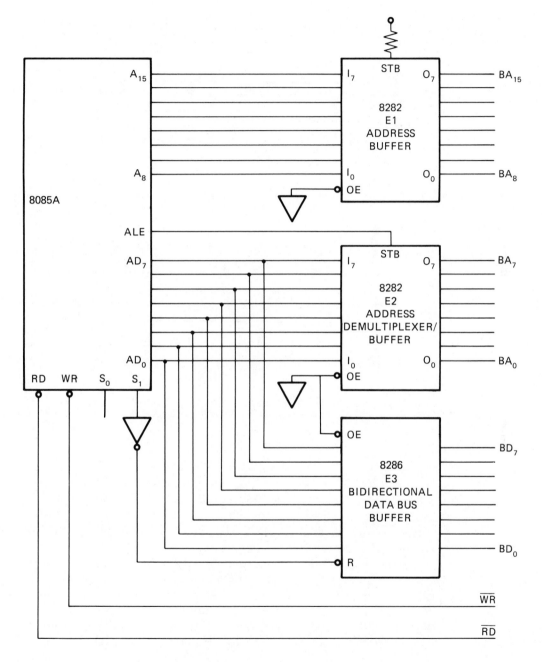

Figure 9–6. The 8085A expanded bus.

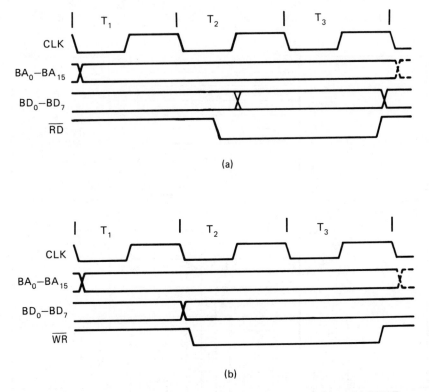

Figure 9–7. Timing diagrams as related to the expanded bus. (a) READ
machine cycle; (b) WRITE machine cycle.

9.4 S_0 AND S_1

The 8085A has two signals, S_0 and S_1, which Intel calls "Status." We
will refer to these signals as "Control" because it is generally understood
that in processor I/O, control signals are generated by the processor
whereas status signals are generated by peripherals. These two signal lines
are shown in Figure 9–1.

Whenever the bus is used to input data, S_1 is HIGH; whenever the
bus is used to output data, S_1 is LOW. For the READ cycle, S_1 is HIGH for
the entire duration of the cycle. The opposite is true for a WRITE cycle.
Therefore, S_1 can be used to control the direction of data through the 8286
(Figure 9–6). Only an inverter is required. You might ask, "Why not use the
control signals $\overline{RD}$ or $\overline{WR}$?" These signals are only active while data is being
transferred. It is much better to use a signal that is active for the entire cycle, thus allowing time for the circuits to be set up before data is transferred.

9.5   A MICROCOMPUTER SYSTEM

Now that we have buffered the address and address/data buses, let's implement the hardware for a complete system. The system we have chosen will have 8 K bytes of RAM (Random Access Memory), 8 K bytes of ROM (Read Only Memory), control and status ports, and an I/O port.

9.5.1   Memory

We have buffered the address and data buses so that we can connect many memory and I/O circuits to the processor. For the RAM portion of memory, we have chosen the 2141. The 2141 is a 4096 × 1 bit static RAM that requires no special circuitry to implement. Its data sheet may be found in Appendix C. Eight devices connected as shown in Figure 9–8 create a 4 K byte page of memory. Additional identical pages can be added to create as much memory as is desired by the user, up to 64 K bytes. Our system uses two 4 K byte pages or sixteen devices.

Each 2141 contains one bit at the specified address. Twelve address lines are required for 4096 memory locations. The low twelve lines of address, BA_0–BA_{11}, are connected to A_0 through A_{11} of each of the 2141s. Each device has one input line and one output line. The output line is three-stated and is enabled by $\overline{CS}$ when $\overline{RD}$ and $\overline{MS}$ are active. If $\overline{WR}$ and $\overline{MS}$ are active, the 2141s are activated for the write mode of operation. This allows the input and output lines to be connected in common to the bus. The chip select line ($\overline{CS}$) is activated for either a read or write operation.

Figure 9–8 shows the address lines connected in parallel to each of the eight 2141s. Notice that the write enable lines are connected in common to the control line $\overline{WR}$. The chip select lines are connected in common and are enabled by either $\overline{RD}$ and $\overline{MS}$ or $\overline{WR}$ and $\overline{MS}$. This line is activated whenever this particular block (page) of memory is addressed. Address decoding for $\overline{MS}$ will be covered later in the chapter.

The data lines are not connected in common. Each data line is connected to a specific chip. However, the input (DI) and the output (DO) lines are connected in common because the data bus is bidirectional.

The 2732 is a 4 K × 8 erasable PROM. It is the device we have chosen for our system. Two such devices provide the required 8 K bytes of ROM. The logic symbol for the 2732 appears in Figure 9–9; its data sheet can be found in Appendix C. Notice in Figure 9–9 that there are twelve address lines, an output enable (OE) line, and a chip enable (CE) line as inputs to the device. The eight output lines connect to the data bus. When $\overline{CE}$ and $\overline{OE}$ are both LOW, data from the selected address is placed on the data bus.

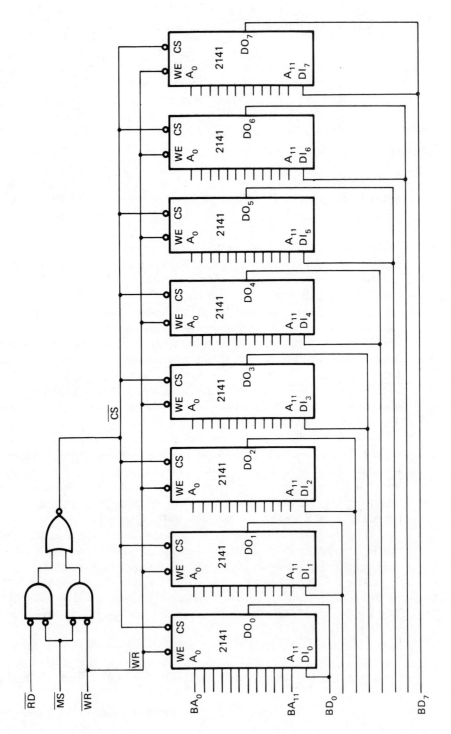

Figure 9–8. Eight 2141s used as a 4 K byte page of RAM.

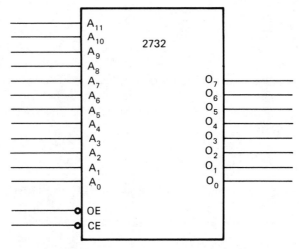

Figure 9-9. Logic symbol for the 2732 4 K byte PROM.

9.5.2 Decoding Memory

Assuming that all pages are 4 K bytes, sixteen pages are possible (64 K bytes). Because twelve address lines are required to select addresses within a page, the remaining four address lines are used to select each of sixteen pages. Figure 9-10 shows how two 8205 decoders can be used to decode sixteen 4 K pages, which is the maximum memory that can be addressed by the 8085A. The 8205 data sheet can be found in Appendix C.

The 8205 is a "1 of 8" binary decoder. There are three input lines (A_0, A_1, and A_2), which, when decoded, select one of eight output lines. There are three enable lines: $\overline{E}_1$, $\overline{E}_2$, and E_3. All three of these lines must be active in order to select one of the eight outputs. The 8205 in Figure 9-10(a) is used to decode pages 0-7. These are the addresses between 0000H and

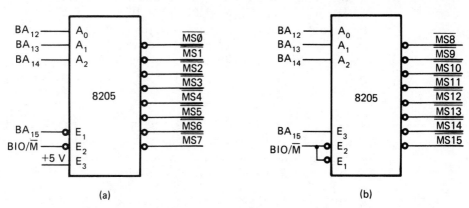

Figure 9-10. 8205 decoder: (a) decoding pages 0-7, (b) decoding pages 8-15.

7FFFH or 0 to 32 K. For these addresses, bit 15 must equal 0. Therefore you will notice that BA_{15} is used as one of the three enable lines. In addition, a second input is enabled by $BIO/\overline{M}$. When $BIO/\overline{M}$ is LOW and BA_{15} is LOW, this chip is selected—which selects one of eight pages of memory. The page selected is determined by the lines BA_{12}, BA_{13}, and BA_{14}, which are decoded by the 8205. Recall that when $BIO/\overline{M}$ is HIGH, a port is being selected and all memory should be disabled. The third enable input is tied HIGH.

Figure 9–10(b) shows a second 8205 used to select pages 8–15 (8000H–FFFFH). BA_{15} for these addresses must be HIGH. Therefore, BA_{15} is connected to the active HIGH enable input, E_3. Both active LOW enable inputs are tied to $BIO/\overline{M}$. When BA_{15} AND $BIO/\overline{M}$ are active, one of the pages, 8 through 15, is selected.

In Figure 9–11, we show how two 4 K pages of ROM and two 4 K pages of RAM are connected to the bus and how each page is decoded. Notice that the output enable lines, $\overline{OE}$, of the 2732s connect to $\overline{BRD}$. The write enable lines, $\overline{WR}$, of RAM connect to $\overline{BWR}$; and the read enable lines, $\overline{RD}$, connect to $\overline{BRD}$. The function of the decoder here is exactly as described previously. This decoder is enabled only when $BIO/\overline{M}$ is LOW; therefore, only memory addresses are selected.

9.5.3   System I/O

Our system is completed with the addition of I/O ports. In this system, we are using ports that input or output data under program control only. Another method, using interrupts, is discussed in Chapter 11.

Figure 9–12 shows two 74LS373s connected as an Input/Output port. The data sheet for the 74LS373 is included in Appendix C. It is an 8-bit gated D-type latch. It uses a three-state output circuit that is enabled with the $\overline{OE}$ input. Another input, E, is used to gate data into the latch. Because it is gated, it has a transparent mode that occurs when the E input is maintained at a HIGH level. For input, the transparent mode is used and the three-state output is enabled with the read control signal $\overline{RD}$ and the port select signal $\overline{PS}$. For output, the second 74LS373 has its $\overline{OE}$ input tied to ground, which makes its stored data always available at its output. The write control ($\overline{WR}$) and $\overline{PS}$ are used to gate the signal into the latches by activating the E input.

Two paralled I/O ports are shown in Figure 9–13. Their symbols represent the circuit in Figure 9–12. The first is used as a status and control port. It provides eight control lines and eight status lines. The second port is used to input and output data in parallel. Additional ports may be added to the system. The decoder, an 8205, provides decoding for eight ports. If more than eight ports are used, additional decoding will be required. Notice that the control signal $IO/\overline{M}$ activates the decoder when it is HIGH. Therefore, only port addresses are decoded.

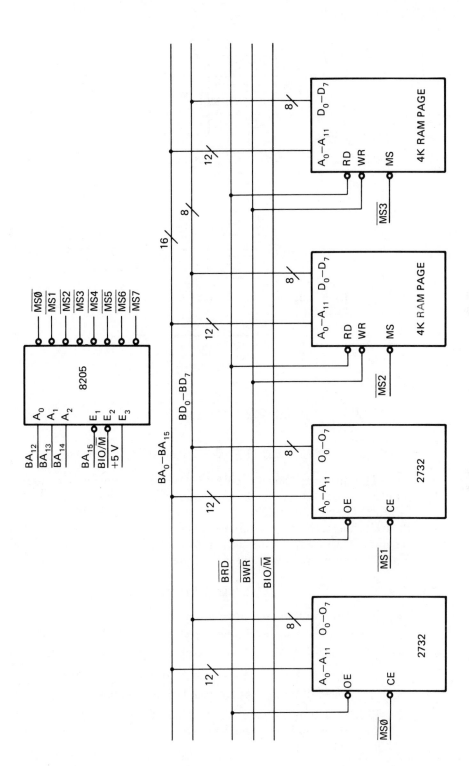

Figure 9-11. Bus and decoding connections for memory.

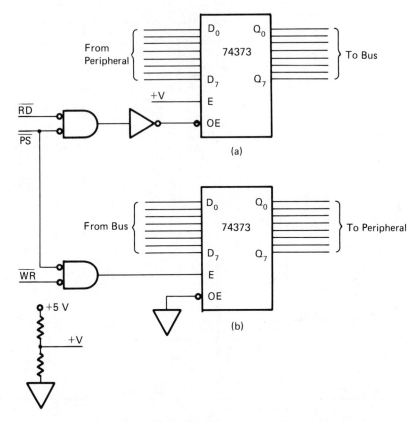

Figure 9–12. Parallel I/O port: (a) input port; (b) output port.

The third port shown is a UART (Universal Asynchronous Receiver/Transmitter). It is used to communicate with peripherals in serial. Data is outputted to it or inputted from it as if it were a parallel port. However, the device converts the data to serial and transmits it to the peripheral. It also receives data in serial and makes it available to the processor in parallel. Serial communication is discussed in Chapter 12.

Questions and Problems

1. Name the working registers in the 8085A.
2. During what T state is address asserted on the bus?
3. During what T state is address valid on the address/data bus?
4. During what T state is data valid on the address/data bus?
5. How many T states does an opcode fetch require?
6. Refer to Figure 9–6. During what T state is address latched into the address demultiplexer/buffer (E2)?

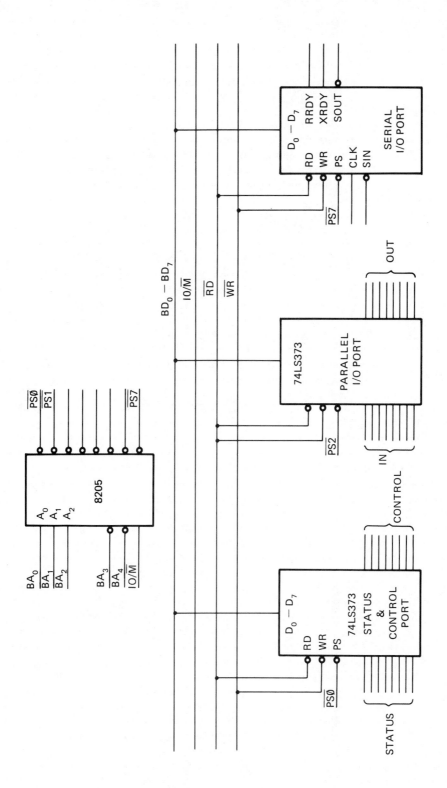

Figure 9-13. Bus and decoding connections for I/O.

7. For a memory write bus cycle, what is the state of S_0, S_1, and IO/$\overline{M}$?

8. For an opcode fetch, what is the state of S_0, S_1, and IO/$\overline{M}$?

9. For an I/0 write bus cycle, what is the state of S_0, S_1, and IO/$\overline{M}$?

10. In an I/O write bus cycle:
    a) When is address valid on the buffered address bus?
    b) When is data available on the buffered data bus?
    c) Is the 8286 (Figure 9–6) in the receive or transmit mode?
    d) During which time period/s is $\overline{RD}$ active?

11. In an opcode fetch bus cycle:
    a) When is address valid on the buffered address bus?
    b) When is data available on the buffered data bus?
    c) Is the 8286 (Figure 9–6) in the receive or transmit mode?
    d) During which time period/s is $\overline{RD}$ active?

12. Which registers can be used together as a register pair?

13. What's the difference between a machine cycle and an instruction cycle?

14. During an opcode fetch, when is the instruction decoded?

15. Refer to Figure 9–5. The conditions are: $\overline{OE} = 0$, $\overline{R} = 0$. Is the machine cycle a read or a write?

16. Refer to Figure 9–6. Is the 8282 labeled E1 being used as an electrical buffer or a logical buffer?

Programming
the 8085A

Programming the LIMP microprocessor was discussed in Chapter 7; this chapter is devoted to programming the 8085A. Although the basic concepts of programming LIMP and the 8085A are the same, it is important to realize that because of the hardware differences in the two processors, the instructions will also differ. Because instructions that a processor can execute depend on the hardware that makes up that particular processor, machine and assembly languages are referred to as machine dependent languages.

10.1 8085A REGISTERS

The architecture of the 8085A was discussed in Chapter 9. However, let's review the functions of the various registers—this is necessary because most of them are affected by the instructions. Figure 10–1 diagrams the registers that are affected by the 8085A instructions. One additional register, the interrupt mask, is affected by two instructions. We will refer to the interrupt mask when we discuss I/O programming.

PAIRS	REGISTERS	
PSW	A	FLAGS
B	B	C
D	D	E
H	H	L
SP	SP	
PC	PC	

Figure 10–1. Registers addressed by the 8085A instructions.

The A register is the accumulator. It stores the results of arithmetic and logical operations. In addition, data is inputted to, or outputted from, the A register.

The B, C, D, E, H, and L registers are GPRs (general purpose registers). They may be used to store 8-bit data, or used in pairs to store 16-bit data or addresses. If used in pairs, they are organized as the B and C, the D and E, or the H and L pair. Together, the A register and the flags are called the PSW. The instruction opcode specifies whether an 8-bit register or a 16-bit register pair is to be used. The functions of the SP and PC are the same as with LIMP; however, they are both 16-bit registers in the 8085A.

10.2 ADDRESSING MODES

What is an addressing mode? Within the instruction set, many techniques are used to locate an operand. In general, operands are found in registers or memory locations. Memory addresses may be included in the instruction; they may appear in registers (register pairs); or they may be calculated. The specific technique used is called an *addressing mode*.

The addressing modes used by the 8085A are easy to understand and easy to use because operands that reside in memory are always specified with a 16-bit absolute address. This address may appear either in the instruction word or in a register pair.

10.2.1   Register Mode

The register mode is used when the operand is located in a register. For example, the instruction

MOV   A,B

specifies a source (B) and a destination operand (A). It causes the processor to duplicate the contents of the B register in the A register. Notice that the instruction specifies the location of the operand rather than the operand itself.

Another example of the register mode is

ADD   C

which causes the processor to add the contents of the C register to the contents of the A register and save the sum in the A register. In this case the A register is not specified but is implied. This is possible because there is only one accumulator.

10.2.2   Direct Mode

The address of the operand appears in the instruction itself when the direct mode is used. The instruction must contain three bytes for the direct mode: the first for the opcode and the second and third for the address.

STA ADDR is an example of the direct mode of addressing. The processor executes this instruction by loading the A register with the contents of ADDR. The label ADDR is a symbolic address. Suppose ADDR has been equated to the address 1000. The following instruction would then have the same meaning.

STA   1000H   (H means hexadecimal)

Another example of direct addressing is

LHLD   LABL

which means: "Load the H and L register pair directly (direct mode) with the contents of LABL." Because the H and L pair contain sixteen bits, two bytes are loaded. The contents of LABL are loaded into the L register and the contents of LABL + 1 (the next address) are loaded into the H register. It is the convention that the low byte of a 2-byte word appears at the lower of the two addresses.

10.2.3   Indirect Mode

This mode is sometimes called the deferred mode. A register pair is specified either implicitly or explicitly. The register pair does not contain the operand, but rather, the address of the operand. For example the instruction

LDAX   B

specifies the B and C pair explicitly. The A register is loaded with the contents of an address that is stored in the B and C pair when this instruction is executed. Note that the address is stored in the register pair. The use of the letter X in the instruction reminds us that the instruction deals with a register pair in some manner. In this case a 16-bit number is contained in the B and C pair. However, this is only a 1-byte instruction. Another example is

MOV   D,M

M in this instruction specifies implicitly that the H and L pair contain the address of the operand. The processor moves the operand to the D register from memory when the instruction is executed. When using the indirect mode, the register pair is referred to as a pointer. The H and L pair are the most convenient to use as a pointer because this pair can be specified in many more ways than the B and C or D and E pairs can.

10.2.4 Immediate Mode

The fourth mode of addressing used by the 8085A is called the *immediate mode*. In this mode, the operand itself is contained in the instruction. It is called the immediate mode because the data is found immediately following the opcode. It is either the second byte of the instruction with an 8-bit operand, or it is the second and third bytes if a 16-bit operand is used. The immediate mode is commonly used to initialize registers or memory locations with constants or addresses. The instruction

MVI   A,05

is interpreted as "Move immediate to the A register the number 5." This is a 2-byte instruction. The second byte contains the number 5. The immediate mode is specified in the opcode whenever the letter I is used. A register pair may be initialized with the LXI instruction. For example,

LXI   H,ADDR

initializes the H and L pair with the 16-bit address ADDR. This is a 3-byte instruction: the first for the opcode and the second and third for the 16-bit address or number. Remember that the letter X in the instruction is used to remind us that a register pair is somehow used.

The immediate mode may also be used for arithmetic or logical instructions. For example, the contents of the A register may be tested with

CPI   41H

which is interpreted as, "Compare immediate the contents of the A register with the hexadecimal number 41." As with other compare instructions, only the contents of the flag byte are changed when this instruction is executed. In this case, the Z flag will be set if the contents of the A register equals 41.

The student should find that learning the 8085A's instruction set is easy because only four addressing modes are used.

10.3 CONDITION FLAGS

The 8085A uses five flags to indicate conditions that exist after the execution of each instruction. Programs test these flags when conditional jumps, calls, or returns are executed. It is important for you to know how each instruction affects these flags. Some affect all flags, some affect most, some affect only one, and some affect no flags at all. For example, suppose that a program is to input data to the A register. Further, suppose that if the data is positive, one routine is to be executed, and if negative, another routine should be executed. The code might look like this:

```
          IN     PORT
          JP     TWO
ONE:      .
          .
          .
TWO:      .
          .
          .
```

The JP (jump if positive) instruction will produce erroneous results because the IN instruction does not affect the flags at all. Until you are familiar with how each instruction affects the flags, it would be prudent to refer to the reference material each time you use a conditional jump, call, or return instruction!

10.3.1 S Flag

The S flag occupies bit position 7 of the flag byte, as shown in Figure 10-2. Generally this flag is affected by the execution of arithmetic and logical instructions. If the result of such an instruction is negative, the S flag is set; otherwise it is cleared. In other words, the S flag takes on the state of the sign bit (bit 7 of the accumulator) when arithmetic or logical instructions are executed.

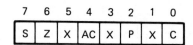

Figure 10-2. Bit positions of the 8085A flags.

10.3.2   Z Flag

The Z flag occupies bit position 6 of the flag byte. The Z flag is set if the contents of the A register is zero after the execution of arithmetic or logical instructions. Any other result with these instructions will clear the Z flag. General purpose registers may be incremented or decremented. If the result contained in any 8-bit GPR is zero after executing either the increment (INR) or decrement (DCR) instruction, the Z flag will be set. For these two instructions, any other result will clear the Z flag.

10.3.3   AC Flag

Bit position 4 of the flag byte contains the auxiliary carry (AC) flag. This flag is tested by only one of the 8085A's instructions. It is used when converting mathematical results to decimal with the DAA (decimal adjust accumulator) instruction. When performing an addition, if there is a carry in the result from bit position 3 to bit position 4, the AC flag will be set; otherwise, it will be cleared.

10.3.4   P Flag

The P (parity) flag appears in bit position 2 of the flag byte. This flag is used to test or create parity bits, which are used in some systems that employ the use of redundant check bits. For the execution of those instructions that affect this flag, if the result in the A register contains an even number of one bits, the P flag is set. It is cleared if there are an odd number of one bits. An example of an even number of one bits is the binary number 11000011, which contains 4 one bits.

10.3.5   CY Flag

The CY flag appears in bit position 0 of the flag byte. The CY flag may be considered as an extension of the A register for the execution of arithmetic instructions. For example, if the result of an ADD instruction is a number too large to be contained in the A register, the CY flag will be set; otherwise, it will be cleared. This flag is used when multibyte numbers are processed.

Bits 1, 3, and 5 of the flag byte have not been defined by INTEL *.

The student is reminded that not all instructions affect the flags in the same manner.

* Registered trademark of Intel Corporation.

10.4   THE 8085A INSTRUCTIONS

The 8085A instructions can be divided into four groups: data transfer, arithmetic and logical, branch control, and I/O and machine control. These instructions are listed in Figure 10–3.

10.4.1   Data Transfer Instructions

The first group, data transfer, includes all of the move (MOV) instructions, the move immediate (MVI), the 16-bit load immediate (LXI), and various other load and store instructions. The term *load* refers to registers and the term *store* refers to memory. Data is loaded into registers, and data is stored in memory. None of the instructions in this group affects the condition flags.

10.4.2   Arithmetic and Logic Instructions

The second group, arithmetic and logical, includes various forms of the add and subtract instructions, including increment and decrement. Logical instructions that perform AND, OR, EXCLUSIVE–OR, and compare operations are in this group. In addition, there are some special instructions for complementing and rotating the contents of the A register as well as instructions for setting or clearing the CY flag. Finally, the DAD (double add) instruction allows for arithmetic operations with 16-bit words. Most of the instructions in this group affect the condition flags.

10.4.3   Branch Control Instructions

The branch control group includes all of the jump, call, and return instructions. All of the call and jump instructions use the direct mode of addressing except one: the PCHL instruction. It moves the contents of the H and L pair to the PC, which in effect causes a jump to the address in the H and L pair. This is the indirect mode. In a sense, all of the return instructions use the indirect mode, too. Actually, the mode is indirect-deferred because a register, the SP, contains the address of the address of the next instruction to be executed. This is only academic because we understand how the address of the next instruction is popped from the stack when a return is executed. None of the instructions in the branch control group affects the condition flags, even though most of these instructions use the flags.

10.4.4   I/O and Machine Control Instructions

The fourth group, I/O and machine control, contains two I/O instructions, IN and OUT; four stack manipulation instructions; the enable and disable interrupt instructions; a no operation (NOP) instruction; and

DATA TRANSFER GROUP

MOV — Move

A,A	7F		E,A	5F
A,B	78		E,B	58
A,C	79		E,C	59
A,D	7A		E,D	5A
A,E	7B		E,E	5B
A,H	7C		E,H	5C
A,L	7D		E,L	5D
A,M	7E		E,M	5E

MOV — Move / Move (cont)

Move		Move (cont)	
B,A	47	H,A	67
B,B	40	H,B	60
B,C	41	H,C	61
B,D	42	H,D	62
B,E	43	H,E	63
B,H	44	H,H	64
B,L	45	H,L	65
B,M	46	H,M	66
C,A	4F	L,A	6F
C,B	48	L,B	68
C,C	49	L,C	69
C,D	4A	L,D	6A
C,E	4B	L,E	6B
C,H	4C	L,H	6C
C,L	4D	L,L	6D
C,M	4E	L,M	6E
D,A	57	M,A	77
D,B	50	M,B	70
D,C	51	M,C	71
D,D	52	M,D	72
D,E	53	M,E	73
D,H	54	M,H	74
D,L	55	M,L	75
D,M	56		

XCHG   EB

MVI — Move Immediate

A, byte	3E
B, byte	06
C, byte	0E
D, byte	16
E, byte	1E
H, byte	26
L, byte	2E
M, byte	36

LXI — Load Immediate

B, dble	01
D, dble	11
H, dble	21
SP, dble	31

Load/Store

LDAX B	0A
LDAX D	1A
LHLD adr	2A
LDA adr	3A
STAX B	02
STAX D	12
SHLD adr	22
STA adr	32

ARITHMETIC AND LOGICAL GROUP

Add* / **Logical***

ADD			ANA	
A	87		A	A7
B	80		B	A0
C	81		C	A1
D	82		D	A2
E	83		E	A3
H	84		H	A4
L	85		L	A5
M	86		M	A6
ADC			XRA	
A	8F		A	AF
B	88		B	A8
C	89		C	A9
D	8A		D	AA
E	8B		E	AB
H	8C		H	AC
L	8D		L	AD
M	8E		M	AE

Subtract* / **Logical***

SUB			ORA	
A	97		A	B7
B	90		B	B0
C	91		C	B1
D	92		D	B2
E	93		E	B3
H	94		H	B4
L	95		L	B5
M	96		M	B6
SBB			CMP	
A	9F		A	BF
B	98		B	B8
C	99		C	B9
D	9A		D	BA
E	9B		E	BB
H	9C		H	BC
L	9D		L	BD
M	9E		M	BE

Double Add † — DAD

B	09
D	19
H	29
SP	39

Increment** / **Decrement****

INR			DCR	
A	3C		A	3D
B	04		B	05
C	0C		C	0D
D	14		D	15
E	1C		E	1D
H	24		H	25
L	2C		L	2D
M	34		M	35
INX			DCX	
B	03		B	0B
D	13		D	1B
H	23		H	2B
SP	33		SP	3B

Specials

DAA*	27
CMA	2F
STC†	37
CMC†	3F

Rotate †

RLC	07
RRC	0F
RAL	17
RAR	1F

Arith & Logical Immediate

ADI byte	C6
ACI byte	CE
SUI byte	D6
SBI byte	DE
ANI byte	E6
XRI byte	EE
ORI byte	F6
CPI byte	FE

byte = constant, or logical/arithmetic expression that evaluates to an 8-bit data quantity. (Second byte of 2-byte instructions).

dble = constant, or logical/arithmetic expression that evaluates to a 16-bit data quantity. (Second and Third bytes of 3-byte instructions).

adr = 16-bit address (Second and Third bytes of 3-byte instructions).

* = all flags (C, Z, S, P, AC) affected.

** = all flags except CARRY affected; (exception: INX and DCX affect no flags).

† = only CARRY affected.

All mnemonics copyright ©Intel Corporation 1976.

Figure 10-3. The 8085A instruction set. (Courtesy Intel Corporation)

Name	Code	Restart Address
RST 0	C7	0000_{16}
RST 1	CF	0008_{16}
RST 2	D7	0010_{16}
RST 3	DF	0018_{16}
RST 4	E7	0020_{16}
TRAP	Hardware* Function	0024_{16}
RST 5	EF	0028_{16}
RST 5 5	Hardware* Function	$002C_{16}$
RST 6	F7	0030_{16}
RST 6 5	Hardware* Function	0034_{16}
RST 7	FF	0038_{16}
RST 7 5	Hardware* Function	$003C_{16}$

*NOTE The hardware functions refer to the on-chip interrupt feature of the 8085 only

USE OF THE A REGISTER BY RIM AND SIM INSTRUCTIONS (8085 ONLY)

A REGISTER AFTER EXECUTING RIM

D_7 | SID | I7 5 | I6 5 | I5 5 | IE | M7 5 | M6 5 | M5 5 | D_0

- SERIAL INPUT DATA
- INTERRUPTS PENDING
- INTERRUPT ENABLE FLAG
- INTERRUPT MASKS

A REGISTER BEFORE EXECUTING SIM

D_7 | SOD | SOE | X | R7 5 | MSE | M7 5 | M6 5 | M5 5 | D_0

- RST 5 5 MASK
- RST 6 5 MASK
- RST 7 5 MASK
- MASK SET ENABLE
- RESET RST 7 5
- UNDEFINED
- SOD ENABLE
- SERIAL OUTPUT DATA

BRANCH CONTROL GROUP

Jump

JMP adr	C3
JNZ adr	C2
JZ adr	CA
JNC adr	D2
JC adr	DA
JPO adr	E2
JPE adr	EA
JP adr	F2
JM adr	FA
PCHL	E9

Call

CALL adr	CD
CNZ adr	C4
CZ adr	CC
CNC adr	D4
CC adr	DC
CPO adr	E4
CPE adr	EC
CP adr	F4
CM adr	FC

Return

RET	C9
RNZ	C0
RZ	C8
RNC	D0
RC	D8
RPO	E0
RPE	E8
RP	F0
RM	F8

Restart

RST-	0	C7
	1	CF
	2	D7
	3	DF
	4	E7
	5	EF
	6	F7
	7	FF

I/O AND MACHINE CONTROL

Stack Ops

PUSH	B	C5
	D	D5
	H	E5
	PSW	F5
POP	B	C1
	D	D1
	H	E1
	PSW*	F1
XTHL		E3
SPHL		F9

Input/Output

OUT byte	D3
IN byte	DB

Control

DI	F3
EI	FB
NOP	00
HLT	76

New Instructions (8085 Only)

RIM	20
SIM	30

ASSEMBLER REFERENCE

Operators

(.) NUL
LOW, HIGH
*/. MOD, SHL, SHR
+, −
NOT
AND
OR, XOR

ASSEMBLER REFERENCE (Cont.)

Pseudo Instruction

General:
ORG
END
EQU
SET
DS
DB
DW

Macros:
MACRO
ENDM
LOCAL
REPT
IRP
IRPC
EXITM

Relocation:
ASEG   NAME
DSEG   STKLN
CSEG   STACK
PUBLIC   MEMORY
EXTRN

Conditional Assembly:
IF
ELSE
ENDIF

Constant Definition

0BDH	Hex
1AH	
105D	Decimal
105	
72O	Octal
72Q	
11011B	Binary
00110B	
'TEST'	ASCII
'A''B'	

235

INTEL® 8080/8085 INSTRUCTION SET REFERENCE TABLES

INTERNAL REGISTER ORGANIZATION

A Reg. (8)

B Reg. (8)	C Reg. (8)
D Reg. (8)	E Reg. (8)
H Reg. (8)	L Reg. (8)
Program Counter (16)	
Stack Pointer (16)	

FLAG BYTE

D_7 → S | Z | X | AC | X | P | X | C ← D_0

- CARRY
- PARITY
- AUX. CARRY
- ZERO
- SIGN

X: UNDEFINED

REGISTER-PAIR ORGANIZATION

PSW

A (8)	FLAGS (8)

B	(B/C) (16)
D	(D/E) (16)
H	(H/L) (16)
Prog. Ctr.	(16)
Stack Ptr.	(16)

NOTE: Leftmost Byte is high-order byte for arithmetic operations and addressing. Left byte is pushed on stack first. Right byte is popped first.

BRANCH CONTROL INSTRUCTIONS

Flag Condition	Jump		Call		Return	
Zero=True	JZ	CA	CZ	CC	RZ	C8
Zero=False	JNZ	C2	CNZ	C4	RNZ	C0
Carry=True	JC	DA	CC	DC	RC	D8
Carry=False	JNC	D2	CNC	D4	RNC	D0
Sign=Positive	JP	F2	CP	F4	RP	F0
Sign=Negative	JM	FA	CM	FC	RM	F8
Parity=Even	JPE	EA	CPE	EC	RPE	E8
Parity=Odd	JPO	E2	CPO	E4	RPO	E0
Unconditional	JMP	C3	CALL	CD	RET	C9

ACCUMULATOR OPERATIONS

	Code	Function
XRA A	AF	Clear A and Clear Carry
ORA A	B7	Clear Carry
CMC	3F	Complement Carry
CMA	2F	Complement Accumulator
STC	37	Set Carry
RLC	07	Rotate Left
RRC	0F	Rotate Right
RAL	17	Rotate Left Thru Carry
RAR	1F	Rotate Right Thru Carry
DAA	27	Decimal Adjust Accum.

REGISTER PAIR AND STACK OPERATIONS

	Register Pair						Function
	PSW (A/F)	B (B/C)	D (D/E)	H (H/L)	SP	PC	
INX		03	13	23	33		Increment Register Pair
DCX		0B	1B	2B	3B		Decrement Register Pair
LDAX		0A	1A	7E(1)			Load A Indirect (Reg. Pair holds Adrs)
STAX		02	12	77(2)			Store A Indirect (Reg. Pair holds Adrs)
LHLD				2A			Load H/L Direct (Bytes 2 and 3 hold Adrs)
SHLD				22			Store H/L Direct (Bytes 2 and 3 hold Adrs)
LXI		01	11	21	31	C3(3)	Load Reg. Pair Immediate (Bytes 2 and 3 hold immediate data)
PCHL						E9	Load PC with H/L (Branch to Adrs in H/L)
XCHG			EB				Exchange Reg. Pairs D/E and H/L
DAD		09	19	29	39		Add Reg. Pair to H/L
PUSH	F5	C5	D5	E5			Push Reg. Pair on Stack
POP	F1	C1	D1	E1			Pop Reg. Pair off Stack
XTHL				E3			Exchange H/L with Top of Stack
SPHL					F9		Load SP with H/L

Notes: 1. This is MOV A,M.   2. This is MOV M,A.   3. This is JMP.

00	NOP		2B	DCX H	81	ADD C	D7	RST 2
01	LXI B,dble		2C	INR L	82	ADD D	D8	RC
02	STAX B		2D	DCR L	83	ADD E	D9	- - -
03	INX B		2E	MVI L,byte	84	ADD H	DA	JC adr
04	INR B		2F	CMA	85	ADD L	DB	IN byte
05	DCR B		30	SIM*	86	ADD M	DC	CC adr
06	MVI B,byte		31	LXI SP,dble	87	ADD A	DD	- - -
07	RLC		32	STA adr	88	ADC B	DE	SBI byte
08	- - -		33	INX SP	89	ADC C	DF	RST 3
09	DAD B		34	INR M	8A	ADC D	E0	RPO
0A	LDAX B		35	DCR M	8B	ADC E	E1	POP H
0B	DCX B		36	MVI M,byte	8C	ADC H	E2	JPO adr
0C	INR C		37	STC	8D	ADC L	E3	XTHL
0D	DCR C		38	- - -	8E	ADC M	E4	CPO adr
0E	MVI C,byte		39	DAD SP	8F	ADC A	E5	PUSH H
0F	RRC		3A	LDA adr	90	SUB B	E6	ANI byte
10	- - -		3B	DCX SP	91	SUB C	E7	RST 4
11	LXI D,dble		3C	INR A	92	SUB D	E8	RPE
12	STAX D		3D	DCR A	93	SUB E	E9	PCHL
13	INX D		3E	MVI A,byte	94	SUB H	EA	JPE adr
14	INR D		3F	CMC	95	SUB L	EB	XCHG
15	DCR D		40	MOV B,B	96	SUB M	EC	CPE adr
16	MVI D,byte		41	MOV B,C	97	SUB A	ED	- - -
17	RAL		42	MOV B,D	98	SBB B	EE	XRI byte
18	- - -		43	MOV B,E	99	SBB C	EF	RST 5
19	DAD D		44	MOV B,H	9A	SBB D	F0	RP
1A	LDAX D		45	MOV B,L	9B	SBB E	F1	POP PSW
1B	DCX D		46	MOV B,M	9C	SBB H	F2	JP adr
1C	INR E		47	MOV B,A	9D	SBB L	F3	DI
1D	DCR E		48	MOV C,B	9E	SBB M	F4	CP adr
1E	MVI E,byte		49	MOV C,C	9F	SBB A	F5	PUSH PSW
1F	RAR		4A	MOV C,D	A0	ANA B	F6	ORI byte
20	RIM*		4B	MOV C,E	A1	ANA C	F7	RST 6
21	LXI H,dble		4C	MOV C,H	A2	ANA D	F8	RM
22	SHLD adr		4D	MOV C,L	A3	ANA E	F9	SPHL
23	INX H		4E	MOV C,M	A4	ANA H	FA	JM adr
24	INR H		4F	MOV C,A	A5	ANA L	FB	EI
25	DCR H		50	MOV D,B	A6	ANA M	FC	CM adr
26	MVI H,byte		51	MOV D,C	A7	ANA A	FD	- - -
27	DAA		52	MOV D,D	A8	XRA B	FE	CPI byte
28	- - -		53	MOV D,E	A9	XRA C	FF	RST 7
29	DAD H		54	MOV D,H	AA	XRA D		
2A	LHLD adr		55	MOV D,L	AB	XRA E		
			56	MOV D,M	AC	XRA H		
			57	MOV D,A	AD	XRA L		
			58	MOV E,B	AE	XRA M		
			59	MOV E,C	AF	XRA A		
			5A	MOV E,D	B0	ORA B		
			5B	MOV E,E	B1	ORA C		
			5C	MOV E,H	B2	ORA D		
			5D	MOV E,L	B3	ORA E		
			5E	MOV E,M	B4	ORA H		
			5F	MOV E,A	B5	ORA L		
			60	MOV H,B	B6	ORA M		
			61	MOV H,C	B7	ORA A		
			62	MOV H,D	B8	CMP B		
			63	MOV H,E	B9	CMP C		
			64	MOV H,H	BA	CMP D		
			65	MOV H,L	BB	CMP E		
			66	MOV H,M	BC	CMP H		
			67	MOV H,A	BD	CMP L		
			68	MOV L,B	BE	CMP M		
			69	MOV L,C	BF	CMP A		
			6A	MOV L,D	C0	RNZ		
			6B	MOV L,E	C1	POP B		
			6C	MOV L,H	C2	JNZ adr		
			6D	MOV L,L	C3	JMP adr		
			6E	MOV L,M	C4	CNZ adr		
			6F	MOV L,A	C5	PUSH B		
			70	MOV M,B	C6	ADI byte		
			71	MOV M,C	C7	RST 0		
			72	MOV M,D	C8	RZ		
			73	MOV M,E	C9	RET		
			74	MOV M,H	CA	JZ adr		
			75	MOV M,L	CB	- - -		
			76	HLT	CC	CZ adr		
			77	MOV M,A	CD	CALL adr		
			78	MOV A,B	CE	ACI byte		
			79	MOV A,C	CF	RST 1		
			7A	MOV A,D	D0	RNC		
			7B	MOV A,E	D1	POP D		
			7C	MOV A,H	D2	JNC adr		
			7D	MOV A,L	D3	OUT byte		
			7E	MOV A,M	D4	CNC adr		
			7F	MOV A,A	D5	PUSH D		
			80	ADD B	D6	SUI byte		

*8085 Only.

Figure 10-3. The 8085A instruction set. (Courtesy Intel Corporation)

the halt (HLT) instruction. Finally, two instructions, RIM and SIM, are used for reading and setting the interrupt mask register. The I/O and machine control instructions do not affect the condition flags.

10.5   THE 8085A INSTRUCTION SET

Appendix B contains an expanded description of the 8085A instruction set. This is a direct reprint from the INTEL* 8080/8085 Assembly Language Programming manual. Each instruction is described in detail. Where it is helpful, diagrams and/or examples are used to clarify the use of the instruction.

When you find it necessary to investigate a particular instruction, it may be easily found because they appear in alphabetical order. In addition to the description of the instruction, the following information is always given:

1.   The mnemonic code format

2.   The machine language format including the opcode, which is shown in binary

3.   Number of machine cycles

4.   Number of machine states

5.   Addressing mode used

6.   The flags that are affected

Probably the information that you will find most useful at first deals with the flags. You will notice that how the flags are affected is not necessarily given, but which flags are affected is always given. You may refer to section 10.3 of this chapter to determine how the flags are affected.

The number of machine cycles and the number of states are useful particularly when you are writing routines that control external events and precise timing is required. In these situations it is necessary to know the period of each state (T). Each state is the reciprocal of the clock frequency. Therefore, if the clock frequency is 3 MHz, then T will equal 333 ns. The time for the routine, then, is the product of T and the total number of states.

Sometimes you will find it useful to evaluate the bit structure of the opcode. This information is also included in Appendix B. The 8-bit registers are assigned binary numbers as follows:

Register	Binary number
A	111
B	000
C	001

D	010
E	011
H	100
L	101
M	110

You will notice that M is included in this group. Recall that M specified the indirect mode using the H and L pair as a pointer. One may think of M as being a register in memory. The instruction set specifies M just as it would specify any other 8-bit register. The machine language specifies M as 110 in binary.

If we look through the instruction set, we will notice (in the binary code given) the use of the letters SSS and DDD. These letters indicate the bit positions that specify the registers used for source (SSS) and destination (DDD) operands. For example, consider the instruction ADC reg. ADC is the opcode meaning "Add to the accumulator with carry," and reg means that one of the 8-bit registers must be specified as containing the source operand. The binary code appears like this:

1	0	0	0	1	S	S	S

If the B register is specified as the source operand, the mnemonic code would look like this:

ADC   B

and the machine language code:

1	0	0	0	1	0	0	0

Notice that the three LSBs are 000, specifying the B register. If the source operand is M, then the mnemonic code would be:

ADC   M

and the machine language code:

1	0	0	0	1	1	1	0

In this case the three LSBs are 110, specifying M as containing the source operand.

Register pairs are also specified in some instructions. Because there are four pairs, only two bits are required for the binary code. The assignment is as follows:

	Binary	*Pair*
B	00	B,C
D	01	D,E
H	10	H,L
SP	11	SP
PSW	11	A,F

You may wonder about the binary code 11, which specifies either the SP or the PSW. No conflict occurs because the opcodes that specify the SP do not specify the PSW and vice versa. Let's consider the INX instruction, which causes a 16-bit number contained in a register pair to be incremented. From Appendix B, we find that the binary code is given like this:

1	0	R	P	0	0	1	1

The letters RP indicate the two bit positions that specify the register pair containing the operand. If the number in the D and E pair is to be incremented, the opcode would be:

INX   D

and the machine code would be:

0	0	0	1	0	0	1	1

Notice that bits 4 and 5 equal 01, which specifies the D and E pair.

Two instructions, LDAX and STAX, can only specify one of two register pairs; therefore, only one bit is used for this purpose. If bit 4 of either of these instructions equals 0, the B and C pair is specified. If bit 4 equals 1, the D and E pair is specified.

10.6 ASSEMBLING PROGRAMS

Programs that use only mnemonic instructions are called assembly language programs. They are the source for the machine language (binary) programs that the processor can execute. The process of converting assembly language programs to machine language is called assembling. You may recall that we discussed this procedure for assembling programs for LIMP in Chapter 7.

If you assemble a program without the aid of a program called an *assembler,* then you are the assembler and we will call the procedure "assembling by hand." This procedure requires that you refer to a programmer's card and substitute a machine language word for each instruction in the program. Figure 10–3 is a copy of the 8080/8085 Assembly Language Reference Card, or programmer's card.

Care must be taken so that correct addresses are assigned to each instruction. Some instructions require one byte, some two bytes, and some require three bytes of machine language code. If the register mode is used, only one byte is required because the register or registers can be specified in the byte containing the opcode. If the direct addressing mode is used, then three bytes are required: one for the opcode and two more for the 16-bit address. When 16-bit numbers are assembled, remember that the low byte must appear in the first of the two addresses. Let's assemble the load instruction LDA 2050H, which uses the direct addressing mode. The first byte must contain the opcode 3A, which we find by referring to the programmer's card. The second and third bytes contain the address with the low byte first. Therefore, the complete machine language instruction is:

3A   50   20

Suppose the address of this instruction is 1037; then, the address of the next instruction must be 103A because this is a 3-byte instruction.

Instructions that use the indirect addressing mode are 1-byte instructions because, like the register mode, only a register pair needs to be specified.

Instructions using the immediate mode may be 2-byte or 3-byte instructions, depending upon the immediate data. If the immediate data is an 8-bit number, then the instruction word is two bytes long. If the immediate data is a 16-bit number or address, three bytes are required in the word. Remember, when assembling 16-bit numbers, "low byte first!"

Follow how the program in Figure 10–4 is assembled. This is a simple program which prints "HELLO" on a terminal. The port address of the terminal is 1 and the address of the status port is 0. The terminal printer ready bit appears in bit position 0 of the status byte. We will describe how the program works as we go through it.

The first consideration is where the program is to be loaded into memory. Locations below address 40 are used for the RST vectors. A stack must be initialized, so let's reserve locations 40 to 80 for the stack. Therefore, the first address of our program is 80 and is identified with the label START.

The first instruction initializes the SP to the starting address. This is logical because the program will grow toward the higher addresses, and the stack will grow toward the lower addresses. Remember that the SP is decremented before anything is moved to the stack. This is a 3-byte instruction. The opcode for LXI SP is 31, the first byte of the instruction. The second byte is the low byte of the address START, which is 80. The third byte

0080	31	80	00	START:	LXI	SP,START
0083	21	9C	00		LXI	H,MSG
0086	OE	05			MVI	C,5
0088	CD	8C	00		CALL	PRINT
008B	76				HLT	
008C	DB	00		PRINT:	IN	0
008E	E6	01			ANI	1
0090	CA	8C	00		JZ	PRINT
0093	7E				MOV	A,M
0094	D3	01			OUT	1
0096	23				INX	H
0097	OD				DCR	C
0098	C2	8C	00		JNZ	PRINT
009B	C9				RET	
009C	48	45	4C	MSG:	DB	'HELLO'
009F	4C	4F				
00A1						

Figure 10-4. Program that prints the message 'HELLO.'

is the high byte of the address START, which is 00. The next address is 0083. So far so good!

The next instruction initializes the H and L pair as a pointer. The op-code for LXI H is 21, which goes to address 0083. But what are the next two bytes? Because we have not yet determined the physical address of MSG, we do not know. There are two possible procedures to follow. One, we could go ahead and assign addresses to all of the instructions; or two, we could leave these two bytes blank until we have assembled the program to the label MSG, at which time we will know the address of MSG. Care must be taken in either case because it is easy to forget the second and third bytes and assign the wrong address to the next instruction.

The next instruction (MVI C,5) initializes a counter with the number of characters to be printed. This is another instruction that uses the immediate mode. It is a 2-byte instruction because an 8-bit register is the destination. The first byte is the opcode and specifies the C register. The second byte is the number 5.

The CALL instruction uses the direct addressing mode; therefore, it is a 3-byte instruction. The second and third bytes contain the address of the subroutine being called.

The next instruction, HLT, is the last instruction to be executed in the program. This instruction is part of the machine control group and causes the processor to halt. It is a 1-byte instruction.

The next address, 008C, is the first address of the subroutine. If you understand subroutines correctly, you know that the subroutine could appear anywhere in memory. The first three instructions of the subroutine test the ready bit of the terminal's printer to determine if it is ready to accept the next character to be printed. The IN instruction is one of the two I/O instructions. The destination of the data inputted is the A register. The memory map contains all addresses from O-FFFFH. In the 8085A, these locations are referred to using 16-bit addresses. For the IN and OUT instructions, a separate range of addresses (I/O map) is used to address ports. Because the 8085A has an I/O map of addresses from 00 to FF in addition to the memory map, only one byte is required for the address. You guessed it, this is a special 2-byte instruction using the direct mode.

The ANI 1 instruction performs the logical AND operation on the contents of the A register and the immediate number 1. It has two purposes. The first is to mask away all bits except bit 0 in the A register. Bit 0 is the ready bit being tested. Bits 1 through 7 may be status bits for other peripherals and should not be allowed to influence the results of this test. The second purpose is to set or clear the Z flag, depending on the results of the test. Because a conditional jump instruction follows this, it is necessary to know how the flags are affected. Referring to Appendix B, we discover that the ANI instruction affects all flags. In this case, we are specifically concerned with the Z flag. If the Z flag equals 1, it means that the contents of the A register equals 0 and, more specifically, the value of the ready bit is 0. The ANI 1 instruction is a 2-byte instruction. The first contains the opcode and implies the use of the A register. The second contains the number 1.

The JZ PRINT instruction tests the contents of the Z flag. If the Z flag equals 1, a jump is executed and the next instruction to be executed is the IN instruction at address 008C. The purpose of this jump is to test the ready bit again because the test just made indicated that the printer is not yet ready. If the Z flag equals 0, it indicates that the printer is ready and execution falls through the jump instruction to the next instruction. The JZ PRINT instruction uses the direct mode of addressing and requires three bytes.

Next, a byte of data is read from memory with the MOV A,M instruction. The data is one of the characters of the message. The letter M in the instruction specifies the source operand using the indirect mode. The H and L pair contains the address of the character. The destination, A, uses the register mode. This instruction requires one byte.

The OUT 1 instruction causes the data to be outputted to the printer at port address 1. The OUT instruction is the second of the two I/O instructions. Like the IN instruction, it requires two bytes.

After a byte of data has been outputted, the INX H instruction causes the pointer (the H and L pair) to be incremented. This is a 1-byte instruction.

Next, the DCR C instruction subtracts 1 from the C register. This instruction affects some of the flags. Specifically, if the result of executing the instruction causes the C register to equal 0, the Z flag will be set; otherwise it will be cleared. The purpose of this instruction and the JNZ instruction that follows is to determine if all of the characters have been outputted. The DCR C instruction is a 1-byte instruction.

The JNZ instruction is exactly the same as the JZ instruction except that the jump occurs if the Z flag equals 0. When the Z flag equals 1, it means that the contents of the C register equals 0 and all characters have been printed. The JNZ PRINT instruction is assembled just like the JZ instruction, except that the first byte equals C2 instead of CA.

The RET instruction is a 1-byte instruction that causes execution to return to the main program.

Following the RET instruction is the label MSG, which is the symbolic address of 009C. The letters DB (define byte) do not represent an instruction but rather indicate that bytes of data are to be assembled in the program at this point. The single quotes that appear before and after the message HELLO tell the assembler that the ASCII code for the letters in the message are to be used. Notice that the five bytes assembled here represent the message in ASCII.

10.7 ASSEMBLER

What is an assembler? It is a program! It runs on a computer system usually intended for program development. Its purpose is to simplify the task of writing programs. Its basic function is to read source programs written by a programmer who is using the mnemonics described in the instruction set. The programmer uses another program called a text editor to write the source program.

Assembling programs by hand is a tedious job, so why do it? Assembling by hand should only be considered if the programs are short and a system with an assembler is not available. Another reason is that these assembler systems are expensive. However, writing and assembling programs for small controller-type systems where the programs reside in ROM is appropriate.

When using a text editor and an assembler, the task of debugging or making modifications in the program is made simpler. Source programs are usually maintained in files. Therefore in order to make a change, the programmer uses the text editor to read the file, edit in the changes, and write the program back into the file. He then uses the assembler to reassemble the program—and the task is complete.

10.7.1 Source Code Format

Writing programs in assembly language is similar to writing in English in that there are rules of grammar. Spelling is most important. For example, if the mnemonic instruction code is misspelled, the assembler will reject it and generate an error. Remember, the assembler is a program, not a person. It cannot guess what we mean, it can only interpret precisely written instructions.

Each line of source code produces one instruction word. The word may be one, two, or three bytes in length. Rules dictate that each line of source code consist of four fields as follows:

LABEL: OPCODE OPERAND   ;COMMENT

The first field, the label field, may contain a symbolic address called a label. It consists of one to six alphanumeric characters. However, the first character must be alphabetic. The label is optional, depending on whether the programmer needs to identify this address. The programmer identifies addresses symbolically. The assembler assigns physical addresses to these symbols. Remember, the purpose of the assembler is to relieve the programmer of tedious tasks like calculating addresses. When possible, let the assembler do the work for you! Each label is terminated with a colon (:). The label field is eight character positions wide. If the label is not used, leave the label field blank by typing a tab.

The opcode field starts at the ninth character position and also occupies eight character positions. This field contains the mnemonic opcode.

Next is the operand field. It starts in the seventeenth character position and occupies sixteen character positions. More room is required in this field because some operand expressions can be lengthy.

The comment field starts in the thirty-third character position and uses the remainder of the line. The comment field is optional and is used to document the purpose of the instructions in the program. This field starts with a semicolon (;), which delimits the comment from the instruction. Comments may occupy an entire line or a number of lines, but each line of comments must begin with a semicolon. The assembler does not attempt to assemble anything on a line beyond the semicolon.

How does the assembler interpret numbers? The programmer has the option of using decimal, octal, hexadecimal, or even binary numbers in his program, but he must specify which base he is using. A letter following the number does the job. The letter D is used for decimal, Q for octal, H for hexadecimal, and B for binary. If no letter is used, the default interpretation is decimal. The following are some examples:

Assembled Number in Hex	Source
0A	10
0A	10D
08	10Q
10	10H
02	10B
FF	0FFH
FACE	0FACEH
FFFF	65535

Notice that the hexadecimal number FF is specified as 0FFH. The leading 0 is required because without it the assembler would assume FFH is a label. Recall that labels consist of from one to six alphanumeric characters and the first character must be alphabetic. A 0 must be placed in front of all hexadecimal numbers that use A through F as the most significant digit. The assembler will then take the number as a number, not a label. An example of a 16-bit number is 0FACEH, which the assembler takes as hexadecimal FACE.

10.8 ASSEMBLER DIRECTIVES

When writing a program, the programmer not only supplies the mnemonic instructions, but he must also tell the assembler specifically how he wants it assembled. Where the program is to reside, the meaning of certain labels that the programmer uses, how to assemble some required data, and even when the end of the program has been reached, are examples of information that the programmer must supply to the assembler. He does this by using assembler directives, sometimes called pseudo instructions. They appear in the program in the same way as the mnemonic instructions do. Assembler directives are not executable by the processor as instructions are, but are instructions to the assembler that are used to communicate to the assembler how the program is to be assembled.

10.8.1 ORG Directive

The ORG directive is used to inform the assembler where to set its location counter. This counter contains the address of the instruction being assembled. For example, the following code

```
        ORG     38H
        JMP     2000H
        ORG     1000H
START:  LXI     SP,START
```

will cause the assembler to assemble the JMP instruction at address 0038 and the LXI instruction at location 1000.

10.8.2 EQU Directive

Sometimes the programmer wishes to use a label to represent some expression. He uses the EQU directive to do this. The following:

```
VALUE   EQU     5000H
```

assigns 5000 to the label VALUE. In the above example, VALUE appears in the label field, EQU in the opcode field, and 5000H in the operand field. After this line, whenever the assembler finds the label VALUE referenced in the program, it will assemble the number 5000. In the following example

XVALUE   EQU   VALUE + 100

the label XVALUE has been assigned the value of 5100. One special note: When using the EQU directive, a colon (:) must not be used to terminate the label.

10.8.3   SET Directive

The SET directive is identical to the EQU directive with one important difference. A label that has been assigned using the EQU directive cannot be changed. However, if the label has been assigned a value using the SET directive, it can be changed later in the program with another SET directive.

10.8.4   DB Directive

The DB (define byte) directive asks the assembler to assemble the binary code for numbers, expressions, or ASCII strings. The numbers and expressions must be evaluated to 8-bit numbers. If the expression THIS has been equated to 10H and THAT to 0FFH, then the following examples can be used. Assume that the assembler's location counter contains 1000H.

Address	Assembled Code	Opcode	Operand
1000	10	DB	THIS
1001	FF	DB	THAT
1002	0F	DB	THIS + THAT
1003	EF	DB	THAT – THIS
1004	10 FF AB	DB	THIS,THAT,0ABH
1007			

Notice that in the last case, three expressions were given and separated by commas.

ASCII strings can also be evaluated by the assembler as follows:

Address	Assembled Code	Label	Opcode	Operand
009C	48 45 4C 4C	MSG:	DB	'HELLO'
00A0	4F			

The single quote symbol must be used to indicate that ASCII is to be assembled and that a label was not indicated.

10.8.5 DW Directive

The DW directive causes the assembler to evaluate 16-bit numbers or expressions and assemble them. Each number assembled requires two bytes. For the following examples assume that the assembler's location counter contains 1000H.

Address	Assembled Code	Opcode	Operand
1000	CE FA	DW	0FACEH
1002	34 12 01 00	DW	1234H,1,0FFFFH
1006	FF 0F		

Notice that the low byte of the 2-byte number is assembled in the first of two locations. Also notice that commas can be used to separate the different values.

10.8.6 DS Directive

The DS (define storage) directive is used to define a block of storage. It is used to reserve locations in memory that the program will use to store data. For example, suppose we wish to reserve a block of 256 (decimal) bytes for a data buffer in memory. Assume that the assembler's location counter contains 2050H. The following directive does the job:

Address	Label	Opcode	Operand
2050	BUF:	DS	256D
2150			

Notice that we did not specify what to assemble, we only specified that the assembler was to reserve 100H locations. You will notice that the assembler changed the contents of its location counter to 2150 as indicated on the second line.

10.8.7 IF, ELSE, and ENDIF Directives

The IF, ELSE, and ENDIF directives allow the programmer to assemble portions of a program only if certain specified conditions are met. The IF directive evaluates an expression as being either true or false. If the least significant bit (LSB) of the expression equals 1, then the expression is considered to be true. If the LSB equals 0, then it is false. For example, suppose that there are three versions of a particular program to be assembled. Perhaps the differences in the programs have to do with the peripherals that exist on various systems. If version 1 is to be assembled, then the programmer can select that version by using the EQU directive in the first three lines of the program as follows:

```
VER1     EQU     1
VER2     EQU     0
VER3     EQU     0
```

VER1 will be interpreted by the assembler as being true, whereas VER2 and VER3 will be false. In the following example, only that part of the program between the label VER1 and the label VER2 will be assembled.

```
ROUT1:   IF        VER1     EQ     1
         .
         .                           (version one routine)
         .
         ENDIF
ROUT2:   IF        VER2     EQ     0
         .
         .                           (version two routine)
         .
         ENDIF
ROUT3:   IF        VER3     EQ     0
         .
         .                           (version three routine)
         .
         ENDIF
```

Notice that the directives are used in a portion of the program—called an IF–ENDIF, or conditional assembly block. The block must start with the IF directive and end with the ENDIF directive. The ELSE directive has the opposite meaning of the IF directive and is optional.

10.8.8   END Directive

The END directive is used to tell the assembler that it has reached the end of the source code to be assembled. Only one END directive appears in the program. The END directive has an optional argument that is called the transfer address. The transfer address is used by the system's loader program to allow it to start the program at the appropriate address.

10.9   ASSEMBLER EXPRESSION OPERATORS

The assembler has the ability to evaluate expressions. One must realize that this evaluation takes place only at the time of assembly. There are a number of operators available; the most common are arithmetic and logical. Here is a partial list:

Operator	Meaning
+	addition
–	subtraction
*	multiplication
/	divide
NOT	logical one's complement
AND	logical AND
OR	logical OR
XOR	logical exclusive OR

The following instruction demonstrates how the arithmetic operators work:

MVI   A,3 + 20*4

The source operand 3 + 20*4 is evaluated as 83 decimal, or 53 hexadecimal. The above instruction moves 53H to the accumulator. The following instruction demonstrates how the operator may be used in a program.

JMP   LABL + 8

When executed, this instruction causes a jump to the address eight locations past the address assigned to LABL. Suppose a list of items is contained in a table. The label TABL appears at the address of the first item, and the label TEND appears at the address after the last item. The instruction

MVI   C,TEND-TABLE

initializes the C register with the number of items in the table.

The logical operators are useful for manipulating control words where the bit structure has importance. In the following instruction,

LXI   D,CONTRL XOR 0FFH

suppose CONTRL has been equated to 5A5AH. The eight LSBs of this number are complemented by the XOR 0FFH operation, and the D and E pair is initialized with 5AA5H. Remember that the assembler can only evaluate expressions at the time the program is assembled. Calculations that are made when the program is executed must be performed by the program itself. Use the assembler to make the job of programming easier!

10.10 MACROS

In assembly language programming, it is often desirable to invoke a single statement that causes a sequence of code to be generated by the assembler. The programmer must write this code and make it available to the assembler. The form in which it is written is called a macro definition.

Suppose that a sequence of instructions causes two numbers to be multiplied and the product stored in memory. Further suppose that it is desired that this routine be written as a macro. First, the programmer writes the definition and gives it a macro name such as MULT. When the assembler has read the definition, the macro may be repeatedly invoked in the program. The programmer merely inserts the macro, MULT, in the source code as if it were another instruction. Because the assembler has been "taught" how to interpret the macro, it inserts the correct sequence of code in the program.

Perhaps the greatest advantage of using macros is the ability to pass parameters to the macro. Passing parameters means to provide the macro with required information such as constants or addresses. This information may differ each time the macro is used. In the above example, the macro definition can be written so that the programmer can specify the source of the two numbers being multiplied and where the product is to be stored. The macro statement might look like this:

    MULT   NUM1,NUM2,PROD

NUM1 is the symbolic address of the first number, NUM2 is the address of the second number, and PROD is the address where the product is to be stored.

Macro definitions can be written and stored on file where a system program called a librarian can make them available to the assembler. This provides the programmer with a technique for saving routines and easy access to them when writing programs in the future.

10.10.1 Macro Directives

Directives are used when writing macro definitions. A macro directive is the same as an assembler directive except that it is associated with the macro definitions. Macro directives tell the assembler how the programmer wishes the definition to be written. MACRO and ENDM are examples of macro directives. All definitions must start with the MACRO directive and end with the ENDM directive. The following simple example demonstrates how a macro definition is written.

When the CMP instruction is executed, jump instructions that test the Z, CY, or S flags usually follow. Suppose that we wish to execute a jump if the contents of a register is equal to or greater than the contents of the A register. In the 8080/8085 instruction set, this will require the use of two instructions. The sequence of instructions would probably look like this:

```
CMP     C               ;compare C to A
JC      THERE           ;if C is greater than A, execute jump
JZ      THERE           ;if C equals A, execute jump
```

The first of the two instructions, JC, will effect the jump if the contents of the C register is greater than the contents of the A register. The second, JZ, will effect the jump if the two operands are equal.

A macro that can simplify the procedure follows:

```
MACRO    JHIS    DST
         JC      DST
         JZ      DST
ENDM
```

The first line has three parts. The first is the directive, MACRO. Second is the macro name, JHIS, "Jump if HIgher or the Same". The third part is a dummy label for the destination operand. The assembler will take any legal label in this position of the line as the destination operand. Therefore, in the second line, JC DST, the dummy operand will be replaced by the operand that the programmer specifies in the first line. The same is true for the third line. Now, to invoke the macro, the programmer's code might look like this:

```
CMP     C           ;compare C to A
JHIS    THERE       ;if C is a higher value or the same, jump
```

Do you understand that the JHIS macro has caused the assembler to assemble six bytes? Two instructions for the basic instruction set are assembled for the macro, JHIS. Assuming that THERE equals 5000H, the following shows what is assembled.

```
B9              CMP     C
DA  00  50      JHIS    THERE
CA  00  50
```

Do you have the feeling that we have created a new instruction? In a sense, that is exactly what macros do! The machine language code that is generated is probably no shorter than it would otherwise be; however, macros make the tedious job of programming much easier!

The preceding macro is intended to be used with unsigned numbers because the C flag is tested. The following macro can be used in the same manner to test signed numbers because it tests the S flag:

```
MACRO    JGT    DST    ;jump if greater than
         JM     DST    ;or equal to
         JZ     DST
ENDM
```

Sometimes all we wish to do is redefine an existing instruction because we may have difficulty remembering how the instruction works in a given case. The following redefines the JNC instruction so that we may remember its effect when following the CMP instruction.

```
    MACRO    JLO     DST      ;jump if lower
             JNC     DST
    ENDM
```

Finally, let's look at how the first example, MULT, may be defined as a macro:

```
    MACRO    MULT    NUM1,NUM2,PROD    ;macro name,
                                       arguments
             PUSH    PSW      ;save registers
             PUSH    B        ;
             PUSH    H        ;
             LDA     NUM1     ;get multipli-
                              cand
             MOV     H,A      ;
             LDA     NUM2     ;get multiplier
             MOV     C,A      ;
             MVI     B,0      ;for most sig-
                              ;nificant byte
             MVI     L,9      ;bit counter
    ZERO:    MOV     A,C      ;rotate LSB of
             RAR              ;multiplier to C
                              ;flag and shift
             MOV     C,A      ;low byte of re-
                              ;sult
             DCR     L        ;done?
             JZ      DONE     ;yes, jump out
                              ;of routine
             MOV     A,B
             JNC     ONE
             ADD     H        ;add multipli-
                              ;cand to high
                              ;byte if
                              ;bit was a one
    ONE:     RAR              ;shift high byte
                              ;of result
             MOV     B,A
             JMP     ZERO
    DONE:    SHLD    PROD     ;save two byte
                              ;result
             POP     H        ;restore regis-
                              ;ters
             POP     B        ;
             POP     PSW      ;
    ENDM
```

Notice that this macro saves all registers and restores them so that they contain exactly what they did before the macro was invoked. Further, notice that all operands appear in memory. The product is a 16-bit number. It requires the use of two locations in memory. Remember, NUM1, NUM2, and PROD are dummy labels. The programmer may use any legal labels he chooses. For example, the macro may be invoked with the following line of code:

MULT   HRS,DAYS,TIME

The assembler will replace NUM1 with HRS, NUM2 with DAYS, and PROD with TIME. The macro may be invoked in other parts of the same program using other labels. Other directives are used by the macro programmer but are not included in this text. We believe that macro programming is outside of the context of this book, but we have included an introduction to help the student interpret programs written by others.

10.10.2   Macros vs Subroutines

What is the difference between macros and subroutines? When a subroutine is used, only one version is contained in the program. It may be called from various places in the program. Macros, on the other hand, generate inline machine language code each time they are invoked. However, different versions may be generated each time because different parameters may be passed to the macro. In general, using subroutines has the advantage of using less machine language code, while using macros has the advantage of more versatility.

10.11   RELOCATABLE MODULES

Sometimes the programmer writes his programs in program blocks or modules. This technique is used for large programs where the various tasks of the program can be broken into modules. Smaller modules are easier to debug than large programs. These modules are each assembled with a temporary address of zero. The various modules are "linked" together with a feature of the assembler, or by another program called a *linker*. The linker readjusts all the addresses contained within the modules so that the memory references will be correct. The student is reminded that the 8080/8085 instructions contain absolute addresses and that the programs cannot arbitrarily be moved in memory without correction of the references to them. The programmer uses directives in the program to control the linking procedure.

10.12   INTERPRETERS AND COMPILERS

Most computer programming is accomplished by using high level languages such as BASIC (Beginner's All-purpose Instruction Code) or FORTRAN (FORmula TRANslator). These languages use programs called *interpreters* or *compilers* to produce the machine language code. Of course, this is what an assembler does. However, the assembler produces one machine language instruction word for each line of source code. With high level languages, many machine language instructions are produced with each line of source code. This is their nature because the high level instructions are very powerful. Entire mathematical expressions may be written on a single line!

Interpreters read one line of source code at a time, then substitute the appropriate machine language code and execute it. Remember, the processor can only execute machine language instructions! This procedure is continued throughout the entire program.

Compilers, on the other hand, read the entire source program and produce a machine language program that can be executed later.

High level languages are created with the user in mind. The instructions may be English-like or they may be mathematically oriented. Generally, high level languages are easier to write, are very powerful, use a great deal of memory, and execute slowly. Assembly language programs are more difficult to write because the instructions are oriented to the hardware of the processor. However, they make the best use of memory and execute rapidly.

The student is encouraged to take courses in both assembly and high level languages.

Questions

1. Name the four addressing modes used with the 8085A. Give an example of each.

2. For the instruction STA 2050H:
    a) What is the addressing mode?
    b) How many bytes are there in the instruction?
    c) How many T states are required?
    d) What does the instruction do?

3. For the instruction MOV M,A:
    a) What is the addressing mode?
    b) How many bytes are there in the instruction?
    c) How many T states are required?
    d) What does the instruction do?

4. What is the machine language code for MOV B,C? Which register contains the source operand? Which bits of the instruction code describe the destination register?

5. What's the difference between a CALL and a JMP?

6. Explain the difference between a conditional and an unconditional jump.

7. In a subroutine, what should the last instruction be?

8. At some point in a program, the A register contains 7FH and the C register contains 0A3H. If the next instruction is ADD C:
   a) What is the condition of the flags after the instruction has been executed?
   b) What is the contents of the A register?
   c) What is the contents of the C register?

9. At some point in a program, the A register contains 3CH and the D register contains 0B4H. If the next instruction is ADD D:
   a) What is the condition of the flags after the instruction has been executed?
   b) What is the contents of the A register?
   c) What is the contents of the D register?

10.

```
START    LXI    C,43H    ;load C with 43
         MVI    A,C4     ;load A with C4
2WAY:    ADI    5        ;add 5 to A
         JZ     2WAY     ;if 0, go to 2WAY
         HLT
```

In the program above, there are a number of formatting errors. List them.

11. The flag byte is A6H. What is the condition of the flags?

12. We divided the 8085A's instructions into groups. What are they? Give an example of each.

13. The machine code for an instruction is 01010000.
   a) Where is the source operand?
   b) Where is the destination operand?
   c) What is the instruction?
   d) What do bits 6 and 7 tell us?

14. What is a source program?

15. What is an object program?

Interrupts
for the
8085A

The 8085A uses two methods for implementing interrupts. The first is identical to the method used in the preceding generation (the 8080). We will refer to this method as the INTR interrupts. The INTR interrupts use the RST 0 through RST 7 instructions in the instruction set. These interrupts require the implementation of an input port called an *interrupt controller.*

The second method for implementing interrupts utilizes the 8085A hardwired interrupts, which we will call the "point 5's": RST 5.5, RST 6.5, RST 7.5, and TRAP. These interrupts do not require the use of an interrupt controller because that function is part of the 8085A hardware. Both methods are discussed in this chapter.

11.1   RST 0 THROUGH RST 7

The first method used for interrupts depends on the use of instructions that exist in the 8085A instruction set. These are the instructions RST 0 through RST 7. These are one-byte instructions that execute exactly like the CALL instruction with the following exception: only one address may be called by each instruction because the instruction word does not contain the two bytes of address. For example, when the RST 0 instruction is executed, the contents of the PC (the return address) are saved on the stack and zero is placed in the PC. Therefore, 0000 is the address called by the RST 0 instruction. RST 1 CALLs 0008, RST 2 CALLs 0010, and so on to RST 7, which CALLs 0038. All of the RST instructions and their addresses are listed in Table 11-1.

Table 11-1.   List of RST Instructions and Their Addresses

RST Instruction	Address
RST 0	0000
RST 1	0008
RST 2	0010
RST 3	0018
RST 4	0020
RST 5	0028
RST 6	0030
RST 7	0038

Notice that there are eight memory locations between each of these addresses. Jump instructions are usually placed in these locations causing the processor to execute a routine that may be located anywhere in memory. The RST instructions may be used anywhere within a program. However, their importance lies in their use with interrupts.

The 8085A has an input called INTR (INTerrupt Request), which is used to initiate the interrupt. In addition, the 8085A contains a flip-flop (INTE) which, when set, enables the processor to be interrupted when INTR is activated. This flip-flop is set by executing the EI (Enable Interrupt) instruction. The flip-flop is reset in one of two ways: (1) when the interrupt request is honored, (2) by executing the instruction DI (Disable Interrupt).

11.1.1   INA Cycle

Figure 11-1 shows a flow diagram of an instruction cycle. The first block in the diagram represents an opcode fetch. Normally the opcode fetch consists of four states. During T_1, the contents of the PC are placed

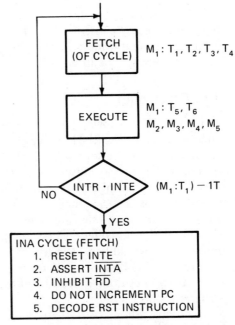

Figure 11-1. Flow diagram of an instruction cycle.

on the address bus. During T_2, the PC is incremented. $\overline{RD}$ is asserted during T_2 and T_3, causing the instruction to be transferred to the instruction register where it is decoded during T_4. Some instructions are executed during T_4. However, many instructions require additional states or machine cycles for execution—as indicated in the block labeled EXECUTE. INTR is sampled during the final state of an instruction cycle just prior to M_1 and T_1 of the next opcode fetch. If INTE is set *and* INTR is active, then a special machine cycle called INA (INterrupt Acknowledge) is entered. Otherwise, the program continues with the next opcode fetch cycle (OF). Testing the INTR line at the end of each instruction cycle assures that the instruction cycle is complete before an interrupt is allowed.

When the INA cycle is entered, the processor

1.   Resets the INTE flip-flop

2.   Fetches the next instruction from the interrupt controller by asserting $\overline{INTA}$ rather than $\overline{RD}$

3.   Inhibits the PC from being incremented

4.   Decodes the instruction

The INA cycle causes the next instruction to be fetched from the interrupt controller (the interrupt port) rather than from memory. If the interrupt controller has been implemented so that it asserts a valid instruction on the data bus, then that instruction will be the next instruction to be executed (even three-byte instructions). The RST instruction was intended for this purpose. The routine called by the RST instruction provides the appropriate service for the interrupt.

11.1.2   Interrupt Controller

Figure 11–2 shows how an interrupt controller could be implemented. Assume that the lines REQ0 through REQ7 are strobes (pulses) from eight different peripheral devices. If a peripheral is ready to input or output data, it will issue an interrupt by pulsing one of these lines. For example, suppose a peripheral has data to be inputted at port 3 and request line 3 (REQ3) has been assigned to this peripheral. The peripheral asserts a short pulse on this line. This causes one of the eight peripheral request (PR) latches to set. The encoder encodes the particular request into a three-bit number, which would be 011 in this example. In addition, REQ3 sets the service request flip-flop (SR F/F) causing the output of the encoder to be latched into bit positions 3, 4, and 5 of the three-state buffer by activating the enable input, E.

Let's look at how the RST instruction is encoded. Figure 11–3 shows the RST instruction byte. Notice that bits 0, 1, 2, 6, and 7 are all 1's. Bits 3, 4, and 5 are a binary number representing the particular RST instruction.

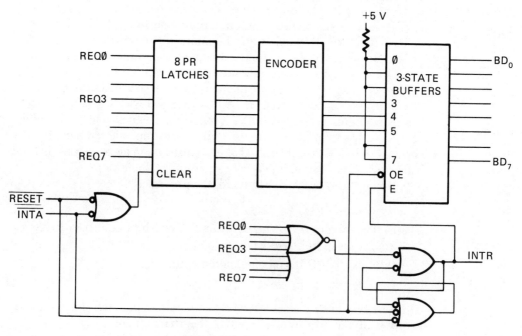

Figure 11–2. An interrupt controller.

7	6	5	4	3	2	1	Ø
1	1	V_2	V_1	V_0	1	1	1

Figure 11-3. Encoding the RST instruction.

For example, RST 0 would be encoded as 11000111, and RST 7 would be encoded as 11111111. Because the peripheral has activated REQ3, and bits 0, 1, 2, 6, and 7 are tied HIGH, 11011111 will be latched into the three-state buffer.

When the SR F/F was set, an interrupt to the processor was made because the interrupt request line to the 8085A, INTR, was activated. As explained before, if the processor honors the request, it will respond by asserting INTA. Asserting INTA will cause the SR F/F and the request latches to be reset. In addition, the output enable line (OE) to the three-state buffer is activated causing the interrupt controller to assert the RST instruction on the data bus. The processor completes the INA cycle by decoding the RST instruction.

Following the INA cycle, two machine cycles are needed to execute the RST instruction. During these two cycles, the return address is saved on the stack; bits 3, 4, and 5 of the RST instruction are transferred to their respective bit positions in the PC; and all other bits of the PC are cleared. Therefore, the next instruction to be executed is at address 0000 through 0038—depending on which RST instruction is being executed. In our example, this instruction would be at address 0018, the address CALLed by the RST 3 instruction.

11.1.3   Interrupt Service Routine

Figure 11-4 shows a flow diagram for a typical Interrupt Service Routine (ISR). This diagram is a continuation of Figure 11-1. It starts after the execution of the RST instruction, which was fetched during the INA cycle. The first block is the execution of a vector (at address 0018 in our example) that is a jump to another location where the remainder of the ISR resides. The first instruction of the service routine should be PUSH PSW because when the interrupt occurs, there is no way of knowing the contents of the PSW. The processor may be in the middle of an arithmetic or decision making routine where the contents of the PSW are vital to the completion of the routine. The next block indicates that all registers used by the ISR should also be saved and for the same reason. Registers not used by the ISR need not be saved.

The block labeled PROVIDE SERVICE represents the sequence of instructions that is the service routine itself. The registers and PSW are then restored. The next block is required so that succeeding interrupts can occur. If, during the execution of the service routine, a second interrupt is requested, it will be ignored until INTE is enabled. Therefore, in this exam-

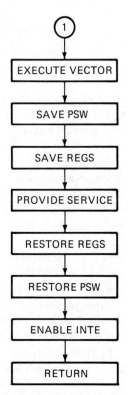

Figure 11-4. Flow diagram for a typical interrupt service routine (ISR).

ple, a second interrupt may occur immediately after the EI instruction (Enable Interrupt) and just before the return. It is possible to allow interrupts during the execution of a service routine by executing the EI instruction earlier in the routine. However, consideration should be given to the volatility of data and to the relative importance of the two routines.

Figure 11-5 shows the source listing of this ISR. The purpose of this routine shall be to input data (an ASCII character) from a video terminal, echo it, and store it in a memory buffer. If the character is a "control C," it indicates that the last character has been entered, and a jump is executed to another routine where something is done with the data stored in the memory buffer. All the initialization for this routine, including enabling the interrupt, must be done in the main program. Because RST 3 is used for this interrupt (at location 0018), there should be a jump instruction to location ISR0. This jump instruction is sometimes called a vector because program execution goes from the main program to the vector address (location 0018), then to the ISR ("vectors" to ISR0).

The first two instructions of the ISR save the PSW and the H and L register pair. No other registers are used in the routine. Next, the H and L

```
ISRØ:   PUSH    PSW         ;Save Acc and Flag
        PUSH    H           ;
        LHLD    PTR         ;Get current buffer adr
        IN      Ø           ;Input character
        OUT     1           ;Echo it
        MOV     M,A         ;Store it
        CPI     3           ;Is it a control C? Then all
        JZ      DOIT        ;Characters have been entered
        INX     H           ;Increment pointer
        SHLD    PTR         ;Save next buffer adr
        POP     H           ;Restore registers
        POP     PSW         ;
        EI                  ;Enable interrupt and
        RET                 ;return to main program

PRT:    DS      2           ;Reserved for buffer adr
BUFF:   DS      5ØH         ;Eighty locations for buffer
```

Figure 11-5. Interrupt service routine (ISR) source listing.

pair are loaded with the current address of the buffer. Notice that this is not necessarily the first address of the buffer but is the address where the byte to be inputted will be stored. Each time an interrupt occurs, this address is incremented. The next two instructions input and echo one character. There is no need to test for a ready bit because if there was not a character ready to be inputted, an interrupt would not have taken place. Of course, it is only assumed that the terminal is ready to print the next character.

Next, the CPI 3 instruction tests to see if the character just inputted is a "control C." If so, a jump to another routine is executed. Although this routine (DOIT) is not shown, it must end by restoring the registers, enabling the interrupt, and executing the RET instruction. It probably will reinitialize PTR with the first address of the buffer (BUFF).

The MOV M,A instruction stores the character in the memory buffer. The H and L pair are then incremented (INX H) and stored in a location called PTR (SHLD PTR). PTR now contains the address where data will be stored after the next interrupt. The registers are restored (POP H and POP PSW), interrupt is enabled (EI), and execution returns to the main program (RET).

Only one character is inputted with each interrupt. One may be concerned about the number of instructions required. However, it is better to think in terms of time. Consider program control I/O. A large percentage of time is wasted testing for ready bits. As was indicated earlier, 833 μs are required to input or output one character at 1200 baud. This ISR requires 46.7 μs to execute if the 8085A's clock frequency is 3 MHz. In addition, the RST instruction cycle and the vector instruction cycle add another 7.3 μs making a total of 54 μs. This leaves 779 μs for the processor to execute other routines before the same interrupt can occur again.

11.2 THE 8085A HARDWIRED INTERRUPTS

The interrupts using RST 0 through RST 7 require the implementation of a special port to handle these interrupts. This port is called an interrupt controller. The 8085A has a set of interrupts that require no additional hardware. These are: RST 5.5, RST 6.5, RST 7.5, and TRAP. These are not instructions but inputs to the 8085A that cause it to initiate an interrupt sequence as follows:

1.   Disable interrupt
2.   Push the contents of the PC (return address)
3.   Execute the instruction at the vector address

The vector addresses and the interrupts are listed in Table 11–2.

Table 11–2.   Vector Addresses and Interrupts

Interrupt	Vector address
TRAP	24H
RST 7.5	3CH
RST 6.5	34H
RST 5.5	2CH

11.2.1   Mask Register

RST 5.5, RST 6.5, and RST 7.5 interrupts are maskable. That is, the interrupts can be individually disabled by setting bits in the MASK register. This register is an integral part of the 8085A. An instruction, SIM, is used to set or clear bits in the mask. Another instruction, RIM, is used to read the contents of the mask. When a bit associated with a particular interrupt is set (masked), the interrupt will not be recognized by the processor. The RST 5.5, RST 6.5, and RST 7.5 inputs are affected by the EI and DI instructions in the same manner as the INTR input is affected. The TRAP input, however, cannot be masked, nor can it be disabled. Therefore, TRAP has the highest priority of all interrupts. This input is usually used by the system to cause an interrupt when some system failure or error exists. Its ISR may print an error message, execute a diagnostic routine, or simply halt.

The RST 7.5 interrupt differs from RST 5.5 and RST 6.5 interrupts in that its service request flip-flop is edge-triggered and sets on the rising edge of the RST 7.5 input. It is reset whenever the RST 7.5 interrupt is honored, by the SIM instruction or by activating the system RESET line. The RST 6.5 and 5.5 inputs are levels that are sensed by the processor in the same manner as the INTR signal is sensed. This means that service request flip-flops (usually part of the input or output ports) are required. These flip-flops are cleared by executing the IN or OUT instructions.

11.2.2 Interrupt Mask

The interrupt mask contains only three bits: one each for the RST 7.5, 6.5, and 5.5 interrupts. Figure 11–6 diagrams the contents of the A register prior to executing the SIM instruction. Bits 0, 1, and 2 are associated with 5.5, 6.5, and 7.5 masks respectively. Bit 3 (mask set enable) must equal 1 in order to change the mask. The use of bit 3 allows the SIM instruction to be used for other purposes without changing the mask. The purpose of bit 4 is to reset the RST 7.5 service request flip-flop.

			RESET 7.5	MSE	7.5	6.5	5.5

Figure 11–6. Contents of the A register associated with setting the interrupt mask.

If the RST 5.5 interrupt is to be used in a program, the following instructions will mask the RST 7.5 and 6.5 interrupts and unmask RST 5.5.

```
MVI     A,0EH
SIM
```

Bit 0 equals 0, which unmasks the 5.5 interrupt. Bits 1 and 2 equal 1, which mask 6.5 and 7.5 interrupts. Bit 3 equals 1, which is required to change the mask.

Sometimes it is desirable to reset the RST 7.5 service request flip-flop under program control. This can be accomplished by the following:

```
MVI     A,10H
SIM
```

The value of bit 3 (mask set enable) can be either 1 or 0, depending on whether we want to change the mask.

After the execution of the RIM instruction, existing information relative to the interrupts is transferred to the A register. The contents of the A register is as shown in Figure 11–7. Bits 0, 1, and 2 indicate the value of the masks. Bit 3 indicates the value of the interrupt enable flip-flop (INTE). Bits 4, 5, and 6 indicate the level of the RST 5.5 and 6.5 inputs while bit 6 indicates the state of the RST 7.5 service request flip-flop. The content of bit 7 will be discussed later.

i7.5	i6.5	i5.5	iE	M7.5	M6.5	M5.5

Figure 11–7. Contents of the A register associated with reading interrupt mask.

Perhaps the best way to show the use of the mask is by example. Let's implement an output port for our system that will interface a video terminal's printer. Figure 11–8 shows such a port. It uses an INTEL 8212 8-bit input or output port. A data sheet for the 8212 appears in Appendix C. This chip contains a service request flip-flop that is set by strobing the STB input of the 8212. This activates the $\overline{\text{INT}}$ output, which in turn activates the RST 6.5 to the 8085A. The 8212 uses three-state outputs. However, for this application, the mode (MD) input is held HIGH, causing the outputs to remain enabled. One device select input, DS2, is activated by an address decoder as shown in Figure 11–9. You will notice that BIO/$\overline{\text{M}}$ is included in the decode, assuring that only port addresses are decoded by this circuit.

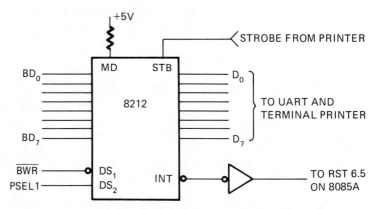

Figure 11–8. Interrupting output port.

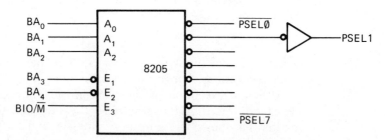

Figure 11–9. Port address decoder.

The other device select input, $\overline{\text{DS1}}$, is activated by the control signal $\overline{\text{BWR}}$. The service request flip-flop is reset when $\overline{\text{DS1}}$ and DS2 are active. Keep in mind that these signals are all available from our bus driver circuit discussed earlier.

When the instruction OUT 1 is executed, the following occurs:

1.   DS2 is activated by the output of the port address decoder.

2. $\overline{\text{DS1}}$ is activated by the control signal $\overline{\text{BWR}}$.

3. Data is latched into the 8212.

4. The printer takes the data.

5. When the printer is ready for more data, it strobes the STB input of the 8212.

6. This sequence causes the service request flip-flop to set and RST 6.5 to become active.

11.2.3 Interrupt Service Routine

Let's now consider the interrupt service routine (ISR) for printing the contents of a buffer. First, consider that if the printer is ready for new data it will interrupt the processor by strobing STB of the 8212. This will occur whether there is data to be printed or not. Leaving the RST 6.5 interrupt masked will prevent the interrupt until there is data to be printed. At that point, the main program unmasks the RST 6.5 interrupt and a series of interrupts will occur until all the data is printed. It is the responsibility of the ISR to mask the RST 6.5 interrupt when all the data has been printed. It is normal practice to terminate strings of ASCII characters in memory with a special character such as a "control C" or a null byte. The ISR can test each character being outputted and mask the RST 6.5 interrupt when this special character is detected. As a result, no more interrupts from the printer will be honored until the main program unmasks the interrupt again.

The following sequence of instructions in the main program will initialize the ISR to print the contents of a memory buffer:

```
LHLD    BUFF        ;initialize the ISR with
SHLD    PTR         ;the first address of the buffer
RIM                 ;get the current mask
ANI     5           ;unmask only RST 6.5
ORI     8           ;mask set enable
SIM                 ;set new mask
```

The first two instructions initialize a pointer buffer in the ISR. This is the first address of data to be printed. The RIM instruction reads the interrupt mask. Notice that the ANI 5 instruction clears all bits except bits 2 and 0, which represent the 7.5 and 5.5 masks respectively. When we unmask RST 6.5 we do not want to change the other two masks! The ORI 8 instruction sets bit 3, which is required by the SIM instruction to change the contents of the interrupt mask. At this point, the main program continues execution until an interrupt occurs.

Figure 11–10 is a source listing of the ISR. Notice that it takes the same general form as described in Figure 11–4. First, the registers used by the ISR are saved. Next, the H and L register pair are loaded with the current pointer address, a character is read from memory, the pointer is in-

```
ISR65:    PUSH    PSW       ;save registers
          PUSH    H         ;
          LHLD    PPTR      ;initialize current pointer address
          MOV     A,M       ;get character
          INX     H         ;increment pointer
          OUT     1         ;output character
          ORA     A         ;null character?
          JNZ     NOMSK     ;no, do not mask
          RIM               ;yes, get interrupt mask
          ANI     5         ;
          ORA     ØAH       ;and set 6.5 mask
          SIM               ;
NOMSK:    SHLD    PPTR      ;save current pointer address
          POP     H         ;restore registers
          POP     PSW       ;
          EI                ;enable interrupt
          RET               ;and return to main program
PPTR:     DS      2         ;location for pointer address
```

Figure 11-10. ISR for printing contents of memory buffer.

cremented, and the character is outputted. The ORA A instruction results in no change to the data in the A register. However, the flags are affected according to the contents of the A register. If a null character (00) is encountered, the Z flag is set; if not, it will be cleared. If the Z flag is set, it indicates that all of the characters in the buffer have been outputted and the 6.5 mask must be set. This is accomplished by reading the interrupt mask (RIM), saving the current mask values (ANI 5), and setting the 6.5 mask (ORA 0AH and SIM).

If a null character was not detected, a jump is executed over the above instructions to the location labeled NOMSK. In either case, the current pointer address is saved (SHLD PTR), the registers are restored (POP H and POP PSW), the interrupt is reenabled (EI), and execution is returned to the main program (RET).

Using this technique for printing data provides the most efficient use of the processor.

Questions

1. What is the purpose of INTR? Where is this signal generated? How long will the signal last?
2. What is the vector address of the RST 4 instruction?
3. What is the vector address of the RST 6.5 instruction?
4. What is the difference between RST 6 and an RST 6.5?
5. What is the difference between RST 5.5 and RST 7.5?
6. When is INTR sampled?
7. List the interrupts in order of priority.

8. Referring to the INTE flip-flop:
   a) What is its purpose?
   b) How is it set?
   c) How is it cleared?
   d) Where is it located?

9. What conditions must be met in order to go into an INA cycle?

10. When an INA cycle is entered:
    a) Where does the next instruction come from?
    b) What happens to the contents of the PC?

11. When entering an interrupt service routine, what should the first instruction be?

12. When an RST 5.5 interrupt occurs, what is the sequence of events that occur?

13. What is the purpose of the MASK register?

14. What instruction is used to set or clear bits in the mask?

15. Which bit in the mask register is used with the RST 6.5 interrupt?

16. Which bit in the mask register is used to set or clear the RST 7.5 service request flip-flop?

17. List the ways RST 7.5 can be reset.

18. In the 8212, what are the active levels of DS1 and DS2?

8085A Special Devices

The 8085A has a low driving capability; this requires our microcomputer system in Chapter 9 to use electrical buffering (see Figure 9–6). Some small systems dedicated to a particular job may use devices specially made to interface directly with the 8085A, thus using a minimum number of interconnections so that an entire system can be implemented on a single circuit board. The 8155, 8185, and 8355 are three such devices and are discussed in this chapter. The 8085A has sufficient driving capability for such systems providing that the bus is physically short, minimizing capacitive loading. In this chapter we will implement the hardware for such a system.

12.1   THE   8185

The 8185 is a 1024 × 8 static RAM. Its logic symbol is found in Figure 12–1; its data sheet can be found in Appendix C. Because 1 K bytes of address are used, ten address lines are required: $2^{10} = 1024$.

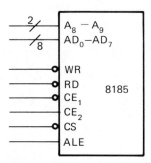

Figure 12–1. Logic symbol for an 8185 1 K static RAM.

Recall that the low eight bits of address and data are multiplexed on the same eight lines. The 8185 takes advantage of this characteristic by latching the low eight bits of address internally during T_1. Then during the T_2 and T_3, it uses the same eight lines for data. The 8185 uses the ALE input to latch these eight bits of address. A_8 and A_9 with these eight lines are used for the ten bits of address.

Two inputs, $\overline{RD}$ and $\overline{WR}$, control the read and write functions of the 8185. One-chip select $(\overline{CS})$ and two chip enable $(\overline{CE1}$ and CE2) facilitate decoding. The status of $\overline{CE1}$ and CE2 as well as address lines A_8 and A_9 are latched internally with ALE. All functions of the 8185 are disabled until $\overline{CS}$ becomes active. Another feature of the 8185 is that it can be placed in a low power state when it is not selected. If it is simply storing data and is not selected for a read or write operation, it draws only 25 mA. When it is selected, it is powered up and draws 100 mA.

Figure 12–2 shows the 8185 connected to the 8085A. Notice that a minimum number of connections are made between the two devices. $\overline{CS}$, $\overline{CE}_1$, and CE_2 must all be active for the 8185 to function. Unless all three lines are needed for decoding, one or two of the lines would be permanently enabled by tying them HIGH or LOW, depending on their active levels.

12.2   THE   8355

Another device that uses the multiplex characteristic of the 8085 is the 8355 ROM with I/O (Appendix C). This device combines the functions of read only memory and I/O ports. As shown in the block diagram in Figure 12–3, the 8355 contains 2 K bytes of ROM and two I/O ports. Notice on the block diagram that there are two Data Direction Registers,

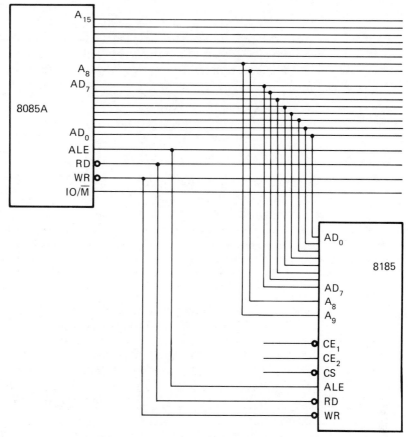

Figure 12–2. 8185 connected to the 8085A.

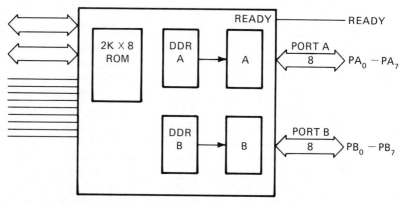

Figure 12–3. Block diagram of the 8355 2 K ROM with I/O.

identified as DDR A and DDR B. They are addressed as ports XXXXXX-10B and XXXXXX11B. The characteristics of the ports are programmable. The device uses three-state drivers to the bus, and all signals are compatible with the 8085, which simplifies the task of interfacing.

The port addresses are selected by the two least significant bits of address. They are as follows:

XXXXXX00B	Port A
XXXXXX01B	Port B
XXXXXX10B	DDR A
XXXXXX11B	DDR B

Data may be set in a data direction register (DDR) by the OUT instruction. Each bit in the DDR programs the direction of data for the corresponding bit in the port. A one bit in the DDR causes the corresponding bit position to be used for output. A zero bit in the DDR causes the corresponding bit position to be used for input. For example, the following instructions

MVI	A,7
OUT	2

cause port A to be programmed so that the three LSBs are used for output and the five MSBs are used for input. The DDRs are cleared by activating the RESET line.

The values of the signals: AD_0–AD_7, A_8–A_{10}, CE_2, $\overline{CE_1}$, and $IO/\overline{M}$ are all latched into the 8355 on the trailing edge of ALE. If CE_2 and $\overline{CE_1}$ are both active during ALE, the device can be accessed. If not, the device is not selected and its outputs, AD_0–AD_7 and READY, remain in the high impedance state.

Assuming that the device has been selected, the ROM function of the device is active when $\overline{IOW}$ and $\overline{IOR}$ are both HIGH and $IO/\overline{M}$ is LOW during ALE. The contents of the address that was latched during ALE (AD_0–AD_7, A_8–A_{10}) is asserted on the AD_0–AD_7 lines when $\overline{RD}$ becomes active.

The two-chip enable inputs (CE_2, $\overline{CE_1}$) are activated to select that particular memory page where the ROM is to exist.

Data is outputted to the selected port by activating $\overline{IOW}$. In this case, the level of $IO/\overline{M}$ has no meaning. Therefore, it is possible to connect the $\overline{IOW}$ input of the 8355 to the $\overline{WR}$ line of the 8085. However, consideration should be given to the instructions used. If an instruction is executed that writes to the 2 K block of ROM in this device (which is not logical), data will be written to a port or a DDR.

Data may be inputted from the selected port by using either $\overline{RD}$ or $\overline{IOR}$. If $\overline{RD}$ is used, then $IO/\overline{M}$ must be HIGH. However, if $\overline{IOR}$ is used, the level of $IO/\overline{M}$ does not matter. This feature can allow the ports to be addresses outside of the range of the ROM addresses. Further decoding can even allow the ports to be memory mapped. You will recall that LIMP used memory mapped I/O.

The ROM in the 8355 is mask programmable; that is, programming is part of the fabrication process. Therefore, the program must be supplied when the device is ordered. Another device, the 8755, contains an erasable and electrically reprogrammable ROM (EPROM). This device is otherwise similar to the 8355. A data sheet for the 8755 appears in Appendix C.

Figure 12-4 shows the 8355 connected to the 8085A. Notice that $\overline{\text{IOW}}$ connects to the $\overline{\text{WR}}$ control line of the 8085A. This line is activated only when outputting data to one of its ports.

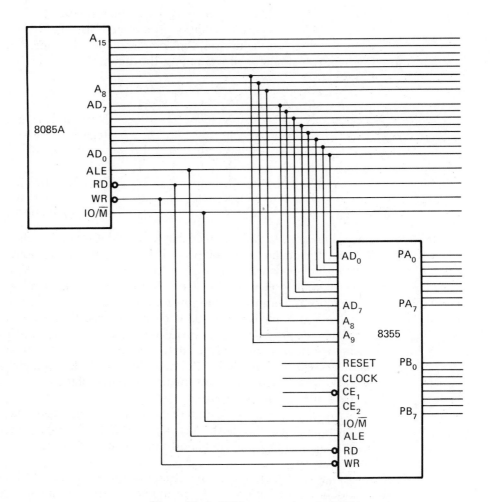

Figure 12-4. 8355 connected to the 8085A.

12.3 THE 8155

Another device that interfaces directly with the 8085A is the 8155. A block diagram appears in Figure 12–5; its data sheet can be found in Appendix C. The 8155 contains the following features:

1. Two ports that can be programmed for either input or output

2. One 6-bit port that can be programmed in a number of ways including interrupt handshaking for the other two ports

3. 256 bytes of RAM

4. A programmable counter/timer

The device has eight address lines $(A_0–A_7)$, which are used to select each of the 256 RAM locations. In addition, the three LSBs $(A_0–A_2)$, are used to select the three port addresses, the command and status register, and the two registers used for programming the timer. These addresses are as follows:

A_7	A_6	A_5	A_4	A_3	A_2	A_1	A_0	
X	X	X	X	X	0	0	0	Command and Status Register
X	X	X	X	X	0	0	1	I/O Port A
X	X	X	X	X	0	1	0	I/O Port B
X	X	X	X	X	0	1	1	Control or I/O Port C
X	X	X	X	X	1	0	0	LSBs of Timer Count
X	X	X	X	X	1	0	1	MSBs of Timer Count

The values of $AD_0–AD_7$, chip enable $(\overline{CE})$, and IO/$\overline{M}$ are latched into the 8155 on the trailing edge of ALE. If $\overline{CE}$ and IO/$\overline{M}$ are both LOW, a memory address is selected. If $\overline{CE}$ is LOW and IO/$\overline{M}$ is HIGH, an I/O or timer function is selected. The signals $\overline{RD}$ and $\overline{WR}$ control reads and writes for memory and inputs and outputs for the ports.

Ports A, B, and C may be used in various ways, depending on how the 8155 has been programmed. The 8155 is programmed by outputting a command byte to the command and status register. The command and status register is selected if IO/$\overline{M}$ is HIGH and the three LSBs equal 000. Ports A, B, and C are selected in the same manner except that the three LSBs equal 001, 010, and 011 respectively.

Notice in the block diagram that each of the three ports may be used as either input or output ports. Although port C is only a 6-bit port, it can be programmed to provide the handshaking (control and status signals) for ports A and B.

Figure 12–6 shows the bit structure for the command byte. Bit 0 defines how port A is used. A 0 causes port A to become an input port; a 1 causes it to become an output port. Bit 1 is used in the same way to define

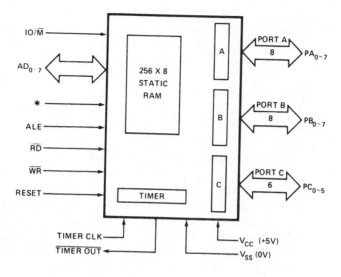

*: 8155/8155-2 = $\overline{CE}$, 8156/8156-2 = CE

Figure 12–5. Block diagram of the 8155 1/4 K RAM with I/O ports and timer. (Courtesy of INTEL Corp.)

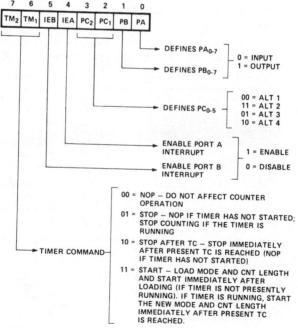

Figure 12–6. Command register bit assignment. (Courtesy of INTEL Corp.)

port B. Bits 2 and 3 define the use of port C. Four alternative options are provided. Alternative 1 is programmed when bits 2 and 3 both equal 0. This causes port C to become a 6-bit input port. Alternative 2 occurs when bits 2 and 3 both equal 1 and port C becomes a 6-bit output port. Alternative 3 is programmed when bit 2 equals 1 and bit 3 equals 0. This causes the three LSBs of port C to take on special meaning. They become the interrupt control or program control handshaking signals for port A. Bit 0 of port C becomes an output to be used to interrupt the processor. It is called port A interrupt request (A INTR). Bit 1 is an output that can be used as a ready bit for port A. It is called port A buffer full (A BF). Bit 2 is an input to the 8155 causing data to be strobed into port A if port A has been programmed for input. If port A has been programmed for output, bit 2 is used to acknowledge that the data has been received by the peripheral and is requesting new data. It is active LOW and is called port A strobe ($\overline{\text{A STB}}$). The three MSBs of port C, for alternative 3, are used for output, possibly as control bits. The fourth alternative is the same as alternative 3, except that bits 3, 4, and 5 are used in the same manner for port B as bits 0, 1, and 2 are used for port A. Figure 12–7 is a diagram showing how the 8155 may be used when it is programmed with alternative 4. Notice that port A has been programmed for input and port B has been programmed for output. The four LSBs of the command byte equaled 1010 when the 8155 was programmed. Bit 3 equals 1 and bit 2 equals 0, which selects alternative 4. Bit 1 equals 1, which programs port B for output while bit 0 equals 0, which programs port A for input.

When alternative 4 is used, the 8155 uses internal circuits to provide the functions of a service request flip-flop and an enable interrupt flip-flop for each of the two ports. In addition, data is latched in a buffer when input-

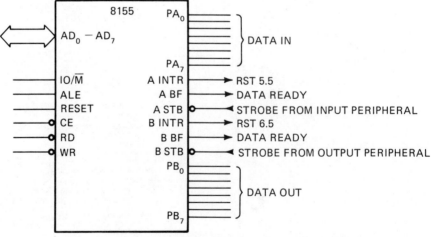

Figure 12–7. 8155 programmed for alternative 4. Command register contains 00111010.

ting or outputting. For example, when port A is used for input, data is gated into the buffer (input buffer) and the service request flip-flop is set. This is accomplished when the peripheral activates the $\overline{\text{A STB}}$ input. If port A's interrupt enable flip-flop is set, then A INTR is issued to the processor, causing an interrupt. The service request flip-flop is then cleared when the processor inputs the data from the input buffer.

Now, let's consider an example where port B is used as an output port and the 8155 has been programmed for alternative 4. We will start with the processor outputting data to the port. Data is gated into the output buffer with the $\overline{\text{WR}}$ control signal. This causes the B buffer full signal (B BF) to become active, which signals the peripheral that data is ready to take. After the peripheral takes the data, it strobes the $\overline{\text{B STB}}$ input, causing the interrupt service flip-flop to set, which activates the B INTR line if the enable flip-flop is set. The processor responds to the interrupt by outputting the next byte of data, which in turn causes the service request flip-flop to be reset.

The interrupts for ports A and B are set with the command byte that is stored in the command register. If bit 4 of the command register equals 1, the interrupt for port A is enabled. If the bit equals 0, the interrupt is disabled. Bit 5 of the command register is used in the same way for enabling or disabling port B's interrupt. The contents of the command register are diagrammed in Figure 12–8.

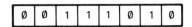

Figure 12–8. Contents of command register for alternative 4.

The 8155 also contains a status register. Its address is the same as the command register (I/O address XXXXX000B); therefore, it is a read-only register. It contains seven flip-flops, which are diagrammed in Figure 12–8. This register may be polled at any time to indicate the status of the 8155. For example, bits 1 (A BF—A Buffer Full) and 4 (B BF—B Buffer Full) may be used as ready bits when only a single interrupt has been implemented for the two service routines that are required. The ISR simply polls these two bits to determine which routine is to be used.

12.3.1   8155 Timer

The 8155 includes a timer that may be used for controlling various events. The timer is programmed by loading the count length register with a 14-bit binary number representing the length of the desired count as shown in Figure 12–9. When the timer is started, the number in the count length register is loaded into another register, which is decremented with each input (TIMER IN). The output (TIMER OUT) is a function of the mode of operation. See Figure 12–10. The bits are loaded into the count

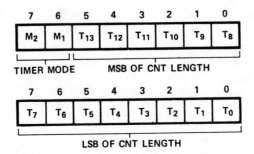

Figure 12-9. Timer format.

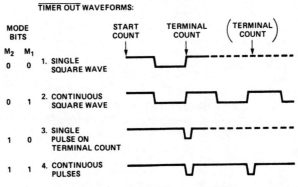

Figure 12-10. Timer modes.

length register one byte at a time. The address of the low byte is XXXXX-100B and XXXXX101B for the high byte. The two MSBs of the high byte, M_1 and M_2, set the mode as follows:

M_2	M_1	
0	0	Outputs a LOW during second half of count
0	1	Outputs a square wave equaling the count length programmed with automatic reload at terminal count
1	0	Outputs a single pulse when the terminal count is reached
1	1	Outputs a single pulse each time the terminal count is reached with automatic reload

The counter is controlled by bits 6 and 7 of the command byte. There are four commands to choose from as follows:

C_7	C_6	
0	0	NOP - Does not affect the counter's operation
0	1	STOP - Causes the timer to stop if it is running
1	0	STOP AFTER TC - Stop immediately when terminal count is reached
1	1	START - Load mode and count length from the count length register and start immediately. If timer is running, start the new mode and count length immediately after present terminal count is reached

The principal purpose of the timer is that of a square-wave timer or frequency divider. To achieve this, it decrements by two twice while completing one cycle. If the LSB equals 1, it repeats the process. Therefore, special care must be given for determining the initial count.

12.4 8085A SERIAL I/O

The 8085A has two data lines that are used with devices such as a VDT (Video Data Terminal). The first line (pin 4 of the 8085A) is called SOD, Serial Output Data. It is used to output data, one bit at a time, by the use of the SIM (Set Interrupt Mask) instruction. The second line (pin 5), is called SID, Serial Input Data. It is used to input data, one bit at a time, using the RIM (Read Interrupt Mask) instruction.

Data transmitted to video terminals or printers is in the form of an interchange code such as ASCII (American Standard Code for Information Interchange), which was discussed in Chapter 2. This data is usually communicated in serial. Bits of data are transmitted in sequence, one bit at a time. First, a start bit is transmitted for a precise period of time called a Bit Time. Then the least significant bit is transmitted for the same period. This is followed by the next significant bit and continued until all eight bits of the byte are transmitted. Finally, a stop bit is transmitted.

The rate at which the start, data, and stop bits are transmitted is called *baud*. For example, if each bit time is 833 μs, the baud is 1200. Since ten bits are required (one start, eight data, and one stop), 120 characters per second are transmitted when 1200 baud is used.

For some terminals, particularly the older mechanical types, two stop bits are required. This additional time allows the mechanical system to settle before it is required to receive the next character. Therefore, eleven bit times are required per character. An example would be 110 baud, which is equal to 10 characters per second.

Figure 12–11 shows the waveform produced when the ASCII character "A" is transmitted. The waveform would appear at the SOD output of the 8085A. A similar waveform would appear at the SID input when data is being received by the 8085A. First, notice that the start bit is LOW level. The start bit always follows an idle condition (no characters being transmitted or received) or a stop bit. Each of these two conditions produce a HIGH level on the signal line. Following the start bit, the least significant bit is transmitted, then the next significant bit, and so on until the most significant bit, bit 7 is transmitted. The signal is HIGH when a 1 is transmitted and LOW when a 0 is transmitted. Transmission of the character is terminated when the stop bit is transmitted.

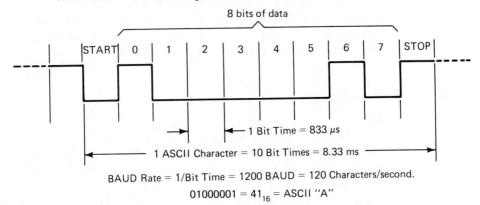

BAUD Rate = 1/Bit Time = 1200 BAUD = 120 Characters/second.

01000001 = 41_{16} = ASCII "A"

Figure 12–11. Waveform at the SOD output of the 8085A representing the letter "A."

When sending ASCII data in serial, the bits are transmitted asynchronously (that is, no synchronizing pulses are used). Therefore, some method must be devised that allows the receiver to distinguish one bit from another. The method is flowcharted in Figure 12–12 and is described below.

The receiver first detects the start bit. When the receiver has completed the reception of the previous character, it senses the beginning of a start bit when the line goes LOW again. Next, after detecting the start bit, the receiver waits one bit time and takes the LSB. It waits another bit time and takes the next significant bit. This procedure continues until all bits are received. The receiver does not take the stop bit as data. It is only transmitted so that the receiver can accurately detect the next start bit.

Figure 12–13 shows how the 8085A may be interfaced to a VDT. The signals are compatible with RS–232C standards. These standards require that a logical 1 be represented by a negative voltage level between − 3 volts and − 12 volts and that a logical 0 be represented by a positive voltage level between + 3 volts and + 12 volts. The waveforms representing the ASCII character "A" are shown in Figure 12–14. Two special devices, the

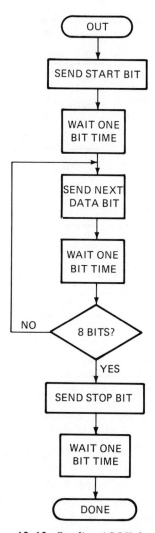

Figure 12–12. Sending ASCII data in serial.

MC1489 line receiver and the MC1488 line transmitter, are used for this purpose. The data sheets for these devices appear in Appendix C. The MC1488 requires two supplies: +15 and −15 volts.

12.4.1   Serial Output Routine for the 8085A

The SIM instruction causes the datum in bit position 7 of the A register to be transferred to the SOD output if bit 6 of the A register equals 1. The SOD output is latched; therefore, the output level remains until the next SIM instruction is executed.

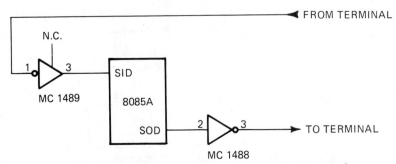

Figure 12-13. Interfacing the 8085A to a video data terminal.

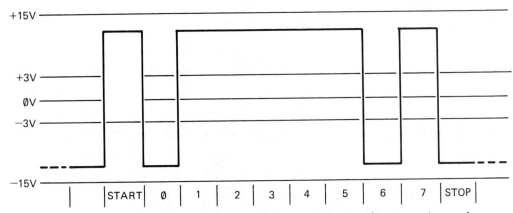

Figure 12-14. RS232 compatible signal between line transmitter and
line receiver for the ASCII letter "A."

Figure 12-15 is a flow diagram showing one possible method of out-putting data in serial using the SIM instruction. It represents the subroutine labeled OUT, shown in the assembly listing in Figure 12-16. The routine saves all registers, including the A register that contains the ASCII character to be outputted. One important requirement of the routine is that bit 7 of the ASCII character must equal 0 because this bit is also used as a start bit. Sometimes bit 7 is used as a parity bit, but this routine does not allow for parity.

The first block of the flowchart indicates that the registers used in the routine are saved. This is accomplished by using the PUSH instructions. Next, the C register is initialized with the number 9. This is a loop counter that counts the start bit and the eight data bits to be outputted. The stop bit is transmitted separately.

Next, let's consider the loop in the routine. The first instruction, RRC, rotates the bit in the LSB position to position 7 so that it becomes the next bit to be outputted. This bit pattern is saved (MOV B,A) in the B register to be used later. The ANI 80H instruction strips all bits except bit 7

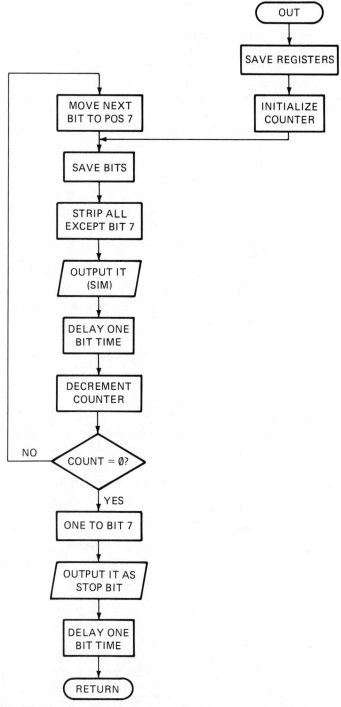

Figure 12-15. Flow diagram for outputting data in serial using the SIM
instruction.

from the A register. This is done so that the SIM instruction will not affect other functions of the Interrupt Mask register. Next, bit 6 is set to equal 1 with the ORI 40H instruction, which is required to enable the SOD function.

The SIM instruction outputs the bit to the SOD latch. The output level produced remains until the next SIM instruction is executed. Therefore, the bit time can be accurately established by executing the appropriate delay after the execution of each SIM instruction. A delay subroutine is used for this purpose.

The bits that were previously saved in the B register are now returned to the A register (MOV A,B). Next, the C register is decremented to determine if all the bits have been transmitted. If not, the loop is reentered by executing the JNZ instruction.

Finally, the stop bit is transmitted by setting bit 6 and bit 7 in the A register (MVI A,0C0H), outputting it (SIM), and calling the delay subroutine again. Notice that the SOD output will remain HIGH if no more characters are immediately outputted. This will allow the receiver to detect the next start bit when a character is outputted again. The registers are then restored (POP), and execution returns to the calling program (RET).

How did the start bit get transmitted? The program loop was entered at the label GO. This is the address of the second instruction in the loop. Notice that initially the bits to be transmitted occupied their proper positions in the A register and that bit 7 equaled 0. By entering the loop after the rotate instruction, all data bits were saved and the 0 at bit position 7 was transmitted. This is also the last data bit to be transmitted because although ASCII uses only 7 bits, a full byte of data is transmitted.

12.4.2   Serial Input Routine for the 8085A

The RIM instruction causes the datum at the SID input of the 8085A to be transferred to bit position 7 of the A register. No other bits affect this function. Other bits from the Interrupt Mask, however, will also be transferred. These bits may be removed by executing a mask operation.

Figure 12–17 is a flow diagram showing one possible method of inputting data in serial using the RIM instruction. It represents the subroutine (IN) shown in the assembly listing in Figure 12–16.

This routine starts by saving the registers used in the routine. The PSW is not saved because new data will appear in the A register after the subroutine is executed. A buffer, the B register, is initialized to 0. The bits will be assembled in this register, one bit at a time, as they are received. A counter, the C register, is initialized to the number of data bits to be inputted—seven. The eighth bit, bit 7, will not be inputted because no parity is used; therefore, it will remain equal to 0.

```
 1                              TITLE    IO SUBROUTINES
 2                              ;subroutines for outputting and inputting data from/to V
 3
 4                 BTIM   EQU     39D              ;delay for bit time at 4800
 5                                                 ;T = 333
 6
 7                              ;output routine
 8     0000  F5      OUT:   PUSH    PSW              ;save character
 9     0001  C5             PUSH    B                ;save registers used
10     0002  D5             PUSH    D                ;
11     0003  0E 09          MVI     C,9              ;1 stop and 8 data bits
12     0005  C3 09 00       JMP     GO               ;output bit-7 = start bit
13     0008  0F      OLP:   RRC                      ;next bit to position 7
14     0009  47      GO:    MOV     B,A              ;save rest of bits
15     000A  E6 80          ANI     80H              ;strip other bits
16     000C  F6 40          ORI     40H              ;enable SOD
17     000E  30             SIM                      ;output bit
18     000F  CD 41 00       CALL    DELAY            ;wait one bit time
19     0012  78             MOV     A,B              ;get rest of bits
20     0013  0D             DCR     C                ;done?
21     0014  C2 08 00       JNZ     OLP              ;no - continue outputting bits
22     0017  3E C0          MVI     A,0C0H           ;output stop bit
23     0019  30             SIM                      ;
24     001A  CD 41 00       CALL    DELAY            ;
25     001D  D1             POP     D                ;restore registers
26     001E  C1             POP     B                ;
27     001F  F1             POP     PSW              ;restore character
28     0020  C9             RET                      ;return to calling program
29
30                              ;input routine
31     0021  C5      IN:    PUSH    B                ;save registers
32     0022  D5             PUSH    D                ;
33     0023  06 00          MVI     B,0              ;buffer for assembling byte
34     0025  0E 07          MVI     C,7              ;7 bits for ASCII
35     0027  20      SBIT:  RIM                      ;find start bit
36     0028  17             RAL                      ;is this it?
37     0029  D2 27 00       JNC     SBIT             ;no, try again
38     002C  16 13          MVI     D,BTIM/2         ;yes, wait for middle of period
39     002E  CD 43 00       CALL    DEL              ;one half bit time
40     0031  CD 41 00 DBIT: CALL    DELAY            ;wait one bit time for next bit
41     0034  20             RIM                      ;input next bit
42     0035  E6 80          ANI     80H              ;strip garbage
43     0037  B0             ORA     B                ;assemble bit in byte
44     0038  0F             RRC                      ;right one bit position
45     0039  47             MOV     B,A              ;and save partial byte
46     003A  0D             DCR     C                ;got all bits?
47     003B  C2 31 00       JNZ     DBIT             ;no, keep going
48     003E  D1             POP     D                ;restore registers
49     003F  C1             POP     B                ;
50     0040  C9             RET                      ;return to calling program
51
52                              ;delay subroutine
53     0041  16 27   DELAY: MVI     D,BTIM           ;initiate delay = 1 bit time
54     0043  15      DEL:   DCR     D                ;delay
55     0044  C2 43 00       JNZ     DEL              ;
56     0047  C9             RET                      ;return to calling program
57                          END
```

Figure 12-16. Assembly listing for serial I/O routines.

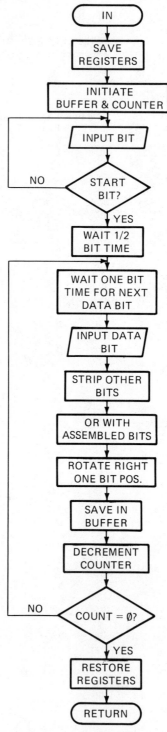

Figure 12–17. *Flow diagram for inputting data in serial using the RIM instruction.*

The next task of the routine is to find the start bit. Remember, the last bit transmitted was a stop bit that left the SID input HIGH. When the input goes LOW again, it must be the start bit. The program loop at address SBIT detects the start bit. The RIM instruction inputs the value of SID. Then the RAL instruction moves it to the carry flag where a JC SBIT instruction continues the procedure until the start bit is detected. At that time, a delay of one half of a bit time is executed. The purpose of this delay is to provide a reference to the middle of the start-bit-time. Therefore, after the next delay is executed, the RIM instruction will input the LSB of data precisely at the middle of its bit time. It is important to input bits in the middle of their bit times so that there will be no chance of spurious data due to the change of levels that occurs at the start and end of each bit time.

After the bit has been inputted, all other bits in the A register are stripped (ANI 80H). The bit is then assembled into the byte by ORing it with the contents of the B register (ORA B). This bit occupies the MSB position of the A register. The rotate instruction, RRC, moves all bits right one bit position before they are saved again in the B register (MOV B,A).

The DCR C and JNZ DBIT instructions cause the loop to be executed seven times. Seven loops cause the seven bits of the ASCII character to be inputted, assembled, and rotated to their appropriate positions in the byte.

The subroutine execution completes by restoring the registers that have been saved (POPs) and returning to the calling program (RET). Notice that the ASCII character just inputted appears in the A register.

12.4.3   Timing for Serial I/O

The subroutine, DELAY, was called from the IN and OUT subroutines and establishes the bit time and, therefore, the baud rate of the serial data. In the case of the OUT subroutine, the bit time is the time between the execution of one SIM instruction and the execution of the next. Conversely, in the IN subroutine, the bit time is the time between the execution of one RIM instruction and the execution of the next. Both bit times must be the same.

A delay of time is required to extend the time of the program loop to that required for a particular baud rate. The delay is accomplished by repeating the execution of the DCR D and the JNZ DEL instructions in the DELAY subroutine. The number of times that these two instructions are repeated in the program is called BTIM. This delay does not constitute all of the bit time. For example, in the OUT subroutine, part of the bit time is used by the execution of the program loop. The same is true for the IN subroutine.

The following is a discussion of how the number of loops, BTIM, in the DELAY subroutine is determined.

First, let's determine the number of states used by the execution of the respective program loops. Figure 12–18 shows each loop with the number of states indicated for each instruction. Notice that for the OUT loop there are 62 states and for the IN loop there are 55 states. It is desirable for both routines to have the same numbers of states. However, a difference of 7 states, or 2.3 μs, will probably make no difference in this example. If it did, a dummy instruction, like ORI 0, could be included in the IN loop. If this instruction were placed just before the DCR D instruction, it would not affect the program but would extend its execution time to equal the OUT loop.

	IN Loop:		States:		OUT Loop:		States:
DBIT:	CALL	DELAY	18	OLP:	RRC		4
	RIM		4		MOV	B,A	4
	ANI	80H	7		ANI	80H	7
	ORA	B	4		ORI	40H	7
	RRC		4		SIM		4
	MOV	B,A	4		CALL	DELAY	18
	DCR	C	4		MOV	A,B	4
	JNZ	DBIT	10		DCR	C	4
			55		JNZ	OLP	10
							62

DELAY:	MVI	D,BTIM	7	;executed once
DEL:	DCR	D	4	;executed BTIM times
	JNZ	DEL	10	;executed BTIM times
	RET		10	;executed once

Figure 12–18. Program loops including machine states.

If we choose a baud rate of 4800, the bit time equals one over 4800 or 208 μs. Suppose the 8085A has a clock frequency of 3 MHz. Then each state has a duration of 333 μs. Therefore, 625 states are required for one bit time. Notice that in the DELAY subroutine, two instructions are executed only once. If we add the number of states required for these two instructions, 17, to the number of states in the OUT loop, we have a total of 79. This leaves 546 states (625 − 79 = 546) that must be provided by the loop in DELAY. Each loop uses 14 states; therefore, 39 loops are required. You will notice in the program listing that BITIM has been equated to 39D.

12.5 SYSTEM USING 8085A SPECIAL DEVICES

The following is a discussion of a small stand-alone system for a dedicated application using 8085A special devices. The system can be fabricated on a single PC board and can be packaged in a small area wherever it is convenient for its application. The system is shown in Figure 12–19.

The system uses 4 K bytes of ROM for the operating system. An operating system is the collection of programs that are necessary to carry out the functions of the system's application. The ROM is contained in two 8355 devices; two 8755s could be used if EROMS are desirable.

The system also uses 2 K bytes of RAM, contained in two 8185s for temporary storage of data. The 8156 contains 256 bytes of RAM, which are normally used for the stack and small buffers. The 8156 is identical to the 8155 except that the chip select input is active HIGH.

The two 8355s provide four 8-bit ports that may be programmed as desired. A total of 32 lines for these two devices may be individually programmed for input or output. The 8156 is connected so that two ports are used with the RST 5.5 and 6.5 interrupts. These may also be programmed as desired for input or output. Serial I/O is also provided for communications with a video terminal.

12.5.1 Decoding Memory and Ports

Notice that a separate decoder is not used. Instead, decoding for device selection is accomplished with the CE and CS inputs and one 7402 at the devices themselves. The range of addresses for the first 8355 (ROM0) is 0000H through 07FFH. It is selected when A_{11}, A_{12}, and A_{13} are all LOW. A_{14} and A_{15} are not used in this system.

Remember, when the IN or OUT instructions are executed, the port address is duplicated on both the high and low bytes. Therefore, bits 5, 6, and 7 of the port address must each be 0. Bits 2, 3, and 4 may have any value. This means, for example, that port address 00H, 04H, 0CH, 10H, 14H, and 1CH will each select the A port of the first 8355 (ROM0). The programmer must be aware of this overlapping of port addresses. Therefore, definite addresses that do not select other devices must be used. Let's assume then that the first 8355 uses port addresses 00H, 01H, 02H, and 03H for port A, port B, DDR A, and DDR B respectively.

Notice that the second 8355 requires that bit 11 must be HIGH and that bits 12 and 13 must be LOW. This provides a memory address range of 0800H through 0FFFH and port addresses 08H, 09H, 0AH and 0BH. There may be memory address redundancy depending on the values of bits 14 and 15. However, if the programmer always uses addresses that cause bits 14 and 15 to equal 0, no problem will exist. Notice that for I/O, if bit 2 equals 0, one of the port addresses in the first 8355 is selected and if bit-2 equals 1, one of the port addresses in the second 8355 is selected.

RAM0 or RAM1 is selected if A_{12} is HIGH (CE) and A_{13} is LOW ($\overline{CS}$). A_{10} is used to determine which RAM device is selected. If A_{12} is HIGH, A_{13} is LOW, and A_{10} is LOW, the range of addresses is 1000H through 13FFH. If on the other hand, A_{10} is HIGH, the range of addresses is 1400H through 17FFH. The following may be helpful for understanding how memory is decoded:

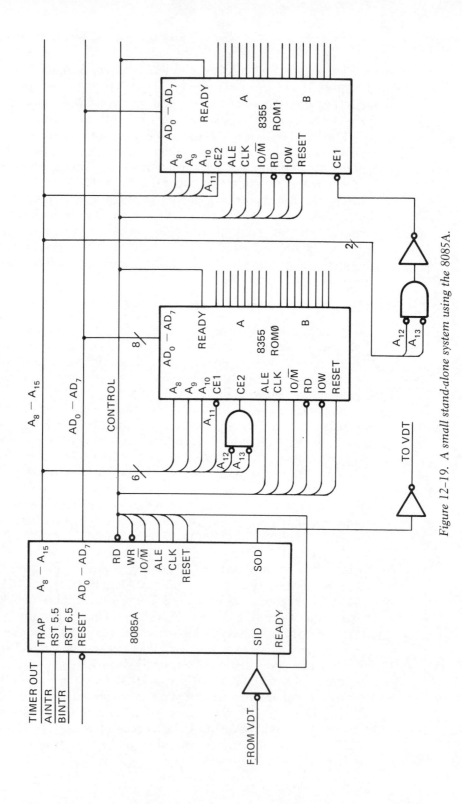

Figure 12–19. A small stand-alone system using the 8085A.

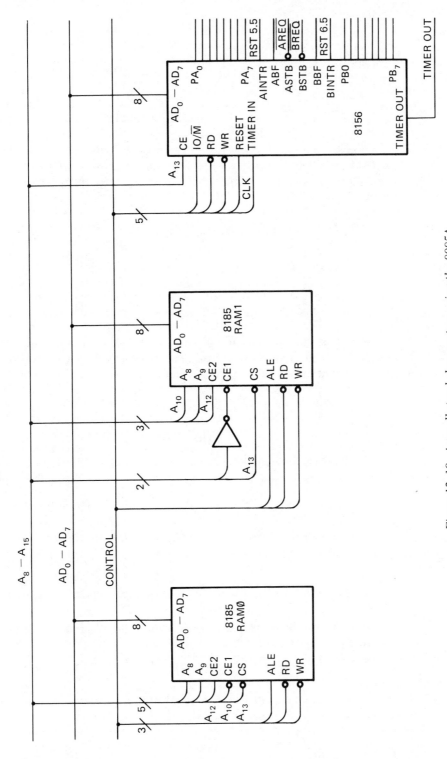

Figure 12-19. A small stand-alone system using the 8085A.

A_{11}	A_{10}	A_9	A_8	
0	0	X	X	ROM0
0	1	X	X	ROM1
1	X	0	X	RAM0
1	X	1	X	RAM1

The 8156 is selected whenever A_{13} equals 1. This will set the range of its RAM to 2000H through 20FFH. Be aware that there are many redundant addresses in this situation. The port and control registers are as follows:

Control and Status Register	=	20H
Port A	=	21H
Port B	=	22H
Port C	=	23H
Timer Low Count	=	24H
Timer High Count	=	25H

This is an example of a minimum hardware system that can be located exactly where it is needed. Its purpose is probably that of controlling various operations in other systems. It may be modified for almost any similar application.

Questions

1. When does the 8185 latch the low eight bits of address?
2. What control signal is used to latch the low eight bits of address?
3. What lines were chosen for chip enable and chip select of the 8185's in the system we implemented in Figure 12–19?
4. Why did we avoid using A_{11} as a CE or CS line for the 8185s?
5. Which of the CE and CS lines must be active in order for the 8185 to function?
6. What conditions must exist for RAM1 to be selected for a memory write?
7. What conditions must exist for ROM0 to be selected for a memory read?
8. What conditions must exist for ROM1 to be selected for a memory read?
9. What conditions must exist for RAM0 to be selected for a memory write?

10. In the 8355, what control line is used to select either memory or I/O operations?

11. During what time must $\overline{CE1}$ and CE2 be active if ROM1 is to be selected?

12. What is the range of addresses of ROM in our system?

13. What is the range of addresses of RAM in our system?

14. How would we output data through port A of the 8155?

15. How many I/O ports does our system have?

16. How is address line A_{13} used in our system?

17. In what way is $\overline{A\ STB}$ used in the 8155?

Chapter

13

The 6502 Microprocessor

When making comparisons between microprocessors, it is probably a good idea to consider their similarities rather than their differences. After all, they are basically the same; they all have an address bus, a data bus, and a control bus. Some of the differences are: the number of lines in a bus, the control signals, the active levels, the instruction set, I/O interrupts, and the modes used to address data. Therefore, after learning about one processor, understanding other processors should be easy.

13.1 THE 6502

The second processor we have selected to study is the 6502 made by MOS Technology, Inc., and by Synertek, Inc. We have chosen this processor because it is different from the 8085A and because it is widely used. The Apple II personal computer illustrated in Figure 13–1 is a well-known application of the 6502.

Figure 13–1. Apple II Personal Computer. (Courtesy Apple Computer)

Like the 8085A, the 6502 has sixteen address lines and an 8-bit bidirectional data bus. The 6502 has a minimal number of control lines (outputs), which are as follows:

ϕ_0	Phase 1 clock
ϕ_2	Phase 2 clock
$R/\overline{W}$	Read, NOT Write
SYNC	Occurs during opcode fetch cycle

Inputs to the 6502 are the following:

$\phi/0$	Crystal input
$\overline{RES}$	Reset

RDY	Ready
IRQ	Interrupt request
NMI	Non-maskable Interrupt
S.O.	Set Overflow

Pinouts of the 6502 are shown in Figure 13–2.

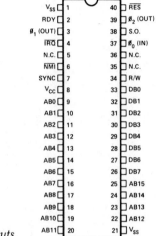

Figure 13–2. 6502 Pinouts.

Figure 13–3 shows a block diagram of the 6502. Notice that the diagram has two sections: the REGISTER SECTION and the CONTROL SECTION. The registers that are directly involved with the instruction register are:

Y	Index Y
X	Index X
S	Stack Pointer
A	Accumulator
PCL	Program Counter Low Byte
PCH	Program Counter High Byte

These are all 8-bit registers. You may have noticed that there are no general purpose registers. All arithmetic and logic operations are carried out using the accumulator (A) and a memory location.

13.2   ZERO PAGE ADDRESSING

For the 6502, when the high byte of the address equals 0, page zero is being addressed. Page zero has special meaning for the 6502. It usually contains small buffers or memory registers. A special mode of addressing, called

SY6500 INTERNAL ARCHITECTURE

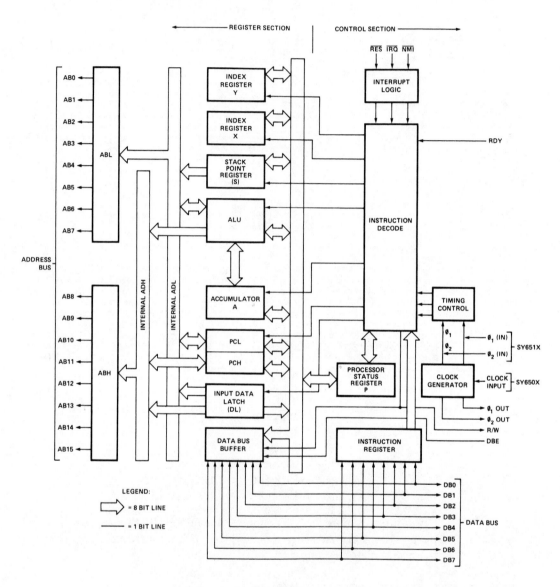

Figure 13–3. Block diagram of the 6502.

zero page addressing, allows 8-bit memory addresses for page zero. Therefore, 2-byte instructions are used for zero page addressing. Recall that the 8085A uses a number of GPRs. In the 6502, GPRs are not used; rather, addresses in page zero are used like GPRs.

Memory-mapped I/O is used for the 6502. It is possible to implement the I/O ports on page zero. Decoding I/O addresses will be discussed later.

One special situation occurs because the stack pointer is an 8-bit register. Whenever the processor addresses the stack, it asserts the contents of the stack pointer (S) as the low byte of the address onto the address bus. In addition, it asserts a 01 onto the high byte of the address bus. Therefore, the stack is created on page one.

13.3 ADDRESSING MODES

Perhaps the greatest difference between the 8085A and the 6502 concerns the addressing modes. When the 8085A addresses memory, it always does so by using a 16-bit absolute address, either directly or indirectly. This includes the immediate mode, where the PC points to the operand. The 6502, on the other hand, has many modes. They are specified either implicitly in the opcode or explicitly in the operand. The following is a list of the modes and the operand format used to specify each. The letters "a" or "d" each represent four bits of address or data.

Mode	Operand Format
Immediate	# dd
Absolute	aaaa
Zero Page	aa
Implied	
Indirect Absolute	(aaaa)
Absolute Indexed,X	aaaaX
Absolute Indexed,Y	aaaaY
Zero Page Indexed,X	aaX
Zero Page Indexed,Y	aaY
Indexed Indirect	(aaX)
Indirect Indexed	(aa)Y
Relative	aa or aaaa
Accumulator	A

This may seem like a lot of modes; however, there is a certain amount of redundancy in the list, depending on whether or not the zero page is used and if index register X or Y is used.

13.3.1   Immediate Mode

The immediate mode is the same as with the 8085A except that only one byte of data can be specified. The use of the # sign specifies the immediate mode, which seems to be a universal method. Recall that LIMP uses the # sign in the same manner.

13.3.2   Absolute Mode

The absolute mode is identical to the direct mode used by the 8085A. The second and third bytes of the instruction contain the address of the operand. As before, the low byte appears at the lower of the two addresses. Because a 16-bit address is specified in the operand, the assembler knows to use the absolute mode.

13.3.3   Zero Page Mode

The zero page mode is specified when the address can be equated to an 8-bit address. This mode is identical to the absolute mode except that the operand is in page zero. The assembler recognizes that the zero page mode is to be used because the address can be equated to an 8-bit number. Using this mode makes more efficient use of memory because only one byte is required for the address.

13.3.4   Implied Mode

Some instructions, like INY (INcrement the contents of the Y register) or SEC (SEt Carry flag) specify the operand in the opcode; therefore, no other operand is specified. In these instructions the mode is implied by the opcode.

13.3.5   Indirect Absolute Mode

Only the jump (JMP) instruction uses the indirect absolute mode. As with the absolute mode, this is a three-byte instruction. The second and third bytes of the instruction, which JMP also uses, contain an address where the low byte of the destination address is contained. The next address contains the address of the high byte of the destination address. This mode allows the programmer to have a table of addresses. Jumps may then be executed through the table.

With some other processors, this mode is called the deferred mode. Notice the use of the parens. They enclose an address, which means that this is not the address of the operand but is the address of the address of the operand. In this case, the operand is the destination of the jump. The use of the parens tends to be a universal method of specifying the indirect or deferred mode.

13.3.6 Absolute Indexed Mode

This mode is used in conjunction with the X and Y index registers. The effective address of the operand is determined by adding the contents of the index register to the address contained in the second and third byte of the instruction. This mode allows the programmer to create buffers where the index register contains the index or count value and the instruction contains the base address of the buffer. This is referred to as the "Absolute,X" or "Absolute,Y" modes.

Using an address followed by a register when specifying the operand is a universal method of indicating the index mode.

13.3.7 Zero Page Indexed Mode

The "Zero Page,X" and "Zero Page,Y" modes are the same as "Absolute,X" and "Absolute,Y" modes except that the operand appears on page zero. This is a two-byte instruction where the second byte is the base address and is indexed by either the X or Y index registers to obtain the effective address. When the base and index are added, no carry is produced so that crossing of the page boundary does not occur. That is, page one is not entered.

13.3.8 Indexed Indirect Mode

For this mode, only the X index register is used. The address of the operand must be located in memory page zero, low byte first. The second byte of the two-byte instruction is indexed with the X index register to produce the address in page zero. Then the effective address of the operand is read from the two locations. Crossing of the zero page boundary cannot occur in this mode.

Notice that in this mode parens are used to indicate the indirect or deferred mode (aaX). In addition, the letter X is used with the address to indicate the index mode. It is useful to recognize that because the parens enclose the entire expression, indexing is performed first. Then, the result is the address of the operand.

13.3.9 Indirect Indexed Mode

In this mode, the second byte of the instruction points to a location in page zero. The contents of this location is added to the contents of the Y index register. The result is the low order address of the effective address. The carry from this addition is added to the contents of the next location in memory page zero, which contains the high byte of the effective address.

Once again, notice how the operand is specified (aa)Y. Because the parens enclose only the address, the indirect or deferred operation is performed first. Then, the address thus obtained is indexed with the Y register.

13.3.10   Relative Mode

The relative mode of addressing is used only with branch instructions. Branch instructions are two-byte instructions. The first byte contains the op-code and the second byte contains the offset, or in other words, the relative address of the destination of the branch. When the processor has fetched the op-code and read the offset, the PC is pointing to the next address, which contains the next sequential instruction. The processor executes the branch by adding the offset to the PC. The result is that the PC now contains the effective destination address. The relative address is a signed 8-bit number. If the number is negative, the offset is negative— meaning that the branch will be backwards. The range of the offset is – 128 to + 127 bytes from the next address after the branch instruction.

13.3.11   Accumulator Mode

This mode is used when a one-byte instruction implies the use of the accumulator. An example is TAX, which means, "Transfer the contents of the A register to the X index register."

13.4   INTERFACING THE 6502

The timing diagram for the 6052s read bus cycle is shown in Figure 13–4. It shows ϕ_1, ϕ_2, address, R/$\overline{W}$, and data. When ϕ_1 goes HIGH, an address is asserted by the processor on the address bus. The R/$\overline{W}$ control signal remains HIGH, indicating a read cycle. The result is that a memory location or port is selected and made ready to place data on the bus. The phase 2 (ϕ_2) clock is a strobe, used to determine the time the event is to take place.

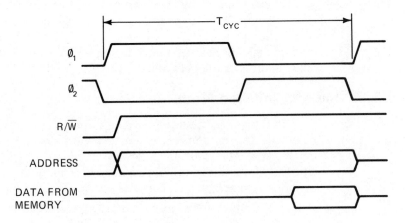

Figure 13–4. READ bus cycle for the 6502.

Figure 13–5 is the timing diagram for the write cycle. The control signal R/$\overline{\text{W}}$ goes LOW and address is asserted at the beginning of the cycle when ϕ_1 goes HIGH. Later, when ϕ_2 goes HIGH, the processor asserts data on the data bus. ϕ_2 is used to gate the data to memory or an output port.

The R/$\overline{\text{W}}$ signal is used by memory or a port to determine the direction of the data transfer. The ϕ_2 clock is used as a data bus enable and determines when the transfer takes place.

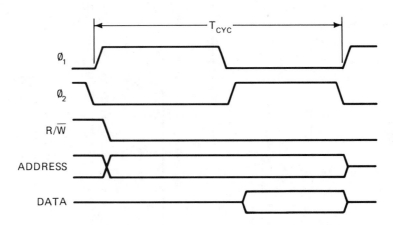

Figure 13–5. WRITE bus cycle for the 6502.

13.4.1   Memory Interface

A diagram showing how the 6502 is connected to two 2114 1 K × 4 static RAM devices to form 1 K bytes of read/write memory appears in Figure 13–6. Notice how the processor's R/$\overline{\text{W}}$ signal is connected to the 2114's write enable ($\overline{\text{WE}}$) inputs. When this signal is HIGH, the 2114 is conditioned to place data on the bus. When it is LOW, memory is conditioned to accept data from the bus. When ϕ_2 goes HIGH, one of the two events will occur. The decoded memory select signal (MS) is ANDed with ϕ_2 to activate the $\overline{\text{CS}}$ input. Decoding of the high order bits of address for the select signals is accomplished in the same manner as with other processors and as previously described.

The advantage of this interface is that a minimum number of control lines are required. This is possible because memory-mapped I/O is used.

For addressing other types of memory or ports, it may be necessary to develop two separate control signals, $\overline{\text{RD}}$ and $\overline{\text{WR}}$, as shown in Figure 13–7. Two NAND gates are used. R/$\overline{\text{W}}$ is ANDed with ϕ_2 to produce $\overline{\text{RD}}$, and NOT R/$\overline{\text{W}}$ is ANDed with ϕ_2 to produce $\overline{\text{WR}}$.

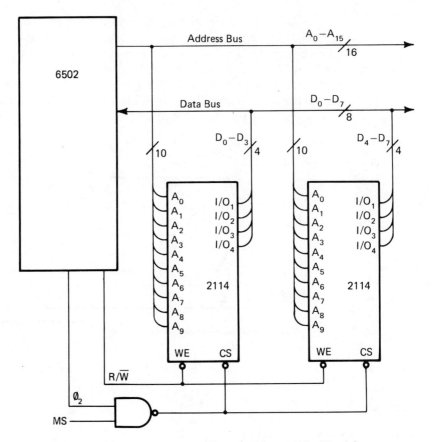

Figure 13-6. 2 - 2114's connected to a 6502 to provide 4K x 1 byte of RAM.

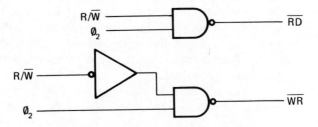

Figure 13-7. Generating two separate control signals.

13.4.2 I/O Interface

Two 74LS373 8-bit D-type latches are shown in Figure 13–8 forming an I/O port for the 6502. For the output port, the three-state outputs are enabled by grounding the OE input. A NOR gate is used to AND R/$\overline{W}$, port address select ($\overline{PS}$), and ϕ_2 to latch the data from the data bus. The data remains latched until the next output to this port occurs.

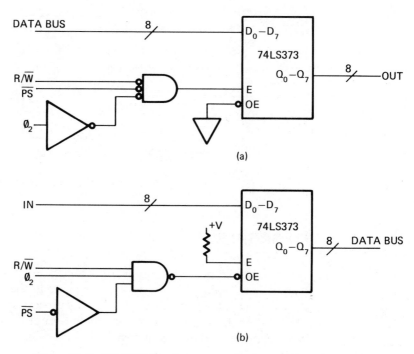

Figure 13–8. 74LS373 Octal three-state latches used as I/O ports for the 6502. (a) Output port; (b) Input port.

The second 74LS373 is used for input and operates in the transparent mode. This mode is established by maintaining the latch enable (E) input at a HIGH level. Data is gated onto the bus by ANDing R/$\overline{W}$, $\overline{PS}$, and ϕ_2.

When port addresses are decoded, all sixteen bits of address must be considered. Remember, memory mapped I/O is used and almost any addresses can be used for ports. Page zero addresses may be desirable because the zero page addressing modes can speed the I/O process.

Figure 13–9 shows how addresses $00 through $07 on page zero may be decoded. Because RAM also exists at these addresses, it must be disabled when the port addresses are selected. This circuit provides a signal (DMEM) for this purpose.

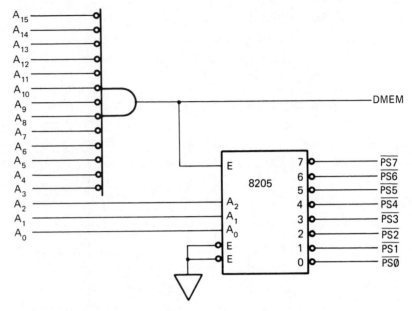

Figure 13–9. Decoding memory mapped port addresses on page zero.

13.5   6502 INTERRUPTS

The 6502 has two interrupt request inputs: $\overline{\text{IRQ}}$ and $\overline{\text{NMI}}$. The $\overline{\text{IRQ}}$ input is maskable; that is, a mask bit exists in the processor status register (P). If the mask bit is set (equal to 1), the processor ignores the interrupt. If it is not set, the processor begins the interrupt sequence after completing execution of the current instruction by using the following procedure:

1. Set Interrupt Mask (I)
2. Push high byte of PC (PCH)
3. Push low byte of PC (PCL)
4. Push processor status word (P)
5. Move the contents of location $FFFE to PCL
6. Move the contents of location $FFFF to PCH

The dollar sign ($) is used by the 6502 assembler to denote hexadecimal numbers; therefore, we will also use it. Memory must exist at locations $FFFE and $FFFE to contain the address of the ISR. First the processor sets the interrupt mask (I). This prevents any further interrupts and is necessary so that the sequence can be completed without error. The mask,

I, is cleared when a RTI (ReTurn from Interrupt) is executed at the end of the ISR.

An interrupt may also be initiated by activating the non-maskable input ($\overline{\text{NMI}}$). In this case, there is no mask and an interrupt will always take place. The interrupt vector addresses for $\overline{\text{NMI}}$ are $FFFA and $FFFB.

Addresses $FFFC and $FFFD are used to initiate execution of the system when a reset ($\overline{\text{RES}}$ is activated) is executed. Reset causes the processor to move the contents of these two addresses to the PC, which will start the systems program.

Interrupts for the 6502 are much like the interrupts used by LIMP except that the 6502 has only two inputs. The $\overline{\text{NMI}}$ input is intended for high priority interrupts like that from a disk controller; therefore, in many system configurations it may be dedicated to that application.

13.5.1 Polled Interrupts

There may be various peripherals like terminals, printers, instruments, etc., that interrupt the processor when they require service. How is this accomplished with just one input ($\overline{\text{IRQ}}$) and only one vector address? The 6502 relies to a great extent on polling to determine which device has interrupted.

All interrupt request lines are "ORed" to activate the $\overline{\text{IRQ}}$ input to the processor. When any interrupt occurs, the processor vectors to a single ISR. The ISR inputs status through a status port from the various peripherals, determines which peripheral has interrupted, and then branches to the routine that will service that particular peripheral.

Figure 13-10 shows how the 74LS348 (see Appendix C) priority encoder can be used for generating the interrupt and how the status may be inputted.

Study the truth table on the data sheet. Notice that if more than one input is active, only the input representing the higher number will be en-

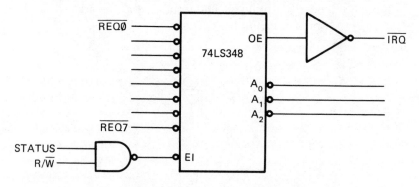

Figure 13-10. Priority Encoder used for interrupt polling.

coded. Therefore, a priority may be assigned to each input with 7 being the highest.

Notice in the functional diagram that if any input is active (LOW), the OE output will be HIGH. This signal is used to generate the interrupt (Figure 13–10) by activating the $\overline{\text{IRQ}}$ input to the processor.

When interrupted, the processor initiates the interrupt sequence and vectors to the ISR. Instructions in the ISR are executed that read the status at a memory location called STATUS. When the EI input of the 74LS348 is activated, the three-state output is enabled, which places the encoded number representing the interrupted peripheral on the data bus. After this number is inputted, the processor branches to the required service routine. It is the responsibility of the peripheral to terminate the request line to the encoder when the peripheral has been serviced.

13.5.2   Vectored Interrupts

Polling tends to slow the response time for interrupts. When speed is essential, vectored interrupts may be used. But wait, only one vector address is available for each interrupt input!

The solution is to fool the processor by modifying the vector addresses. Figure 13–11 is a diagram showing how this may be accomplished. Two 8-bit NAND gates are used to decode the vector addresses $FFFE and $FFFF. A 74LS157 Quadruple 2-input Multiplexer is used. The data sheet for this device is in Appendix C. This device modifies the four bits of the address of a ROM that appears in the top 2 K of memory. Notice that A_0 is not modified. This is because we want to select two addresses for each vector. Bits 1, 2, 3, and 4 of the ROM address are obtained from the output of the multiplexer. Normally the select input (S) to the multiplexer is LOW, which selects the A inputs from the data bus causing no modification of address. When either $FFFE or $FFFF are addressed by the processor, the S input goes HIGH and bits 1, 2, and 3 are obtained from the output of the priority encoder. Bit 4 will equal 0 in this case because that input to the encoder is grounded. The result is that the address is modified according to which interrupt has occurred as follows:

Interrupt	Vector Addresses
$\overline{\text{IRQ0}}$	$FFF0 and $FFF1
$\overline{\text{IRQ1}}$	$FFF2 and $FFF3
$\overline{\text{IRQ2}}$	$FFF4 and $FFF5
$\overline{\text{IRQ3}}$	$FFF6 and $FFF7
$\overline{\text{IRQ4}}$	$FFF8 and $FFF9
$\overline{\text{IRQ5}}$	$FFFA and $FFFB
$\overline{\text{IRQ6}}$	$FFFC and $FFFD
$\overline{\text{IRQ7}}$	$FFFE and $FFFF

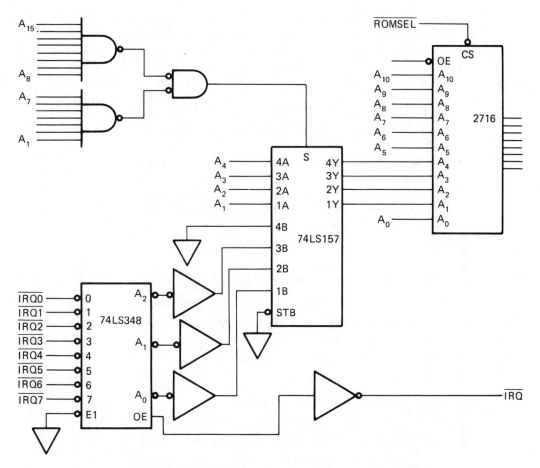

Figure 13-11. Modifying the vector addresses of the 6502.

The sixteen highest addresses in ROM must be reserved for vector addresses. As many vectored interrupts may be implemented as needed using this method. Using vectored interrupts provides the fastest means of servicing interrupts possible.

13.6 SPECIAL DEVICES

Like with the 8085A, there are a number of special peripheral devices that are intended for use with the 6502. These devices simplify the implementation on a 6502 microcomputer system. Data sheets for three of the devices, the 6520, the 6522, and the 6530 appear in Appendix C.

The 6520 is called a Peripheral Interface Adapter (PIA). The PIA has two I/O ports with data direction registers (DDRs) that control the direction of I/O lines individually. Handshaking signals are also provided.

The 6522, called a Versatile Interface Adapter (VIA), has two bidirectional ports, two 16-bit programmable timers, and a serial data port.

The 6530 has 1 K bytes of ROM, 64 bytes of RAM, two programmable ports, an interval timer, and a programmable interval timer with interrupt.

In addition to the 6502, there are a number of other processors in the 6502 family all capable of executing the same instructions. They are designated 6503 through 6515. Some have an on-chip clock like the 6502, and others require an external clock. Most are packaged in 28-pin packages and have either twelve or thirteen address lines, allowing them to address 4 to 8 K of memory. Along with the special peripheral devices, these are ideal for small controller-type applications.

Questions

1. List the registers in the register section of the 6502.
2. Where in memory is the stack pointer located?
3. How many bytes are there in a page of memory?
4. Which mode of addressing is used with branch instructions?
5. What does the # sign mean?
6. What is ϕ_2 used for?
7. When is R/$\overline{\text{W}}$ asserted on the bus?
8. The 6502 has two interrupt request inputs. What are they?
9. Which of the interrupt request inputs are maskable?
10. What does the symbol $ mean as used by the 6502 assembler?

In Chapters 9 through 12 we discussed the 8085A processor and developed an 8085A based computer. It is impractical to discuss, in depth, more than one processor in a single text. However, we do want to introduce and discuss 16-bit processors. Our discussion of these processors will concentrate primarily on those concepts not yet developed and on differences between the 8086 and 8088 processors and the 8085A. Those concepts or circuits previously developed will only be highlighted and references to them may be made.

The 8088 is a 16-bit processor that uses an 8-bit data bus. It is called a 16-bit processor because its internal architecture is like a 16-bit processor and because it processes 16-bit data words. Its bus is like the one used with the 8085A. However, it can address 1 million bytes of memory. Twenty bits of address are derived from the multiplexed bus.

Another 16-bit processor that uses a 16-bit data bus is the 8086. We have chosen to discuss the 8086 and the 8088 in this chapter because of the natural progression of Intel processors. Many of the control signals and the bus structure are familiar to us from our study of the 8085A. Further, the 8086 and the 8088 are very similar processors with few differences. Because of these similarities, a separate discussion of each processor would be redundant. Most of the following discussions will be with reference to both processors—whenever there are differences, we will treat the processors individually.

The 8086 and 8088 Microprocessors

14.1   COMMON ARCHITECTURE

The functional block diagrams of the 8086 and 8088 are shown in Figure 14-1. We will discuss them together because, as you can see, they are identical except for the number of words in the queue. Both the 8086 and the 8088 may be divided functionally into two parts: the Bus Interface Unit (BIU) and the Execution/control Unit (EU). You may look at these units, the BIU and the EU, as being two separate processors. The BIU fetches instructions from memory and buffers them in the queue. The queue is a 2-word (8088) or a 3-word (8086) location in the BIU. Sometimes

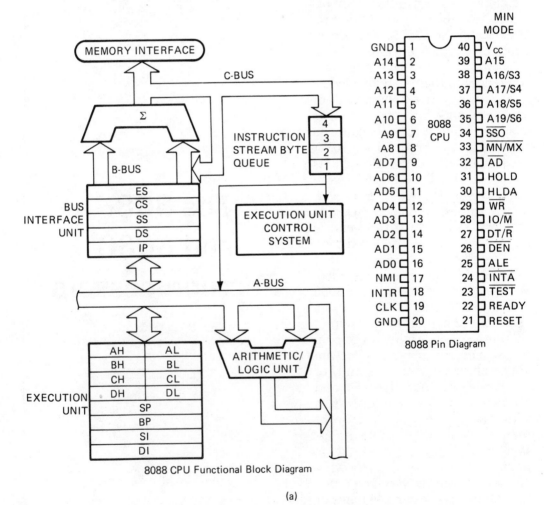

8088 CPU Functional Block Diagram

8088 Pin Diagram

(a)

Figure 14-1. Functional block diagrams and pinouts for
(a) 8088,

referred to as the instruction pipeline, the BIU fills this space with instructions awaiting execution by the EU. The 8088 fetches bytes and provides the EU with words. The 8086 fetches words and provides the EU with words. The EU takes the pre-fetched instructions from the queue and executes them. This system has a great advantage over the 8085A or the 6502 because, while the EU is executing an instruction, the BIU is fetching and storing in the queue the next instructions. You can see how much more efficient this parallel fetching and executing is compared to the processors we discussed earlier, which fetch and then execute each instruction.

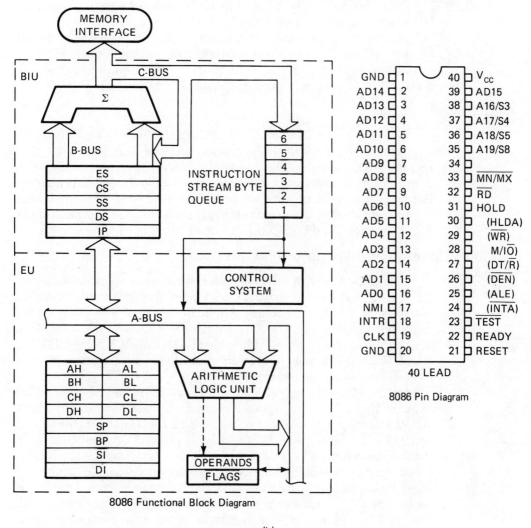

8086 Functional Block Diagram

40 LEAD

8086 Pin Diagram

(b)

(b) 8086. (Courtesy Intel Corporation)

The BIU also contains the segment registers and the instruction pointer. The EU contains the general purpose registers, the ALU, and the flags.

14.1.1   Address and Data Bus Structure

Pinouts for the 8086 and the 8088 are shown in Figure 14-1. The 8088 has an 8-bit data bus that is multiplexed with the low byte of the address and is identified as AD0–AD7. The high byte of the address is labeled A8–A15. This is nothing new. We found the same lines in the 8085A.

The 8086 has a 16-bit data bus that is multiplexed with the low sixteen bits of address and is identified as AD0–AD15.

Both processors use A16–19, which are four multiplexed lines used for the high four bits of address and for certain status information. These four additional address lines allow the processors to assert twenty bits of address on the address bus during each memory reference operation.

14.1.2   Control Bus

Pins 24, 25, and 28 through 32 contain control signals whose function is the same as in the 8085A. These control signals are ALE, IO/$\overline{\text{M}}$, $\overline{\text{RD}}$, $\overline{\text{WR}}$, $\overline{\text{INTA}}$, HLDA, and HOLD. Even though they are functionally alike, some of them are asserted at different times than in the 8085A. These differences will be evident when we discuss the bus cycles. These and other control signals will be discussed as they are used. With the exception of pin 34, all pin names and their functions are identical in the two processors.

14.1.3   Minimum and Maximum Modes

To support 8088 or 8086 systems, two modes of operation are possible. These modes are referred to as minimum or maximum modes (or minimum or maximum systems). A minimum system refers to a system where pin 33, labeled MN/$\overline{\text{MX}}$, is tied HIGH. With MN/$\overline{\text{MX}}$ tied HIGH, the control signals at pins 24 through 31—$\overline{\text{INTA}}$, ALE, $\overline{\text{DEN}}$, DT/$\overline{\text{R}}$, IO/$\overline{\text{M}}$, $\overline{\text{WR}}$, HLDA, and HOLD—are generated by the processor. Pins 35 through 38 are used as address lines.

In the maximum mode, MN/$\overline{\text{MX}}$, is tied LOW and a bus controller (typically the 8288) is used. This bus controller decodes three inputs, 20, S1 and S2 which are available at pins 26 through 28, and generates the control signals $\overline{\text{INTA}}$, ALE, $\overline{\text{DEN}}$, DT/$\overline{\text{R}}$, IO/$\overline{\text{M}}$, $\overline{\text{WR}}$, HLDA, and HOLD. In the maximum mode, the 8088 (or the 8086) is a much more powerful processor. This mode is used where multiprocessor operations are required, or where bus arbitration is used. Bus arbitration is required for multiprocessor applications. We should not be misled by the word "minimum." We can address 1 M byte of memory in either mode. In our discussions we will limit ourselves to a minimum system, realizing that maximum systems are not that much different.

14.1.4 Segment Addressing

As mentioned earlier, both processors assert twenty bits of address on the address bus during each memory reference operation. This results in a range of addresses from 0 to FFFFFH. All registers that contain addresses are 16-bit registers. The direct addressing mode specifies a 16-bit number. How, then, can a 20-bit address be accommodated?

Through the various modes, a 16-bit address is determined which provides a range of 64 K bytes or one segment of addresses. These sixteen bits are sometimes referred to as the logical address. The logical address is added to the contents of one of four segment registers as shown in Figure 14-2. Each segment register contains sixteen bits. However, the contents of the segment register are shifted left 4 bit positions as shown in Figure 14-3. The result is a 20-bit number which is the physical memory address.

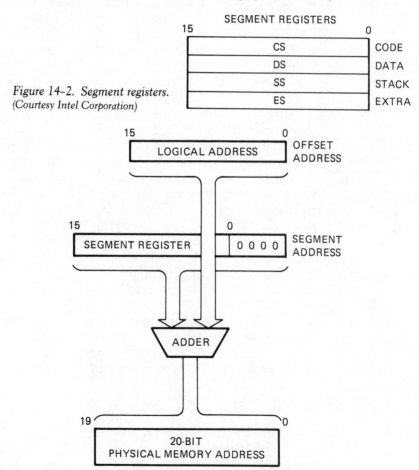

Figure 14-2. Segment registers.
(Courtesy Intel Corporation)

Figure 14-3. Scheme used to address 1 M bytes. (Courtesy Intel Corporation)

The contents of the segment register including the four least significant 0-bits is the base for a segment of addresses. Changing the contents of the segment register allows the base of a segment to exist anywhere in the physical memory.

One of the four segment registers, called the code segment register (CS), is used to establish the current base for the segment containing instructions. In this case, the logical address is contained in the instruction pointer (IP). The IP is another name for the PC used in other processors.

Another segment register is used when making reference to data in memory. It is called the data segment register (DS). A third segment register called the stack segment register (SS) is used for stack operations. The fourth is called the extra segment register (ES). This one is dedicated to string operations, which will be explained later. All references to memory by the processor are done so through the use of the segment registers. Therefore, no matter what addressing mode is used, an effective (logical) address is first determined and then added with the contents of one of the segment registers as shown in Figure 14-3 to produce the 20-bit physical address.

There are no restrictions on the contents of the segment registers. Therefore, at any one time, four segments of memory may be defined. They do not need to occupy contiguous memory locations and they may overlap each other.

You may wonder how so much memory can be used. Consider a system where the entire operating system resides in ROM! ROM has become inexpensive enough to make this possible. A monitor or executive, an assembler, an editor, a Basic interpreter, possibly a FORTRAN or Pascal compiler, various utility programs, and the required I/O drivers can all reside in ROM.

Assume that the programs have been assembled so their starting (logical) address equals zero. To execute a particular program, the code segment register is initialized with the physical address of the program. Since this sets the base of the segment, clearing the IP causes the program to execute.

A system like this will execute much faster than a disk operating system because there is no need to transfer programs to memory from the disk. The only mass media required would be for user data files. As the system grows, new ROM may be added to the system.

14.1.5   Data Registers

The data group registers are called the AX, BX, CX, and DX registers. Each contains sixteen bits. The block diagram in Figure 14-1 shows them broken up into high and low bytes. They are more fully described in Figure 14-4. These are the general purpose registers. They can be referenced as

AX:	AH	AL	ACCUMULATOR
BX:	BH	BL	BASE
CX:	CH	CL	COUNT
DX:	DH	DL	DATA

Figure 14-4. Data registers (GPRs).

either 8-bit or 16-bit registers. These registers are similar in function to the register pairs in the 8085A. Although AX is referred to as the accumulator, and is most easily used by the processor in that role, any one of the GPRs can be used as the accumulator. Any of these registers can be used to contain operands in all of the arithmetic and logical operations.

Some of the data registers have dedicated purposes as well as acting as GPRs. These include:

AX   All I/O operations use this register as the accumulator.

BX   The only GPR used in calculating memory addresses.

CX   Used by string and loop operations as a counter.

DX   Provides I/O addresses for I/O instructions when required.

14.1.6   Pointer and Index Registers

The pointer and index registers are identified in Figure 14–5. These registers usually store offset addresses used for addressing within a segment. They can be used in arithmetic and logical operations just like the GPRs.

The SP is used like the SPs we have studied in the past. In addition to the SP, the BP can also be used to point to locations in the stack. It can point to items in the stack independent of the SP pointer. This feature increases the flexibility of the instruction set considerably. Both registers are used in conjunction with the stack segment register.

SP	STACK POINTER
BP	BASE POINTER
SI	SOURCE INDEX
DI	DESTINATION INDEX

Figure 14-5. Pointer and index registers.

The index registers, SI and DI, have autoincrement and autodecrement capabilities. They are special registers also used in string manipulation instructions. Autoincrement and autodecrement modes are discussed in Chapter 15.

14.1.7   Control Registers

This grouping refers to the instruction pointer (IP) and the flags. The IP points to the next instruction to be fetched. The flags are the condition codes. The flags are shown as a 16-bit register in Figure 14-6. These flags are identified as follows:

OF   Overflow Flag. This flag is set if the operation results in a carry into but not out of the MSB position; otherwise it is cleared.

DF   Direction Flag. If this flag is set, the contents of the index registers, SI and DI, will be decremented after each operation, once for byte operations and twice for word operations. If the flag is clear, the registers will be incremented, once for byte operations and twice for word operations.

IF   Interrupt Flag. If this flag is set, interrupt is enabled. If clear, interrupts are disabled.

TF   Trap Flag. If this flag is set, the processor generates a type 1 interrupt after each instruction. The flag is cleared by the push flags step of the interrupt sequence.

SF   Sign Flag. This flag is set if an arithmetic operation causes the MSB to equal 1; otherwise it is cleared.

ZF   Zero Flag. This flag is set if the result of an arithmetic or logical operation is 0; otherwise it is cleared.

AF   Auxiliary Carry Flag. This flag is set when there is a carry out of the bit 3 position in an arithmetic operation; otherwise it is cleared.

PF   Parity Flag. This flag is set if the result of an arithmetic or logical operation results in an even number of 1 bits; otherwise it is cleared.

CF   Carry Flag. This flag is set if there is a carry out of the MSB in an ADD, or a borrow is generated in a SUBtract; otherwise it is cleared.

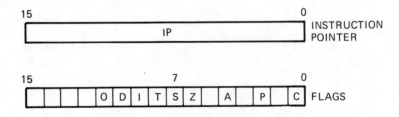

Figure 14-6. Instruction pointer and flag registers.

The sign, zero, auxiliary carry, parity, and carry flags function like the same flags in the 8085A. They even occupy the same bit positions in the low byte of the flag register. Only the overflow, direction, interrupt enable/disable and trap flags are new.

14.2 THE 8088 BUS CYCLE

The 8088 bus cycle is very similar to the 8085A bus cycle and is interpreted in much the same manner. All 8088 bus cycles have four time periods—T1, T2, T3, and T4. See Figure 14-7. If there is a WAIT state, it occurs between T3 and T4. Each WAIT state is one time period long. Each time period represents the duration of each clock cycle. In the 8088, each clock cycle is from 200 to 500 ns long depending on the crystal frequency being used.

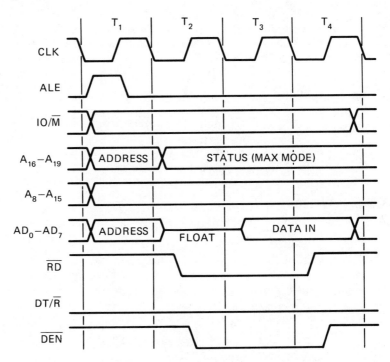

Figure 14-7. READ bus cycle for the 8088.

14.2.1 Read Bus Cycle

ALE is asserted at the beginning of T1 and returns to its inactive state toward the end of T1. The trailing edge of ALE is typically used to latch the multiplexed address lines, AD0–AD7 and A16–A19.

IO/$\overline{M}$ is asserted on the bus at the beginning of T1 and lasts for the entire bus cycle. The line is HIGH for I/O READ or WRITE operations and is LOW when addressing memory.

A16–A19 are four multiplexed lines used for the high four bits of address and certain status information. Address is asserted at the beginning of T1 and remains valid until the beginning of T2. In the maximum mode system, certain status information is asserted on the bus during T2. In the minimum mode system, no valid data is present on these lines during T2, T3, and T4.

As in the 8085A, address is valid on lines A8–A15 throughout the bus cycle and need not be latched. However, electrical buffering may be necessary depending on the system. In that case, the address would be latched using ALE in the same way that the multiplexed lines are latched.

Address is valid on the AD0–AD7 lines from the beginning of T1 until the beginning of T2 and is latched with the trailing edge of ALE. Then, approximately one time period lapses during which time the lines are in the high impedance state. This delay exists to allow the bus time to adjust to the change in direction of data. Data is then asserted during T3 and is valid through T4.

$\overline{RD}$ is asserted toward the beginning of T2 and is valid through the middle of T4, allowing ample time for data on the address/data bus to be read by the processor.

DT/$\overline{R}$, Data transmit/receive, and $\overline{DEN}$, Data Enable, are required when data bus buffering is required. DT/$\overline{R}$ is LOW when a READ bus cycle is occurring. $\overline{DEN}$ is asserted about the middle of T2 and remains valid to the middle of T4.

14.2.2   Write Bus Cycle

READ and WRITE bus cycles are identical through the first five waveforms. Notice in Figure 14–8 that data is asserted on the address/data immediately after the address is removed at the beginning of T2. No recovery time is required because the processor has control of the timing. $\overline{WR}$ is asserted on the bus at about the same time as data and is valid until the end of T4.

DT/$\overline{R}$ is HIGH for WRITE bus cycles. Notice that $\overline{DEN}$ is asserted early in T2 (since data is present) and is valid through the middle of T4.

14.3   8086 BUS CYCLE

The 8086 bus cycle is similar to the 8088 bus cycle with three notable exceptions.

First, in the 8086, two signals are developed that were not required in the 8088. These are $\overline{BHE}$ and A0. $\overline{BHE}$ (Bus Enable High) together with

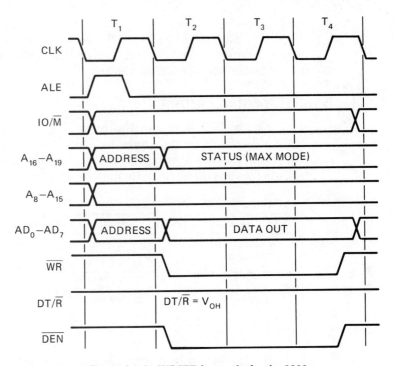

Figure 14–8. WRITE bus cycle for the 8088.

the LSB of the address/data bus are used to select the proper byte(s) of address according to the following table:

$\overline{BHE}$	A0	
0	0	whole word
0	1	upper byte from/to odd address
1	0	lower byte from/to even address
1	1	none

Second, the 8088 signal $IO/\overline{M}$ is replaced in the 8086 with its complement $M/\overline{IO}$. Memory is selected when $M/\overline{IO}$ is HIGH. I/O is selected when $M/\overline{IO}$ is LOW.

Third, because the 8086 has a 16-bit data bus, bits 0–15 must be multiplexed. The address/data bus, then, is AD0–AD15.

14.4 8086/8088 ADDRESSING MODES

The full understanding of the 8086/8088 addressing modes requires a concerted study of the instruction set and programming techniques. We will limit our discussion to some of the features provided by the 8086 and

8088 addressing modes. The modes are basically the same as those used by the 8085A. The difference lies in the versatility provided by indexing the various registers. Direct, indirect, immediate, and register modes are all used in the 8086–8088 instruction set.

14.4.1 Single Operand Format

Figure 14-9 illustrates the format for various instruction words. Figure 14-9(a) shows the format for a single operand instruction. Notice that five bytes are shown. Even though they are all not always used, the following discussion refers to them as bytes 1 through 5.

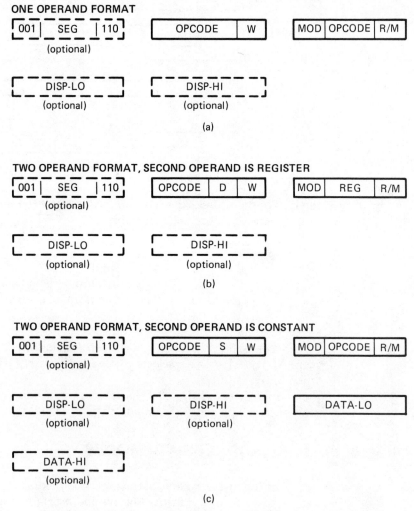

Figure 14-9. Instruction word formats. a) Single operand b) Double operand c) Double operand where second operand is immediate data.

The first byte is optional. Because the operand need not be restricted to the current data or stack segment, the first byte is used to indicate a different segment. This byte has an unique pattern (001SS110); bits 3 and 4 specify the segment register that is to be used. These bits are defined in Figure 14–10(a).

The second byte contains the first part of the opcode. The least significant bit of this byte (W) indicates whether the operand is a byte or a word. If it equals 0, the operand is a byte. If it equals 1, the operand is a 16-bit word.

Bits 3, 4, and 5 of the third byte contain the remainder of the opcode. For example, if the opcode is INC, bits 1 through 7 of byte 2 will equal 1111111 and bits 3, 4, and 5 of byte 3 will equal 000. Bits 6 and 7 of byte 3 (MOD field) specify one of four ways that the remainder of the instruction is to be interpreted. For example, if the MOD field contains 11, then the operand is in a register (register mode). In this case the R/M field (bits 0, 1, and 2) specifies the particular register. The register assignments are shown in Figure 14–10(b).

Bytes 4 and 5 are optional. If they are required, they will contain a displacement. The displacement may be either eight or sixteen bits long. If

BIT FIELDS:

SEG:	SEGMENT REG
00	ES
01	CS
10	SS
11	DS

(a)

	REGISTER	
REG:	8-BIT (W = 0)	16-BIT (W = 1)
000	AL	AX
001	CL	CX
010	DL	DX
011	BL	BX
100	AH	SP
101	CH	BP
110	DH	SI
111	BH	DI

(b)

```
W = 0: 8-BIT OPERAND(S)
    1: 16-BIT OPERAND(S)

D = 0: DESTINATION IS FIRST OPERAND
    1: DESTINATION IS SECOND OPERAND

S = 0: DATA = DATA HI, DATA LO        APPLIES IF
    1: DATA = DATA-LO SIGN EXTENDED      W = 1
```

(c)

Figure 14–10. Field bit assignments for instruction words. a) SEG field b) REG field c) W, D, and S fields.

it is eight bits long, byte 5 will not be required. The displacement is added in various ways to the contents of registers to find the effective address of the operand. See Figure 14–11.

FIRST OPERAND CHOICE DEPENDS ON ADDRESSING MODE:

FIRST OPERAND IN MEMORY		FIRST OPERAND IN REGISTER		
INDIRECT ADDRESSING	DIRECT ADDRESSING			
00* : DISP = 0 MOD = 01 : DISP = DISP-LO SIGN EXTENDED 10 : DISP = DISP-HI, DISP-LO	MOD = 00 AND R/M = 110	MOD = 11		
	OPERAND EFFECTIVE ADDRESS = DISP-HI, DISP-LO		REGISTER	
OPERAND *R/M:* *EFFECTIVE ADDRESS*		*R/M:*	8-BIT (W = 0)	16-BIT (W = 1)
000 (BX) + (SI) + DISP		000	AL	AX
001 (BX) + (DI) + DISP		001	CL	CX
010 (BP) + (SI) + DISP		010	DL	DX
011 (BP) + (DI) + DISP		011	BL	BX
100 (SI) + DISP		100	AH	SP
101 (DI) + DISP		101	CH	BP
110 (BP) + DISP		110	DH	SI
111 (BX) + DISP		111	BH	DI

Where ( ) means "contents of"
*Exception—direct addressing mode

Figure 14–11. Determining first operand.

If the MOD field contains 00, 01, or 10 the R/M field is used to specify how the displacement is used. The MOD field contains 01 when the displacement is 8 bits long. In this case, after the displacement has been fetched, it is converted to a 16-bit number by sign extending. That is, the value of bit 7 is duplicated in bits 8 through 15. This maintains the sign of the number.

The MOD field contains 10 when the displacement is 16 bits long. In this case the displacement is fetched as bytes 4 and 5 of the instruction. As is the convention, the low byte is assembled first and appears before the high byte.

When the MOD field contains 00, it means that no displacement is required. However, a special case exists when MOD equals 00 and R/M equals 110. This indicates the direct addressing mode and bytes 4 and 5 are taken directly as the address of the operand.

14.4.2   Double Operand Format

The double operand format is illustrated in Figure 14–9(b). As before, the instruction may require from two to five bytes. Byte one is used if necessary to specify a different segment register. If byte 1 is not used, the segment register is selected by default. Figure 14–12 shows how the segment registers are assigned when byte 1 is not used (default segment base). For example, if a string operation is specified by the opcode, the DS register is assigned by default for the source operand. The CS, ES, or SS registers can be assigned by using byte one. Notice that the ES register is assigned by default for the destination operand and no other register (alternate segment base) can be specified for this purpose.

TYPE OF MEMORY REFERENCE	DEFAULT SEGMENT BASE	ALTERNATE SEGMENT BASE	LOGICAL ADDRESS
Instruction Fetch	CS	NONE	IP
Stack Operation	SS	NONE	SP
String Source	DS	CS, ES, SS	SI
String Destination	ES	NONE	DI
BP Used As Base Register	SS	CS, DS, ES	Effective Address
General Data Read/Write	DS	CS, ES, SS	Effective Address

Figure 14–12. Assignment of the segment registers for default and alternate bases.

In general, when the operand is data, the default segment register is DS and any other segment register may be specified by using byte 1.

For the double operand instruction, one of the operands must be in a register except when the immediate mode is used.

Either the source or the destination operand may be contained in the register. In either case the contents of the register is called the second operand. Bit 1 of byte 2 (D) specifies whether the register (second operand) contains the source or the destination operand. See Figure 14–10(c). If D equals zero the destination is the first operand. If D equals one the destination is the second operand. Bits 3, 4, and 5 of byte 3 is the register field (REG). This field specifies the register containing the second operand. The first operand is specified the same way as it is in the single operand instruction. Bytes 4 and 5 are used as required for the displacement.

Figure 14–9(c) illustrates the format for a double operand instruction when the second operand is a constant (immediate mode). Seven bytes are possible. Bytes 6 and 7 are used for the immediate data. Byte 7 is used only when a 16-bit data word is required and is indicated by bit 1 of byte 2 (S). See Figure 14–10(c).

It is obvious that assembling the 8086/8088 instructions "by hand" can be very difficult. Using an assembler is almost necessary.

14.5 THE 8086/8088 INSTRUCTION SET

The 8086/8088 instruction set is listed in Appendix E. You will notice that most of the instructions are like those found in the 8085A set. However, some "powerful" instructions have been added. For example, in the arithmetic group, there are multiply (MUL and IMUL) and divide (DIV and IDIV) instructions. There are instructions that are used when ASCII digits are added, subtracted, or multiplied (AAD, AAS, and AAM).

There is a set of instructions that allow strings of bytes or words to be manipulated. As mentioned before, the DS and ES segment registers are used to contain the base addresses for the strings. These instructions are particularly useful for manipulating strings of ASCII text material.

The study of programming the 8086 and 8088 processors is out of the scope of this text. However, the student is encouraged to take on this task because these processors are in wide use in the industry today.

As with other 16-bit processors, the 8086 and 8088 are intended to be used in larger systems than the 8-bit processors like the 8085A. Because larger instruction words are used, it follows that the instruction set should be more sophisticated to match the characteristics of the larger systems.

Questions

1. Name the GPRs in the 8086/8088.
2. What is the purpose of the Index Registers?
3. What is the purpose of the Pointer Registers?
4. What is the purpose of the Instruction Pointer?
5. How do the address/data buses differ between the 8086 and 8088?
6. How long is address valid on lines A_{16}–A_{19}?
7. What is the purpose of the queue?
8. How many words does the queue store in the 8086?
9. How do we select minimum vs maximum mode?
10. During which time period(s) of a bus cycle is $\overline{\text{DEN}}$ active?
11. What is the state of DT/$\overline{\text{R}}$ for a WRITE bus cycle?
12. Name the hardware interrupts.
13. Which of the hardware interrupts is maskable?
14. Which instructions are used to generate software interrupts?
15. In the 8286, what signal controls the direction of data?
16. What were the addresses of RAM in the 8088 system we implemented?

Chapter

15

The
LSI–11
Microcomputer

A 16-bit microcomputer system, developed by Digital Equipment Corp. (DEC*), executes the same PDP–11 programs that run on the larger PDP–11 family of minicomputers produced by that company. The system is modularized as shown in Figure 15–1. Various systems can be configured by plugging modules into the LSI–11 back plane that implements the LSI–11 bus. This bus is standardized so that options or peripherals are simply inserted into the back plane as required. A back plane with various LSI–11 modules is shown in Figure 15–2.

Software packages are available that implement and integrate the various hardware options into a working system. The assembly language used is called PDP–11, Programmed Data Processing–11. The system can support high level languages like BASIC, FORTRAN, COBOL, DIBOL, and PASCAL.

*Registered trademark of Digital Equipment Corporation

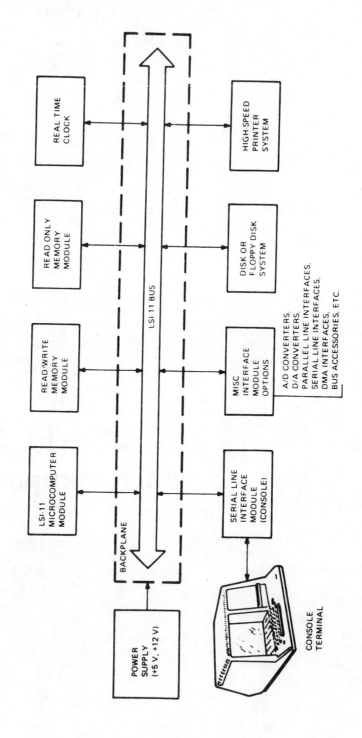

Figure 15–1. Block diagram showing modularized characteristics of the LSI-11 system. (Courtesy Digital Equipment Corporation)

Figure 15-2. Back plane with various LSI–11 modules.

15.1 THE LSI–11 BUS

An important feature of the PDP–11 family of computers is the master-slave relationship between the peripherals and the processor. The processor and any peripheral except memory can become the master so that it can initiate a transfer of data to or from a slave. A slave can be a peripheral, processor, or memory and must be addressed by the master. The concept allows a peripheral to take over the sole use of the bus to communicate with the processor, memory, or any other peripheral.

When a device is designated as a master, it must supply the address of memory or a peripheral. For example, it is possible for a disk controller to output data directly to a printer. The controller requests use of the bus from the bus arbitrator, which is located on the processor board. It is the purpose of the bus arbitrator to accept requests for the use of the bus and grant them based on the current use of the bus and a priority scheme. When the disk controller receives the grant, it places the address of the printer on the bus and completes a data transfer cycle (bus cycle) in the same manner that the processor would. The bus arbitrator grants the use of the bus when it is not being used, which can be between read and write bus cycles of the processor. This technique makes maximum use of the bus.

Data from a magnetic tape drive may be printed while other data on disk may be transferred to memory.

15.1.1   The Processor

The KDF11–AA processor board, which is one of the LSI–11 processors, is shown in Figure 15–3. It is implemented using three MOS/LSI chips. Two of the chips are required for the basic processor and are contained in a single package as shown in the figure.

One of the two chips, called the data chip, performs all arithmetic and logic operations as well as data and address transfers outside of the basic processor itself.

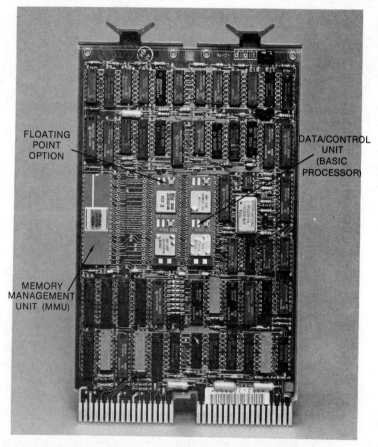

FLOATING
POINT
OPTION

DATA/CONTROL
UNIT
(BASIC
PROCESSOR)

MEMORY
MANAGEMENT
UNIT (MMU)

*Figure 15–3. KDF11–AA processor module (M8186) shown
with optional floating point. (Courtesy Digital Equipment
Corporation)*

The second of the two chips, the control chip, contains a ROM that controls the operations required for the processor to execute the PDP-11 instructions. The microcode contained in the ROM also implements a basic monitor program that automatically is executed when the processor is halted. The program is used instead of the switch register that was used by earlier processors.

The third chip is a memory management unit (MMU). The MMU provides the necessary logic circuitry to control the extended address lines (bits 16 and 17). In addition, it contains registers that are used to manage the use of the extended memory.

Figure 15-3 also shows an optional chip used to implement an extended set of instructions that perform floating point operations. This chip contains additional ROM that extends the microcode.

A functional block diagram is shown in Figure 15-4. The basic processor chips appear in the lower left portion of the diagram with the MMU just above them. The various other block functions are implemented with TTL MSI and SSI circuits. The bus connections are shown on the right side of the diagram.

15.1.2 Signal Names

In keeping with the modular approach to LSI-11 systems, bus lines, pin numbers, and signal names must be standardized. First, let's discuss the signal names. An example, BBS7 L, shown in the upper right-hand corner of the block diagram, is interpreted as "bus bank select 7." The first letter, B, signifies that this is a bus signal. Most bus signal names start with the letter B. The next three characters describe the purpose of the signal. The last letter, L, signifies that the active level of the signal is LOW. No bars are used when specifying any LSI-11 signal name. Only a letter, L (LOW) or H (HIGH), is used to specify which level is active.

In the block diagram, to the left of BBS7 L, are the characters AP2. This specifies the back plane pin connection. The letter, A, specifies the edge connector slot A, P specifies the pin, and 2 specifies the solder side of the board.

The following signals, BDAL0 L through BDAL15 L, comprise the multiplexed address/data bus. BDAL16 L and BDAL17 L are used for extended memory addressing and parity error and enable bits if the parity testing option is incorporated.

Notice the DAL18 through DAL21 lines. They are not used in the LSI-11/23 or earlier processors but are used by the LSI-11/23 PLUS and future processors. Until we discuss memory management, we will consider the bus as having only sixteen address/data lines (BDAL < 15:00 > L).

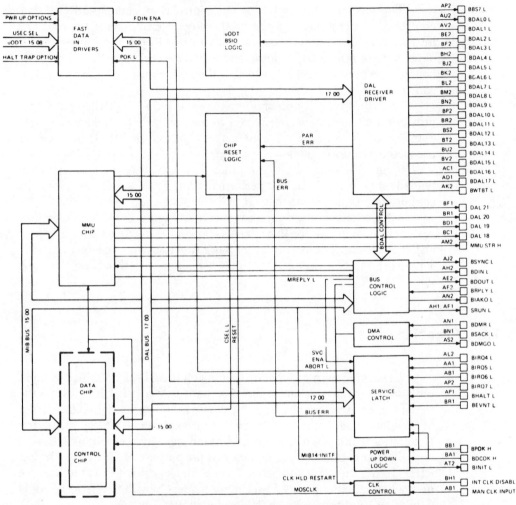

Figure 15-4. Processor functional block diagram. (Courtesy Digital Equipment Corporation)

15.1.3 Bytes and Words in Memory

Data is organized in memory as 16-bit words or 8-bit bytes. The LSB of the address is used in a unique manner. Normally, when addressing words, the LSB equals zero; therefore, words must be located at even numbered addresses. When a byte operation is to be performed, which is specified in the opcode, the LSB is used to address either the high or low byte of the word. The low byte of the address is the even-numbered address and the high byte is the odd address. Words must appear at even addresses while bytes may appear at either even or odd addresses. All instructions are contained in words; therefore, all instructions must appear at word addresses (even addresses).

15.1.4   I/O Page

All I/O devices for PDP-11 systems that are supported by DEC must have standardized addresses. This is required so that standardized software can be used. For example, all the various programs that are available from DEC expect that the console terminal is at address 177560 (octal). Therefore, the upper 4 K words of memory are reserved for I/O.

All control and status registers and input and output buffers are addressed as if they are part of the highest 4 K words of memory.

15.1.5   Bus Cycles

Whenever data is inputted to a master, the bus cycle required is called a DATI cycle. DATI cycles always transfer words; therefore, the master takes the entire word from the bus if a word operation is specified. However, if a byte operation is specified, the master takes either the high or low byte. Because the bus cycle was initiated by the master, it knows which byte to take.

A DATO bus cycle is used when a master transfers a word to a slave. The address is always even and a word is always transferred. If a byte is to be transferred, a DATOB bus cycle is used. In this case, the LSB of the address is used by the slave to determine if the address is even or odd.

Sometimes an input cycle and an output cycle may be combined into one operation. An example is when the contents of a memory location is to be incremented. First, a read cycle is used to read the data; next, the data is incremented; finally a write cycle is used to put the data back in memory. The common factor in the above example is the address. In the DATIO bus cycle, the address is asserted on the bus only once. Data is transferred to the master and then back to the slave without readdressing. A DATIOB bus cycle is used to accomplish the same thing when the data is a byte.

15.1.6   Data Transfers

In addition to the BDAL lines, six other signal lines are required to execute data transfers using the five bus cycles just described. They are:

Signal	Description
BSYNC L	Bus Cycle Control
BDIN L	Data Input Control
BDOUT L	Data Output Control
BRPLY L	Slave's Acknowledge of Bus Cycle
BWTBT L	Write/Byte Control
BBS7 L	I/O Device Select

A definite protocol must exist between the master and slave for a data transfer. The protocol is closed loop; that is, the master must receive a response from the slave in order to continue in a normal manner. The dialogue for a DATI bus cycle follows. The numbers in the dialogue refer to the waveforms in Figure 15–5.

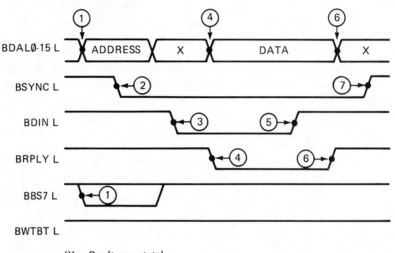

BDALØ-15 L

BSYNC L

BDIN L

BRPLY L

BBS7 L

BWTBT L

(X = Don't care state)

Figure 15–5. The DATI bus cycle.

DATI Bus Cycle

Device	Dialogue	Signal Activity
Master:	1. "Hello, here's an address"	Asserts Address on BDAL< 15:00 > L Asserts BBS7 L if I/O page
Master:	2. "If it's yours, get ready"	Asserts BSYNC L
Master:	3. "I want some data"	Asserts BDIN L
Slave:	4. "OK, here it is"	Asserts Data on BDAL< 15:00 > L Asserts BRPLY L
Master:	5. "I got it"	Terminates BDIN L
Slave:	6. "OK, goodbye"	Terminates DATA Terminates BRPLY L
Master:	7. "Goodbye"	Terminates BSYNC L End of bus cycle

Notice that the master waits for a response from the slave twice. The first time is after it has asserted the input control signal, BDIN L. It waits until the slave has placed data on the BDAL lines and has asserted BRPLY

L. If the slave is slow, it may delay the assertion of BRPLY L allowing a greater period of time for the data to settle on the bus. This allows the bus to operate at the most efficient speed possible.

The second time the master waits is after it has terminated BDIN L. The master will not continue until the slave terminates BRPLY L, which acknowledges to the master that it has removed data from the BBDAL lines.

During the time that address appears on the BDAL lines, BBS7 L is asserted if the address is in the upper 4 K words of memory. This signal disables memory and enables I/O. BBS7 L is active if bits 15, 14, and 13 of the address all equal 1. Therefore, the I/O page ranges in addresses from 160000 to 177776 (octal). The signal, BWTBT L, is never asserted during a DATI bus cycle.

The DATO bus cycle is similar to the DATI cycle except that at the time the address is asserted, BWTBT L is also asserted. This tells the slave, in advance of the BDOUT L control signal, that a DATO or DATOB bus cycle has started.

If, while BDOUT L is asserted BWTBT L is still asserted, it tells the slave that a write byte operation is in effect. Otherwise, the slave takes a word from the bus. If it is a byte operation, the slave must use the LSB of the address to decide which of the two bytes has been addressed.

The following is the dialogue for a DATO or DATOB bus cycle. The associated waveforms are shown in Figure 15–6.

DATO(B) Bus Cycle

Device	Dialogue	Signal Activity
Master:	1. "Hello, here's an address and I'm outputting"	Asserts Address on BDAL< 15:00 > L Asserts BWTBT L Asserts BBS7 L if I/O page
Master:	2. "If it's yours, get ready"	Asserts BSYNC L
Master:	3. "Here's some data"	Asserts Data on BDAL< 15:00 > L Asserts BDOUT L Terminates BWTBT L if word
Slave:	4. "It's mine!"	Asserts BRPLY L
Master:	5. "OK, take it"	Terminates BDOUT L Terminates BWTBT L if byte Terminates DATA
Slave:	6. "I have it - Goodbye"	Terminates BRPLY L
Master:	7. "Goodbye"	Terminates BSYNC L End of bus cycle

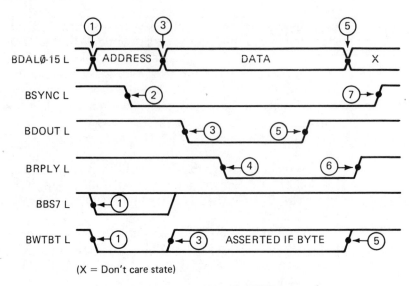

(X = Don't care state)

Figure 15-6. The DAT0 or DATOB bus cycle

For the DATI, DATO, or DATOB bus cycles, if the slave is memory, it must latch the address when BSYNC L is asserted so that it can select the appropriate memory location. If the address is an I/O device, it may use a comparator at the time BSYNC L is asserted and set a single latch (device selected). A second latch must be used to save the LSB of the address for byte operations.

Figure 15-7 shows the waveforms for a DATIO or DATIOB bus cycle. Basically, the DATIO bus cycle is the combination of the DATI cycle followed by a DATO cycle with the address asserted only once. This cycle is used when the source and destination operands are specified at the same location. Notice that BSYNC L is asserted when the address is on the BDAL lines. It remains asserted until the entire cycle is complete. This prevents the slave from terminating the cycle too soon. Also notice that BRPLY L is asserted twice by the slave, once in response to the read portion on the cycle and once in response to the write portion. The slave can detect that a DATIO cycle is beginning by detecting that BWTBT L is asserted with the address and is followed immediately by BDIN L instead of BDOUT L.

15.1.7   Direct Memory Access

Some peripheral devices communicate directly with memory. A good example of such a device is a controller for a disk drive.

The controller needs to know the starting address in memory, the starting address in the disk drive (cylinder, track, sector, etc.), the length of the data to be transferred, and the direction the transfer is to take place

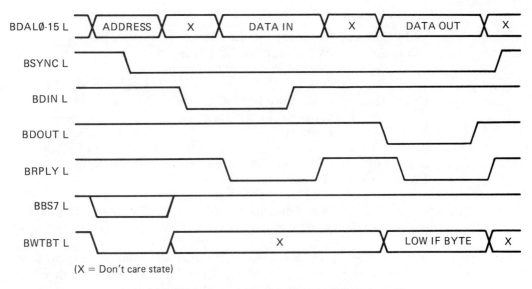

(X = Don't care state)

Figure 15–7. Waveforms for DATIO(B) bus cycle.

(read or write). This information is supplied, under program control, from the processor.

To make the transfer, the controller must issue a request to use the bus. When it receives a grant from the bus arbitrator, it takes over the bus as bus master. If the processor is executing a program at the time of the request, the arbitrator will issue grants between processor bus cycles. In this manner the controller and the processor share the use of the bus with the greatest efficiency.

Four signals on the bus are used for the requests and grants:

BDMR L	DMA Request line
BDMGI L	DMA Grant Input
BDMGO L	DMA Grant Output
BSACK L	Bus Grant Acknowledge

Because more than one DMA device may be on the bus, two grant lines are used. Each board plugged into the back plane receives the grant as BDMGI L and must pass it on to the next board as BDMGO L. When the grant is received by the device that issued the request, it does not pass it on. Therefore, if two DMA devices are on the bus, the device that is closer to the processor will have the higher priority. It is important that DMA devices have a high priority because they transfer data rapidly and because the data is volatile. That is, it will be lost if the transfer is not immediately completed.

The dialogue for a typical direct memory data transfer follows:

DMA Cycle	Dialogue	Bus Activity
DMA Device:	"I want to use the bus"	Asserts BDMR L
Arbitrator:	(Waits until BRPLY L is terminated in current bus cycle) "OK"	Asserts BDMGO L
DMA Device:	(Waits until BSYNC L is terminated) "I have the grant - I'm next!"	Asserts BSACK L Terminates BDMR L
Arbitrator:	"OK, you may use the bus"	Terminates BDMGO L
DMA Device:	(Transfers up to 4 words DATI or DATO bus cycles) "I'm done, thank you"	Terminates BSACK L

(Processor becomes master)

The signal BSACK L prevents the arbitrator from granting any other requests. Grants are issued between bus cycles of the processor; therefore, they may occur during the execution of an instruction.

15.1.8 Interrupts

Two kinds of priorities are provided for interrupts. The first, called horizontal priority, is like that used by DMA requests. When two devices have issued interrupt requests simultaneously, the device that is electrically closer to the processor receives the grant and does not pass it on. Therefore, devices that are closest to the processor have the highest priority.

The second, or vertical priority, is determined by the particular request line used. Four priorities are provided. They are priorities 4, 5, 6, and 7 with 7 being the highest. Priorities 0, 1, 2, and 3 are software priorities and no hardware is associated with them.

The processor status word (PSW) uses three bits for saving the current level of priority. For example, if a device configured to have a priority of 4 requests an interrupt, the bus arbitrator (part of the processor) compares the level of priority with 4. If the current level is equal to or greater than 4, the interrupt will be ignored. If, on the other hand, the current level is less than 4, the interrupt will be granted.

The following signals are required for the interrupt transaction.

BIRQ4 L	Interrupt request priority level 4
BIRQ5 L	Interrupt request priority level 5
BIRQ6 L	Interrupt request priority level 6
BIRQ7 L	Interrupt request priority level 7
BIAKI L	Interrupt acknowledge input

BIAKO L	Interrupt acknowledge output
BDAL< 15:00 > L	Data/Address lines
BDIN L	Data input control
BRPLY L	Slave reply

BIAKI L and BIAKO L are "daisy chained" from device to device. The priority level is configured on the device board by wiring the request to the appropriate request line. Assuming that a device has been configured for a priority level of 4, the dialogue goes as follows:

Device:	"I want to interrupt the processor"	Asserts BIRQ4 L
Arbitrator:	Interrupts processor (ignores request if current level is 4 or greater)	
Processor:	"OK, wait"	Asserts BDIN L
	"Request granted"	Asserts BIAKO L
Device:	"OK, for me only!"	(Doesn't assert BIAKO L)
	"This is what I want you to do"	Asserts Vector Address on BDAL< 7:00 > L
	"Please"	Asserts BRPLY L Terminates BIRQ4 L
Processor:	"OK, It will be done"	Terminates BDIN L Terminates BIAKO L
Device:	"Thank you"	Terminates BRPLY

The device requesting the interrupt is asking to become bus master and to use the bus long enough to transfer an address to the processor. This address is in the range of 60 to 400 (octal) and is called a vector address. The device only transfers the eight LSBs of the vector address and the processor assumes that the eight MSBs are all zero.

A vector address contains the address of the interrupt service routine. The very next address after the vector address contains the value of the PSW to be used by the ISR. Recall that the PSW contains the priority of the particular interrupt.

After the interrupt has been granted, the processor pushes the PSW and the PC on the stack, saving their values. It then loads the PC with the contents of the vector address (address of ISR) and the PSW with the contents of the second vector address (vector + 2). In the above example, the new PSW contains the priority of 4. The old priority level is saved on the stack.

The last instruction in the ISR, RTI (ReTurn from Interrupt), causes the saved values of the PC and PSW to be restored, and program execution continues from the point where the interrupt occurred. The main program must initialize the vector addresses with the addresses of the ISRs and their priorities. There are no special instructions required to save the PSW, allowing the interrupts to occur automatically.

15.2 PROGRAMMING THE LSI–11

Perhaps the greatest feature of the LSI–11 is the software that it executes. There are many instructions in the PDP–11 instruction set (Appendix D), but the addressing modes used give the PDP–11 Assembly Language its greatest advantage. Another important feature is that any register or any memory location can be used as an accumulator.

The processor contains eight registers, R0 through R7. Each register contains sixteen bits. R0 through R5 are known as general purpose registers (GPRs). They may be used to contain data, addresses of data, or addresses of addresses. R6 is also known as the hardware stack pointer and is used in the same way as the SP in the 8085A. It is called a hardware stack because the processor contains the hardware necessary for it to be used automatically on calls to subroutines or interrupts.

R7 is the program counter (PC). As with other processors, the PC contains the address of the next instruction to be executed.

15.2.1 Instruction Format

During the discussion that follows, examples of modes will be used with the move (MOV) instruction; therefore it is necessary to understand its format. The format of the move instruction is shown in Figure 15–8. That part of the word called the source operand contains three bits specifying a mode (MMM) and three bits specifying a register (RRR). Together these six bits provide the information necessary to locate the source operand. The six LSBs are used in the same way to locate the destination operand. Because of the eight modes and eight registers, octal is convenient and is used in PDP–11. For the remainder of the chapter, all numbers will be octal unless otherwise specified. Expressing the format in Figure 15–9 will take this form: 01SSDD. Six digits are used. The SS is used for the source operand and the DD for the destination operand.

In PDP–11, either words (16 bits) or bytes may be operands. The four MSBs of the instruction word specify the opcode. To move a word, the

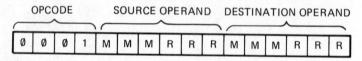

Figure 15–8. Format for the double operand instruction move (MOV).

OPCODE   SOURCE   DESTINATION

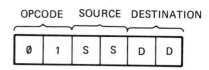

| 0 | 1 | S | S | D | D |

Figure 15-9. Octal format for the MOV instruction.

mnemonic is MOV and the four MSBs are 0001 binary (01 octal). To move a byte, the mnemonic is MOVB and the four MSBs of the instruction word are 1001 binary (11 octal). Notice that the MSB of the instruction word specifies whether the operation is on a byte or a word.

15.3 ADDRESSING MODES

The register mode is used when operands are in registers. The deferred mode is used when the register contains an address. There is a mode called autoincrement and another called autodecrement that automatically increment or decrement the registers that are used as pointers. These are used when data appears in sequence in memory. Another mode called autoincrement deferred uses a table of addresses to locate operands scattered about memory.

Relative, index, immediate, and absolute are some of the other modes that exist in PDP-11. Learning these modes is the main task of learning PDP-11. Once you learn the addressing modes, using the instruction set becomes rather easy! So, let's study the modes one by one.

15.3.1 The Register Mode

The instruction, MOV R0,R1 is an example of the register mode. An operand is contained in R0. Execution of the instruction duplicates it in R1. Both operand locations specified are in the processor. Only a fetch bus cycle is required; no bus cycles are required to execute the instruction.

The register mode is also called mode 0, because it is specified by a zero in the instruction word. For MOV R0,R1, the source operand, bits 6–11, contain 00 (octal), which specifies mode 0, register 0. This means that R0 contains the source operand. The destination operand is specified by bits 0–5. In this case, they contain 01, which specifies mode 0, register 1, meaning that R1 contains the destination operand. In other words, the destination operand is specified by mode 0, register 1.

When a byte operation is specified in the opcode and mode 0 is specified for the destination, special consideration must be given to the contents of the destination register. Registers can only contain words. Therefore, when a byte is moved to a register, it must be converted to a 16-bit number. This is done by sign extention. If bit 7 of the byte (the sign bit) equals zero, then zeros are extended through bit positions 8–15. If bit 7 equals one, then ones are extended through bit positions 8–15. For example, if the value of the byte moved to R1 equals 100 (bit 7 = 0), then R1 will contain 000100 after the move. On the other hand, if the number 200 is moved to R1 (bit 7 = 1), then it will contain 177600 after the move. The following are examples of the register mode.

Octal	Mnemonics		Comments
010100	MOV	R1,R0	;move the word from R1 to R0
010200	MOV	R2,R0	;move the word from R2 to R0
010300	MOV	R3,R0	;move the word from R3 to R0
110300	MOVB	R3,R0	;move the byte from R3 to R0
110401	MOVB	R4,R1	;move the byte from R4 to R0

15.3.2   The Deferred Mode

With mode 1, called the deferred mode, the specified register contains the address of the operand instead of the operand itself. Parens or the "at" symbol (@) are used in the mnemonic code to signify the deferred mode. For example, (R1), specifies that R1 contains the address of the operand and is encoded as 001001 in binary (11 octal). The above can be specified as @R1 also. In either case, the register contains the address of the operand.

When a byte operation is specified, a byte of data is moved to or from memory. Some examples are:

Octal	Mnemonic		Comments
011100	MOV	(R1),R0	;move the word from memory to R0
011203	MOV	(R2),R3	;move the word from memory to R3
110415	MOVB	R4,(R5)	;move the byte from R4 to memory ;only the 8 LSBs of R4 are moved
010415	MOV	R4,@R5	;same as above, except word operation
111213	MOVB	(R2),(R3)	;move the byte from memory to memory

Some of the above examples combine modes 1 and 0. The meaning of deferred can be interpreted as, "The data is not here. Take this address and go there to find the data."

15.3.3   The Autoincrement Mode

Mode 2, called the autoincrement mode, is identical to mode 1, except that the contents of the specified register are incremented after they are used to find the operand. Although the name does not say so, it is implied that this is a deferred mode. Mode 2 is identified in the mnemonic code by using parens to enclose the operand as is the case with mode 1. In addition, a plus sign follows to indicate the autoincrement mode.

Mode 2 is ideally used when operands appear in consecutive locations in memory. The instruction MOV R0,(R1)+ moves the contents of R0 to a location in memory. R1 contains the address of that location. After the address has been used, R1 is incremented by two, causing it to point to the next word location. The instruction specifies a word operation; therefore, the location in memory is a word location, containing two bytes.

If a byte operation had been specified, only a byte would be moved and R1 would be incremented by only one, causing it to point to the next byte. Word locations always have even addresses, while byte locations may have either even or odd addresses. Some examples of the autoincrement mode are:

Octal	Mnemonics		Comments
012100	MOV	(R1)+,R0	;move from memory to R0, then increment R1
010322	MOV	R3,(R2)+	;move from R3 to memory, then increment R2
112204	MOVB	(R2)+,R4	;move from memory to R4, then increment R2
112122	MOVB	(R1)+,(R2)+	;move from memory to memory, then increment R1, R2

15.3.4 The Autoincrement Deferred Mode

In mode 3, called the autoincrement deferred mode, the register contains the address of an address of the operand. That may sound a bit confusing, but you may look at it like this: This mode is the same as mode 2, except that what would be the operand is the address of the operand. After the operand is obtained, the register is always incremented by two.

Mode 3 is identified in the mnemonic code by using the @ symbol followed by the register enclosed in parens. As before, the plus sign is used to indicate that the register is incremented after the operand is obtained.

When operands do not appear in sequence but are scattered around in memory, it is convenient to use a table of addresses and a register initialized with the address of the first entry in the table. Using mode 3 allows the programmer to access the first operand, wherever it is. This register automatically increments so that it points to the second entry in the table, which contains the address of the next operand.

Both word or byte operands can be accessed using mode 3; however, the register specified always increments by two because it always contains an address of an address.

The name of mode 3, autoincrement deferred, implies that the operand is doubly deferred. Some examples:

Octal	Mnemonics		Comments
013300	MOV	@(R3)+,R0	;move at memory to R0, increment register 3
113112	MOVB	@(R1)+,(R2)	;move at memory to memory, increment register 1
011421	MOV	(R4),(R1)+	;move memory to at memory, increment register 1

The term "at memory" means that the memory location contains an address and the operand is "at" that location. The meaning of doubly deferred can be interpreted as: "The data is not here, take this address, go there, and find another address—use that address to find the data."

15.3.5   The Autodecrement Mode

Mode 4, called the autodecrement mode, is like mode 2 with this exception: the specified register decrements before the operand is obtained. In mode 2, the register is incremented after the operand is obtained and points to the next operand. In mode 4, the register decrements and points to the next operand, which appears at the next lower address. After the operand is obtained, the register remains pointing to this address.

This mode is useful when operands are located in reverse sequence in memory. You may recall that the SP works in this manner.

Mode 4 is indicated in the mnemonic code by placing parens around the specifying register, which is preceded by a minus sign. Placing the minus sign first reminds us that the register is decremented before it contains the address of the operand. For byte operations the register is decremented by one; for word operations, by two.

Here are some examples of mode 4, the autodecrement mode.

Octal	Mnemonics		Comments
010041	MOV	R0,−(R1)	;decrement R1, move R0 to memory
110142	MOVB	R1,−(R2)	;decrement R2, move byte R1 to memory
014311	MOV	−(R3),(R1)	;decrement R3, move memory to memory
010046	MOV	R0,−(SP)	;push R0

In the last example, R6, which is called SP, is used to point to the top of the stack. A push operation is performed. The stack pointer is first decremented and then the contents of R0 is moved to the top of the stack. Because of the nature of the stack, only words may be pushed or popped. The stack may be popped by using mode 2, the autoincrement mode: MOV (SP)+,R0.

15.3.6 The Autodecrement Deferred Mode

The autodecrement deferred mode, mode 5, is like mode 3, the auto-increment mode except that the specifying register is decremented first. This mode is used when operands are scattered about memory and a table of addresses is used in reverse order. Some examples using the autodecrement deferred mode are:

Octal	Mnemonic		Comments
015100	MOV	@ − (R1),R0	;decrement R1, move at memory to R0
110153	MOVB	R1,@ − (R3)	;decrement R3, move byte R1 to at memory
115114	MOVB	@ − (R1),(R4)	;decrement R1, move byte at memory to memory

Notice that mode 5 is indicated by using the @ symbol followed by a minus sign and the specifying register enclosed in parens. As with mode 3, mode 5 is doubly deferred.

15.3.7 The Index Mode

With mode 6, called the index mode, a base address is added to an index word to produce the effective address of the operand. The base address specifies the starting memory location of a table or list. A specific entry in the table or list can then be represented by the index word. The base address can be stored in a register. The index word is the second word of the instruction. The locations of the base and index may be reversed, depending on how the programmer wishes to use them.

Assume that R4 contains the address 5000. When the processor fetches the instruction, MOV 100(R4),R0, it knows that it must read a second word because it has decoded mode 6 for the source operand. After it has fetched the second word, 100, it adds the word to R4 to produce the effective address. The contents of R4 does not change, but the contents of location 5100 is read and loaded into R0.

Recall that when the processor fetches an instruction word, it increments the PC automatically. It always increments the PC by two in the LSI–11 because instruction words exist only at even addresses. The PC also increments by two when reading the second word of the instruction, causing it to point to the next instruction.

For the following examples, assume that R1 contains 1000, R2 contains 2000, and R3 contains 3000.

Octal	Word 2	Mnemonic		Comments
016100	000002	MOV	2(R1),R0	;move the contents of 1002 to R0
116201	000100	MOVB	100(R2),R1	;move the contents of byte address 2100 to R1
016304	177776	MOV	− 2(R3),R4	;move the contents of 2776 to R4
016600	000002	MOV	2(SP),R0	;move the word under top of stack to R0

In the example where the index is − 2, the second word of the instruction equals 177776 because 2's complement arithmetic is used to calculate negative indexes. Because the SP (R6) points to the top of the stack, 2(SP) points to the next word location or the preceding word pushed on the stack.

15.3.8 The Index Deferred Mode

The index deferred mode, or mode 7, is simply a deferred version of mode 6. The @ symbol is used to indicate that mode 7 is doubly deferred. For the following examples, assume that R1 contains 1000 and R2 contains 2000. Further assume that location 1000 contains 5000, 2000 contains 10000, 5000 contains 7000, and 10000 contains 20000.

Octal	Word 2	Mnemonic		Comments
017200	003000	MOV	@3000(R2),R0	;7000 is address of operand
117100	007000	MOVB	@7000(R1),R0	;20000 is address of operand
010072	177000	MOV	R0,@ − 1000(R2)	;7000 is the actual operand

Perhaps it is easiest to consider mode 6 first and then just use another deferral for mode 7.

15.3.9 The Immediate Mode

The immediate mode is actually mode 2 using register 7, the PC. To execute the following instruction, MOV (R7)+ ,R0, the processor fetches the instruction first. Recall the nature of the PC. It points to the next word because the PC always increments by two when executing a fetch. Because R7 is the specified register and mode 2 is used, then it is pointing to the operand. Notice that it is the immediate mode because the operand appears immediately after the word containing the opcode.

The problem with the above example is that a word must be reserved between the instruction word and the next instruction for the data. The PDP-11 assembler recognizes another mnemonic code for the immediate mode. It uses the pound sign (#) to indicate the immediate data. The instruction, MOV # DATA,R0, is the same as the above example, except that the assembler makes provision for the immediate data. You may recall that LIMP uses the pound sign in the same manner to indicate data. Some examples of the immediate mode are:

Octal	Word 2	Mnemonic	Comments
012700	177777	MOV # 177777,R0	;fill R0 with all 1's
012706	001000	MOV # START,SP	;initialize SP with stack address, 1000
012701	005000	MOV # 5000,R1	;init. R1 as a pointer to adr 5000

The immediate mode is often used for initialization of registers or memory locations.

15.3.10 The Absolute Mode

The absolute mode also uses the PC. However, in this case the PC points to the address of the operand instead of the operand itself. The absolute mode is mode 3 using register 7, the PC. In PDP-11, the absolute mode can be thought of as immediate deferred and is symbolized that way. The form of the mnemonic code for the move instruction is: MOV @ # ADDR,R0, where ADDR is a symbolic label.

This mode works in the same way as the direct mode in the 8085. The address of the operand follows the instruction word. The following are some examples using the absolute mode. Assume HERE is equated to 1000 and THERE is equated to 4000.

Octal	Word 2	Mnemonic		Comments
013700	001000	MOV	@ # HERE,R0	;contents of location 1000 to R0
110137	004000	MOVB	R1,@ # THERE	;low byte of R1 to 4000
011237	004000	MOV	(R2),@ # THERE	;at R2 to 4000

15.3.11 The Relative Mode

The relative mode uses mode 6 with register 7, the PC. In this case, the second word of the instruction is indexed with the PC to produce the effective address of the operand. The assembler recognizes the following mnemonic form for the move instruction: MOV R0,THERE, where THERE is a symbolic address for the operand. Notice that for the relative mode, the label stands alone with no # or @ symbols used.

As with the immediate and absolute modes, the assembler makes provision for a second word in the instruction. This word is the relative address between the next instruction to be executed and the address of the operand, hence the name, relative mode. The relative address may be calculated by subtracting the current value of the PC from the address of the operand. Remember the nature of the PC—it automatically increments by two each time a read or fetch is executed.

For each of the following examples, assume that the initial value of the PC is 1000 and that HERE is equated to 5000 and THERE is equated to 500.

Octal	Word 2	Word 3	Mnemonic	Comments
016700	003774		MOV HERE,R0	;contents of 5000 to R0
010167	177474		MOV R1,THERE	;contents of R1 to 500
016767	177474	003776	MOV THERE,HERE	;contents of 500 to 5000

The last example requires three words because two addresses are used. When calculating the first relative address, remember that the PC is pointing to the third word of the instruction. When the second relative address is calculated, the PC is pointing to the next instruction. The address THERE must equate to a negative number because it appears before the current instruction. Two's complement arithmetic is used.

15.3.12 The Relative Deferred Mode

The relative deferred mode uses mode 7 and register 7. It is the deferred form of the relative mode. That is, where the operand is found using the relative mode, an address of the operand appears using the relative deferred mode. For each of the following examples, assume that the initial value of the PC is 1000 and that HERE is equated to 5000 and THERE is equated to 500. Further, assume that 500 contains 3000 and 5000 contains 6000.

Octal	Word 2	Word 3	Mnemonic	Comments
010077	003774		MOV R0,@HERE	;R0 to 6000
017701	177474		MOV @THERE,R1	;contents of 3000 to R1
017777	003774	177472	MOV @HERE,@THERE	;contents of 6000 to 3000

This completes the discussion on the PDP-11 modes. We believe that careful study of the PDP-11 addressing modes before you attempt to study the instruction set will make that study easier.

15.4 THE PDP-11 INSTRUCTION SET

PDP-11 systems are very powerful because of the versatility of the hardware and because of the many features of the instruction set. The following list demonstrates some of the features of the PDP-11 instruction set.

1. Any memory location can be used as an accumulator.
2. Memory to memory operations are allowed. For example, the contents of one memory location can be added to the contents of a second memory location without using any of the GPRs.
3. I/O addresses are memory-mapped and can be handled just like any other memory address. Data can be moved directly between the I/O device and memory without using any GPRs.
4. It has the ability to manipulate data in either 16-bit words or bytes.
5. Versatility is provided by the large number of addressing modes.

In this section, our discussion will emphasize the differences or special features of the instructions. Because many of the PDP-11 instructions are very similar to those used by other previously discussed processors, there is little need for additional discussion.

15.4.1 The Processor Status Word

Figure 15-10 shows a diagram of the LSI-11 Processor Status word, or PS. It is contained in a 16-bit register. Bits 8 through 15 are used when memory management is employed. We will not discuss these bits now. Bits 0 through 3 are the flags, called Condition Codes in PDP-11. Bit 0 is the carry (C); bit 1, the overflow (V); bit 2, the zero (Z); and bit 3, the negative, or N condition code.

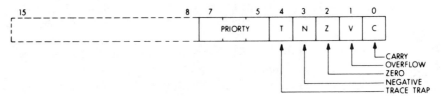

Figure 15-10. Diagram of the LSI-11 Processor Status word.
(Courtesy Digital Equipment Corporation)

The N-bit indicates a negative condition when it equals 1. The Z-bit indicates a zero condition; the V-bit, an overflow condition; and the C-bit, a carry when they are equal to 1.

Most instructions in the PDP-11 instruction set affect the condition codes with the exception of branches, jumps, calls, and returns. The branch instructions are the only ones to use the condition codes because there are no conditional jumps, calls, or returns.

Bit 4 of the PS, called the T-bit, is used for debug purposes. It allows a debug program to execute—which can make tests between each instruction of the program being debugged.

Bits 5, 6, and 7 contain the priority bits and were discussed earlier. Now that we know where the condition codes are, let's continue with the branch instructions.

15.4.2 Branch Instructions

Figure 15-11 shows a list of the branch instructions with a diagram of the format for the instructions. Each is a one-word instruction. The high byte of the word contains the opcode; the low byte contains the offset. The offset for PDP-11 is very similar to that used in the 6502 branch instructions except that it contains the number of words rather than the number of bytes the branch will take. The offset must be multiplied by two before it is indexed with the PC.

When the branch instruction is fetched, the PC is pointing to the next instruction. The offset is removed from the instruction word, sign extended to convert it to a 16-bit number and rotated left to multiply it by two. The result is indexed with the PC to produce the destination address of the branch.

When considering the machine language instruction, it is easy to remember that the number in the offset is the number of words that the branch will take. If the offset is positive, the branch will be forward; if negative, the branch will be backwards.

In the column under Base Code in Figure 15-11 you will find the opcode for each of the branch instructions. Notice that the offset equals 0 in every case. Once the offset has been calculated, it is simply added to the base to produce the instruction word. The offset may be calculated by finding the difference between the destination of the branch and the current value of the PC (the PC is pointing to the next instruction after the branch instruction).

All decisions are made using the branch instructions because they are the only conditional instructions in PDP-11.

There is a set of branches: BLT (branch if less than), BLE (branch if less than or equal to), BGT (branch if greater than), and BGE (branch if greater than or equal to) that are intended to be used only when testing signed numbers. These branches all use the N bit of the condition codes.

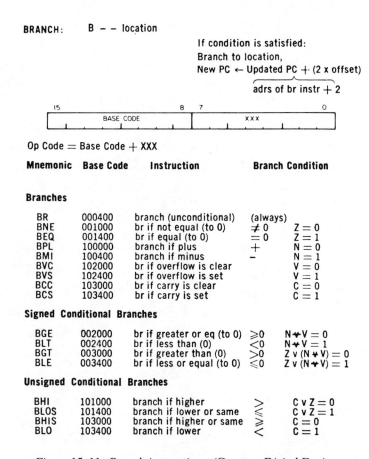

Figure 15-11. Branch instructions. (Courtesy Digital Equipment Corporation)

Another set: BHI (branch if higher), BHIS (branch if higher or the same), BLO (branch if lower), and BLOS (branch if lower or the same) do not test the N bit, but test the C bit instead. This set is intended for testing unsigned numbers.

15.4.3 Single Operand Instructions

Figure 15-12 is a list of single operand instructions including the single operand format. The opcode is contained in bits 6 through 15. The six LSBs specify the mode and register for locating the destination address.

For those instructions that can specify either a word or byte operation (whether single or double operand), bit 15 is used as an indicator. For word operations, bit 15 equals zero; for byte operations, bit 15 equals one. Notice

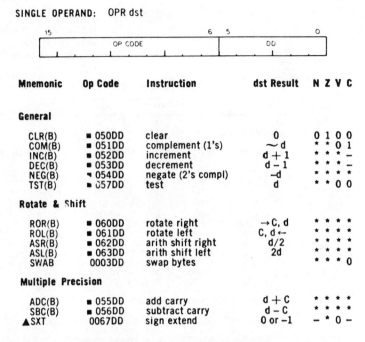

SINGLE OPERAND: OPR dst

Mnemonic	Op Code	Instruction	dst Result	N Z V C
General				
CLR(B)	■ 050DD	clear	0	0 1 0 0
COM(B)	■ 051DD	complement (1's)	~ d	* * 0 1
INC(B)	■ 052DD	increment	d + 1	* * * —
DEC(B)	■ 053DD	decrement	d − 1	* * * —
NEG(B)	◄ 054DD	negate (2's compl)	−d	* * * *
TST(B)	■ 057DD	test	d	* * 0 0
Rotate & Shift				
ROR(B)	■ 060DD	rotate right	→ C, d	* * * *
ROL(B)	■ 061DD	rotate left	C, d ←	* * * *
ASR(B)	■ 062DD	arith shift right	d/2	* * * *
ASL(B)	■ 063DD	arith shift left	2d	* * * *
SWAB	0003DD	swap bytes		* * * 0
Multiple Precision				
ADC(B)	■ 055DD	add carry	d + C	* * * *
SBC(B)	■ 056DD	subtract carry	d − C	* * * *
▲SXT	0067DD	sign extend	0 or −1	− * 0 −

Figure 15-12. Single operand instructions. (Courtesy Digital Equipment Corporation)

that a square block is shown in the MSB position for those instructions that have this option. Also notice that the instructions can indicate a byte operation by including the letter B in the mnemonic.

Notice the four columns to the right in Figure 15-12. They indicate how the condition code bits are affected by each instruction. An asterisk (*) indicates that the particular bit depends on the data that results from the instruction just executed. A 0 indicates that the particular bit is always cleared, while a 1 indicates that the bit is always set. A dash (–) indicates that the instruction did not affect that bit.

The column to the left of these bits is a simple notation indicating the operation performed by the instruction.

There are two complement instructions. The first, COM, is a logical or 1's complement while NEG is a mathematical or 2's complement. The TST instruction does not change the operand itself but does affect the condition codes. The overflow (V) and the carry (C) bits are both cleared. The N and Z bits are set according to value of the operand.

One of the single operand instructions is rather special. It is the SWAB (SWAp Bytes) instruction. It causes the high and low bytes in the operand to change positions. Notice that the C bit is cleared while all other condition codes are affected by the results of the particular data.

The two rotate instructions are familar. They cause the bits in the operand to be rotated either left or right through the C bit. These instructions may either rotate a byte or a word; however, the bits rotate through the C bit in either case.

The arithmetic shift right (ASR) instruction causes the bits in a word or byte to be shifted right one bit position. The MSB is duplicated. That is, if the MSB was a 1, it will reproduce a 1 in that position. If it was a 0, it will reproduce a 0. This is necessary to maintain the correct sign of the word. The ASL (Arithmetic Shift Left) instruction shifts the bits to the left while moving a 0 in the LSB position.

The ADC (ADd Carry) and SBC (SuBtract Carry) are used to manipulate the C bit when using multiple precision (words with more than 16 bits) arithmetic.

Finally, the sign extend (SXT) instruction fills an operand with all 1's or all 0's, depending on the value of the N bit. It is also used for multiple precision arithmetic.

15.4.4   Double Operand Instructions

The double operand instructions are listed in Figure 15–13. The format for these instructions is included.

The first four instructions listed are like those you have already studied except for the way they affect the condition codes. Notice that they all affect the condition codes in some manner.

The next three instructions are in the logical group. The first of these, BIT (BIt Test), is used to test the value of particular bits in a word or byte. For example, the instruction BIT #100,R0, tests the value of bit 6 in R0. Regardless of the values of the other bits in R0, the Z bit will be cleared if bit 6 equals 1 and will be set if bit 6 equals 0. The contents of R0 are not affected.

This instruction is executed by ANDing the source operand with the destination operand and setting the condition codes accordingly. The destination operand is not changed.

The BIC (BIt Clear) instruction clears each bit in the destination operand that corresponds to each 1-bit in the source operand. For example, the instruction BIC #400,R0 will clear bit 8 in R0 without affecting the value of the other bits.

The processor executes this instruction by ANDing the 1's complement of the source operand with the destination operand and setting the condition code bits accordingly.

The BIS (BIt Set) instruction is executed by ORing the source operand with the destination operand. For example, the instruction BIS #300,R0 will set bits 6 and 7 in R0 regardless of the value of the other bits.

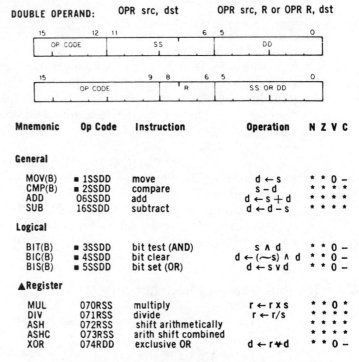

DOUBLE OPERAND: OPR src, dst   OPR src, R or OPR R, dst

Mnemonic	Op Code	Instruction	Operation	N Z V C
General				
MOV(B)	∎ 1SSDD	move	d ← s	* * 0 –
CMP(B)	∎ 2SSDD	compare	s – d	* * * *
ADD	06SSDD	add	d ← s + d	* * * *
SUB	16SSDD	subtract	d ← d – s	* * * *
Logical				
BIT(B)	∎ 3SSDD	bit test (AND)	s ∧ d	* * 0 –
BIC(B)	∎ 4SSDD	bit clear	d ← (~s) ∧ d	* * 0 –
BIS(B)	∎ 5SSDD	bit set (OR)	d ← s ∨ d	* * 0 –
▲**Register**				
MUL	070RSS	multiply	r ← r x s	* * 0 *
DIV	071RSS	divide	r ← r/s	* * * *
ASH	072RSS	shift arithmetically		* * * *
ASHC	073RSS	arith shift combined		* * * *
XOR	074RDD	exclusive OR	d ← r ⊻ d	* * 0 –

Figure 15-13. Double operand instructions. (Courtesy Digital Equipment Corporation)

15.4.5 Jump Instructions

Figure 15-14 shows a list of instructions including a jump (JMP) and a jump to subroutine (JSR). These instructions are all different, so let's start with JMP.

The JMP instruction is unconditional, which means that it is not used in decision making. Because the branch instructions have a limited range, the JMP instructions are required so that program control can be changed to any place in memory. Although it is included in Figure 15-14, this instruction is really a single operand instruction and it uses that format.

The jump to subroutine instruction uses the format shown in Figure 15-14. A register is specified in the instruction word in bits 6, 7, and 8. The register is called a *link register*. It is used to save the return address so that execution of the main program can continue after the subroutine has been executed. When the JSR instruction is executed, the contents of the link register are pushed on to the stack and the return address is moved to the link register automatically. The RTS (ReTurn from Subroutine) instruction moves the contents of the link register back to the PC, and then the top of

JUMP & SUBROUTINE:

Mnemonic	Op Code	Instruction	Notes
JMP	0001DD	jump	PC ← dst
JSR	004RDD	jump to subroutine	} use same R
RTS	00020R	return from subroutine	
▲MARK	0064NN	mark	aid in subr return
▲SOB	077RNN	subtract 1 & br (if ≠ 0)	(R) − 1, then if (R) ≠ 0: PC ← Updated PC − (2 x NN)

Figure 15–14. Jump instructions. (Courtesy Digital Equipment Corporation)

the stack is popped to the link register. This procedure allows the link register to be used to pass parameters to and from the subroutine. In case you were wondering—yes, any number of subroutine calls may be nested. The same register specified as the link in the JSR instruction must also be specified in the return. Any register except the SP may be used as the link including the PC.

MARK is an instruction used to clean the stack when a number of parameters have been passed to the subroutine using the stack.

A special instruction, SOB (Subtract One and branch Back if not zero) is used for program loops. A register is initialized with the number of times the program is to loop. Each time the SOB instruction is executed, the register is decremented. If the contents of the register is not zero, a branch back to the loop is executed. Finally, when the register contents equal zero, execution falls through the instruction and the following instruction is executed. The offset is always positive and is contained in the six LSBs of the instruction. The branch must always be backwards.

15.4.6 Condition Code Operators

The group of instructions that allow the programmer to manipulate the condition codes are shown in Figure 15–15. The first five instructions are used to clear the various bits. The next five instructions are used to set the bits. Notice that the bits to be cleared or set correspond to the bits in the PSW. Also notice that there is an instruction that clears all bits and another that sets all bits. Using a bit of ingenuity, you can devise an instruction word that will clear or set two or three bits.

15.4.7 Miscellaneous Instructions

A set of miscellaneous instructions is shown in Figure 15–16. They include HALT, WAIT, RESET, and a NOP. You remember the NOP, it does nothing. The HALT instruction causes the processor to suspend execution of the program and to execute the ODT microcode. The processor cannot be interrupted when halted. On the other hand, the WAIT instruction will allow an interrupt while program execution has suspended.

CONDITION CODE OPERATORS:

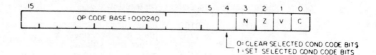

Mnemonic	Op Code	Instruction	N Z V C
CLC	000241	clear C	– – – 0
CLV	000242	clear V	– – 0 –
CLZ	000244	clear Z	– 0 – –
CLN	000250	clear N	0 – – –
CCC	000257	clear all cc bits	0 0 0 0
SEC	000261	set C	– – – 1
SEV	000262	set V	– – 1 –
SEZ	000264	set Z	– 1 – –
SEN	000270	set N	1 – – –
SCC	000277	set all cc bits	1 1 1 1

Figure 15–15. Condition code operators. (Courtesy Digital Equipment Corporation)

The RESET instruction causes the processor to activate the bus signal BINIT L, which initiates the various I/O boards on the bus.

15.4.8 Trap and Interrupt Instructions

The PDP–11 systems rely on the use of software traps for various purposes. The trap instructions are shown in Figure 15–17.

One trap instruction, EMT (EMulator Trap), is used in system programs. It causes the processor to trap and vector through location 30 to a service routine called a trap handler. The low byte of the trap instruction carries a logical number representing one of the system's subroutines. The purpose of the trap handler is to convert the logical number to an address and call the subroutine at that address. The advantage of this technique is that users of the system can access the various subroutines without know-

MISCELLANEOUS:

Mnemonic	Op Code	Instruction
HALT	000000	halt
WAIT	000001	wait for interrupt
RESET	000005	reset external bus
NOP	000240	(no operation)
● SPL	00023N	set priority level (to N)
▲ MFPI	0065SS	move from previous instr space
▲ MTPI	0066DD	move to previous instr space
● MFPD	1065SS	move from previous data space
● MTPD	1066DD	move to previous data space

Figure 15–16. Miscellaneous instructions. (Courtesy Digital Equipment Corporation)

TRAP & INTERRUPT:

Mnemonic	Op Code	Instruction	Notes
EMT	104000 to 104377	emulator trap (not for general use)	PC at 30, PS at 32
TRAP	104400 to 104777	trap	PC at 34, PS at 36
BPT	000003	breakpoint trap	PC at 14, PS at 16
IOT	000004	input/output trap	PC at 20, PS at 22
RTI	000002	return from interrupt	
▲RTT	000006	return from interrupt	inhibit T bit trap

Figure 15–17. Trap and interrupt instructions. (Courtesy Digital Equipment Corporation)

ing the address of the subroutine. Because system programs are modified frequently and addresses are changed, only logical numbers of the subroutines are published.

The instruction TRAP is used in the same manner, but it is intended for user routines instead of system routines.

The BPT (Break Point Trap) is used with debug programs. The RTT (ReTurn from Trap) is also used in debug routines.

The IOT (Input/Output Trap) is used with a set of input and output routines called an I/O executive. The I/O executive may be used with the user programs and provides the necessary routines to communicate with the peripherals.

When an interrupt occurs, the processor pushes the PSW and the return address (PC). When the service routine is completed, the instruction, RTI (ReTurn from Interrupt), causes the saved values to be returned to the PC and the PSW respectively and execution of the main program to continue.

Notice that in all of the trap instructions a specified address is indicated for the vectors. These addresses are absolute and cannot be changed. Device vectors are configured on the interface boards and can be changed.

Questions

Name the bus signal in questions 1–12.

1. Causes the slave to place data on the bus.
2. Indicates that a valid address is on the bus.
3. Generated by BDAL13, BDAL14, and BDAL15.
4. Indicates that the bus cycle is complete.
5. Control Signal for DATI bus cycle.

6. Asserted immediately following sync on DATO bus cycles.

7. Asserted in response to an IN or OUT control signal.

8. Indicates that the bus is used for a byte operation.

9. Issued by the processor when data is valid on the bus.

10. This signal has the longest duration.

11. This signal is terminated by the slave in response to the termination of a read or write control signal.

12. Indicates a DATO or DATOB cycle has started.

13. In the master/slave relationship, who can be master? Who can be slave?

14. What part of the processor grants bus requests?

15. When are bus grants issued?

16. How does a device request use of the bus?

17. What do vector addresses contain?

18. How does the bus arbitrator let a device know it has granted its request?

19. How would you interpret the instruction 010103?

20. How would you interpret the instruction 010304?

21. How would you interpret the instruction 012102?

22. How would you interpret the instruction 010415?

23. How would you interpret the instruction 113402?

24. How would you interpret the instruction 111231?

Appendix A

Answers to Odd-Numbered Problems

CHAPTER 1

1. Through interface circuits.
3. The data bus.
5. Address 40 is a peripheral device address and we are going to read data from this device.
7. READ
9. In the processor.
11. The program counter (PC).
13. The peripheral address was 30, and data was to be input from that peripheral.
15. The IR contains the instruction that was fetched from memory.

CHAPTER 2

Problem Set 2–1

1. 7	3. 13	5. 38	7. 101	9. 240	11. 12
13. 63	15. 190	17. 2174	19. 26	21. 76	23. 512
25. 4522					

Problem Set 2–2

1. a) 101   b) 5   c) 5
3. a) 1100   b) 14   c) C
5. a) 1001101   b) 115   c) 4D
7. a) 1100100   b) 144   c) 64
9. a) 10000010   b) 202   c) 82
11. a) 100000000   b) 400   c) 100
13. a) 100101100   b) 454   c) 12C
15. a) 1010100001   b) 1241   c) 2A1
17. a) 46   b) 26
19. a) 342   b) 2E
21. a) 210   b) 88
23. a) 134476   b) D93E
25. a) 176013   b) FC0B
27. $10111101_2 = 189_{10} = BD_{16}$
29. $101010_2 = 52_8 = 42_{10}$
31. $11111100100000_2 = 37440_8 = 16160_{10}$
33. $00111011.00110000_2 = 3B.30_{16}$
35. $00101010.00001100_2 = 52.03_8$
37. 00101011.01000000_2
39. $265.152_8 = B5.35_{16}$

Problem Set 2–3

1. a) $1177_8 = 639_{10}$ b) $1140_8 = 608_{10}$ c) $1352_8 = 746_{10}$
3. a) $11B6_{16} = 4534_{10}$ b) $19ACE_{16} = 105166_{10}$ c) $3DB6_{16} = 15798_{10}$
5. a) $1011_2 = 11_{10}$ b) $11000_2 = 24_{10}$ c) $1010110_2 = 86_{10}$
7. a) 15   b) 77   c) 337
9. a) 7AC   b) 6A1A   c) CE9F
11. a) 101   b) 1011   c) 1101

Problem Set 2–4

1. a) –3; –0000011   b) 18; 00010010   c) 5; 00000101
   d) –21; –00010101   e) 3; 00000011
3. $0001\ 0111_{BCD}$
5. $1000\ 0011.0100\ 0111_{BCD}$

CHAPTER 3

Problems 3-1

1. AND, OR, NOT

3. Two or more

5.

4-input AND gate

7.

B	C	D	$\overline{D}$	$BC\overline{D}$
0	0	0	1	0
0	0	1	0	0
0	1	0	1	0
0	1	1	0	0
1	0	0	1	0
1	0	1	0	0
1	1	0	1	1
1	1	1	0	0

9.

A	B	C	ABC	$\overline{ABC}$
0	0	0	0	1
0	0	1	0	1
0	1	0	0	1
0	1	1	0	1
1	0	0	0	1
1	0	1	0	1
1	1	0	0	1
1	1	1	1	0

11.

A	B	$\overline{A}$	$\overline{A}B$
0	0	1	0
0	1	1	1
1	0	0	0
1	1	0	0

13.

A	B	C	B+C	A(B+C)
0	0	0	0	0
0	0	1	1	0
0	1	0	1	0
0	1	1	1	0
1	0	0	0	0
1	0	1	1	1
1	1	0	1	1
1	1	1	1	1

15.

A	B	C	$\overline{B}$	$\overline{C}$	$\overline{B}\,\overline{C}$	$A\overline{B}\,\overline{C}$	$\overline{A\,\overline{B}C}$
0	0	0	1	1	1	0	1
0	0	1	1	0	0	0	1
0	1	0	0	1	0	0	1
0	1	1	0	0	0	0	1
1	0	0	1	1	1	1	0
1	0	1	1	0	0	0	1
1	1	0	0	1	0	0	1
1	1	1	0	0	0	0	1

Problems 3-2

1. a) $\overline{(A+B)}$ b) $A + B + \overline{C}$ c) $AB + C$ d) $CDE(A + B)$
   e) $(A + B)(C + D)$ f) $\overline{(A+B+CDE+F)}$

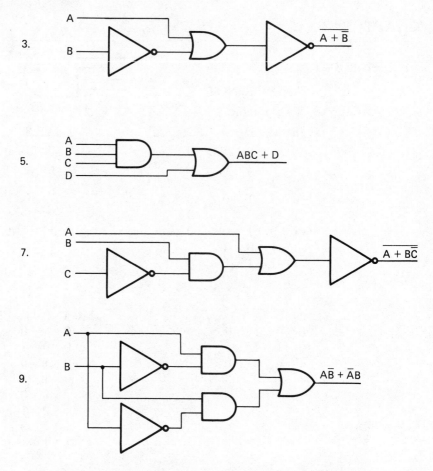

Figure A 3-2. Answers to problems 3, 5, 7, and 9 of Problem Set 3-2.

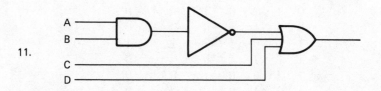

Problems 3–3

1. Q_2 is turned off when Q_1 is turned on allowing the output to go HIGH.
3. If A is HIGH, one of the transistors is turned on resulting in a LOW output.

5.

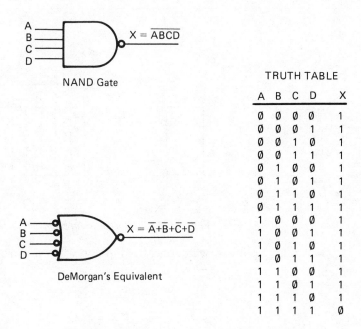

A	B	C	D	X
0	0	0	0	1
0	0	0	1	1
0	0	1	0	1
0	0	1	1	1
0	1	0	0	1
0	1	0	1	1
0	1	1	0	1
0	1	1	1	1
1	0	0	0	1
1	0	0	1	1
1	0	1	0	1
1	0	1	1	1
1	1	0	0	1
1	1	0	1	1
1	1	1	0	1
1	1	1	1	0

Figure A 3-3. Answer to problem 5, Problem Set 3-3.

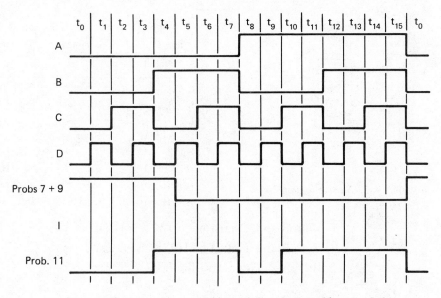

Figure A 3-4. Answers to problems 7, 9 and 11, Problem Set 3-3.

CHAPTER 4

Problems 4–1

1.

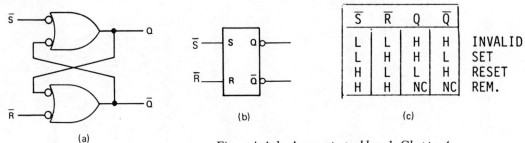

Figure A 4–1. Answer to problem 1, Chapter 4.

3. A timing pulse, or gate, tells the flip-flop when it can change state.

5.

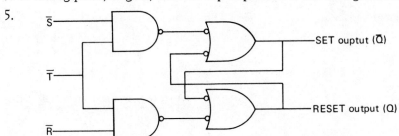

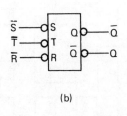

(b)

Figure A 4–2. Answer to problem 5.
Chapter 4.

Input			Command	Output	
$\overline{S}$	$\overline{R}$	$\overline{T}$		Q	$\overline{Q}$
L	L	L		NC	NC
L	L	H	Remember	NC	NC
L	H	L		NC	NC
L	H	H	Reset	L	H
H	L	L		NC	NC
H	L	H	Set	H	L
H	H	L		NC	NC
(c) H	H	H	Invalid	H	H

7. Both R and T must be LOW. S is HIGH.

9. Both R and T must be HIGH. S is LOW.

11. By using master-slave flip-flops.

13. When the flip-flop is "cocked," the master has gone to the state of the input (set or reset). When the flip-flop has "triggered," the slave has gone to the state of the master.

15. The J-K flip-flop has no invalid state.

17. When a flip-flop complements, that means its output changes state.

19.
21.

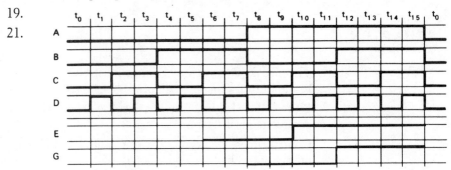

Figure A 4-3. Answers to problems 19 and 21, Chapter 4.

Problems 4–2

1. Depends on the number of flip-flops that make up the register. One bit is stored per flip-flop.

3. Buffer registers are registers used between two systems where there are differences that prevent direct access between the two.

5. In jam entry, new data may be entered when a timing pulse, called ENTER in our diagram, becomes active.

CHAPTER 5

1. The PC stores the address of the next instruction.

3. 4

5. To temporarily store addresses of data.

7. 8,8,2

9. $Z = 0; S = 1$

11. 01101001; $C = 1; S = 0; Z = 0$

13. $01001101 = 115_8 = 4D_{16}$

15. 11001000   00011100
      310   34
       C8   1C

17. MOV A,M. The contents of A (the source) are moved to the memory location (the destination) pointed to by P.

19. Bit 7 = 0 because XOR E is a 1-byte instruction. Bit 6 = 0 because XOR E is not a move instruction.

21. 10111101   10100011
    275   213
    BD   A3

CHAPTER 6

1. The $\overline{\text{TRAN C}}$ and $\overline{\text{RCV D}}$ lines must be active to transfer DATA C to the output of gate 8. All other lines must be inactive.

3. If the DISABLE line is not active, the output of the circuit will be the complement of its input.

5. Control lines $\overline{\text{TRAN C}}$, $\overline{\text{RCV A}}$, and $\overline{\text{RCV D}}$ must be active. All other control lines must be inactive.

7. The processor is the source if the control signal is HIGH.

9. The $\overline{\text{READ}}$ and $\overline{\text{PS1}}$ signals must be activated to input data via port 1.

11. The data must be placed at the inputs to the 8-bit latch. Then the peripheral provides a clock pulse that latches the data. This must be followed by activating the $\overline{\text{READ}}$ and $\overline{\text{PS0}}$ control signals.

13. The A/D converter must have finished its conversion process. Then it issues a ready signal to the status port. The processor then reads and detects the READY signal.

15. Address lines A_1 AND A_2 through A_7 must be HIGH and A_0 must be LOW to select port 2.

17. Any combination of active lines will select a memory location so long as lines A_2 through A_7 are not all active.

19. The READ and $\overline{\text{PSEL}}$ lines must be activated to read memory.

CHAPTER 7

1. Decision-making symbol.

3. The opcode field. This field contains the mnemonic op-codes.

5. Comments field is optional.

7. 01000010

9. a) 2A   b) CD   c) 49

11. a) 8A   b) 8A   c) C5   d) 3B

13. a) (A) = 5C (C) = 4B (P) = 27 (PC) = 18

 b) MOV M,C

 c) (A) = 47 (C) = 4B

 d) The instruction at address 22 will be executed because Z = 1.

15. Assuming hex, the beginning address is 50 and the last address is B4.

17.
60	F0	69	START: MOV #NUM1,P
62	C0	00	MOV #00,A
64	55		MOV M,C
65	22		AND C
66	85	69	STA NUM1
68	07		HLT
69			NUM1:

This program merely clears the contents of NUM1.

19.
50	E0	50	MOV #BEGIN,C	;initialize C reg
52	C8	05	MOV #SIZE,B	;initialize counter
54	32		XOR C	;A + C (XOR)
55	F0	65	MOV #DATA1,P	;initialize P
57	45		MORE: MOV M,A	;(M) to A
58	16		INC P	;incr the pointer
59	BF	70	CALL SUM	;call subroutine
61	19		DEC B	;decr counter
62	BE	56	BNZ MORE	;go to MORE if Z = 0
64	07		HLT	
65			DATA1	
66			DATA2	
67			DATA3	
68			DATA4	
70	0A		SUM: ADD C	;(A) + (C) to A
71	50		MOV A,C	;store result in C
72	06		RET	;return to main program
			END	

CHAPTER 8

1. A CALL instruction saves the contents of the PC on the stack and then jumps to the address specified in the CALL instruction. A PUSH saves the contents.

3. a) At address 9F. Remember, the SP is first decremented and then the data is stored. b) 78, the sum of (A) and (D).

5. By issuing IRDY, the ready bit.

7. A status port is the interface circuitry used to let the program know a peripheral is ready to input data. A control port is the interface circuitry that allows the processor to control the flow of data from a peripheral to the processor.

9. $\overline{\text{WRITE}}$ AND $\overline{\text{PSEL 3}}$ (if port 3 is the selected port) AND Bit 7 (because Bit 7 has been designated as the EI bit). The EI signal is used to set the INTE flip-flop, which allows the processor to be interrupted whenever a port wishes to input or output data.

11. On the stack.

13. The background program is the main program. We always return to this program after an interrupt.

CHAPTER 9

1. A, B, C, D, E, H, L

3. During T_1

5. Minimum of 4, maximum of 6 depending on the instruction.

7. $S_0 = 0, S_1 = 1, \text{IO}/\overline{\text{M}} = 0$

9. $S_0 = 1, S_1 = 0, \text{IO}/\overline{\text{M}} = 1$

11. a) During the entire cycle.   b) During T_2 and T_3.   c) Receive mode   d) T_2 and T_3.

13. An instruction cycle is the time required to complete an instruction. A machine cycle is typically any read or write operation (except for the DMA and RST instructions). An instruction cycle will have from one to five machine cycles depending on the instruction.

15. READ

CHAPTER 10

1. Register (MOV C,H); Immediate (MVI B,4CH); Direct (LDA 2060); Indirect (STAX D).

3. a) Register   b)1   c) 4   d) Moves data from the A reg to the memory address pointed to by the H and L register pair.

5. A call is a special kind of jump. It causes the contents of the PC (the address of the next instruction in sequence) to be saved on the stack so that program execution will continue in that sequence after the subroutine is completed. A jump causes program execution to continue in sequence from the address contained in the jump instruction.

7. RETurn

9. a) $S = 1, Z = 0, C = 0, AC = 1, P = 1$.   b) F0H   c) B4H

11. $S = 1, Z = 0, C = 0, AC = 1, P = 0$

13. a) In the B reg.   b) In the D reg.   c) MOV D,B   d) These bits identify the kind of instruction to be executed. 01 always indicates a MOVe instruction.

15. The machine language program that will be stored by the computer.

CHAPTER 11

1. a) Used to initiate one of the interrupts RST0 through RST7.   b) In the Interrupt Controller.   c) Until $\overline{\text{INTA}}$ or $\overline{\text{RESET}}$ is activated.

3. 34H

5. The RST 5.5 Service Request F/F is part of the interface circuit. The RST 7.5 Service Request F/F is internal to the processor.

7. TRAP, RST 7.5, RST 6.5, RST 5.5, INTR

9. INTE set, INTR active

11. Save PSW and all regs used by the Interrupt Service Routine.

13. Allows the "point 5's" to be individually disabled (but not TRAP).

15. Bit 1

17. 1) Whenever an RST 7.5 can be reset; 2) By the SIM instruction; 3)RESET

CHAPTER 12

1. During T_1

3. A_{10}, A_{12}, and A_{13} were used. Since A_{14} and A_{15} are not used in the system they could have been used.

5. A_{11}

7. A_{11}, A_{12}, and A_{13} all LOW.

9. A_{10} and A_{13} LOW, A_{12} HIGH

11. During ALE (T_1)

13. 1000 – 1BFF (RAM0), 1400 – 1FFF (RAM1)

15. Four plus Port C of the 8155, which is a special 6-bit port.

17. $\overline{\text{A STB}}$ is bit 2 of Port C and is used to acknowledge that data has been received by a peripheral and new data is being requested.

CHAPTER 13

1. Index X, Index Y, SP, Accumulator, PCL, PCH
3. 1 K bytes
5. Specifies immediate mode and precedes the value of the data (or a label that represents its value).
7. At the beginning of the bus cycle
9. $\overline{\text{IRQ}}$

CHAPTER 15

1. BDIN L
3. BBS7 L
5. BDIN L
7. BRPLY L
9. BDOUT L
11. BRPLY L
13. The processor or any I/O device can be the master. Memory cannot be the master. The processor, any I/O device, or memory can be the slave.
15. Between bus cycles
17. Address of interrupt service routines.
19. MOV R1,R3
21. MOV (R1)+,R2
23. MOVB @(R4)+,R2

Intel 8080/8085
Instruction Set

HOW TO USE THIS CHAPTER

This chapter is a dictionary of 8080 and 8085 instructions. The instruction descriptions are listed alphabetically for quick reference. Each description is complete so that you are seldom required to look elsewhere for additional information.

This reference format necessarily requires repetitive information. If you are reading this manual to learn about the 8080 or the 8085, do not try to read this chapter from ACI (add immediate with Carry) to XTHL (exchange top of stack with H and L registers). Instead, read the description of the processor and instruction set in Chapter 1 and the programming examples in Chapter 6. When you begin to have questions about particular instructions, look them up in this chapter.

TIMING INFORMATION

The instruction descriptions in this manual do not explicitly state execution timings. This is because the basic operating speed of your processor depends on the clock frequency used in your system.

The 'state' is the basic unit of time measurement for the processor. A state may range from 480 nanoseconds (320 nanoseconds on the 8085) to 2 microseconds, depending on the clock frequency. When you know the length of a state in your system, you can determine an instruction's basic execution time by multiplying that figure by the number of states required for the instruction.

Notice that two sets of cycle/state specifications are given for 8085 conditional call and jump instructions. This is because the 8085 fetches the third instruction byte only if it is actually needed; i.e., the specified condition is satisfied.

This basic timing factor can be affected by the operating speed of the memory in your system. With a fast clock cycle and a slow memory, the processor can outrun the memory. In this case, the processor must wait for the memory to deliver the desired instruction or data. In applications with critical timing requirements, this wait can be significant. Refer to the appropriate manufacturer's literature for memory timing data.

ACI   **ADD IMMEDIATE WITH CARRY**

ACI adds the contents of the second instruction byte and the carry bit to the contents of the accumulator and stores the result in the accumulator.

Opcode	Operand
ACI	data

The operand specifies the actual data to be added to the accumulator except, of course, for the carry bit. Data may be in the form of a number, an ASCII constant, the label of a previously defined value, or an expression. The data may not exceed one byte.

The assembler's relocation feature treats all external and relocatable symbols as 16-bit addresses. When one of these symbols appears in the operand expression of an immediate instruction, it must be preceded by either the HIGH or LOW operator to specify which byte of the address is to be used in the evaluation of the expression. When neither operator is present, the assembler assumes the LOW operator and issues an error message.

1	1	0	0	1	1	1	0
data							

Cycles: 2
States: 7
Addressing: immediate
Flags: Z,S,P,CY,AC

Example:

Assume that the accumulator contains the value 14H and that the carry bit is set to one. The instruction ACI 66 has the following effect:

$$
\begin{array}{rcl}
\text{Accumulator} & = 14H & = 00010100 \\
\text{Immediate data} & = 42H & = 01000010 \\
\text{Carry} & = & \underline{\qquad 1} \\
& & 01010111 = 57H
\end{array}
$$

ADC   **ADD WITH CARRY**

The ADC instruction adds one byte of data plus the setting of the carry flag to the contents of the accumulator. The result is stored in the accumulator. ADC then updates the setting of the carry flag to indicate the outcome of the operation.

The ADC instruction's use of the carry bit enables the program to add multi-byte numeric strings.

Add Register to Accumulator with Carry

Opccde	Operand
ADC	reg

The operand must specify one of the registers A through E, H or L. This instruction adds the contents of the specified register and the carry bit to the accumulator and stores the result in the accumulator.

1	0	0	0	1	S	S	S

Cycles:	1
States:	4
Addressings:	register
Flags:	Z,S,P,CY,AC

Add Memory to Accumulator with Carry

Opcode	Operand
ADC	M

This instruction adds the contents of the memory location addressed by the H and L registers and the carry bit to the accumulator and stores the result in the accumulator. M is a symbolic reference to the H and L registers.

1	0	0	0	1	1	1	0

Cycles:	2
States:	7
Addressing:	register indirect
Flags:	Z,S,P,CY,AC

Example:

Assume that register C contains 3DH, the accumulator contains 42H, and the carry bit is set to zero. The instruction ADC C performs the addition as follows:

```
   3DH  =  00111101
   42H  =  01000010
 CARRY  =         0
           01111111 = 7FH
```

The condition flags are set as follows:

Carry	= 0
Sign	= 0
Zero	= 0
Parity	= 0
Aux. Carry	= 0

If the carry bit is set to one, the instruction has the following results:

$$
\begin{array}{rl}
3DH = & 00111101 \\
42H = & 01000010 \\
CARRY = & \underline{\qquad 1} \\
& 10000000 = 80H
\end{array}
$$

Carry	=	0
Sign	=	1
Zero	=	0
Parity	=	0
Aux. Carry	=	1

ADD   ADD

The ADD instruction adds one byte of data to the contents of the accumulator. The result is stored in the accumulator. Notice that the ADD instruction excludes the carry flag from the addition but sets the flag to indicate the outcome of the operation.

Add Register to Register

Opcode	Operand
ADD	reg

The operand must specify one of the registers A through E, H or L. The instruction adds the contents of the specified register to the contents of the accumulator and stores the result in the accumulator.

1	0	0	0	0	S	S	S

Cycles:	1
States:	4
Addressing:	register
Flags:	Z,S,P,CY,AC

Add From Memory

Opcode	Operand
ADD	M

This instruction adds the contents of the memory location addressed by the H and L registers to the contents of the accumulator and stores the result in the accumulator. M is a symbolic reference to the H and L registers.

1	0	0	0	0	1	1	0

Cycles:	2
States:	7
Addressing:	register indirect
Flags:	Z,S,P,CY,AC

Examples:

Assume that the accumulator contains 6CH and register D contains 2EH. The instruction ADD D performs the addition as follows:

$$2EH = 00101110$$
$$6CH = 01101100$$
$$\overline{9AH = 10011010}$$

The accumulator contains the value 9AH following execution of the ADD D instruction. The contents of the D register remain unchanged. The condition flags are set as follows:

Carry	= 0
Sign	= 1
Zero	= 0
Parity	= 1
Aux. Carry	= 1

The following instruction doubles the contents of the accumulator:

ADD A

ADI   ADD IMMEDIATE

ADI adds the contents of the second instruction byte of the contents of the accumulator and stores the result in the accumulator.

Opcode	Operand
ADI	data

The operand specifies the actual data to be added to the accumulator. This data may be in the form of a number, an ASCII constant, the label of a previously defined value, or an expression. The data may not exceed one byte.

The assembler's relocation feature treats all external and relocatable symbols as 16-bit addresses. When one of these symbols appears in the operand expression of an immediate instruction, it must be preceded by either the HIGH or LOW operator to specify which byte of the address is to be used in the evaluation of the expression. When neither operator is present, the assembler assumes the LOW operator and issues an error message.

1	1	0	0	0	1	1	0
data							

Cycles:	2
States:	7
Addressing:	immediate
Flags:	Z,S,P,CY,AC

Example:

Assume that the accumulator contains the value 14H. The instruction ADI 66 has the following effect:

$$Accumulator = 14H = 00010100$$
$$Immediate\ data = 42H = \underline{01000010}$$
$$01010110 = 56H$$

Notice that the assembler converts the decimal value 66 into the hexadecimal value 42.

ANA   LOGICAL AND WITH ACCUMULATOR

ANA performs a logical AND operation using the contents of the specified byte and the accumulator. The result is placed in the accumulator.

Summary of Logical Operations

AND produces a one bit in the result only when the corresponding bits in the test data and the mask data are ones.

OR produces a one bit in the result when the corresponding bits in either the test data or the mask data are ones.

Exclusive OR produces a one bit only when the corresponding bits in the test data and the mask data are different; i.e., a one bit in either the test data or the mask data — but not both — produces a one bit in the result.

AND	OR	EXCLUSIVE OR
1010 1010	1010 1010	1010 1010
0000 1111	0000 1111	0000 1111
0000 1010	1010 1111	1010 0101

AND Register with Accumulator

Opcode	Operand
ANA	reg

The operand must specify one of the registers A through E, H or L. This instruction ANDs the contents of the specified register with the accumulator and stores the result in the accumulator. The carry flag is reset to zero.

1	0	1	0	0	S	S	S

Cycles: 1
States: 4
Addressing: register
Flags: Z,S,P,CY,AC

AND Memory with Accumulator

Opcode	Operand
ANA	M

This instruction ANDs the contents of the specified memory location with the accumulator and stores the result in the accumulator. The carry flag is reset to zero.

1	0	1	0	0	1	1	0

Cycles:	2
States:	7
Addressing:	register indirect
Flags:	Z,S,P,CY,AC

Example:

Since any bit ANDed with a zero produces a zero and any bit ANDed with a one remains unchanged, AND is frequently used to zero particular groups of bits. The following example ensures that the high-order four bits of the accumulator are zero, and the low-order four bits are unchanged. Assume that the C register contains 0FH:

```
Accumulator = 1 1 1 1   1 1 0 0 = 0FCH
C Register  = 0 0 0 0   1 1 1 1 = 0FH
              0 0 0 0   1 1 0 0 = 0CH
```

ANI   **AND IMMEDIATE WITH ACCUMULATOR**

ANI performs a logical AND operation using the contents of the second byte of the instruction and the accumulator. The result is placed in the accumulator. ANI also resets the carry flag to zero.

Opcode	Operand
ANI	data

The operand must specify the data to be used in the AND operation. This data may be in the form of a number, an ASCII constant, the label of some previously defined value, or an expression. The data may not exceed one byte.

The assembler's relocation feature treats all external and relocatable symbols as 16-bit addresses. When one of these symbols appears in the operand expression of an immediate instruction, it must be preceded by either the HIGH or LOW operator to specify which byte of the address is to be used in the evaluation of the expression. When neither operator is present, the assembler assumes the LOW operator and issues an error message.

1	1	1	0	0	1	1	0
data								

Cycles: 2
States: 7
Addressing: immediate
Flags: Z,S,P,CY,AC

Summary of Logical Operations

AND produces a one bit in the result only when the corresponding bits in the test data and the mask data are ones.

OR produces a one bit in the result when the corresponding bits in either the test data or the mask data are ones.

Exclusive OR produces a one bit only when the corresponding bits in the test data and the mask data are different; i.e., a one bit in either the test data or the mask data — but not both — produces a one bit in the result.

AND	OR	EXCLUSIVE OR
1010 1010	1010 1010	1010 1010
0000 1111	0000 1111	0000 1111
0000 1010	1010 1111	1010 0101

Example:

The following instruction is used to reset OFF bit six of the byte in the accumulator:

        ANI   10111111B

Since any bit ANDed with a one remains unchanged and a bit ANDed with a zero is rest to zero, the ANI instruction shown above sets bit six OFF and leaves the others unchanged. This technique is useful when a program uses individual bits as status flags.

CALL   CALL

The CALL instruction combines functions of the PUSH and JMP instructions. CALL pushes the contents of the program counter (the address of the next sequential instruction) onto the stack and then jumps to the address specified in the CALL instruction.

Each CALL instruction or one of its variants implies the use of a subsequent RET (return) instruction. When a call has no corresponding return, excess addresses are built up in the stack.

Opcode	Operand
CALL	address

The address may be specified as a number, a label, or an expression. (The label is most common.) The assembler inverts the high and low address bytes when it assembles the instruction.

1	1	0	0	1	1	0	1
low addr							
high addr							

Cycles:	5
States:	17 (18 on 8085)
Addressing:	immediate/register indirect
Flags:	none

Example:

When a given coding sequence is required several times in a program, you can usually conserve memory by coding the sequence as a subroutine invoked by the CALL instruction or one of its variants. For example, assume that an application drives a six-digit LED display; the display is updated as a result of an operator input or because of two different calculations that occur in the program. The coding required to drive the display can be included in-line at each of the three points where it is needed, or it can be coded as a subroutine. If the label DISPLY is assigned to the first instruction of the display driver, the following CALL instruction is used to invoke the display subroutine:

CALL   DISPLY

This CALL instruction pushes the address of the next program instruction onto the stack and then transfers control to the DISPLY subroutine. The DISPLY subroutine must execute a return instruction or one of its variants to resume normal program flow. The following is a graphic illustration of the effect of CALL and return instructions:

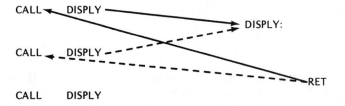

Consideration for Using Subroutines

The larger the code segment to be repeated and the greater the number of repetitions, the greater the potential memory savings of using a subroutine. Thus, if the display driver in the previous example requires one hundred bytes, coding it in-line would require three hundred bytes. Coded as a subroutine, it requires one hundred bytes plus nine bytes for the three CALL instructions.

Notice that subroutines require the use of the stack. This requires the application to include random access memory for the stack. When an application has no other need for random access memory, the system designer might elect to avoid the use of subroutines.

CC   **CALL IF CARRY**

The CC instruction combines functions of the JC and PUSH instructions. CC tests the setting of the carry flag. If the flag is set to one, CC pushes the contents of the program counter onto the stack and then jumps to the address specified in bytes two and three of the CC instruction. If the flag is reset to zero, program execution continues with the next sequential instruction.

Opcode	*Operand*
CC	address

Although the use of a label is most common, the address may also be specified as a number or expression.

1	1	0	1	1	1	0	0
low addr							
high addr							

Cycles:	3 or 5 (2 or 5 on 8085)
States:	11 or 17 (9 or 18 on 8085)
Addressing:	immediate/register indirect
Flags:	none

Example:

For the sake of brevity, an example is given for the CALL instruction but not for each of its closely related variants.

CM   **CALL IF MINUS**

The CM instruction combines functions of the JM and PUSH instructions. CM tests the setting of the sign flag. If the flag is set to one (indicating that the contents of the accumulator are minus), CM pushes the contents of the program counter onto the stack and then jumps to the address specified by the CM instruction. If the flag is set to zero, program execution simply continues with the next sequential instruction.

Opcode	*Operand*
CM	address

Although the use of a label is most common, the address may also be specified as a number or an expression.

1	1	1	1	1	1	0	0
low addr
high addr

Cycles:	3 or 5 (2 or 5 on 8085)
States:	11 or 17 (9 or 18 on 8085)
Addressing:	immediate/register indirect
Flags:	none

Example:

For the sake of brevity, an example is given for the CALL instruction but not for each of its closely related variants.

CMA   **COMPLEMENT ACCUMULATOR**

CMA complements each bit of the accumulator to produce the one's complement. All condition flags remain unchanged.

Opcode   *Operand*

CMA

Operands are not permitted with the CMA instruction.

0	0	1	0	1	1	1	1

Cycles:	1
States:	4
Flags:	none

To produce the two's complement, add one to the contents of the accumulator after the CMA instructions has been executed.

Example:

Assume that the accumulator contains the value 51H; when complemented by CMA, it becomes 0AEH:

51H	=	01010001
0AEH	=	10101110

CMC   COMPLEMENT CARRY

If the carry flag equals zero, CMC sets it to one. If the carry flag is one, CMC resets it to zero. All other flags remain unchanged.

Opcode	Operand
CMC	

Operands are not permitted with the CMC instruction.

0	0	1	1	1	1	1	1

Cycles:	1
States:	4
Flags:	CY only

Example:

Assume that a program uses bit 7 of a byte to control whether a subroutine is called. To test the bit, the program loads the byte into the accumulator, rotates bit 7 into the carry flag, and executes a CC (Call if Carry) instruction. Before returning to the calling program, the subroutine reinitializes the flag byte using the following code:

```
CMC        ;SET BIT 7 OFF
RAR        ;ROTATE BIT 7 INTO ACCUMULATOR
RET        ;RETURN
```

CMP   COMPARE WITH ACCUMULATOR

CMP compares the specified byte with the contents of the accumulator and indicates the result by setting the carry and zero flags. The values being compared remain unchanged.

The zero flag indicates equality. No carry indicates that the accumulator is greater than or equal to the specified byte; a carry indicates that the accumulator is less than the byte. However, the meaning of the carry flag is reversed when the values have different signs or one of the values is complemented.

The program tests the condition flags using one of the conditional Jump, Call, or Return instructions. For example, JZ (Jump if Zero) tests for equality.

Functional Description:

Comparisons are performed by subtracting the specified byte from the contents of the accumulator, which is why the zero and carry flags indicate the result. This subtraction uses the processor's internal registers so that source data is preserved. Because subtraction uses two's complement addition, the CMP instruction recomplements the carry flag generated by the subtraction.

Compare Register with Accumulator

Opcode	Operand
CMP	reg

The operand must name one of the registers A through E, H or L.

1	0	1	1	1	S	S	S

Cycles:	1
States:	4
Addressing:	register
Flags:	Z,S,P,CY,AC

Compare Memory with Accumulator

Opcode	Operand
CMP	M

This instruction compares the contents of the memory location addressed by the H and L registers with the contents of the accumulator. M is a symbolic reference to the H and L register pair.

1	0	1	1	1	1	1	0

Cycles:	2
States:	7
Addressing:	register indirect
Flags:	Z,S,P,CY,AC

Example 1:

Assume that the accumulator contains the value 0AH and register E contains the value 05H. The instruction CMP E performs the following internal subtraction (remember that subtraction is actually two's complement addition):

$$
\begin{array}{lll}
\text{Accumulator} & = & 00001010 \\
+(-\text{E Register}) & = & \underline{11111011} \\
& & 00000101 \ +(-\text{carry})
\end{array}
$$

After the carry is complemented to account for the subtract operation, both the zero and carry bits are zero, thus indicating A greater than E.

Example 2:

Assume that the accumulator contains the value −1BH and register E contains 05H:

$$
\begin{array}{lll}
\text{Accumulator} & = & 11100101 \\
+(-\text{E Register}) & = & \underline{11111011} \\
& & 11100000 \ +(-\text{carry})
\end{array}
$$

After the CMP instruction recomplements the carry flag, both the carry flag and zero flag are zero. Normally this indicates that the accumulator is greater than register E. However, the meaning of the carry flag is reversed since the values have different signs. The user program is responsible for proper interpretation of the carry flag.

CNC   CALL IF NO CARRY

The CNC instruction combines functions of the JNC and PUSH instructions. CNC tests the setting of the carry flag. If the flag is set to zero, CNC pushes the contents of the program counter onto the stack and then jumps to the address specified by the CNC instruction. If the flag is set to one, program execution simply continues with the next sequential instruction.

Opcode	Operand
CNC	address

Although the use of a label is most common, the address may also be specified as a number or an expression.

1	1	0	1	0	1	0	0
low addr								
high addr								

Cycles: 3 or 5 (2 or 5 on 8085)
States: 11 or 17 (9 or 18 on 8085)
Addressing: immediate/register indirect
Flags: none

Example:

For the sake of brevity, an example is given for the CALL instruction but not for each of its closely related variants.

CNZ   CALL IF NOT ZERO

The CNZ instruction combines functions of the JNZ and PUSH instructions. CNZ tests the setting of the zero flag. If the flag is off (indicating that the contents of the accumulator are other than zero), CNZ pushes the contents of the program counter onto the stack and then jumps to the address specified in the instruction's second and third bytes. If the flag is set to one, program execution simply continues with the next sequential instruction.

Opcode	Operand
CNZ	address

Although the use of a label is most common, the address may also be specified as a number or an expression.

```
┌─────────────────────────────────┐
│ 1   1   0   0   0   1   0   0   │
├─────────────────────────────────┤
│           low addr              │
├─────────────────────────────────┤
│           high addr             │
└─────────────────────────────────┘
```

Cycles: 3 or 5 (2 or 5 on 8085)
States: 11 or 17 (9 or 18 on 8085)
Addressing: immediate/register indirect
Flags: none

Example:

For the sake of brevity, an example is given for the CALL instruction but not for each of its closely related variants.

CP   **CALL IF POSITIVE**

The CP instruction combines features of the JP and PUSH instructions. CP tests the setting of the sign flag. If the flag is set to zero (indicating that the contents of the accumulator are positive), CP pushes the contents of the program counter onto the stack and then jumps to the address specified by the CP instruction. If the flag is set to one, program execution simply continues with the next sequential instruction.

        Opcode   *Operand*

          CP   address

Although the use of a label is more common, the address may also be specified as a number or an expression.

```
┌─────────────────────────────────┐
│ 1   1   1   1   0   1   0   0   │
├─────────────────────────────────┤
│           low address           │
├─────────────────────────────────┤
│           high addr             │
└─────────────────────────────────┘
```

Cycles: 3 or 5 (2 or 5 on 8085)
States: 11 or 17 (9 or 18 on 8085)
Addressing: immediate/register indirect
Flags: none

Example:

For the sake of brevity, an example is given for the CALL instruction but not for each of its closely related variants.

CPE   CALL IF PARITY EVEN

Parity is even if the byte in the accumulator has an even number of one bits. The parity flag is set to one to indicate this condition. The CPE and CPO instructions are useful for testing the parity of input data. However, the IN instruction does not set any of the condition flags. The flags can be set without altering the data by adding 00H to the contents of the accumulator.

The CPE instruction combines functions of the JPE and PUSH instructions. CPE tests the setting of the parity flag. If the flag is set to one, CPE pushes the contents of the program counter onto the stack and then jumps to the address specified by the CPE instruction. If the flag is set to zero, program execution simply continues with the next sequential instruction.

Opcode	*Operand*
CPE	address

Although the use of a label is more common, the address may also be specified as a number or an expression.

1	1	1	0	1	1	0	0
low addr						
high addr						

Cycles:	3 or 5 (2 or 5 on 8085)
States:	11 or 17 (9 or 18 on 8085)
Addressing:	immediate/register indirect
Flags:	none

Example:

For the sake of brevity, an example is given for the CALL instruction but not for each of its closely related variants.

CPI   COMPARE IMMEDIATE

CPI compares the contents of the second instruction byte with the contents of the accumulator and sets the zero and carry flags to indicate the result. The values being compared remain unchanged.

The zero flag indicates equality. No carry indicates that the contents of the accumulator are greater than the immediate data; a carry indicates that the accumulator is less than the immediate data. However, the meaning of the carry flag is reversed when the values have different signs or one of the values is complemented.

Opcode	*Operand*
CPI	data

The operand must specify the data to be compared. This data may be in the form of a number, an ASCII constant, the label of a previously defined value, or an expression. The data may not exceed one byte.

The assembler's relocation feature treats all external and relocatable symbols as 16-bit addresses. When one of these symbols appears in the operand expression of an immediate instruction, it must be preceded by either the HIGH or LOW operator to specify which byte of the address is to be used in the evaluation of the expression. When neither operator is present, the assembler assumes the LOW operator and issues an error message.

1	1	1	1	1	1	1	0
data								

Cycles: 2
States: 7
Addressing: register indirect
Flags: Z,S,P,CY,AC

Example:

The instruction CPI 'C' compares the contents of the accumulator to the letter C (43H).

CPO   CALL IF PARITY ODD

Parity is odd if the byte in the accumulator has an odd number of one bits. The parity flag is set to zero to indicate this condition. The CPO and CPE instructions are useful for testing the parity of input data. However, the IN instruction does not set any of the condition flags. The flags can be set without altering the data by adding 00H to the contents of the accumulator.

The CPO instruction combines functions of the JPO and PUSH instructions. CPO tests the setting of the parity flag. If the flag is set to zero, CPO pushes the contents of the program counter onto the stack and then jumps to the address specified by the CPO instruction. If the flag is set to one, program execution simply continues with the next sequential instruction.

Opcode	Operand
CPO	address

Although the use of a label is more common, the address may also be specified as a number or an expression.

1	1	1	0	0	1	0	0
low addr								
high addr								

Cycles: 3 or 5 (2 or 5 on 8085)
States: 11 or 17 (9 or 18 on 8085)
Addressing: immediate/register indirect
Flags: none

Example:

For the sake of brevity, an example is given for the CALL instruction but not for each of its closely related variants.

CZ   **CALL IF ZERO**

The CZ instruction combines functions of the JZ and PUSH instructions. CZ tests the setting of the zero flag. If the flag is set to one (indicating that the contents of the accumulator are zero), CZ pushes the contents of the program counter onto the stack and then jumps to the address specified in the CZ instruction. If the flag is set to zero (indicating that the contents of the accumulator are other than zero), program execution simply continues with the next sequential instruction.

Opcode	Operand
CZ	address

Although the use of a label is most common, the address may also be specified as a number or an expression.

1	1	0	0	1	1	0	0
low addr							
high addr							

Cycles: 3 or 5 (2 or 5 on 8085)
States: 11 or 17 (9 or 18 on 8085)
Addressing: immediate/register indirect
Flags: none

Example:

For the sake of brevity, an example is given for the CALL instruction but not for each of its closely related variants.

DAA   **DECIMAL ADJUST ACCUMULATOR**

The DAA instruction adjusts the eight-bit value in the accumulator to form two four-bit binary coded decimal digits.

Opcode	Operand
DAA	

Operands are not permitted with the DAA instruction.

DAA is used when adding decimal numbers. It is the only instruction whose function requires use of the auxiliary carry flag. In multi-byte arithmetic operations, the DAA instruction typically is coded immediately after the arithmetic instruction so that the auxiliary carry flag is not altered unintentionally.

DAA operates as follows:

1.   If the least significant four bits of the accumulator have a value greater than nine, or if the auxiliary carry flag is ON, DAA adds six to the accumulator.

2.   If the most significant four bits of the accumulator have a value greater than nine, or if the carry flag is ON, DAA adds six to the most significant four bits of the accumulator.

0	0	1	0	0	1	1	1

Cycles: 1
States: 4
Addressing: register
Flags: Z,S,P,CY,AC

Example:

Assume that the accumulator contains the value 9BH as a result of adding 08 to 93:

```
CY     AC
0      0

1001   0011
0000   1000
1001   1011  = 9BH
```

Since 0BH is greater than nine, the instruction adds six to contents of the accumulator:

```
CY     AC
0      1
1001   1011
0000   0110
1010   0001  = A1H
```

Now that the most significant bits have a value greater than nine, the instruction adds six to them:

```
CY     AC
1      1
1010   0001
0110   0000
0000   0001
```

When the DAA has finished, the accumulator contains the value 01 in a BCD format; both the carry and auxiliary carry flags are set ON. Since the actual result of this addition is 101, the carry flag is probably significant to the program. The program is responsible for recovering and using this information. Notice that the carry flag setting is lost as soon as the program executes any subsequent instruction that alters the flag.

DAD   **DOUBLE REGISTER ADD**

DAD adds the 16-bit value in the specified register pair to the contents of the H and L register pair. The result is stored in H and L.

	Opcode	Operand
	DAD	$\begin{Bmatrix} B \\ D \\ H \\ SP \end{Bmatrix}$

DAD may add only the contents of the B&C, D&E, H&L, or the SP (Stack Pointer) register pairs to the contents of H&L. Notice that the letter H must be used to specify that the H&L register pair is to be added to itself.

DAD sets the carry flag ON if there is a carry out of the H and L registers. DAD affects none of the condition flags other than carry.

0	0	R	P	1	0	0	1

Cycles:	3
States:	10
Addressing:	register
Flags:	CY

Examples:

The DAD instruction provides a means for saving the current contents of the stack pointer.

```
LXI    H,00H     ;CLEAR H&L TO ZEROS
DAD    SP        ;GET SP INTO H&L
SHLD   SAVSP     ;STORE SP IN MEMORY
```

The instruction DAD H doubles the number in the H and L registers except when the operation causes a carry out of the H register.

DCR   **DECREMENT**

DCR subtracts one from the contents of the specified byte. DCR affects all the condition flags *except* the carry flag. Because DCR preserves the carry flag, it can be used within multi-byte arithmetic routines for decrementing character counts and similar purposes.

Decrement Register

	Opcode	Operand
	DCR	reg

The operand must specify one of the registers A through E, H or L. The instruction subtracts one from the contents of the specified register.

0	0	D	D	D	1	0	1

Cycles: 1
States: 5 (4 on 8085)
Addressing: register
Flags: Z,S,P,AC

Decrement Memory

Opcode	Operand
DCR	M

This instruction subtracts one from the contents of the memory location addressed by the H and L registers. M is a symbolic reference to the memory byte addressed by the H and L registers.

0	0	1	1	0	1	0	1

Cycles: 3
States: 10
Addressing: register indirect
Flags: Z,S,P,AC

Example:

The DCR instruction is frequently used to control multi-byte operations such as moving a number of characters from one area of memory to another:

```
        MVI   B,5H     ; set control counter
        LXI   H,250H   ; load H & L with source address
        LXI   D,900H   ; load D & E with destination address
LOOP:   MOV   A,M      ; load byte to be moved
        STAX  D        ; store byte
        DCX   D        ; decrement destination address
        DCX   H        ; decrement source address
        DCR   B        ; decrement control counter
        XRA   A        ; clear accumulator
        CMP   B        ; compare control counter to zero
        JNZ   LOOP     ; move another byte if counter not zero
```

DCX

DECREMENT REGISTER PAIR

DCX decrements the contents of the specified register pair by one. DCX affects none of the condition flags. Because DCX preserves all the flags, it can be used for address modification in any instruction sequence that relies on the passing of the flags.

Opcode   *Operand*

DCX $\left\{\begin{array}{c} B \\ D \\ H \\ SP \end{array}\right\}$

DCX may decrement only the B&C, D&E, H&L, or the SP (Stack Pointer) register pairs. Notice that the letter H must be used to specify the H and L pair.

Exercise care when decrementing the stack pointer as this causes a loss of synchronization between the pointer and the actual contents of the stack.

0	0	R	P	1	0	1	1

Cycles:	1
States:	5 (6 on 8085)
Addressing:	register
Flags:	none

Example:

Assume that the H and L registers contain the address 9800H when the instruction DCX H is executed. DCX considers the contents of the two registers to be a single 16-bit value and therefore performs a borrow from the H register to produce the value 97FFH.

DI

DISABLE INTERRUPTS

The interrupt system is disabled when the processor recognizes an interrupt or immediately following execution of a DI instruction.

In applications that use interrupts, the DI instruction is commonly used only when a code sequence must not be interrupted. For example, time-dependent code sequences become inaccurate when interrupted. You can disable the interrupt system by including a DI instruction at the beginning of the code sequence. Because you cannot predict the occurrence of an interrupt, include an EI instruction at the end of the time-dependent code sequence.

Opcode   *Operand*

DI

Operands are not permitted with the DI instruction.

1	1	1	1	0	0	1	1

Cycles: 1
States: 4
Flags: none

NOTE

The 8085 TRAP interrupt cannot be disabled. This special interrupt is intended for serious problems that must be serviced regardless of the interrupt flag such as power failure or bus error. However, no interrupt including TRAP can interrupt the execution of the DI or EI instruction.

EI   ENABLE INTERRUPTS

The EI instruction enables the interrupt system following execution of the next program instruction. Enabling the interrupt system is delayed one instruction to allow interrupt subroutines to return to the main program before a subsequent interrupt is acknowledged.

In applications that use interrupts, the interrupt system is usually disabled only when the processor accepts an interrupt or when a code sequence must not be interrupted. You can disable the interrupt system by including a DI instruction at the beginning of the code sequence. Because you cannot predict the occurrence of an interrupt, include an EI instruction at the end of the code sequence.

Opcode	*Operand*

EI

Operands are not permitted with the EI instruction.

1	1	1	1	1	0	1	1

Cycles: 1
States: 4
Flags: none

NOTE

The 8085 TRAP interrupt cannot be disabled. This special interrupt is intended for serious problems that must be serviced regardless of the interrupt flag such as power failure or bus failure. However, no interrupt including TRAP can interrupt the execution of the DI or EI instruction.

Example:

The EI instruction is frequently used as part of a start-up sequence. When power is first applied, the processor begins operating at some indeterminate address. Application of a RESET signal forces the program counter to zero. A common instruction sequence at this point is EI, HLT. These instructions enable the interrupt system (RESET also disables the interrupt system) and halt the processor. A subsequent manual or automatic interrupt then determines the effective start-up address.

HLT   HALT

The HLT instruction halts the processor. The program counter contains the address of the next sequential instruction. Otherwise, the flags and registers remain unchanged.

0	1	1	1	0	1	1	0

Cycles: 1
States: 7 (5 on 8085)
Flags: none

Once in the halt state, the processor can be restarted only by an external event, typically an interrupt. Therefore, you should be certain that interrupts are enabled before the HLT instruction is executed. See the description of the EI (Enable Interrupt) instruction.

If an 8080 HLT instruction is executed while interrupts are disabled, the only way to restart the processor is by application of a RESET signal. This forces the program counter to zero. The same is true of the 8085, except for the TRAP interrupt, which is recognized even when the interrupt system is disabled.

The processor can temporarily leave the halt state to service a direct memory access request. However, the processor reenters the halt state once the request has been serviced.

A basic purpose for the HLT instruction is to allow the processor to pause while waiting for an interrupt from a peripheral device. However, a halt wastes processor resources and should be used only when there is no useful processing task available.

IN   INPUT FROM PORT

The IN instruction reads eight bits of data from the specified port and loads it into the accumulator.

NOTE

This description is restricted to the exact function of the IN instruction. Input/output structures are described in the *8080 or 8085 Microcomputer Systems User's Manual.*

Opcode	Operand
IN	exp

The operand expression may be a number or any expression that yields a value in the range 00H through 0FFH.

```
| 1  1  0  1  1  0  1  1 |
|          exp           |
```

Cycles: 3
States: 10
Addressing: direct
Flags: none

INR   INCREMENT

INR adds one to the contents of the specified byte. INR affects all of the condition flags *except* the carry flag. Because INR preserves the carry flag, it can be used within multi-byte arithmetic routines for incrementing character counts and similar purposes.

Increment Register

Opcode   Operand

INR   reg

The operand must specify one of the registers A through E, H or L. The instruction adds one to the contents of the specified register.

```
| 0  0 | D  D  D | 1  0  0 |
```

Cycles: 1
States: 5 (4 on 8085)
Addressing: register
Flags: Z,S,P,AC

Increment Memory

Opcode   Operand

INR   M

This instruction increments by one the contents of the memory location addressed by the H and L registers. M is a symbolic reference to the H and L registers.

```
| 0  0  1  1  0  1  0  0 |
```

Cycles: 3
States: 10
Addressing: register indirect
Flags: Z,S,P,AC

Example:

If register C contains 99H, the instruction INR C increments the contents of the register to 9AH.

INX   INCREMENT REGISTER PAIR

INX adds one to the contents of the specified register pair. INX affects none of the condition flags. Because INX preserves all the condition flags, it can be used for address modification within multi-byte arithmetic routines.

Opcode	*Operand*
INX	$\begin{Bmatrix} B \\ D \\ H \\ SP \end{Bmatrix}$

INX may increment only the B&C, D&E, H&L, or the SP (Stack Pointer) register pairs. Notice that the letter H must be used to specify the H and L register pair.

Exercise care when incrementing the stack pointer. Assume, for example, that INX SP is executed after a number of items have been pushed onto the stack. A subsequent POP instruction accesses the high-order byte of the most recent stack entry and the low-order byte of the next older entry. Similarly, a PUSH instruction adds the two new bytes to the stack, but overlays the low-order byte of the most recent entry.

0	0	R	P	0	0	1	1

Cycles: 1
States: 5 (6 on 8085)
Addressing: register
Flags: none

Example:

Assume that the D and E registers contain the value 01FFH. The instruction INX D increments the value to 0200H. By contrast, the INR E instruction ignores the carry out of the low-order byte and produces a result of 0100H. (This condition can be detected by testing the Zero condition flag.)

If the stack pointer register contains the value 0FFFFH, the instruction INX SP increments the contents of SP to 0000H. The INX instruction sets no flags to indicate this condition.

JC   JUMP IF CARRY

The JC instruction tests the setting of the carry flag. If the flag is set to one, program execution resumes at the address specified in the JC instruction. If the flag is reset to zero, execution continues with the next sequential instruction.

Opcode	Operand
JC	address

The address may be specified as a number, a label, or an expression. The assembler inverts the high and low address bytes when it assembles the instruction.

1	1	0	1	1	0	1	0
low addr							
high addr							

Cycles:	3 (2 or 3 on 8085)
States:	10 (7 or 10 on 8085)
Addressing:	immediate
Flags:	none

Example:

Examples of the variations of the jump instruction appear in the description of the JPO instruction.

JM   **JUMP IF MINUS**

The JM instruction tests the setting of the sign flag. If the contents of the accumulator are negative (sign flag = 1), program execution resumes at the address specified in the JM instruction. If the contents of the accumulator are positive (sign flag = 0), execution continues with the next sequential instruction.

Opcode	Operand
JM	address

The address may be specified as a number, a label, or an expression. The assembler inverts the high and low address bytes when it assembles the instructions.

1	1	1	1	1	0	1	0
low addr							
high addr							

Cycles:	3 (2 or 3 on 8085)
States:	10 (7 or 10 on 8085)
Addressing:	immediate
Flags:	none

Example:

Examples of the variations of the jump instruction appear in the description of the JPO instruction.

JMP   JUMP

The JMP instruction alters the execution sequence by loading the address in its second and third bytes into the program counter.

Opcode	Operand
JMP	address

The address may be specified as a number, a label, or an expression. The assembler inverts the high and low address bytes when it assembles the address.

1	1	0	0	0	0	1	1
low addr							
high addr							

Cycles:	3
States:	10
Addressing:	immediate
Flags:	none

Example:

Examples of the variations of the jump instruction appear in the description of the JPO instruction.

JNC   JUMP IF NO CARRY

The JNC instruction tests the setting of the carry flag. If there is no carry (carry flag = 0), program execution resumes at the address specified in the JNC instruction. If there is a carry (carry flag = 1), execution continues with the next sequential instruction.

Opcode	Operand
JNC	address

The address may be specified as a number, a label, or an expression. The assembler inverts the high and low address bytes when it assembles the instruction.

1	1	0	1	0	0	1	0
low addr							
high addr							

Cycles:	3 (2 or 3 on 8085)
States:	10 (7 or 10 on 8085)
Addressing:	immediate
Flags:	none

Example:

Examples of the variations of the jump instruction appear in the description of the JPO instruction.

JNZ   JUMP IF NOT ZERO

The JNZ instruction tests the setting of the zero flag. If the contents of the accumulator are not zero (zero flag = 0), program execution resumes at the address specified in the JNZ instruction. If the contents of the accumulator are zero (zero flag = 1), execution continues with the next sequential instruction.

Opcode	Operand
JNZ	address

The address may be specified as a number, a label, or an expression. The assembler inverts the high and low address bytes when it assembles the instruction.

1	1	0	0	0	0	1	0
low addr
high addr

Cycles: 3 (2 or 3 on 8085)
States: 10 (7 or 10 on 8085)
Addressing: immediate
Flags: none

Example:

Examples of the variations of the jump instruction appear in the description of the JPO instruction.

JP   JUMP IF POSITIVE

The JP instruction tests the setting of the sign flag. If the contents of the accumulator are positive (sign flag = 0), program execution resumes at the address specified in the JP instruction. If the contents of the accumulator are minus (sign flag = 1), execution continues with the next sequential instruction.

Opcode	Operand
JP	address

The address may be specified as a number, a label, or an expression. The assembler inverts the high and low order address bytes when it assembles the instruction.

1	1	1	1	0	0	1	0
low addr							
high addr							

Cycles: 3 (2 or 3 on 8085)
States: 10 (7 or 10 on 8085)
Addressing: immediate
Flags: none

Example:

Examples of the variations of the jump instruction appear in the description of the JPO instruction.

JPE   JUMP IF PARITY EVEN

Parity is even if the byte in the accumulator has an even number of one bits. The parity flag is set to one to indicate this condition.

The JPE instruction tests the setting of the parity flag. If the parity flag is set to one, program execution resumes at the address specified in the JPE instruction. If the flag is reset to zero, execution continues with the next sequential instruction.

Opcode	Operand
JPE	address

The address may be specified as a number, a label, or an expression. The assembler inverts the high and low address bytes when it assembles the instruction.

The JPE and JPO (jump if parity odd) instructions are especially useful for testing the parity of input data. However, the IN instruction does not set any of the condition flags. The flags can be set by adding 00H to the contents of the accumulator.

1	1	1	0	1	0	1	0
low addr							
high addr							

Cycles: 3 (2 or 3 on 8085)
States: 10 (7 or 10 on 8085)
Addressing: immediate
Flags: none

Example:

Examples of the variations of the jump instruction appear in the description of the JPO instruction.

JPO   **JUMP IF PARITY ODD**

Parity is odd if the byte in the accumulator has an odd number of one bits. The parity flag is set to zero to indicate this condition.

The JPO instruction tests the setting of the parity flag. If the parity flag is reset to zero, program execution resumes at the address specified in the JPO instruction. If the flag is set to one, execution continues with the next sequential instruction.

Opcode	Operand
JPO	address

The address may be specified as a number, a label, or an expression. The assembler inverts the high and low address bytes when it assembles the instruction.

The JPO and JPE (jump if parity even) instructions are especially useful for testing the parity of input data. However, the IN instruction does not set any of the condition flags. The flags can be set by adding 00H to the contents of the accumulator.

1	1	1	0	0 · 0	1	0
low addr						
high addr						

Cycles:	3 (2 or 3 on 8085)
States:	10 (7 or 10 on 8085)
Addressing:	immediate
Flags:	none

Example:

This example shows three different but equivalent methods for jumping to one of two points in a program based upon whether or not the Sign bit of a number is set. Assume that the byte to be tested is the C register.

Label	Code	Operand
ONE:	MOV	A,C
	ANI	80H
	JZ	PLUS
	JNZ	MINUS
TWO:	MOV	A,C
	RLC	
	JNC	PLUS
	JMP	MINUS
THREE:	MOV	A,C
	ADI	0
	JM	MINUS
PLUS:	—	;SIGN BIT RESET
MINUS:	—	;SIGN BIT SET

The AND immediate instruction in block ONE zeroes all bits of the data byte except the Sign bit, which remains unchanged. If the Sign bit was zero, the Zero condition bit will be set, and the JZ instruction will cause program control to be transferred to the instruction at PLUS. Otherwise, the JZ instruction will merely update the program counter by three, and the JNZ instruction will be executed, causing control to be transferred to the instruction at MINUS. (The Zero bit is unaffected by all jump instructions.)

The RLC instruction in block TWO causes the Carry bit to be set equal to the Sign bit of the data byte. If the Sign bit was reset, the JNC instruction causes a jump to PLUS. Otherwise the JMP instruction is executed, unconditionally transferring control to MINUS. (Note that, in this instance, a JC instruction could be substituted for the unconditional jump with identical results.)

The add immediate instruction in block THREE causes the condition bits to be set. If the sign bit was set, the JM instruction causes program control to be transferred to MINUS. Otherwise, program control flows automatically into the PLUS routine.

JZ   JUMP IF ZERO

The JZ instruction tests the setting of the zero flag. If the flag is set to one, program execution resumes at the address specified in the JZ instruction. If the flag is reset to zero, execution continues with the next sequential instruction.

Opcode	Operand
JZ	address

The address may be specified as a number, a label, or an expression. The assembler inverts the high and low address bytes when it assembles the instruction.

1	1	0	0	1	0	1	0
low addr							
high addr							

Cycles:	3 (2 or 3 on 8085)
States:	10 (7 or 10 on 8085)
Addressing:	immediate
Flags:	none

Example:

Examples of the variations of the jump instruction appear in the description of the JPO instruction.

LDA   LOAD ACCUMULATOR DIRECT

LDA loads the accumulator with a copy of the byte at the location specified in bytes two and three of the LDA instruction.

Opcode	Operand
LDA	address

The address may be stated as a number, a previously defined label, or an expression. The assembler inverts the high and low address bytes when it builds the instruction.

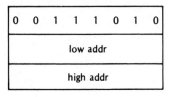

0	0	1	1	1	0	1	0

low addr

high addr

Cycles:	4
States:	13
Addressing:	direct
Flags:	none

Examples:

The following instructions are equivalent. When executed, each replaces the accumulator contents with the byte of data stored at memory location 300H.

```
LOAD:   LDA    300H
        LDA    3*(16*16)
        LDA    200H+256
```

LDAX   LOAD ACCUMULATOR INDIRECT

LDAX loads the accumulator with a copy of the byte stored at the memory location addressed by register pair B or register pair D.

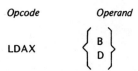

Opcode	Operand
LDAX	B D

The operand B specifies the B and C register pair; D specifies the D and E register pair. This instruction may specify only the B or D register pair.

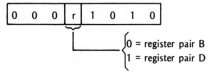

0	0	0	r	1	0	1	0

0 = register pair B
1 = register pair D

Cycles:	2
States:	7
Addressing:	register indirect
Flags:	none

Example:

Assume that register D contains 93H and register E contains 8BH. The following instruction loads the accumulator with the contents of memory location 938BH:

LDAX   D

LHLD   LOAD H AND L DIRECT

LHLD loads the L register with a copy of the byte stored at the memory location specified in bytes two and three of the LHLD instruction. LHLD then loads the H register with a copy of the byte stored at the next higher memory location.

Opcode	Operand
LHLD	address

The address may be stated as a number, a label, or an expression.

Certain instructions use the symbolic reference M to access the memory location currently specified by the H and L registers. LHLD is one of the instructions provided for loading new addresses into the H and L registers. The user may also load the current top of the stack into the H and L registers (POP instruction). Both LHLD and POP replace the contents of the H and L registers. You can also exchange the contents of H and L with the D and E registers (XCHG instruction) or the top of the stack (XTHL instruction) if you need to save the current H and L registers for subsequent use. SHLD stores H and L in memory.

0	0	1	0	1	0	1	0
low addr							
high addr							

Cycles: 5
States: 16
Addressing: direct
Flags: none

Example:

Assume that locations 3000 and 3001H contain the address 064EH stored in the format 4E06. In the following sequence, the MOV instruction moves a copy of the byte stored at address 064E into the accumulator:

LHLD   3000H   ;SET UP ADDRESS
MOV   A,M   ;LOAD ACCUM FROM ADDRESS

LXI   **LOAD REGISTER PAIR IMMEDIATE**

LXI is a three-byte instruction; its second and third bytes contain the source data to be loaded into a register pair. LXI loads a register pair by copying its second and third bytes into the specified destination register pair.

Opcode	Operand
LXI	$\left.\begin{matrix} B \\ D \\ H \\ SP \end{matrix}\right\}$,data

The first operand must specify the register pair to be loaded. LXI can load the B and C register pair, the D and E register pair, the H and L register pair, or the Stack Pointer.

The second operand specifies the two bytes of data to be loaded. This data may be coded in the form of a number, an ASCII constant, the label of some previously defined value, or an expression. The data must not exceed two bytes.

LXI is the only immediate instruction that accepts a 16-bit value. All other immediate instructions require 8-bit values.

Notice that the assembler inverts the two bytes of data to create the format of an address stored in memory. LXI loads its third byte into the first register of the pair and its second byte into the second register of the pair. This has the effect of reinverting the data into the format required for an address stored in registers. Thus, the instruction LXI B,'AZ' loads A into register B and Z into register C.

0	0	R	P	0	0	0	1
low-order data							
high-order data							

Cycles: 3
States: 10
Addressing: immediate
Flags: none

Examples:

A common use for LXI is to establish a memory address for use in subsequent instructions. In the following sequence, the LXI instruction loads the address of STRNG into the H and L registers. The MOV instruction then loads the data stored at that address into the accumulator.

```
LXI    H,STRNG    ;SET ADDRESS
MOV    A,M        ;LOAD STRNG INTO ACCUMULATOR
```

The following LXI instruction is used to initialize the stack pointer in a relocatable module. The LOCATE program provides an address for the special reserved label STACK.

```
LXI    SP,STACK
```

MOV   **MOVE**

The MOV instruction moves one byte of data by copying the source field into the destination field. Source data remains unchanged. The instruction's operands specify whether the move is from register to register, from a register to memory, or from memory to a register.

Move Register to Register

	Opcode	Operand
	MOV	reg1,reg2

The instruction copies the contents of reg2 into reg1. Each operand must specify one of the registers A, B, C, D, E, H, or L.

When the same register is specified for both operands (as in MOV A,A), the MOV functions as a NOP (no operation) since it has no other noticeable effect. This form of MOV requires one more machine state than NOP, and therefore has a slightly longer execution time than NOP. MOV M,M is not permitted.

0	1	D	D	D	S	S	S

Cycles: 1
States: 5 (4 on 8085)
Addressing: register
Flags: none

Move to Memory

	Opcode	Operand
	MOV	M,r

This instruction copies the contents of the specified register into the memory location addressed by the H and L registers. M refers to the byte addressed by the H and L register pair. The second operand must address one of the registers. MOV M,M is not permitted.

0	1	1	1	0	S	S	S

Cycles: 2
States: 7
Addressing: register indirect
Flags: none

Move from Memory

	Opcode	Operand
	MOV	r,M

This instruction copies the contents of the memory location addressed by the H and L registers into the specified register. The first operand must name the destination register. The second operand must be M. M is a symbolic reference to the H and L registers.

0	1	D	D	D	1	1	0

Cycles: 2
States: 7
Addressing: register indirect
Flags: none

Examples:

Label	Opcode	Operands	Comment
LDACC:	MOV	A,M	;LOAD ACCUM FROM MEMORY
	MOV	E,A	;COPY ACCUM INTO E REG
NULOP:	MOV	C,C	;NULL OPERATION

MVI   MOVE IMMEDIATE

MVI is a two-byte instruction; its second byte contains the source data to be moved. MVI moves one byte of data by copying its second byte into the destination field. The instruction's operands specify whether the move is to a register or to memory.

Move Immediate to Register

Opcode	Operand
MVI	reg,data

The first operand must name one of the registers A through E, H or L as a destination for the move.

The second operand specifies the actual data to be moved. This data may be in the form of a number, an ASCII constant, the label of some previously defined value, or an expression. The data must not exceed one byte.

The assembler's relocation feature treats all external and relocatable symbols as 16-bit addresses. When one of these symbols appears in the operand expression of an immediate instruction, it must be preceded by either the HIGH or LOW operator to specify which byte of the address is to be used in the evaluation of the expression. When neither operator is present, the assembler assumes the LOW operator and issues an error message.

0	0	D	D	D	1	1	0
data							

Cycles: 2
States: 7
Addressing: immediate
Flags: none

Move Immediate to Memory

Opcode	Operand
MVI	M,data

This instruction copies the data stored in its second byte into the memory location addressed by H and L. M is a symbolic reference to the H and L register pair.

0	0	1	1	0	1	1	0
data							

Cycles: 3
States: 10
Addressing: immediate/register indirect
Flags: none

Examples:

The following examples show a number of methods for defining immediate data in the MVI instruction. All of the examples generate the bit pattern for the ASCII character A.

MVI	M,01000001B
MVI	M,'A'
MVI	M,41H
MVI	M,101Q
MVI	M,65
MVI	M,5+30*2

NOP   NO OPERATION

NOP performs no operation and affects none of the condition flags. NOP is useful as filler in a timing loop.

Opcode	Operand
NOP	

Operands are not permitted with the NOP instruction.

ORA   INCLUSIVE OR WITH ACCUMULATOR

ORA performs an inclusive OR logical operation using the contents of the specified byte and the accumulator. The result is placed in the accumulator.

Summary of Logical Operations

AND produces a one bit in the result only when the corresponding bits in the test data and the mask data are one.

OR produces a one bit in the result when the corresponding bits in either the test data or the mask data are ones.

Exclusive OR produces a one bit only when the corresponding bits in the test data and the mask data are different; i.e., a one bit in either the test data or the mask data — but not both — produces a one bit in the result.

AND	OR	EXCLUSIVE OR
1010 1010	1010 1010	1010 1010
0000 1111	0000 1111	0000 1111
0000 1010	1010 1111	1010 0101

OR Register with Accumulator

Opcode	Operand
ORA	reg

The operand must specify one of the registers A through E, H or L. This instruction ORs the contents of the specified register and the accumulator and stores the result in the accumulator. The carry and auxiliary carry flags are reset to zero.

1	0	1	1	0	S	S	S

Cycles: 1
States: 4
Addressing: register
Flags: Z,S,P,CY,AC

OR Memory with Accumulator

Opcode	Operand
ORA	M

The contents of the memory location specified by the H and L registers are inclusive-ORed with the contents of the accumulator. The result is stored in the accumulator. The carry and auxiliary carry flags are reset to zero.

1	0	1	1	0	1	1	0

Cycles: 2
States: 7
Addressing: register indirect
Flags: Z,S,P,CY,AC

Example:

Since any bit inclusive-ORed with a one produces a one and any bit ORed with a zero remains unchanged, ORA is frequently used to set ON particular bits or groups of bits. The following example ensures that bit 3 of the accumulator is set ON, but the remaining bits are not disturbed. This is frequently done when individual bits are used as status flags in a program. Assume that register D contains the value 08H:

$$
\begin{array}{lll}
\text{Accumulator} & = & 0\ 1\ 0\ 0\ 0\ 0\ 1\ 1 \\
\text{Register D} & = & \underline{0\ 0\ 0\ 0\ 1\ 0\ 0\ 0} \\
& & 0\ 1\ 0\ 0\ 1\ 0\ 1\ 1
\end{array}
$$

ORI   INCLUSIVE OR IMMEDIATE

ORI performs an inclusive OR logical operation using the contents of the second byte of the instruction and the contents of the accumulator. The result is placed in the accumulator. ORI also resets the carry and auxiliary carry flags to zero.

Opcode	Operand
ORI	data

The operand must specify the data to be used in the inclusive OR operation. This data may be in the form of a number, an ASCII constant, the label of some previously defined value, or an expression. The data may not exceed one byte.

The assembler's relocation feature treats all external and relocatable symbols as 16-bit addresses. When one of these symbols appears in the operand expression of an immediate instruction, it must be preceded by either the HIGH or LOW operator to specify which byte of the address is to be used in the evaluation of the expression. When neither operator is present, the assembler assume the LOW operator and issues an error message.

1	1	1	1	0	1	1	0
data

Cycles:	2
States:	7
Addressing:	immediate
Flags:	Z,S,P,SY,AC

Summary of Logical Operations

AND produces a one bit in the result only when the corresponding bits in both the test data and the mask data are ones.

OR produces a one bit in the result when the corresponding bits in either the test data or the mask data are ones.

Exclusive OR produces a one bit only when the corresponding bits in the test data and the mask data are different; i.e., a one bit in either the test data or the mask data — but not both — produces a one bit in the result.

AND	OR	EXCLUSIVE OR
1010 1010	1010 1010	1010 1010
0000 1111	0000 1111	0000 1111
0000 1010	1010 1111	1010 0101

Example:

See the description of the ORA instruction for an example of the use of the inclusive OR. The following examples show a number of methods for defining immediate data in the ORI instruction. All of the examples generate the bit pattern for the ASCII character A.

ORI	01000001B
ORI	'A'
ORI	41H
ORI	101Q
ORI	65
ORI	5+30*2

OUT   OUTPUT TO PORT

The OUT instruction places the contents of the accumulator on the eight-bit data bus and the number of the selected port on the sixteen-bit address bus. Since the number of ports ranges from 0 through 255, the port number is duplicated on the address bus.

It is the responsibility of external logic to decode the port number and to accept the output data.

NOTE

Because a discussion of input/output structures is beyond the scope of this manual, this description is restricted to the exact function of the OUT instruction. Input/output structures are described in the *8080 or 8085 Microcomputer Systems User's Manual.*

Opcode	*Operand*
OUT	exp

The operand must specify the number of the desired output port. This may be in the form of a number or an expression in the range 00H through 0FFH.

1	1	0	1	0	0	1	1
exp							

Cycles:	3
States:	10
Addressing:	direct
Flags:	none

PCHL   **MOVE H&L TO PROGRAM COUNTER**

PCHL loads the contents of the H and L registers into the program counter register. Because the processor fetches the next instruction from the updated program counter address, PCHL has the effect of a jump instruction.

Opcode	Operand
PCHL	

Operands are not permitted with the PCHL instruction.

PCHL moves the contents of the H register to the high-order eight bits of the program counter and the contents of the L register to the low-order eight bits of the program counter.

The user program must ensure that the H and L registers contain the address of an executable instruction when the PCHL instruction is executed.

1	1	1	0	1	0	0	1

Cycles: 1
States: 5 (6 on 8085)
Addressing: register
Flags: none

Example:

One technique for passing data to a subroutine is to place the data immediately after the subroutine call. The return address pushed onto the stack by the CALL instruction actually addresses the data rather than the next instruction after the CALL. For this example, assume that two bytes of data follow the subroutine call. The following coding sequence performs a return to the next instruction after the call:

```
GOBACK:   POP    H     ;GET DATA ADDRESS
          INR    L     ;ADD 2 TO FORM
          INR    L     ;RETURN ADDRESS
          PCHL         ;RETURN
```

POP   **POP**

The POP instruction removes two bytes of data from the stack and copies them to a register pair or copies the Program Status Word into the accumulator and the condition flags.

POP Register Pair

POP copies the contents of the memory location addressed by the stack pointer into the low-order register of the register pair. POP then increments the stack pointer by one and copies the contents of the resulting address into the high-order register of the pair. POP then increments the stack pointer again so that it addresses the next older item on the stack.

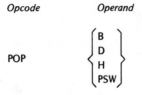

Opcode   Operand

POP

The operand may specify the B&C, D&E, or the H&L register pairs. POP PSW is explained separately.

| 1 | 1 | R | P | 0 | 0 | 0 | 1 |

Cycles: 3
States: 10
Addressing: register indirect
Flags: none

POP PSW

POP PSW uses the contents of the memory location specified by the stack pointer to restore the condition flags. POP PSW increments the stack pointer by one and restores the contents of that address to the accumulator. POP then increments the stack pointer again so that it addresses the next older item on the stack.

| 1 | 1 | 1 | 1 | 0 | 0 | 0 | 1 |

Cycles: 3
States: 10
Addressing: register indirect
Flags: Z,S,P,CY,AC

Example:

Assume that a subroutine is called because of an external interrupt. In general, such subroutines should save and restore any registers it uses so that main program can continue normally when it regains control. The following sequence of PUSH and POP instructions save and restore the Program Status Word and all the registers:

```
PUSH        PSW
PUSH        B
PUSH        D
PUSH        H
             .
             .
subroutine coding
             .
             .
POP         H
POP         D
POP         B
POP         PSW
RET
```

Notice that the sequence of the POP instructions is the opposite of the PUSH instruction sequence.

PUSH   PUSH

The PUSH instruction copies two bytes of data to the stack. This data may be the contents of a register pair or the Program Status Word, as explained below:

PUSH Register Pair

PUSH decrements the stack pointer register by one and copies the contents of the high-order register of the register pair to the resulting address. PUSH then decrements the pointer again and copies the low-order register to the resulting address. The source registers remain unchanged.

Opcode	*Operand*

```
                    ⎧ B  ⎫
                    ⎪ D  ⎪
PUSH                ⎨ H  ⎬
                    ⎩ PSW⎭
```

The operand may specify the B&C, D&E, or H&L register pairs. PUSH PSW is explained separately.

1	1	R	P	0	1	0	1

Cycles: 3
States: 11 (13 on 8085)
Addressing: register indirect
Flags: none

Example:

Assume that register B contains 2AH, the C register contains 4CH, and the stack pointer is set at 9AAF. The instruction PUSH B stores the B register at memory address 9AAEH and the C register at 9AADH. The stack pointer is set to 9AADH:

	Stack Before PUSH	Address	Stack After PUSH	
SP before ──────►	xx	9AAF	xx	
	xx	9AAE	2A	
	xx	9AAD	4C ◄────────── SP after	
	xx	9AAC	xx	

PUSH PSW

PUSH PSW copies the Program Status Word onto the stack. The Program Status Word comprises the contents of the accumulator and the current settings of the condition flags. Because there are only five condition flags, PUSH PSW formats the flags into an eight-bit byte as follows:

7	6	5	4	3	2	1	0
S	Z	0	AC	0	P	1	CY

On the 8080, bits 3 and 5 are always zero; bit one is always set to one. These filler bits are undefined on the 8085.

PUSH PSW decrements the stack pointer by one and copies the contents of the accumulator to the resulting address. PUSH PSW again decrements the pointer and copies the formatted condition flag byte to the resulting address. The contents of the accumulator and the condition flags remain unchanged.

1	1	1	1	0	1	0	1

Cycles: 3
States: 11 (12 on 8085)
Addressing: register indirect
Flags: none

Example:

When a program calls subroutines, it is frequently necessary to preserve the current program status so the calling program can continue normally when it regains control. Typically, the subroutine performs a PUSH PSW prior to execution of any instruction that might alter the contents of the accumulator or the condition flag settings. The subroutine then restores the pre-call system status by executing a POP PSW instruction just before returning control to the calling program.

RAL   **ROTATE LEFT THROUGH CARRY**

RAL rotates the contents of the accumulator and the carry flag one bit position to the left. The carry flag, which is treated as though it were part of the accumulator, transfers to the low-order bit of the accumulator. The high-order bit of the accumulator transfers into the carry flag.

Opcode   *Operand*

RAL

Operands are not permitted with the RAL instruction.

0	0	0	1	0	1	1	1

Cycles: 1
States: 4
Flags: CY only

Example:

Assume that the accumulator contains the value 0AAH and the carry flag is zero. The following diagrams illustrate the effect of the RAL instruction:

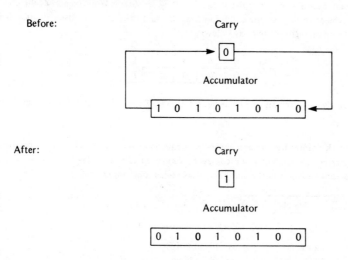

Before: Carry

After: Carry

RAR   ROTATE RIGHT THROUGH CARRY

RAR rotates the contents of the accumulator and the carry flag one bit position to the right. The carry flag, which is treated as though it were part of the accumulator, transfers to the high-order bit of the accumulator. The low-order bit of the accumulator transfers into the carry flag.

        Opcode   *Operand*

        RAR

Operands are not permitted with the RAR instruction.

0	0	0	1	1	1	1	1

Cycles: 1
States: 4
Flags: CY only

Example:

Assume that the accumulator contains the value 0AAH and the carry flag is zero. The following diagrams illustrate the effect of the RAR instruction:

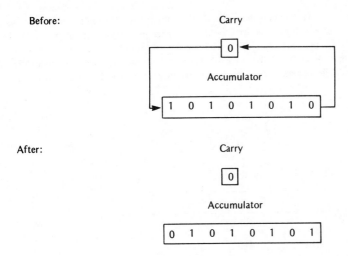

Before: Carry

After: Carry

RC   **RETURN IF CARRY**

The RC instruction tests the carry flag. If the flag is set to one to indicate a carry, the instruction pops two bytes off the stack and places them in the program counter. Program execution resumes at the new address in the program counter. If the flag is zero, program execution simply continues with the next sequential instruction.

Opcode	*Operand*
RC	

Operands are not permitted with the RC instruction.

1	1	0	1	1	0	0	0

Cycles: 1 or 3
States: 5 or 11 (6 or 12 on 8085)
Addressing: register indirect
Flags: none

Example:

For the sake of brevity, an example is given for the RET instruction but not for each of its closely related variants.

RET   **RETURN FROM SUBROUTINE**

The RET instruction pops two bytes of data off the stack and places them in the program counter register. Program execution resumes at the new address in the program counter.

Typically, RET instructions are used in conjunction with CALL instructions. (The same is true of the variants of these instructions.) In this case, it is assumed that the data the RET instruction pops off the stack is a return address placed there by a previous CALL. This has the effect of returning control to the next instruction after the CALL. The user must be certain that the RET instruction finds the address of executable code on the stack. If the instruction finds the address of data, the processor attempts to execute the data as though it were code.

Opcode	Operand
RET	

Operands are not permitted with the RET instruction.

1	1	0	0	1	0	0	1

Cycles: 3
States: 10
Addressing: register indirect
Flags: none

Example:

As mentioned previously, subroutines can be nested. That is, a subroutine can call a subroutine that calls another subroutine. The only practical limit on the number of nested calls is the amount of memory available for stacking return addresses. A nested subroutine can even call the subroutine that called it, as shown in the following example. (Notice that the program must contain logic that eventually returns control to the main program. Otherwise, the two subroutines will call each other indefinitely.)

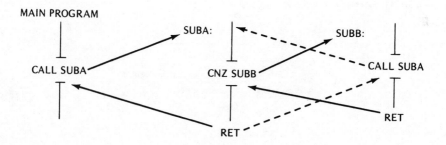

RIM (8085 PROCESSOR ONLY)   **READ INTERRUPT MASK**

The RIM instruction loads eight bits of data into the accumulator. The resulting bit pattern indicates the current setting of the interrupt mask, the setting of the interrupt flag, pending interrupts, and one bit of serial input data, if any.

Opcode   Operand

RIM

Operands are not permitted with the RIM instruction.

The RIM instruction loads the accumulator with the following information:

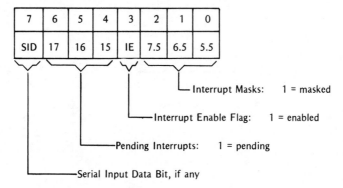

The mask and pending flags refer only to the RST5.5, RST6.5, and RST7.5 hardware interrupts. The IE flag refers to the entire interrupt system. Thus, the IE flag is identical in function and level to the INTE pin on the 8080. A 1 bit in this flag indicates that the entire interrupt system is enabled.

0	0	1	0	0	0	0	0

Cycles: 1
States: 4
Flags: none

RLC   ROTATE ACCUMULATOR LEFT

RLC sets the carry flag equal to the high-order bit of the accumulator, thus overwriting its previous setting. RLC then rotates the contents of the accumulator one bit position to the left with the high-order bit transferring to the low-order position of the accumulator.

Opcode   Operand

RLC

Operands are not allowed with the RLC instruction.

0	0	0	0	0	1	1	1

Cycles: 1
States: 4
Flags: CY only

Example:

Assume that the accumulator contains the value 0AAH and the carry flag is zero. The following diagrams illustrate the effect of the RLC instruction.

Before:

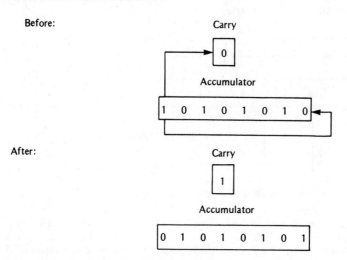

After:

Carry

1

Accumulator

| 0 | 1 | 0 | 1 | 0 | 1 | 0 | 1 |

RM   **RETURN IF MINUS**

The RM instruction tests the sign flag. If the flag is set to one to indicate negative data in the accumulator, the instruction pops two bytes off the stack and places them in the program counter. Program execution resumes at the new address in the program counter. If the flag is set to zero, program execution simply continues with the next sequential instruction.

Opcode   *Operand*

RM

Operands are not permitted with the RM instruction.

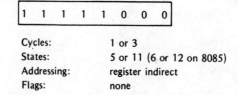

Cycles: 1 or 3
States: 5 or 11 (6 or 12 on 8085)
Addressing: register indirect
Flags: none

Example:

For the sake of brevity, an example is given for the RET instruction but not for each of its closely related variants.

RNC   **RETURN IF NO CARRY**

The RNC instruction tests the carry flag. If the flag is set to zero to indicate that there has been no carry, the instruction pops two bytes off the stack and places them in the program counter. Program execution resumes at the new address in the program counter. If the flag is one, program execution simply continues with the next sequential instruction.

Opcode   *Operand*

RNC

Operands are not permitted with the RNC instruction.

1	1	0	1	0	0	0	0

Cycles: 1 or 3
States: 5 or 11 (6 or 12 on 8085)
Addressing: register indirect
Flags: none

Example:

For the sake of brevity, an example is given for the RET instruction but not for each of its closely related variants.

RNZ   **RETURN IF NOT ZERO**

The RNZ instruction tests the zero flag. If the flag is set to zero to indicate that the contents of the accumulator are other than zero, the instruction pops two bytes off the stack and places them in the program counter. Program execution resumes at the new address in the program counter. If the flag is set to one, program execution simply continues with the next sequential instruction.

Opcode   *Operand*

RNZ

Operands are not permitted with the RNZ instruction.

1	1	0	0	0	0	0	0

Cycles: 1 or 3
States: 5 or 11 (6 or 12 on 8085)
Addressing: register indirect
Flags: none

Example:

For the sake of brevity, an example is given for the RET instruction but not for each of its closely related variants.

RP

RETURN IF POSITIVE

The RP instruction tests the sign flag. If the flag is reset to zero to indicate positive data in the accumulator, the instruction pops two bytes off the stack and places them in the program counter. Program execution resumes at the new address in the program counter. If the flag is set to one, program execution simply continues with the next sequential instruction.

Opcode	Operand
RP	

Operands are not permitted with the RP instruction.

1	1	1	1	0	0	0	0

Cycles: 1 or 3
States: 5 or 11 (6 or 12 on 8085)
Addressing: register indirect
Flags: none

Example:

For the sake of brevity, an example is given for the RET instruction but not for each of its closely related variants.

RPE

RETURN IF PARITY EVEN

Parity is even if the byte in the accumulator has an even number of one bits. The parity flag is set to one to indicate this condition. The RPE and RPO instructions are useful for testing the parity of input data. However, the IN instruction does not set any of the condition flags. The flags can be set without altering the data by adding 00H to the contents of the accumulator.

The RPE instruction tests the parity flag. If the flag is set to one to indicate even parity, the instruction pops two bytes off the stack and places them in the program counter. Program execution resumes at the new address in the program counter. If the flag is zero, program execution simply continues with the next sequential instruction.

Opcode	Operand
RPE	

Operands are not permitted with the RPE instruction.

1	1	1	0	1	0	0	0

Cycles: 1 or 3
States: 5 or 11 (6 or 12 on 8085)
Addressing: register indirect
Flags: none

Example:

For the sake of brevity, an example is given for the RET instruction but not for each of its closely related variants.

RPO   RETURN IF PARITY ODD

Parity is odd if the byte in the accumulator has an odd number of one bits. The parity flag is reset to zero to indicate this condition. The RPO and RPE instructions are useful for testing the parity of input data. However, the IN instruction does not set any of the condition flags. The flags can be set without altering the data by adding 00H to the contents of the accumulator.

The RPO instruction tests the parity flag. If the flag is reset to zero to indicate odd parity, the instruction pops two bytes off the stack and places them in the program counter. Program execution resumes at the new address in the program counter. If the flag is set to one, program execution simply continues with the next sequential instruction.

Opcode   *Operand*

RPO

Operands are not permitted with the RPO instruction.

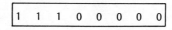

Cycles: 1 or 3
States: 5 or 11 (6 or 12 on 8085)
Addressing: register indirect
Flags: none

Example:

For the sake of brevity, an example is given for the RET instruction but not for each of its closely related variants.

RRC   ROTATE ACCUMULATOR RIGHT

RRC sets the carry flag equal to the low-order bit of the accumulator, thus overwriting its previous setting. RRC then rotates the contents of the accumulator one bit position to the right with the low-order bit transferring to the high order position of the accumulator.

Opcode   *Operand*

RRC

Operands are not permitted with the RRC instruction.

0	0	0	0	1	1	1	1

Cycles: 1
States: 4
Flags: CY only

Example:

Assume that the accumulator contains the value 0AAH and the carry flag is zero. The following diagrams illustrate the effect of the RRC instruction:

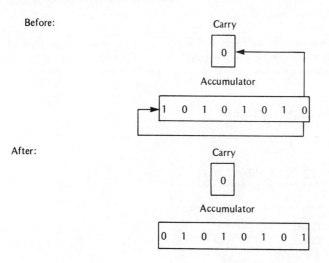

Before: Carry

                              0

                         Accumulator

              1   0   1   0   1   0   1   0

After: Carry

                              0

                         Accumulator

              0   1   0   1   0   1   0   1

RST

RESTART

RST is a special purpose CALL instruction designed primarily for use with interrupts. RST pushes the contents of the program counter onto the stack to provide a return address and then jumps to one of eight predetermined addresses. A three-bit code carried in the opcode of the RST instruction specifies the jump address.

The restart instruction is unique because it seldom appears as source code in an applications program. More often, the peripheral devices seeking interrupt service pass this one-byte instruction to the processor.

When a device requests interrupt service and interrupts are enabled, the processor acknowledges the request and prepares its data lines to accept any one-byte instruction from the device. RST is generally the instruction of choice because its special purpose CALL establishes a return to the main program.

The processor moves the three-bit address code from the RST instruction into bits 3, 4, and 5 of the program counter. In effect, this multiplies the code by eight. Program execution resumes at the new address where eight bytes are available for code to service the interrupt. If eight bytes are too few, the program can either jump to or call a subroutine.

8085 NOTE

The 8085 processor includes four hardware inputs that generate internal RST instructions. Rather than send a RST instruction, the interrupting device need only apply a signal to the RST5.5, RST6.5, RST7.5, or TRAP input pin. The processor then generates an internal RST instruction. The execution depends on the input:

INPUT NAME	RESTART ADDRESS
TRAP	24H
RST5.5	2CH
RST6.5	34H
RST7.5	3CH

Notice that these addresses are within the same portion of memory used by the RST instruction, and therefore allow only four bytes — enough for a call or jump and a return — for the interrupt service routine.

If included in the program code, the RST instruction has the following format:

Opcode	Operand
RST	code

The address code must be a number or expression within the range 000B through 111B.

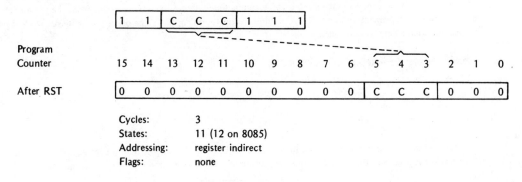

| 1 | 1 | C | C | C | 1 | 1 | 1 |

Program Counter

15 14 13 12 11 10 9 8 7 6 5 4 3 2 1 0

After RST

| 0 | 0 | 0 | 0 | 0 | 0 | 0 | 0 | 0 | 0 | C | C | C | 0 | 0 | 0 |

Cycles:	3
States:	11 (12 on 8085)
Addressing:	register indirect
Flags:	none

RZ   RETURN IF ZERO

The RZ instruction tests the zero flag. If the flag is set to one to indicate that the contents of the accumulator are zero, the instruction pops two bytes of data off the stack and places them in the program counter. Program execution resumes at the new address in the program counter. If the flag is zero, program execution simply continues with the next sequential instruction.

Opcode   Operand

RZ

Operands are not permitted with the RZ instruction.

1	1	0	0	1	0	0	0

Cycles: 1 or 3
States: 5 or 11 (6 or 12 on 8085)
Addressing: register indirect
Flags: none

Example:

For the sake of brevity, an example is given for the RET instruction but not for each of its closely related variants.

SBB   SUBTRACT WITH BORROW

SBB subtracts one byte of data and the setting of the carry flag from the contents of the accumulator. The result is stored in the accumulator. SBB then updates the setting of the carry flag to indicate the outcome of the operation.

SBB's use of the carry flag enables the program to subtract multi-byte strings. SBB incorporates the carry flag by adding it to the byte to be subtracted from the accumulator. It then subtracts the result from the accumulator by using two's complement addition. These preliminary operations occur in the processor's internal work registers so that the source data remains unchanged.

Subtract Register from Accumulator with Borrow

Opcode   Operand

SBB   reg

The operand must specify one of the registers A through E, H or L. This instruction subtracts the contents of the specified register and the carry flag from the accumulator and stores the result in the accumulator.

1	0	0	1	1	S	S	S

Cycles: 1
States: 4
Addressing: register
Flags: Z,S,P,CY,AC

Subtract Memory from Accumulator with Borrow

Opcode	Operand
SBB	M

This instruction subtracts the carry flag and the contents of the memory location addressed by the H and L registers from the accumulator and stores the result in the accumulator.

1	0	0	1	1	1	1	0

Cycles:	2
States:	7
Addressing:	register indirect
Flags:	Z,S,P,CY,AC

Example:

Assume that register B contains 2, the accumulator contains 4, and the carry flag is set to 1. The instruction SBB B operates as follows:

2H + carry = 3H
2's complement of 3H = 11111101

Accumulator = 00000100
                11111101
                00000001 = 1H

Notice that this two's complement addition produces a carry. When SBB complements the carry bit generated by the addition, the carry flag is reset OFF. The flag settings resulting from the SBB B instruction are as follows.

Carry	=	0
Sign	=	0
Zero	=	0
Parity	=	0
Aux. Carry	=	1

SBI   SUBTRACT IMMEDIATE WITH BORROW

SBI subtracts the contents of the second instruction byte and the setting of the carry flag from the contents of the accumulator. The result is stored in the accumulator.

SBI's use of the carry flag enables the program to subtract multi-byte strings. SBI incorporates the carry flag by adding it to the byte to be subtracted from the accumulator. It then subtracts the result from the accumulator by using two's complement addition. These preliminary operations occur in the processor's internal work registers so that the immediate source data remains unchanged.

The assembler's relocation feature treats all external and relocatable symbols as 16-bit addresses. When one of these symbols appears in the operand expression of an immediate instruction, it must be preceded by either the HIGH or LOW operator to specify which byte of the address is to be used in the evaluation of the expression. When neither operator is present, the assembler assumes the LOW operator and issues an error message.

Opcode	Operand
SBI	data

The operand must specify the data to be subtracted. This data may be in the form of a number, an ASCII constant, the label of some perviously defined value, or an expression. The data may not exceed one byte.

1	1	0	1	1	1	1	0

Cycles:	2
States:	7
Addressing:	immediate
Flags:	Z,S,P,CY,AC

Example:

This sequence of instructions replaces a 20-byte array at symbolic location AXLOTL with a logical array consisting of zeros and ones, as follows:

- If an element of AXLOTL is 5 or greater *in absolute value,* it is replaced with 1.
- If an element of AXLOTL is less than 5 in absolute value, it is replaced with 0.

Note that the program flow is governed by how the carry flag is set.

```
                MVI  B,20          ; initialize counter
                XRA  A             ; clear accumulator and carry
                LXI  H,AXLOTL      ; (H,L) point to array AXLOTL
        LOAD:   MOV  A,M           ; load acc. with byte pointed to by (H,L)
                SBI  5             ; subtract 5, set carry if acc. less than 5
                JC   SMALL         ; jump to SMALL if acc. was less than 5
                MVI  M,1           ; store 1 where array element was
                JMP  TEST          ; jump down to test count
        SMALL:  MVI  M,0           ; store 0 where array element was
        TEST:   XRA  A             ; clear accumulator and carry
                DCR  B             ; decrement count
                CMP  B             ; compare B to 0
                JZ   DONE          ; if accum. is zero, all done
                INX  H             ; bump (H,L) to point to next array element
                JMP  LOAD          ; go back and get another array element
        DONE:                      ; remainder of program
```

SHLD   STORE H AND L DIRECT

SHLD stores a copy of the L register in the memory location specified in bytes two and three of the SHLD instruction. SHLD then stores a copy of the H register in the next higher memory location.

SHLD is one of the instructions provided for saving the contents of the H and L registers. Alternately, the H and L data can be placed in the D and E registers (XCHG instruction) or placed on the stack (PUSH and XTHL instructions).

0	0	1	0	0	0	1	0
low addr							
high addr							

Cycles: 5
States: 16
Addressing: direct
Flags: none

Example:

Assume that the H and L registers contain 0AEH and 29H, respectively. The following is an illustration of the effect of the SHLD 10AH instruction:

	MEMORY ADDRESS			
	109	10A	10B	10C
Memory Before SHLD	00	00	00	00
Memory After SHLD	00	29	AE	00

SIM (8085 PROCESSOR ONLY)   SET INTERRUPT MASK

SIM is a multi-purpose instruction that uses the current contents of the accumulator to perform the following functions: Set the interrupt mask for the 8085's RST5.5, RST6.5, and RST7.5 hardware interrupts; reset RST7.5's edge sensitive input; and output bit 7 of the accumulator to the Serial Output Data latch.

Opcode   *Operand*

SIM

Operands are not permitted with the SIM instruction. However, you must be certain to load the desired bit configurations into the accumulator before executing the SIM instruction. SIM interprets the bits in the accumulator as follows:

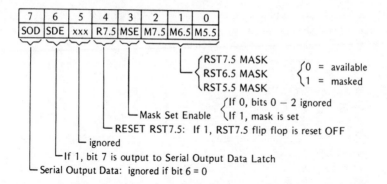

Accumulator bits 3 and 6 function as enable switches. If bit 3 is set ON (set to 1), the set mask function is enabled. Bits 0 through 2 then mask or leave available the corresponding RST interrupt. A 1 bit masks the interrupt making it unavailable; a 0 bit leaves the interrupt available. If bit 3 is set OFF (reset to 0), bits 0 through 2 have no effect. Use this option when you want to send a serial output bit without affecting the interrupt mask.

Notice that the DI (Disable Interrupts) instruction overrides the SIM instruction. Whether masked or not, RST5.5, RST6.5, and RST7.5 are disabled when the DI instruction is in effect. Use the RIM (Read Interrupt Mask) instruction to determine the current settings of the interrupt flag and the interrupt masks.

If bit 6 is set to 1, the serial output data function is enabled. The processor latches accumulator bit 7 into the SOD output where it can be accessed by a peripheral device. If bit 6 is reset to 0, bit 7 is ignored.

A 1 in accumulator bit 4 resets OFF the RST7.5 input flip flop. Unlike RST5.5 and 6.5, RST7.5 is sensed via a processor flip flop that is set when a peripheral device issues a pulse with a rising edge. This edge triggered input supports devices that cannot maintain an interrupt request until serviced. RST7.5 is also useful when a device does not require any explicit hardware service for each interrupt. For example, the program might increment and test an event counter for each interrupt rather than service the device directly.

The RST7.5 flip flop remains set until reset by 1) issuing a RESET to the 8085, 2) recognizing the interrupt, or 3) setting accumulator bit 4 and executing a SIM instruction. The Reset RST7.5 feature of the SIM instruction allows the program to override the interrupt.

The RST7.5 input flip flop is not affected by the setting of the interrupt mask or the DI instruction and therefore can be set at any time. However, the interrupt cannot be serviced when RST7.5 is masked or a DI instruction is in effect.

| 0 | 0 | 1 | 1 | 0 | 0 | 0 | 0 |

Cycles: 1
States: 4
Flags: none

Example 1:   Assume that the accumulator contains the bit pattern 00011100. The SIM instruction resets the RST7.5 flip flop and sets the RST7.5 interrupt mask. If an RST7.5 interrupt is pending when this SIM instruction is executed, it is overridden without being serviced. Also, any subsequent RST7.5 interrupt is masked and cannot be serviced until the interrupt mask is reset.

Example 2: Assume that the accumulator contains the bit pattern 11001111. The SIM instruction masks out the RST5.5, RST6.5, and RST7.5 level interrupts and latches a 1 bit into the SOD input. By contrast, the bit pattern 10000111 has no effect since the enable bits 3 and 6 are not set to ones.

SPHL   MOVE H&L TO SP

SPHL loads the contents of the H and L registers into the SP (Stack Pointer) register.

Opcode	Operand
SPHL	

Operands are not permitted with the SPHL instruction.

SP is a special purpose 16-bit register used to address the stack; the stack must be in random access memory (RAM). Because different applications use different memory configurations, the user program must load the SP register with the stack's beginning address. The stack is usually assigned to the highest available location in RAM. The hardware decrements the stack pointer as items are added to the stack and increments the pointer as items are removed.

The stack pointer must be initialized before any instruction attempts to access the stack. Typically, stack initialization occurs very early in the program. Once established, the stack pointer should be altered with caution. Arbitrary use of SPHL can cause the loss of stack data.

1	1	1	1	1	0	0	1

Cycles:	1
States:	5 (6 on 8085)
Addressing:	register
Flags:	none

Example:

Assume that the H and L registers contain 50H and 0FFH, respectively. SPHL loads the stack pointer with the value 50FFH.

STA   STORE ACCUMULATOR DIRECT

STA stores a copy of the current accumulator contents into the memory location specified in bytes two and three of the STA instruction.

Opcode	Operand
STA	address

The address may be stated as a number, a previously defined label, or an expression. The assembler inverts the high and low address bytes when it builds the instruction.

0	0	1	1	0	0	1	0
low addr							
high addr							

Cycles: 4
States: 13
Addressing: direct
Flags: none

Example:

The following instruction stores a copy of the contents of the accumulator at memory location 5B3H:

STA   5B3H

When assembled, the previous instruction has the hexadecimal value 32 B3 05. Notice that the assembler inverts the high and low order address bytes for proper storage in memory.

STAX   STORE ACCUMULATOR INDIRECT

The STAX instruction stores a copy of the contents of the accumulator into the memory location addressed by register pair B or register pair D.

Opcode   *Operand*

STAX $\begin{Bmatrix} B \\ D \end{Bmatrix}$

The operand B specifies the B and C register pair; D specifies the D and E register pair. This instruction may specify only the B or D register pair.

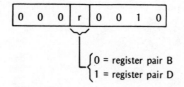

0	0	0	r	0	0	1	0

0 = register pair B
1 = register pair D

Cycles: 2
States: 7
Addressing: register indirect
Flags: none

Example:

If register B contains 3FH and register C contains 16H, the following instruction stores a copy of the contents of the accumulator at memory location 3F16H:

STAX   B

STC   SET CARRY

STC sets the carry flag to one. No other flags are affected.

	Opcode	Operand
	STC	

Operands are not permitted with the STC instruction.

0	0	1	1	0	1	1	1

Cycles: 1
States: 4
Flags: CY

When used in combination with the rotate accumulator through the carry flag instructions, STC allows the program to modify individual bits.

SUB   SUBTRACT

The SUB instruction subtracts one byte of data from the contents of the accumulator. The result is stored in the accumulator. SUB uses two's complement representation of data as explained in Chapter 2. Notice that the SUB instruction excludes the carry flag (actually a 'borrow' flag for the purposes of subtraction) but sets the flag to indicate the outcome of the operation.

Subtract Register from Accumulator

	Opcode	Operand
	SUB	reg

The operands must specify one of the registers A through E, H or L. The instruction subtracts the contents of the specified register from the contents of the accumulator using two's complement data representation. The result is stored in the accumulator.

1	0	0	1	0	S	S	S

Cycles: 1
States: 4
Addressing: register
Flags: Z,S,P,CY,AC

Subtract Memory from Accumulator

	Opcode	Operand
	SUB	M

This instruction subtracts the contents of the memory location addressed by the H and L registers from the contents of the accumulator and stores the result in the accumulator. M is a symbolic reference to the H and L registers.

1	0	0	1	0	1	1	0

Cycles: 2
States: 7
Addressing: register indirect
Flags: Z,S,P,CY,AC

Example:

Assume that the accumulator contains 3EH. The instruction SUB A subtracts the contents of the accumulator from the accumulator and produces a result of zero as follows:

$$
\begin{array}{rl}
3EH = & 00111110 \\
+(-3EH) = & 11000001 \quad \text{one's complement} \\
& \underline{1} \quad \text{add one to produce two's complement} \\
\text{carry out} = 1 & 00000000 \quad \text{result} = 0
\end{array}
$$

The condition flags are set as follows:

Carry	=	0
Sign	=	0
Zero	=	1
Parity	=	1
Aux. Carry	=	1

Notice that the SUB instruction complements the carry generated by the two's complement addition to form a 'borrow' flag. The auxiliary carry flag is set because the particular value used in this example causes a carry out of bit 3.

SUI   SUBTRACT IMMEDIATE

SUI subtracts the contents of the second instruction byte from the contents of the accumulator and stores the result in the accumulator. Notice that the SUI instruction disregards the carry ('borrow') flag during the subtraction but sets the flag to indicate the outcome of the operation.

Opcode	Operand
SUI	data

The operand must specify the data to be subtracted. This data may be in the form of a number, an ASCII constant, the label of some previously defined value, or an expression. The data must not exceed one byte.

The assembler's relocation feature treats all external and relocatable symbols as 16-bit addresses. When one of these symbols appears in the operand expression of an immediate instruction, it must be preceded by either the

HIGH or LOW operator to specify which byte of the address is to be used in the evaluation of the expression. When neither operator is present, the assembler assumes the LOW operator and issues an error message.

1	1	0	1	0	1	1	0

Cycles: 2
States: 7
Addressing: immediate
Flags: Z,S,P,CY,AC

Example:

Assume that the accumulator contains the value 9 when the instruction SUI 1 is executed:

$$Accumulator = 00001001 = 9H$$
$$Immediate\ data\ (2's\ comp) = \underline{11111111} = -1H$$
$$00001000 = 8H$$

Notice that this two's complement addition results in a carry. The SUI instruction complements the carry generated by the addition to form a 'borrow' flag. The flag settings resulting from this operation are as follows:

Carry   =   0
Sign   =   0
Zero   =   0
Parity   =   0
Aux. Carry =   1

XCHG   EXCHANGE H AND L WITH D AND E

XCHG exchanges the contents of the H and L registers with the contents of the D and E registers.

Opcode   *Operand*

XCHG

Operands are not allowed with the XCHG instruction.

XCHG both saves the current H and L and loads a new address into the H and L registers. Since XCHG is a register-to-register instruction, it provides the quickest means of saving and/or altering the H and L registers.

1	1	1	0	1	0	1	1

Cycles: 1
States: 4
Addressing: register
Flags: none

Example:

Assume that the H and L registers contain 1234H, and the D and E registers contain 0ABCDH. Following execution of the XCHG instruction, H and L contain 0ABCDH, and D and E contain 1234H.

XRA   EXCLUSIVE OR WITH ACCUMULATOR

XRA performs an exclusive OR logical operation using the contents of the specified byte and the accumulator. The result is placed in the accumulator.

Summary of Logical Operations

AND produces a one bit in the result only when the corresponding bits in the test data and the mask data are ones.

OR produces a one bit in the result when the corresponding bits in either the test data or the mask data are ones.

Exclusive OR produces a one bit only when the corresponding bits in the test data and the mask data are different; i.e., a one bit in either the test data or the mask data — but not both — produces a one bit in the result.

AND	OR	EXCLUSIVE OR
1010 1010	1010 1010	1010 1010
0000 1111	0000 1111	0000 1111
0000 1010	1010 1111	1010 0101

XRA Register with Accumulator

Opcode	Operand
XRA	reg

The operand must specify one of the registers A through E, H or L. This instruction performs an exclusive OR using the contents of the specified register and the accumulator and stores the result in the accumulator. The carry and auxiliary carry flags are reset to zero.

1	0	1	0	1	S	S	S

Cycles: 1
States: 4
Addressing: register
Flags: Z,S,P,CY,AC

XRA Memory with Accumulator

Opcode	Operand
XRA	M

The contents of the memory location specified by the H and L registers is exclusive-ORed with the contents of the accumulator. The result is stored in the accumulator. The carry and auxiliary carry flags are reset to zero.

1	0	1	0	1	1	1	0

Cycles:	2
States:	7
Addressing:	register indirect
Flags:	Z,S,P,CY,AC

Examples:

Since any bit exclusive-ORed with itself produces zero, XRA is frequently used to zero the accumulator. The following instructions zero the accumulator and the B and C registers.

XRA	A
MOV	B,A
MOV	C,A

Any bit exclusive-ORed with a one bit is complemented. Thus, if the accumulator contains all ones (0FFH), the instruction XRA B produces the one's complement of the B register in the accumulator.

XRI   EXCLUSIVE OR IMMEDIATE WITH ACCUMULATOR

XRI performs an exclusive OR operation using the contents of the second instruction byte and the contents of the accumulator. The result is placed in the accumulator. XRI also resets the carry and auxiliary carry flags to zero.

Opcode	Operand
XRI	data

The operand must specify the data to be used in the OR operation. This data may be in the form of a number, an ASCII constant, the label of some previously defined value, or an expression. The data may not exceed one byte.

The assembler's relocation feature treats all external and relocatable symbols as 16-bit addresses. When one of these symbols appears in the operand expression of an immediate instruction, it must be preceded by either the HIGH or LOW operator to specify which byte of the address is to be used in the evaluation of the expression. When neither operator is present, the assembler assumes the LOW operator and issues an error message.

1	1	1	0	1	1	1	0
			data				

Cycles: 2
States: 7
Addressing: immediate
Flags: Z,S,P,CY,AC

Summary of Logical Operations

AND produces a one bit in the result only when the corresponding bits in the test data and the mask data are ones.

OR produces a one bit in the result when the corresponding bits in either the test data or the mask data are ones.

Exclusive OR produces a one bit only when the corresponding bits in the test data and the mask data are different; i.e., a one bit in either the test data or the mask data — but not both — produces a one bit in the result.

AND	OR	EXCLUSIVE OR
1010 1010	1010 1010	1010 1010
0000 1111	0000 1111	0000 1111
0000 1010	1010 1111	1010 0101

Example:

Assume that a program uses bits 7 and 6 of a byte as flags that control the calling of two subroutines. The program tests the bits by rotating the contents of the accumulator until the desired bit is in the carry flag; a CC instruction (Call if Carry) tests the flag and calls the subroutine if required.

Assume that the control flag byte is positioned normally in the accumulator, and the program must set OFF bit 6 and set bit 7 ON. The remaining bits, which are status flags used for other purposes, must not be altered. Since any bit exclusive-ORed with a one is complemented, and any bit exclusive-ORed with a zero remains unchanged, the following instruction is used:

XRI   11000000B

The instruction has the following results:

Accumulator   = 01001100
Immediate data = 11000000
                  10001100

XTHL   **EXCHANGE H&L WITH TOP OF STACK**

XTHL exchanges two bytes from the top of the stack with the two bytes stored in the H and L registers. Thus, XTHL both saves the current contents of the H and L registers and loads new values into H and L.

Opcode   *Operand*

XTHL

Operands are not allowed with the XTHL instruction.

XTHL exchanges the contents of the L register with the contents of the memory location specified by the SP (Stack Pointer) register. The contents of the H register are exchanged with the contents of SP+1.

1	1	1	0	0	0	1	1

Cycles: 5
States: 18 (16 on 8085)
Addressing: register indirect
Flags: none

Example:

Assume that the stack pointer register contains 10ADH; register H contains 0BH and L contains 3CH; and memory locations 10ADH and 10AEH contain F0H and 0DH, respectively. The following is an illustration of the effect of the XTHL instruction:

	MEMORY ADDRESS				H	L
	10AC	10AD	10AE	10AF		
Before XTHL	FF	F0	0D	FF	0B	3C
After XTHL	FF	3C	0B	FF	0D	F0

The stack pointer register remains unchanged following execution of the XTHL instruction.

Appendix C

Data Sheets for MCS–80/85™

2114A
1024 X 4 BIT STATIC RAM

	2114AL-2	2114AL-3	2114AL-4	2114A-4	2114A-5
Max. Access Time (ns)	120	150	200	200	250
Max. Current (mA)	40	40	40	70	70

- **HMOS Technology**
- **Low Power, High Speed**
- **Identical Cycle and Access Times**
- **Single +5V Supply ±10%**
- **High Density 18 Pin Package**

- **Completely Static Memory - No Clock or Timing Strobe Required**
- **Directly TTL Compatible: All Inputs and Outputs**
- **Common Data Input and Output Using Three-State Outputs**
- **2114 Replacement**

The Intel 2114A is a 4096-bit static Random Access Memory organized as 1024 words by 4-bits using HMOS, a high performance MOS technology. It uses fully DC stable (static) circuitry throughout, in both the array and the decoding, therefore it requires no clocks or refreshing to operate. Data access is particularly simple since address setup times are not required. The data is read out nondestructively and has the same polarity as the input data. Common input/output pins are provided.

The 2114A is designed for memory applications where the high performance and high reliability of HMOS, low cost, large bit storage, and simple interfacing are important design objectives. The 2114A is placed in an 18-pin package for the highest possible density.

It is directly TTL compatible in all respects: inputs, outputs, and a single +5V supply. A separate Chip Select ($\overline{CS}$) lead allows easy selection of an individual package when outputs are or-tied.

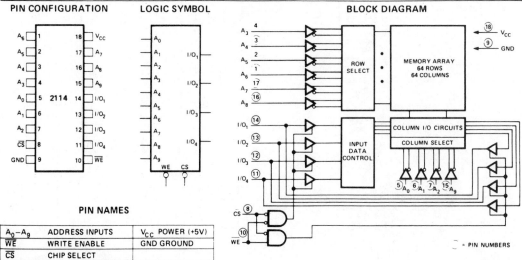

PIN NAMES

A_0–A_9	ADDRESS INPUTS	V_{CC} POWER (+5V)
$\overline{WE}$	WRITE ENABLE	GND GROUND
$\overline{CS}$	CHIP SELECT	
I/O_1–I/O_4	DATA INPUT/OUTPUT	

(Courtesy Intel Corporation)

443

2141
4096 X 1 BIT STATIC RAM

	2141-2	2141-3	2141-4	2141-5	2141L-3	2141L-4	2141L-5
Max. Access Time (ns)	120	150	200	250	150	200	250
Max. Active Current (mA)	70	70	55	55	40	40	40
Max. Standby Current (mA)	20	20	12	12	5	5	5

- ■ **HMOS Technology**
- ■ **Industry Standard 2147 Pinout**
- ■ **Completely Static Memory — No Clock or Timing Strobe Required**
- ■ **Equal Access and Cycle Times**
- ■ **Single +5V Supply**

- ■ **Automatic Power-Down**
- ■ **Directly TTL Compatible — All Inputs and Output**
- ■ **Separate Data Input and Output**
- ■ **Three-State Output**
- ■ **High Density 18-Pin Package**

The Intel® 2141 is a 4096-bit static Random Access Memory organized as 4096 words by 1-bit using HMOS, a high-performance MOS technology. It uses a uniquely innovative design approach which provides the ease-of-use features associated with non-clocked static memories and the reduced standby power dissipation associated with clocked static memories. To the user this means low standby power dissipation without the need for clocks, address setup and hold times, nor reduced data rates due to cycle times that are longer than access times.

$\overline{CS}$ controls the power-down feature. In less than a cycle time after $\overline{CS}$ goes high — deselecting the 2141 — the part automatically reduces its power requirements and remains in this low power standby mode as long as $\overline{CS}$ remains high. This device feature results in system power savings as great as 85% in larger systems, where the majority of devices are deselected.

The 2141 is placed in an 18-pin package configured with the industry standard pinout, the same as the 2147. It is directly TTL compatible in all respects: inputs, output, and a single +5V supply. The data is read out nondestructively and has the same polarity as the input data. A data input and a separate three-state output are used.

PIN CONFIGURATION   LOGIC SYMBOL   BLOCK DIAGRAM

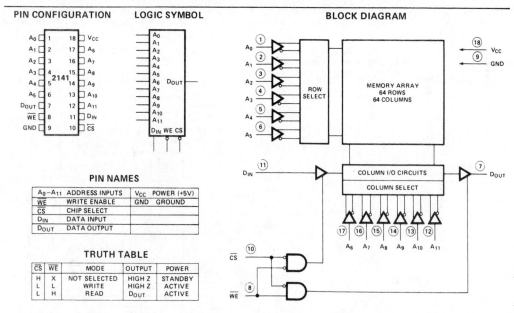

PIN NAMES

A_0–A_{11}	ADDRESS INPUTS	V_{CC}	POWER (+5V)
$\overline{WE}$	WRITE ENABLE	GND	GROUND
$\overline{CS}$	CHIP SELECT		
D_{IN}	DATA INPUT		
D_{OUT}	DATA OUTPUT		

TRUTH TABLE

$\overline{CS}$	$\overline{WE}$	MODE	OUTPUT	POWER
H	X	NOT SELECTED	HIGH Z	STANDBY
L	L	WRITE	HIGH Z	ACTIVE
L	H	READ	D_{OUT}	ACTIVE

(Courtesy Intel Corporation)

2732
32K (4K x 8) UV ERASABLE PROM

- **Fast Access Time:**
  - **— 450 ns Max. 2732**
  - **— 550 ns Max. 2732-6**

- **Single +5V ± 5% Power Supply**

- **Output Enable for MCS-85™ and MCS-86™ Compatibility**

- **Low Power Dissipation:**
  150mA Max. Active Current
  30mA Max. Standby Current

- **Pin Compatible to Intel® 2716 EPROM**

- **Completely Static**

- **Simple Programming Requirements**
  - **— Single Location Programming**
  - **— Programs with One 50ms Pulse**

- **Three-State Output for Direct Bus Interface**

The Intel® 2732 is a 32,768-bit ultraviolet erasable and electrically programmable read-only memory (EPROM). The 2732 operates from a single 5-volt power supply, has a standby mode, and features an output enable control. The total programming time for all bits is three and a half minutes. All these features make designing with the 2732 in microcomputer systems faster, easier, and more economical.

An important 2732 feature is the separate output control, Output Enable ($\overline{OE}$), from the Chip Enable control ($\overline{CE}$). The $\overline{OE}$ control eliminates bus contention in multiple bus microprocessor systems. Intel's Application Note AP-30 describes the microprocessor system implementation of the $\overline{OE}$ and $\overline{CE}$ controls on Intel's 2716 and 2732 EPROMs. AP-30 is available from Intel's Literature Department.

The 2732 has a standby mode which reduces the power dissipation without increasing access time. The maximum active current is 150mA, while the maximum standby current is only 30mA, an 80% savings. The standby mode is achieved by applying a TTL-high signal to the $\overline{CE}$ input.

PIN CONFIGURATION

```
        ┌───┐ ┌───┐
  A7 ▢ 1│   └─┘   │24 ▢ Vcc
  A6 ▢ 2│         │23 ▢ A8
  A5 ▢ 3│         │22 ▢ A9
  A4 ▢ 4│         │21 ▢ A11
  A3 ▢ 5│         │20 ▢ OE/Vpp
  A2 ▢ 6│         │19 ▢ A10
  A1 ▢ 7│         │18 ▢ CE
  A0 ▢ 8│         │17 ▢ O7
  O0 ▢ 9│         │16 ▢ O6
  O1 ▢ 10│        │15 ▢ O5
  O2 ▢ 11│        │14 ▢ O4
 GND ▢ 12│        │13 ▢ O3
        └─────────┘
```

PIN NAMES

A_0–A_{11}	ADDRESSES
$\overline{CE}$	CHIP ENABLE
$\overline{OE}$	OUTPUT ENABLE
O_0–O_7	OUTPUTS

(Courtesy Intel Corporation)

MODE SELECTION

PINS / MODE	$\overline{CE}$ (18)	$\overline{OE}$/V_{PP} (20)	V_{CC} (24)	OUTPUTS (9-11,13-17)
Read	V_{IL}	V_{IL}	+5	D_{OUT}
Standby	V_{IH}	Don't Care	+5	High Z
Program	V_{IL}	V_{PP}	+5	D_{IN}
Program Verify	V_{IL}	V_{IL}	+5	D_{OUT}
Program Inhibit	V_{IH}	V_{PP}	+5	High Z

BLOCK DIAGRAM

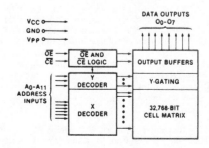

ERASURE CHARACTERISTICS

The erasure characteristics of the 2732 are such that erasure begins to occur when exposed to light with wavelengths shorter than approximately 4000 Angstroms (Å). It should be noted that sunlight and certain types of fluorescent lamps have wavelengths in the 3000-4000Å range. Data show that constant exposure to room level fluorescent lighting could erase the typical 2732 in approximately 3 years, while it would take approximately 1 week to cause erasure when exposed to direct sunlight. If the 2732 is to be exposed to these types of lighting conditions for extended periods of time, opaque labels are available from Intel which should be placed over the 2732 window to prevent unintentional erasure.

The recommended erasure procedure (see Data Catalog page 4-83) for the 2732 is exposure to shortwave ultraviolet light which has a wavelength of 2537 Angstroms (Å). The integrated dose (i.e., UV intensity X exposure time) for erasure should be a minimum of 15 W-sec/cm². The erasure time with this dosage is approximately 15 to 20 minutes using an ultraviolet lamp with a 12000 μW/cm² power rating. The 2732 should be placed within 1 inch of the lamp tubes during erasure. Some lamps have a filter on their tubes which should be removed before erasure.

DEVICE OPERATION

The five modes of operation of the 2732 are listed in Table 1. A single 5V power supply is required in the read mode. All inputs are TTL levels except for $\overline{OE}$/V$_{PP}$ during programming. In the program mode the $\overline{OE}$/V$_{PP}$ input is pulsed from a TTL level to 25V.

TABLE 1. Mode Selection

MODE \ PINS	$\overline{CE}$ (18)	$\overline{OE}$/V$_{PP}$ (20)	V$_{CC}$ (24)	OUTPUTS (9-11,13-17)
Read	V$_{IL}$	V$_{IL}$	+5	D$_{OUT}$
Standby	V$_{IH}$	Don't Care	+5	High Z
Program	V$_{IL}$	V$_{PP}$	+5	D$_{IN}$
Program Verify	V$_{IL}$	V$_{IL}$	+5	D$_{OUT}$
Program Inhibit	V$_{IH}$	V$_{PP}$	+5	High Z

Read Mode

The 2732 has two control functions, both of which must be logically satisfied in order to obtain data at the outputs. Chip Enable ($\overline{CE}$) is the power control and should be used for device selection. Output Enable ($\overline{OE}$) is the output control and should be used to gate data to the output pins, independent of device selection. Assuming that addresses are stable, address access time (t$_{ACC}$) is equal to the delay from $\overline{CE}$ to output (t$_{CE}$). Data is available at the outputs 120ns (t$_{OE}$) after the falling edge of $\overline{OE}$, assuming that $\overline{CE}$ has been low and addresses have been stable for at least t$_{ACC}$ — t$_{OE}$.

Standby Mode

The 2732 has a standby mode which reduces the active power current by 80%, from 150mA to 30mA. The 2732 is placed in the standby mode by applying a TTL high signal to the $\overline{CE}$ input. When in standby mode, the out-puts are in a high impedance state, independent of the $\overline{OE}$ input.

Output OR-Tieing

Because EPROMs are usually used in larger memory arrays, Intel has provided a 2 line control function that accommodates this use of multiple memory connections. The two line control function allows for:

a) the lowest possible memory power dissipation, and
b) complete assurance that output bus contention will not occur.

To most efficiently use these two control lines, it is recommended that $\overline{CE}$ (pin 18) be decoded and used as the primary device selecting function, while $\overline{OE}$ (pin 20) be made a common connection to all devices in the array and connected to the READ line from the system control bus. This assures that all deselected memory devices are in their low power standby mode and that the output pins are only active when data is desired from a particular memory device.

Programming

Initially, and after each erasure, all bits of the 2732 are in the "1" state. Data is introduced by selectively programming "0's" into the desired bit locations. Although only "0's" will be programmed, both "1's" and "0's" can be presented in the data word. The only way to change a "0" to a "1" is by ultraviolet light erasure.

The 2732 is in the programming mode when the $\overline{OE}$/V$_{PP}$ input is at 25V. It is required that a 0.1μF capacitor be placed across $\overline{OE}$/V$_{PP}$ and ground to suppress spurious voltage transients which may damage the device. The data to be programmed is applied 8 bits in parallel to the data output pins. The levels required for the address and data inputs are TTL.

When the address and data are stable, a 50msec, active low, TTL program pulse is applied to the $\overline{CE}$ input. A program pulse must be applied at each address location to be programmed. You can program any location at any time — either individually, sequentially, or at random. The program pulse has a maximum width of 55msec. The 2732 must not be programmed with a DC signal applied to the $\overline{CE}$ input.

Programming of multiple 2732s in parallel with the same data can be easily accomplished due to the simplicity of the programming requirements. Like inputs of the paralleled 2732s may be connected together when they are programmed with the same data. A low level TTL pulse applied to the $\overline{CE}$ input programs the paralleled 2732s.

Program Inhibit

Programming of multiple 2732s in parallel with different data is also easily accomplished. Except for $\overline{CE}$, all like inputs (including $\overline{OE}$) of the parallel 2732s may be common. A TTL level program pulse applied to a 2732's $\overline{CE}$ input with $\overline{OE}$/V$_{PP}$ at 25V will program that 2732. A high level $\overline{CE}$ input inhibits the other 2732s from being programmed.

Program Verify

A verify should be performed on the programmed bits to determine that they were correctly programmed. The verify is accomplished with $\overline{OE}$/V$_{PP}$ and $\overline{CE}$ at V$_{IL}$. Data should be verified t$_{DV}$ after the falling edge of $\overline{CE}$.

8155/8156/8155-2/8156-2
2048 BIT STATIC MOS RAM WITH I/O PORTS AND TIMER

- ■ 256 Word x 8 Bits
- ■ Single +5V Power Supply
- ■ Completely Static Operation
- ■ Internal Address Latch
- ■ 2 Programmable 8 Bit I/O Ports

- ■ 1 Programmable 6-Bit I/O Port
- ■ Programmable 14-Bit Binary Counter/ Timer
- ■ Compatible with 8085A and 8088 CPU
- ■ Multiplexed Address and Data Bus
- ■ 40 Pin DIP

The 8155 and 89156 are RAM and I/O chips to be used in the 8085A and 8088 microprocessor systems. The RAM portion is designed with 2048 static cells organized as 256 x 8. They have a maximum access time of 400 ns to permit use with no wait states in 8085A CPU. The 8155-2 and 8156-2 have maximum access times of 330 ns for use with the 8085A-2 and the full speed 5 MHz 8088 CPU.

The I/O portion consists of three general purpose I/O ports. One of the three ports can be programmed to be status pins, thus allowing the other two ports to operate in handshake mode.

A 14-bit programmable counter/timer is jalso included on chip to provide either a square wave or terminal count pulse for the CPU system depending on timer mode.

PIN CONFIGURATION

PC_3	1	40	V_{CC}
PC_4	2	39	PC_2
TIMER IN	3	38	PC_1
RESET	4	37	PC_0
PC_5	5	36	PB_7
$\overline{TIMER\ OUT}$	6	35	PB_6
$IO/\overline{M}$	7	34	PB_5
$\overline{CE}$ OR CE*	8	33	PB_4
$\overline{RD}$	9	32	PB_3
$\overline{WR}$	10	31	PB_2
ALE	11	30	PB_1
AD_0	12	29	PB_0
AD_1	13	28	PA_7
AD_2	14	27	PA_6
AD_3	15	26	PA_5
AD_4	16	25	PA_4
AD_5	17	24	PA_3
AD_6	18	23	PA_2
AD_7	19	22	PA_1
V_{SS}	20	21	PA_0

8155/8156   8155-2/8156-2

BLOCK DIAGRAM

*: 8155/8155-2 = $\overline{CE}$, 8156/8156-2 = CE

(Courtesy Intel Corporation)

8155/8156 PIN FUNCTIONS

Symbol	Function
RESET (input)	Pulse provided by the 8085A to initialize the system (connect to 8085A RESET OUT). Input high on this line resets the chip and initializes the three I/O ports to input mode. The width of RESET pulse should typically be two 8085A clock cycle times.
AD_{0-7} (input)	3-state Address/Data lines that interface with the CPU lower 8-bit Address/Data Bus. The 8-bit address is latched into the address latch inside the 8155/56 on the falling edge of ALE. The address can be either for the memory section or the I/O section depending on the $IO/\overline{M}$ input. The 8-bit data is either written into the chip or read from the chip, depending on the $\overline{WR}$ or $\overline{RD}$ input signal.
CE or $\overline{CE}$ (input)	Chip Enable: On the 8155, this pin is $\overline{CE}$ and is ACTIVE LOW. On the 8156, this pin is CE and is ACTIVE HIGH.
$\overline{RD}$ (input)	Read control: Input low on this line with the Chip Enable active enables and AD_{0-7} buffers. If $IO/\overline{M}$ pin is low, the RAM content will be read out to the AD bus. Otherwise the content of the selected I/O port or command/status registers will be read to the AD bus.
$\overline{WR}$ (input)	Write control: Input low on this line with the Chip Enable active causes the data on the Address/Data bus to be written to the RAM or I/O ports and command/status register depending on $IO/\overline{M}$.

Symbol	Function
ALE (input)	Address Latch Enable: This control signal latches both the address on the AD_{0-7} lines and the state of the Chip Enable and $IO/\overline{M}$ into the chip at the falling edge of ALE.
$IO/\overline{M}$ (input)	Selects memory if low and I/O and command/status registers if high.
$PA_{0-7}(8)$ (input/output)	These 8 pins are general purpose I/O pins. The in/out direction is selected by programming the command register.
$PB_{0-7}(8)$ (input/output)	These 8 pins are general purpose I/O pins. The in/out direction is selected by programming the command register.
$PC_{0-5}(6)$ (input/output)	These 6 pins can function as either input port, output port, or as control signals for PA and PB. Programming is done through the command register. When PC_{0-5} are used as control signals, they will provide the following: PC_0 — A INTR (Port A Interrupt) PC_1 — ABF (Port A Buffer Full) PC_2 — $\overline{A\ STB}$ (Port A Strobe) PC_3 — B INTR (Port B Interrupt) PC_4 — $\overline{B\ BF}$ (Port B Buffer Full) PC_5 — B STB (Port B Strobe)
TIMER IN (input)	Input to the counter-timer.
$\overline{TIMER\ OUT}$ (output)	Timer output. This output can be either a square wave or a pulse depending on the timer mode.
V_{CC}	+5 volt supply.
V_{SS}	Ground Reference.

DESCRIPTION

The 8155/8156 contains the following:

- 2k Bit Static RAM organized as 256 x 8
- Two 8-bit I/O ports (PA & PB) and one 6-bit I/O port (PC)
- 14-bit timer-counter

The IO/$\overline{M}$ (IO/Memory Select) pin selects either the five registers (Command, Status, PA_{0-7}, PB_{0-7}, PC_{0-5}) or the memory (RAM) portion. (See Figure 1.)

The 8-bit address on the Address/Data lines, Chip Enable input CE or $\overline{CE}$, and IO/$\overline{M}$ are all latched on-chip at the falling edge of ALE. (See Figure 2.)

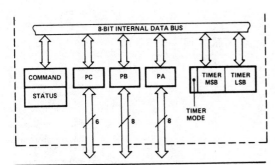

Figure 1. 8155/8156 Internal Registers

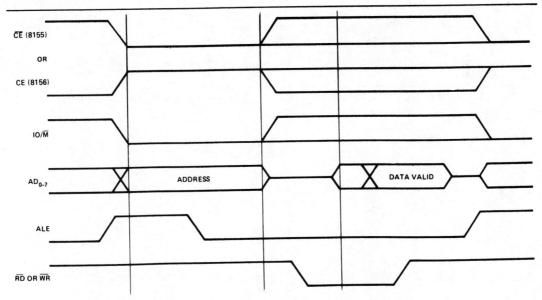

NOTE: FOR DETAILED TIMING INFORMATION, SEE FIGURE 12 AND A.C. CHARACTERISTICS.

Figure 2. 8155/8156 On-Board Memory Read/Write Cycle

PROGRAMMING OF THE COMMAND REGISTER

The command register consists of eight latches. Four bits (0-3) define the mode of the ports, two bits (4-5) enable or disable the interrupt from port C when it acts as control port, and the last two bits (6-7) are for the timer.

The command register contents can be altered at any time by using the I/O address XXXXX000 during a WRITE operation with the Chip Enable active and IO/$\overline{M}$ = 1. The meaning of each bit of the command byte is defined in Figure 3. The contents of the command register may never be read.

READING THE STATUS REGISTER

The status register consists of seven latches, one for each bit; six (0-5) for the status of the ports and one (6) for the status of the timer.

The status of the timer and the I/O section can be polled by reading the Status Register (Address XXXXX000). Status word format is shown in Figure 4. Note that you may never write to the status register since the command register shares the same I/O address and the command register is selected when a write to that address is issued.

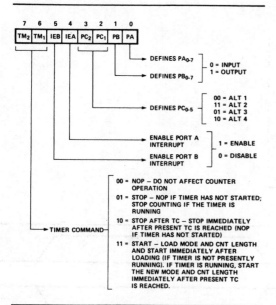

Figure 3. Command Register Bit Assignment

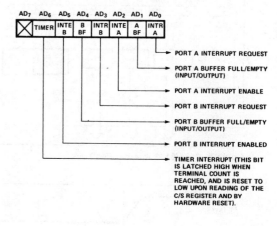

Figure 4. Status Register Bit Assignment

INPUT/OUTPUT SECTION

The I/O section of the 8155/8156 consists of five registers:
(See Figure 5.)

- **Command/Status Register (C/S)** — Both registers are assigned the address XXXXX000. The C/S address serves the dual purpose.

  When the C/S registers are selected during WRITE operation, a command is written into the command register. The contents of this register are *not* accessible through the pins.

  When the C/S (XXXXX000) is selected during a READ operation, the status information of the I/O ports and the timer becomes available on the AD_{0-7} lines.

- **PA Register** — This register can be programmed to be either input or output ports depending on the status of the contents of the C/S Register. Also depending on the command, this port can operate in either the basic mode or the strobed mode (See timing diagram). The I/O pins assigned in relation to this register are PA_{0-7}. The address of this register is XXXXX001.

- **PB Register** — This register functions the same as PA Register. The I/O pins assigned are PB_{0-7}. The address of this register is XXXXX010.

- **PC Register** — This register has the address XXXXX011 and contains only 6 bits. The 6 bits can be programmed to be either input ports, output ports or as control signals for PA and PB by properly programming the AD_2 and AD_3 bits of the C/S register.

  When PC_{0-5} is used as a control port, 3 bits are assigned for Port A and 3 for Port B. The first bit is an interrupt that the 8155 sends out. The second is an output signal indicating whether the buffer is full or empty, and the third is an input pin to accept a strobe for the strobed input mode. (See Table 1.)

When the 'C' port is programmed to either ALT3 or ALT4, the control signals for PA and PB are initialized as follows:

CONTROL	INPUT MODE	OUTPUT MODE
BF	Low	Low
INTR	Low	High
STB	Input Control	Input Control

I/O ADDRESS†								SELECTION
A7	A6	A5	A4	A3	A2	A1	A0	
X	X	X	X	X	0	0	0	Interval Command/Status Register
X	X	X	X	X	0	0	1	General Purpose I/O Port A
X	X	X	X	X	0	1	0	General Purpose I/O Port B
X	X	X	X	X	0	1	1	Port C — General Purpose I/O or Control
X	X	X	X	X	1	0	0	Low-Order 8 bits of Timer Count
X	X	X	X	X	1	0	1	High 6 bits of Timer Count and 2 bits of Timer Mode

X: Don't Care.
†: I/O Address must be qualified by CE = 1 (8156) or $\overline{CE}$ = 0 (8155) and IO/$\overline{M}$ = 1 in order to select the appropriate register.

Figure 5. I/O port and Timer Addressing Scheme

Figure 6 shows how I/O PORTS A and B are structured within the 8155 and 8156:

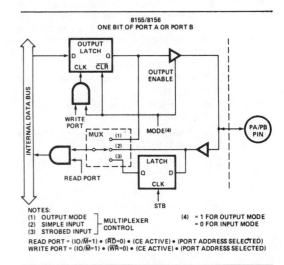

NOTES:
(1) OUTPUT MODE ⎤
(2) SIMPLE INPUT   ⎬ MULTIPLEXER
(3) STROBED INPUT ⎦ CONTROL

(4) = 1 FOR OUTPUT MODE
    = 0 FOR INPUT MODE

READ PORT = (IO/$\overline{M}$=1) • ($\overline{RD}$=0) • (CE ACTIVE) • (PORT ADDRESS SELECTED)
WRITE PORT = (IO/$\overline{M}$=1) • ($\overline{WR}$=0) • (CE ACTIVE) • (PORT ADDRESS SELECTED)

Figure 6. 8155/8156 Port Functions

TABLE 1. TABLE OF PORT CONTROL ASSIGNMENT.

Pin	ALT 1	ALT 2	ALT 3	ALT 4
PC0	Input Port	Output Port	A INTR (Port A Interrupt)	A INTR (Port A Interrupt)
PC1	Input Port	Output Port	A BF (Port A Buffer Full)	A BF (Port A Buffer Full)
PC2	Input Port	Output Port	A $\overline{\text{STB}}$ (Port A Strobe)	A $\overline{\text{STB}}$ (Port A Strobe)
PC3	Input Port	Output Port	Output Port	B INTR (Port B Interrupt)
PC4	Input Port	Output Port	Output Port	B BF (Port B Buffer Full)
PC5	Input Port	Output Port	Output Port	B $\overline{\text{STB}}$ (Port B Strobe)

Note in the diagram that when the I/O ports are programmed to be output ports, the contents of the output ports can still be read by a READ operation when appropriately addressed.

The outputs of the 8155/8156 are "glitch-free" meaning that you can write a "1" to a bit position that was previously "1" and the level at the output pin will not change.

Note also that the output latch is cleared when the port enters the input mode. The output latch cannot be loaded by writing to the port if the port is in the input mode. The result is that each time a port mode is changed from input to output, the output pins will go low. When the 8155/56 is RESET, the output latches are all cleared and all 3 ports enter the input mode.

When in the ALT 1 or ALT 2 modes, the bits of PORT C are structured like the diagram above in the simple input or output mode, respectively.

Reading from an input port with nothing connected to the pins will provide unpredictable results.

Figure 7 shows how the 8155/8156 I/O ports might be configured in a typical MCS-85 system.

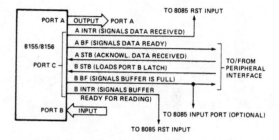

Figure 7. Example: Command Register = 00111001

8205
HIGH SPEED 1 OUT OF 8 BINARY DECODER

- I/O Port or Memory Selector

- Simple Expansion — Enable Inputs

- High Speed Schottky Bipolar Technology — 18 ns Max Delay

- Directly Compatible with TTL Logic Circuits

- Low Input Load Current — 0.25 mA Max, 1/6 Standard TTL Input Load

- Minimum Line Reflection — Low Voltage Diode Input Clamp

- Outputs Sink 10 mA Min

- 16-Pin Dual In-Line Ceramic or Plastic Package

The Intel® 8205 decoder can be used for expansion of systems which utilize input ports, output ports, and memory components with active low chip select input. When the 8205 is enabled, one of its 8 outputs goes "low", thus a single row of a memory system is selected. The 3-chip enable inputs on the 8205 allow easy system expansion. For very large systems, 8205 decoders can be cascaded such that each decoder can drive 8 other decoders for arbitrary memory expansions.

The 8205 is packaged in a standard 16-pin dual in-line package, and its performance is specified over the temperature range of 0°C to +75°C, ambient. The use of Schottky barrier diode clamped transistors to obtain fast switching speeds results in higher performance than equivalent devices made with a gold diffussion process.

PIN CONFIGURATION

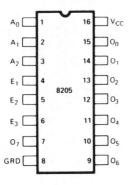

LOGIC SYMBOL

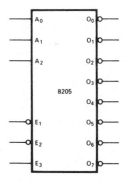

PIN NAMES

$A_0 \cdot A_2$	ADDRESS INPUTS
$\overline{E}_1 \cdot \overline{E}_3$	ENABLE INPUTS
$\overline{O}_0 \cdot \overline{O}_7$	DECODED OUTPUTS

ADDRESS			ENABLE			OUTPUTS							
A_0	A_1	A_2	E_1	E_2	E_3	0	1	2	3	4	5	6	7
L	L	L	L	L	H	L	H	H	H	H	H	H	H
H	L	L	L	L	H	H	L	H	H	H	H	H	H
L	H	L	L	L	H	H	H	L	H	H	H	H	H
H	H	L	L	L	H	H	H	H	L	H	H	H	H
L	L	H	L	L	H	H	H	H	H	L	H	H	H
H	L	H	L	L	H	H	H	H	H	H	L	H	H
L	H	H	L	L	H	H	H	H	H	H	H	L	H
H	H	H	L	L	H	H	H	H	H	H	H	H	L
X	X	X	L	L	L	H	H	H	H	H	H	H	H
X	X	X	H	L	L	H	H	H	H	H	H	H	H
X	X	X	L	H	L	H	H	H	H	H	H	H	H
X	X	X	H	H	L	H	H	H	H	H	H	H	H
X	X	X	H	L	H	H	H	H	H	H	H	H	H
X	X	X	L	H	H	H	H	H	H	H	H	H	H
X	X	X	H	H	H	H	H	H	H	H	H	H	H

(Courtesy Intel Corporation)

FUNCTIONAL DESCRIPTION

Decoder

The 8205 contains a one out of eight binary decoder. It accepts a three bit binary code and by gating this input, creates an exclusive output that represents the value of the input code.

For example, if a binary code of 101 was present on the A0, A1 and A2 address input lines, and the device was enabled, an active low signal would appear on the $\overline{O5}$ output line. Note that all of the other output pins are sitting at a logic high, thus the decoded output is said to be exclusive. The decoders outputs will follow the truth table shown below in the same manner for all other input variations.

Enable Gate

When using a decoder it is often necessary to gate the outputs with timing or enabling signals so that the exclusive output of the decoded value is synchronous with the overall system.

The 8205 has a built-in function for such gating. The three enable inputs ($\overline{E1}$, $\overline{E2}$, E3) are ANDed together and create a single enable signal for the decoder. The combination of both active "high" and active "low" device enable inputs provides the designer with a powerfully flexible gating function to help reduce package count in his system.

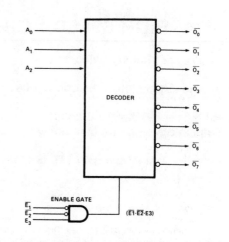

Figure 1. Enable Gate

ADDRESS			ENABLE			OUTPUTS							
A_0	A_1	A_2	E_1	E_2	E_3	0	1	2	3	4	5	6	7
L	L	L	L	L	H	L	H	H	H	H	H	H	H
H	L	L	L	L	H	H	L	H	H	H	H	H	H
L	H	L	L	L	H	H	H	L	H	H	H	H	H
H	H	L	L	L	H	H	H	H	L	H	H	H	H
L	L	H	L	L	H	H	H	H	H	L	H	H	H
H	L	H	L	L	H	H	H	H	H	H	L	H	H
L	H	H	L	L	H	H	H	H	H	H	H	L	H
H	H	H	L	L	H	H	H	H	H	H	H	H	L
X	X	X	L	L	L	H	H	H	H	H	H	H	H
X	X	X	H	L	L	H	H	H	H	H	H	H	H
X	X	X	L	H	L	H	H	H	H	H	H	H	H
X	X	X	H	H	L	H	H	H	H	H	H	H	H
X	X	X	H	L	H	H	H	H	H	H	H	H	H
X	X	X	L	H	H	H	H	H	H	H	H	H	H
X	X	X	H	H	H	H	H	H	H	H	H	H	H

8212
8-BIT INPUT/OUTPUT PORT

- **Fully Parallel 8-Bit Data Register and Buffer**
- **Service Request Flip-Flop for Interrupt Generation**
- **Low Input Load Current — .25mA Max.**
- **Three State Outputs**
- **Outputs Sink 15mA**

- **3.65V Output High Voltage for Direct Interface to 8008, 8080A, or 8085A CPU**
- **Asynchronous Register Clear**
- **Replaces Buffers, Latches and Multiplexers in Microcomputer Systems**
- **Reduces System Package Count**

The 8212 input/output port consists of an 8-bit latch with 3-state output buffers along with control and device selection logic. Also included is a service request flip-flop for the generation and control of interrupts to the microprocessor.

The device is multimode in nature. It can be used to implement latches, gated buffers or multiplexers. Thus, all of the principal peripheral and input/output functions of a microcomputer system can be implemented with this device.

PIN CONFIGURATION

$\overline{DS}_1$	1		24	V_{CC}
MD	2		23	$\overline{INT}$
DI_1	3		22	DI_8
DO_1	4		21	DO_8
DI_2	5		20	DI_7
DO_2	6	8212	19	DO_7
DI_3	7		18	DI_6
DO_3	8		17	DO_6
DI_4	9		16	DI_5
DO_4	10		15	DO_5
STB	11		14	$\overline{CLR}$
GND	12		13	DS_2

PIN NAMES

DI_1-DI_8	DATA IN
DO_1-DO_8	DATA OUT
$\overline{DS}_1$-DS_2	DEVICE SELECT
MD	MODE
STB	STROBE
$\overline{INT}$	INTERRUPT (ACTIVE LOW)
$\overline{CLR}$	CLEAR (ACTIVE LOW)

LOGIC DIAGRAM

(Courtesy Intel Corporation)

FUNCTIONAL DESCRIPTION

Data Latch

The 8 flip-flops that make up the data latch are of a "D" type design. The output (Q) of the flip-flop will follow the data input (D) while the clock input (C) is high. Latching will occur when the clock (C) returns low.

The latched data is cleared by an asynchronous reset input ($\overline{CLR}$). (Note: Clock (C) Overrides Reset ($\overline{CLR}$).)

Output Buffer

The outputs of the data latch (Q) are connected to 3-state, non-inverting output buffers. These buffers have a common control line (EN); this control line either enables the buffer to transmit the data from the outputs of the data latch (Q) or disables the buffer, forcing the output into a high impedance state. (3-state)

The high-impedance state allows the designer to connect the 8212 directly onto the microprocessor bi-directional data bus.

Control Logic

The 8212 has control inputs $\overline{DS1}$, DS2, MD and STB. These inputs are used to control device selection, data latching, output buffer state and service request flip-flop.

DS1, DS2 (Device Select)

These 2 inputs are used for device selection. When $\overline{DS1}$ is low and DS2 is high ($\overline{DS1} \cdot DS2$) the device is selected. In the selected state the output buffer is enabled and the service request flip-flop (SR) is asynchronously set.

MD (Mode)

This input is used to control the state of the output buffer and to determine the source of the clock input (C) to the data latch.

When MD is high (output mode) the output buffers are enabled and the source of clock (C) to the data latch is from the device selection logic ($\overline{DS1} \cdot DS2$).

When MD is low (input mode) the output buffer state is determined by the device selection logic ($\overline{DS1} \cdot DS2$) and the source of clock (C) to the data latch is the STB (Strobe) input.

STB (Strobe)

This input is used as the clock (C) to the data latch for the input mode MD = 0) and to synchronously reset the service request flip-flop (SR).

Note that the SR flip-flop is negative edge triggered.

Service Request Flip-Flop

The (SR) flip-flop is used to generate and control interrupts in microcomputer systems. It is asynchronously set by the $\overline{CLR}$ input (active low). When the (SR) flip-flop is set it is in the non-interrupting state.

The output of the (SR) flip-flop (Q) is connected to an inverting input of a "NOR" gate. The other input to the "NOR" gate is non-inverting and is connected to the device selection logic (DS1 · DS2). The output of the "NOR" gate ($\overline{INT}$) is active low (interrupting state) for connection to active low input priority generating circuits.

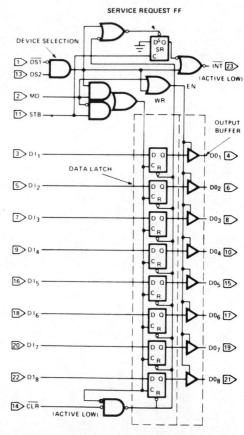

STB	MD	$(DS_1 \cdot DS_2)$	DATA OUT EQUALS
0	0	0	3 STATE
1	0	0	3 STATE
0	1	0	DATA LATCH
1	1	0	DATA LATCH
0	0	1	DATA LATCH
1	0	1	DATA IN
0	1	1	DATA IN
1	1	1	DATA IN

CLR – RESETS DATA LATCH
    SETS SR FLIP FLOP
    (NO EFFECT ON OUTPUT BUFFER)

CLR	$(\overline{DS}_1 \cdot DS_2)$	STB	*SR	INT
0	0	0	1	1
0	1	0	1	0
1	1	⌐	0	0
1	1	0	1	0
1	0	0	1	1
1	1	1	1	0

*INTERNAL SR FLIP FLOP

8282/8283
OCTAL LATCH

- **Fully Parallel 8-Bit Data Register and Buffer**

- **Transparent during Active Strobe**

- **Supports 8080, 8085, 8048, and 8086 Systems**

- **High Output Drive Capability for Driving System Data Bus**

- **3-State Outputs**

- **20-Pin Package with 0.3" Center**

- **No Output Low Noise when Entering or Leaving High Impedance State**

The 8282 and 8283 are 8-bit bipolar latches with 3-state output buffers. They can be used to implement latches, buffers, or multiplexers. The 8283 inverts the input data at its outputs while the 8282 does not. Thus, all of the principal peripheral and input/output functions of a microcomputer system can be implemented with these devices.

PIN CONFIGURATIONS   **LOGIC DIAGRAMS**

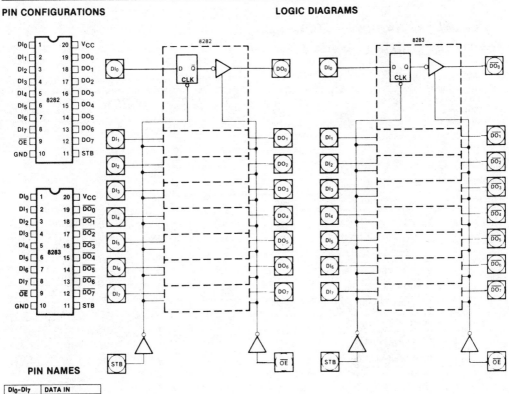

PIN NAMES

DI₀–DI₇	DATA IN
DO₀–DO₇	DATA OUT
OE	OUTPUT ENABLE
STB	STROBE

(Courtesy Intel Corporation)

PIN DEFINITIONS

Pin	Description
STB	STROBE (Input). STB is an input control pulse used to strobe data at the data input pins (A$_0$–A$_7$) into the data latches. This signal is active HIGH to admit input data. The data is latched at the HIGH to LOW transition of STB.
$\overline{OE}$	OUTPUT ENABLE (Input). $\overline{OE}$ is an input control signal which when active LOW enables the contents of the data latches onto the data output pin (B$_0$–B$_7$). OE being inactive HIGH forces the output buffers to their high impedance state.
DI$_0$–DI$_7$	DATA INPUT PINS (Input). Data presented at these pins satisfying setup time requirements when STB is strobed and latched into the data input latches.

DO$_0$–DO$_7$ (8282) $\overline{DO_0}$–$\overline{DO_7}$ (8283) DATA OUTPUT PINS (Output). When $\overline{OE}$ is true, the data in the data latches is presented as inverted (8283) or non-inverted (8282) data onto the data output pins.

OPERATIONAL DESCRIPTION

The 8282 and 8283 octal latches are 8-bit latches with 3-state output buffers. Data having satisfied the setup time requirements is latched into the data latches by strobing the STB line HIGH to LOW. Holding the STB line in its active HIGH state makes the latches appear transparent. Data is presented to the data output pins by activating the $\overline{OE}$ input line. When $\overline{OE}$ is inactive HIGH the output buffers are in their high impedance state. Enabling or disabling the output buffers will not cause negative-going transients to appear on the data output bus.

D.C. AND OPERATING CHARACTERISTICS

ABSOLUTE MAXIMUM RATINGS*

Temperature Under Bias.................0°C to 70°C
Storage Temperature............ –65°C to +150°C
All Output and Supply Voltages........ –0.5V to +7V
All Input Voltages................... –1.0V to +5.5V
Power Dissipation.......................1 Watt

*COMMENT: Stresses above those listed under "Absolute Maximum Ratings" may cause permanent damage to the device. This is a stress rating only and functional operation of the device at these or any other conditions above those indicated in the operational sections of this specification is not implied. Exposure to absolute maximum rating conditions for extended periods may affect device reliability.

D.C. CHARACTERISTICS FOR 8282/8283

Conditions: V$_{CC}$ = 5V ± 5%, T$_A$ = 0°C to 70°C

Symbol	Parameter	Min	Max	Units	Test Conditions
V$_C$	Input Clamp Voltage		–1	V	I$_C$ = –5 mA
I$_{CC}$	Power Supply Current		160	mA	
I$_F$	Forward Input Current		–0.2	mA	V$_F$ = 0.45V
I$_R$	Reverse Input Current		50	μA	V$_R$ = 5.25V
V$_{OL}$	Output Low Voltage		0.50	V	I$_{OL}$ = 32 mA
V$_{OH}$	Output High Voltage	2.4		V	I$_{OH}$ = –5 mA
I$_{OFF}$	Output Off Current		± 50	μA	V$_{OFF}$ = 0.45 to 5.25V
V$_{IL}$	Input Low Voltage		0.8	V	V$_{CC}$ = 5.0V See Note 1
V$_{IH}$	Input High Voltage	2.0		V	V$_{CC}$ = 5.0V See Note 1
C$_{IN}$	Input Capacitance		12	pF	F = 1 MHz V$_{BIAS}$ = 2.5V, V$_{CC}$ = 5V T$_A$ = 25°C

Notes: 1. Output Loading I$_{OL}$ = 32 mA, I$_{OH}$ = –5 mA, C$_L$ = 300 pF

A.C. CHARACTERISTICS FOR 8282/8283

Conditions: $V_{CC} = 5V \pm 5\%$, $T_A = 0°C$ to $70°C$

Loading: Outputs — $I_{OL} = 32$ mA, $I_{OH} = -5$ mA, $C_L = 300$ pF

Symbol	Parameter	Min	Max	Units	Test Conditions
TIVOV	Input to Output Delay —Inverting —Non-Inverting		25 35	ns ns	(See Note 1)
TSHOV	STB to Output Delay —Inverting —Non-Inverting		45 55	ns ns	
TEHOZ	Output Disable Time		25	ns	
TELOV	Output Enable Time	10	50	ns	
TIVSL	Input to STB Setup Time	0		ns	
TSLIX	Input to STB Hold Time	25		ns	
TSHSL	STB High Time	15		ns	

NOTE: 1. See waveforms and test load circuit on following page.

8282/8283 TIMING

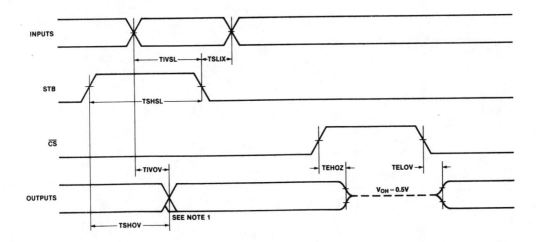

NOTE: 1. 8283 ONLY — OUTPUT MAY BE MOMENTARILY INVALID FOLLOWING THE HIGH GOING STB TRANSITION.
2. ALL TIMING MEASUREMENTS ARE MADE AT 1.5V UNLESS OTHERWISE NOTED

OUTPUT DELAY VS. CAPACITANCE

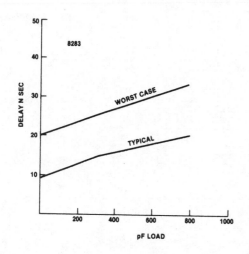
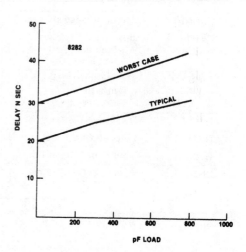

OUTPUT TEST LOAD CIRCUITS

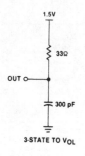

3-STATE TO V$_{OL}$

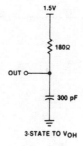

3-STATE TO V$_{OH}$

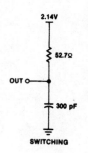

SWITCHING

8286/8287
OCTAL BUS TRANSCEIVER

- **Data Bus Buffer Driver for MCS-86™, MCS-80™, MCS-85™, and MCS-48™ Families**

- **High Output Drive Capability for Driving System Data Bus**

- **Fully Parallel 8-Bit Transceivers**

- **3-State Outputs**

- **20-Pin Package with 0.3" Center**

- **No Output Low Noise when Entering or Leaving High Impedance State**

The 8286 and 8287 are 8-bit bipolar transceivers with 3-state outputs. The 8287 inverts the input data at its outputs while the 8286 does not. Thus, a wide variety of applications for buffering in microcomputer systems can be met.

PIN CONFIGURATIONS

8286

A_0	1	20	V_{CC}
A_1	2	19	B_0
A_2	3	18	B_1
A_3	4	17	B_2
A_4	5	16	B_3
A_5	6	15	B_4
A_6	7	14	B_5
A_7	8	13	B_6
$\overline{OE}$	9	12	B_7
GND	10	11	T

8287

A_0	1	20	V_{CC}
A_1	2	19	$\overline{B_0}$
A_2	3	18	$\overline{B_1}$
A_3	4	17	$\overline{B_2}$
A_4	5	16	$\overline{B_3}$
A_5	6	15	$\overline{B_4}$
A_6	7	14	$\overline{B_5}$
A_7	8	13	$\overline{B_6}$
$\overline{OE}$	9	12	$\overline{B_7}$
GND	10	11	T

PIN NAMES

A_0-A_7	LOCAL BUS DATA
B_0-B_7	SYSTEM BUS DATA
$\overline{OE}$	OUTPUT ENABLE
T	TRANSMIT

LOGIC DIAGRAMS

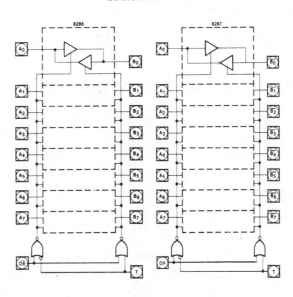

(Courtesy Intel Corporation)

PIN DEFINITIONS

Pin	Description
T	TRANSMIT (Input). T is an input control signal used to control the direction of the transceivers. When HIGH, it configures the transceiver's B_0-B_7 as outputs with A_0-A_7 as inputs. T LOW configures A_0-A_7 as the outputs with B_0-B_7 serving as the inputs.
$\overline{OE}$	OUTPUT ENABLE (Input). $\overline{OE}$ is an input control signal used to enable the appropriate output driver (as selected by T) onto its respective bus. This signal is active LOW.
A_0-A_7	LOCAL BUS DATA PINS (Input/Output). These pins serve to either present data to or accept data from the processor's local bus depending upon the state of the T pin.
B_0-B_7 (8286) $\overline{B_0}$-$\overline{B_7}$ (8287)	SYSTEM BUS DATA PINS (Input/Output). These pins serve to either present data to or accept data from the system bus depending upon the state of the T pin.

OPERATIONAL DESCRIPTION

The 8286 and 8287 transceivers are 8-bit transceivers with high impedance outputs. With T active HIGH and $\overline{OE}$ active LOW, data at the A_0-A_7 pins is driven onto the B_0-B_7 pins. With T inactive LOW and $\overline{OE}$ active LOW, data at the B_0-B_7 pins is driven onto the A_0-A_7 pins. No output low glitching will occur whenever the transceivers are entering or leaving the high impedance state.

D.C. AND OPERATING CHARACTERISTICS
ABSOLUTE MAXIMUM RATINGS*

Temperature Under Bias..................0°C to 70°C
Storage Temperature.............− 65°C to + 150°C
All Output and Supply Voltages........ − 0.5V to + 7V
All Input Voltages..................− 1.0V to + 5.5V
Power Dissipation...........................1 Watt

*COMMENT: Stresses above those listed under "Absolute Maximum Ratings" may cause permanent damage to the device. This is a stress rating only and functional operation of the device at these or any other conditions above those indicated in the operational sections of this specification is not implied. Exposure to absolute maximum rating conditions for extended periods may affect device reliability.

D.C. CHARACTERISTICS FOR 8286/8287

Conditions: V_{CC} = 5V ± 5%, T_A = 0°C to 70°C

Symbol	Parameter	Min	Max	Units	Test Conditions
V_C	Input Clamp Voltage		−1	V	I_C = −5 mA
I_{CC}	Power Supply Current—8287 —8286		130 160	mA mA	
I_F	Forward Input Current		−0.2	mA	V_F = 0.45V
I_R	Reverse Input Current		50	μA	V_R = 5.25V
V_{OL}	Output Low Voltage —B Outputs —A Outputs		0.5 0.5	V V	I_{OL} = 32 mA I_{OL} = 10 mA
V_{OH}	Output High Voltage —B Outputs —A Outputs	2.4 2.4		V V	I_{OH} = −5 mA I_{OH} = −1 mA
I_{OFF} I_{OFF}	Output Off Current Output Off Current		I_F I_R		V_{OFF} = 0.45V V_{OFF} = 5.25V
V_{IL}	Input Low Voltage —A Side —B Side		0.8 0.9	V V	V_{CC} = 5.0V, See Note 1 V_{CC} = 5.0V, See Note 1
V_{IH}	Input High Voltage	2.0		V	V_{CC} = 5.0V, See Note 1
C_{IN}	Input Capacitance		12	pF	F = 1 MHz V_{BIAS} = 2.5V, V_{CC} = 5V T_A = 25°C

Note: 1. B Outputs — I_{OL} = 32 mA, I_{OH} = −5 mA, C_L = 300 pF   A Outputs — I_{OL} = 10 mA, I_{OH} = −1 mA, C_L = 100 pF

A.C. CHARACTERISTICS FOR 8286/8287

Conditions: $V_{CC} = 5V \pm 5\%$, $T_A = 0°C$ to $70°C$

Loading: B Outputs — $I_{OL} = 32$ mA, $I_{OH} = -5$ mA, $C_L = 300$ pF
A Outputs — $I_{OL} = 10$ mA, $I_{OH} = -1$ mA, $C_L = 100$ pF

Symbol	Parameter	Min	Max	Units	Test Conditions
TIVOV	Input to Output Delay Inverting Non-Inverting		25 35	ns ns	(See Note 1)
TEHTV	Transmit/Receive Hold Time	TEHOZ		ns	
TTVEL	Transmit/Receive Setup	30		ns	
TEHOZ	Output Disable Time		25	ns	
TELOV	Output Enable Time	10	50	ns	

Note: 1. See waveforms and test load circuit on following page.

8286/8287 TIMING

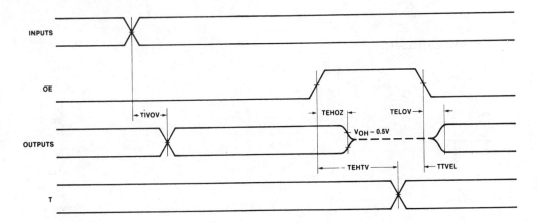

NOTE: 1. ALL TIMING MEASUREMENTS ARE MADE AT 1.5V UNLESS OTHERWISE NOTED.

OUTPUT DELAY VS. CAPACITANCE

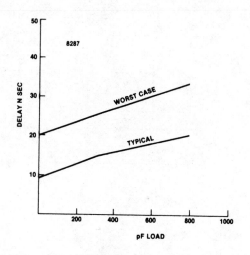

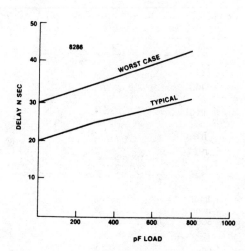

TEST LOAD CIRCUITS

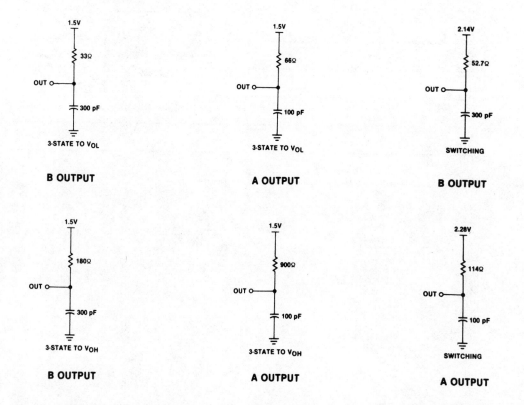

B OUTPUT   A OUTPUT   B OUTPUT

B OUTPUT   A OUTPUT   A OUTPUT

8355/8355-2
16,384-BIT ROM WITH I/O

- **2048 Words × 8 Bits**

- **Single +5V Power Supply**

- **Directly compatible with 8085A and 8088 Microprocessors**

- **2 General Purpose 8-Bit I/O Ports**

- **Each I/O Port Line Individually Programmable as Input or Output**

- **Multiplexed Address and Data Bus**

- **Internal Address Latch**

- **40-Pin DIP**

The Intel® 8355 is a ROM and I/O chip to be used in the 8085A and 8088 microprocessor systems. The ROM portion is organized as 2048 words by 8 bits. It has a maximum acess time of 400 ns to permit use with no wait states in the 8085A CPU.

The I/O portion consists of 2 general purpose I/O ports. Each I/O port has 8 port lines and each I/O port line is individually programmable as input or output.

The 8355-2 has a 300ns access time for compatibility with the 8085A-2 and full speed 5 MHz 8088 microprocessors.

PIN CONFIGURATION

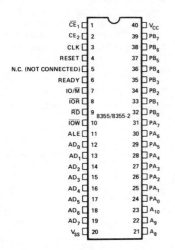

BLOCK DIAGRAM

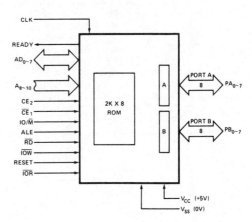

(Courtesy Intel Corporation)

Symbol	Function
ALE (Input)	When ALE (Address Latch Enable is high, AD_{0-7}, IO/$\overline{M}$, A_{8-10}, CE, and $\overline{CE}$ enter address latched. The signals (AD, IO/$\overline{M}$, A_{8-10}, CE, $\overline{CE}$) are latched in at the trailing edge of ALE.
AD_{0-7} (Input)	Bidirectional Address/Data bus. The lower 8-bits of the ROM or I/O address are applied to the bus lines when ALE is high.
	During an I/O cycle, Port A or B are selected based on the latched value of AD_0. If $\overline{RD}$ or $\overline{IOR}$ is low when the latched chip enables are active, the output buffers present data on the bus.
A_{8-10} (Input)	These are the high order bits of the ROM address. They do not affect I/O operations.
$\overline{CE}_1$ CE$_2$ (Input)	Chip Enable Inputs: $\overline{CE}_1$ is active low and CE$_2$ is active high. The 8355 can be accessed only when BOTH Chip Enables are active at the time the ALE signal latches them up. If either Chip Enable input is not active, the AD_{0-7} and READY outputs will be in a high impedance state.
IO/$\overline{M}$ (Input)	If the latched IO/$\overline{M}$ is high when $\overline{RD}$ is low, the output data comes from an I/O port. If it is low the output data comes from the ROM.
$\overline{RD}$ (Input)	If the latched Chip Enables are active when $\overline{RD}$ goes low, the AD_{0-7} output buffers are enabled and output either the selected ROM location or I/O port. When both $\overline{RD}$ and $\overline{IOR}$ are high, the AD_{0-7} output buffers are 3-state.
$\overline{IOW}$ (Input)	If the latched Chip Enables are active, a low on $\overline{IOW}$ causes the output port pointed to by the latched value of AD_0 to be written with the data on AD_{0-7}. The state of IO/$\overline{M}$ is ignored.

Symbol	Function
CLK (Input)	The CLK is used to force the READY into its high impedance state after it has been forced low by $\overline{CE}$ low, CE high and ALE high.
READY (Output)	Ready is a 3-state output controlled by CE$_1$, CE$_2$, ALE and CLK. READY is forced low when the Chip Enables are active during the time ALE is high, and remains low until the rising edge of the next CLK (see Figure 6).
PA_{0-7} (Input/ Output)	These are general purpose I/O pins. Their input/output direction is determined by the contents of Data Direction Register (DDR). Port A is selected for write operations when the Chip Enables are active and $\overline{IOW}$ is low and a 0 was previously latched from AD_0.
	Read operation is selected by either $\overline{IOR}$ low and active Chip Enables and AD_0 low, or IO/$\overline{M}$ high, $\overline{RD}$ low, active chip enables, and AD_0 low.
PB_{0-7} (Input/ Output)	This general purpose I/O port is identical to Port A except that it is selected by a 1 latched from AD_0.
RESET (Input)	An input high on RESET causes all pins in Port A and B to assume input mode.
$\overline{IOR}$ (Input)	When the Chip Enables are active, a low on $\overline{IOR}$ will output the selected I/O port onto the AD bus. $\overline{IOR}$ low performs the same function as the combination IO/$\overline{M}$ high and $\overline{RD}$ low. When $\overline{IOR}$ is not used in a system, $\overline{IOR}$ should be tied to V_{CC} ("1").
V_{CC}	+5 volt supply.
V_{SS}	Ground Reference.

FUNCTIONAL DESCRIPTION

ROM Section

The 8355 contains an 8-bit address latch which allows it to interface directly to MCS-48 and MCS-85 Microcomputers without additional hardware.

The ROM section of the chip is addressed by an 11-bit address and the Chip Enables. The address and levels on the Chip Enable pins are latched into the address latches on the falling edge of ALE. If the latched Chip Enables are active and IO/$\overline{M}$ is low when $\overline{RD}$ goes low, the contents of the ROM location addressed by the latched address are put out through AD_{0-7} output buffers.

I/O Section

The I/O section of the chip is addressed by the latched value of AD_{0-1}. Two 8-bit Data Direction Registers (DDR) in 8355 determine the input/output status of each pin in the corresponding ports. A "0" in a particular bit position of a DDR signifies that the corresponding I/O port bit is in the input mode. A "1" in a particular bit position signifies that the corresponding I/O port bit is in the output mode. In this manner the I/O ports of the 8355 are bit-by-bit programmable as inputs or outputs. The table summarizes port and DDR designation. DDR's cannot be read.

AD_1	AD_0	Selection
0	0	Port A
0	1	Port B
1	0	Port A Data Direction Register (DDR A)
1	1	Port B Data Direction Register (DDR B)

When $\overline{IOW}$ goes low and the Chip Enables are active, the data on the AD_{0-7} is written into I/O port selected by the latched value of AD_{0-1}. During this operation all I/O bits of the selected port are affected, regardless of their I/O mode and the state of IO/$\overline{M}$. The actual output level does not change until $\overline{IOW}$ returns high (glitch free output).

A port can be read out when the latched Chip Enables are active and either $\overline{RD}$ goes low with IO/$\overline{M}$ high, or $\overline{IOR}$ goes low. Both input and output mode bits of a selected port will appear on lines AD_{0-7}.

To clarify the function of the I/O ports and Data Direction Registers, the following diagram shows the configuration of one bit of PORT A and DDR A. The same logic applies to PORT B and DDR B.

Note that hardware RESET or writing a zero to the DDR latch will cause the output latch's output buffer to be disabled, preventing the data in the output latch from being passed through to the pin. This is equivalent to putting the port in the input mode. Note also that the data can be written to the Output Latch even though the Output Buffer has been disabled. This enables a port to be initialized with a value prior to enabling the output.

The diagram also shows that the contents of PORT A and PORT B can be read even when the ports are configured as outputs.

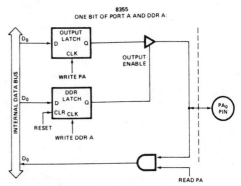

8355
ONE BIT OF PORT A AND DDR A:

WRITE PA = ($\overline{IOW}$=0) • (CHIP ENABLES ACTIVE) • (PORT A ADDRESS SELECTED)
WRITE DDR A = ($\overline{IOW}$=0) • (CHIP ENABLES ACTIVE) • (DDR A ADDRESS SELECTED)
READ PA = {[(IO/$\overline{M}$=1) • ($\overline{RD}$=0)] + ($\overline{IOR}$=0)} • (CHIP ENABLES ACTIVE) • (PORT A ADDRESS SELECTED)

NOTE: WRITE PA IS NOT QUALIFIED BY IO/$\overline{M}$.

System Interface with 8085A and 8088

A system using the 8355 can use either one of the two I/O Interface techniques:

- Standard I/O
- Memory Mapped I/O

If a standard I/O technique is used, the system can use the feature of both CE and $\overline{CE}$. By using a combination of unused address lines A_{11-15} and the Chip Enable inputs, the system can use up to 5 each 8355's without requiring a CE decoder. See Figure 2a and 2b.

If a memory mapped I/O approach is used the 8355 will be selected by the combination of both the Chip Enables and IO/$\overline{M}$ using the AD_{8-15} address lines. See Figure 1.

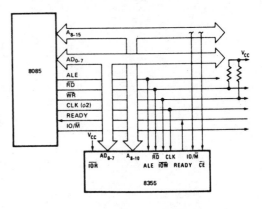

Figure 1. 8355 in 8085A System (Memory-Mapped I/O)

8755A /8755A-2
16,384-BIT EPROM WITH I/O

- **2048 Words × 8 Bits**

- **Single + 5V Power Supply (V$_{CC}$)**

- **Directly Compatible with 8085A and 8088 Microprocessors**

- **U.V. Erasable and Electrically Reprogrammable**

- **Internal Address Latch**

- **2 General Purpose 8-Bit I/O Ports**

- **Each I/O Port Line Individually Programmable as Input or Output**

- **Multiplexed Address and Data Bus**

- **40-Pin DIP**

The Intel® 8755A is an erasable and electrically reprogrammable ROM (EPROM) and I/O chip to be used in the 8085A and 8088 microprocessor systems. The EPROM portion is organized as 2048 words by 8 bits. It has a maximum access time of 450 ns to permit use with no wait states in an 8085A CPU.

The I/O portion consists of 2 general purpose I/O ports. Each I/O port has 8 port lines, and each I/O port line is individually programmable as input or output.

The 8755A-2 is a high speed selected version of the 8755A compatible with the 5 MHz 8085A-2 and the full speed 5 MHz 8088.

PIN CONFIGURATION

BLOCK DIAGRAM

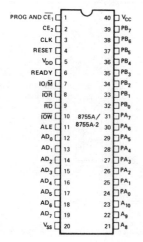

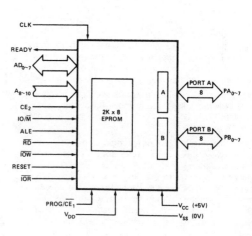

(*Courtesy Intel Corporation*)

8755A FUNCTIONAL PIN DEFINITION

Symbol	Function
ALE (input)	When Address Latch Enable goes high, AD_{0-7}, IO/M, A_{8-10}, CE_2, and $\overline{CE_1}$ enter the address latches. The signals (AD, IO/M, A_{8-10}, CE) are latched in at the trailing edge of ALE.
AD_{0-7} (input/output)	Bidirectional Address/Data bus. The lower 8-bits of the PROM or I/O address are applied to the bus lines when ALE is high. During an I/O cycle, Port A or B are selected based on the latched value of AD_0. If $\overline{RD}$ or $\overline{IOR}$ is low when the latched Chip Enables are active, the output buffers present data on the bus.
A_{8-10} (input)	These are the high order bits of the PROM address. They do not affect I/O operations.
PROG/$\overline{CE_1}$ CE_2 (input)	Chip Enable Inputs: $\overline{CE_1}$ is active low and CE_2 is active high. The 8755A can be accessed only when *BOTH* Chip Enables are active at the time the ALE signal latches them up. If either Chip Enable input is not active, the AD_{0-7} and READY outputs will be in a high impedance state. $\overline{CE_1}$ is also used as a programming pin. (See section on programming.)
IO/$\overline{M}$ (input)	If the latched IO/$\overline{M}$ is high when $\overline{RD}$ is low, the output data comes from an I/O port. If it is low the output data comes from the PROM.
$\overline{RD}$ (input)	If the latched Chip Enables are active when $\overline{RD}$ goes low, the AD_{0-7} output buffers are enabled and output either the selected PROM location or I/O port. When both $\overline{RD}$ and $\overline{IOR}$ are high, the AD_{0-7} output buffers are 3-stated.
$\overline{IOW}$ (input)	If the latched Chip Enables are active, a low on $\overline{IOW}$ causes the output port pointed to by the latched value of AD_0 to be written with the data on AD_{0-7}. The state of IO/$\overline{M}$ is ignored.
CLK (input)	The CLK is used to force the READY into its high impedance state after it has been forced low by $\overline{CE_1}$ low, CE_2 high, and ALE high.

Symbol	Function
READY (output)	READY is a 3-state output controlled by CE_2, $\overline{CE_1}$, ALE and CLK. READY is forced low when the Chip Enables are active during the time ALE is high, and remains low until the rising edge of the next CLK. (See Figure 6.)
PA_{0-7} (input/output)	These are general purpose I/O pins. Their input/output direction is determined by the contents of Data Direction Register (DDR). Port A is selected for write operations when the Chip Enables are active and $\overline{IOW}$ is low and a 0 was previously latched from AD_0, AD_1. Read operation is selected by either $\overline{IOR}$ low and active Chip Enables and AD_0 and AD_1 low, *or* IO/$\overline{M}$ high, $\overline{RD}$ low, active Chip Enables, and AD_0 and AD_1 low.
PB_{0-7} (input/output)	This general purpose I/O port is identical to Port A except that it is selected by a 1 latched from AD_0 and a 0 from AD_1.
RESET (input)	In normal operation, an input high on RESET causes all pins in Ports A and B to assume input mode (clear DDR register).
$\overline{IOR}$ (input)	When the Chip Enables are active, a low on $\overline{IOR}$ will output the selected I/O port onto the AD bus. $\overline{IOR}$ low performs the same function as the combination of IO/$\overline{M}$ high and $\overline{RD}$ low. When $\overline{IOR}$ is not used in a system, $\overline{IOR}$ should be tied to V_{CC} ("1").
V_{CC}	+5 volt supply.
V_{SS}	Ground Reference.
V_{DD}	V_{DD} is a programming voltage, and must be tied to +5V when the 8755A is being read. For programming, a high voltage is supplied with $V_{DD} = 25V$, typical. (See section on programming.)

FUNCTIONAL DESCRIPTION

PROM Section

The 8755A contains an 8-bit address latch which allows it to interface directly to MCS-48 and MCS-85 Microcomputers without additional hardware.

The PROM section of the chip is addressed by the 11-bit address and CE. The address, $\overline{CE}_1$ and CE_2 are latched into the address latches on the falling edge of ALE. If the latched Chip Enables are active and IO/$\overline{M}$ is low when $\overline{RD}$ goes low, the contents of the PROM location addressed by the latched address are put out on the AD_{0-7} lines.

I/O Section

The I/O section of the chip is addressed by the latched value of AD_{0-1}. Two 8-bit Data Direction Registers (DDR) in 8755A determine the input/output status of each pin in the corresponding ports. A "0" in a particular bit position of a DDR signifies that the corresponding I/O port bit is in the input mode. A "1" in a particular bit position signifies that the corresponding I/O port bit is in the output mode. In this manner the I/O ports of the 8755A are bit-by-bit programmable as inputs or outputs. The table summarizes port and DDR designation. DDR's cannot be read.

AD_1	AD_0	Selection
0	0	Port A
0	1	Port B
1	0	Port A Data Direction Register (DDR A)
1	1	Port B Data Direction Register (DDR B)

When $\overline{IOW}$ goes low and the Chip Enables are active, the data on the AD is written into I/O port selected by the latched value of AD_{0-1}. During this operation all I/O bits of the selected port are affected, regardless of their I/O mode and the state of IO/$\overline{M}$. The actual output level does not change until $\overline{IOW}$ returns high. (glitch free output)

A port can be read out when the latched Chip Enables are active and either $\overline{RD}$ goes low with IO/$\overline{M}$ high, or $\overline{IOR}$ goes low. Both input and output mode bits of a selected port will appear on lines AD_{0-7}.

To clarify the function of the I/O Ports and Data Direction Registers, the following diagram shows the configuration of one bit of PORT A and DDR A. The same logic applies to PORT B and DDR B.

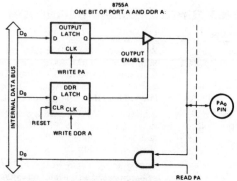

8755A
ONE BIT OF PORT A AND DDR A:

WRITE PA = ($\overline{IOW}$=0) • (CHIP ENABLES ACTIVE) • (PORT A ADDRESS SELECTED)
WRITE DDR A = ($\overline{IOW}$=0) • (CHIP ENABLES ACTIVE) • (DDR A ADDRESS SELECTED)
READ PA = {(IO/$\overline{M}$=1) • ($\overline{RD}$=0)} + ($\overline{IOR}$=0)} • (CHIP ENABLES ACTIVE) • (PORT A ADDRESS SELECTED)

NOTE: WRITE PA IS NOT QUALIFIED BY IO/$\overline{M}$.

Note that hardware RESET or writing a zero to the DDR latch will cause the output latch's output buffer to be disabled, preventing the data in the Output Latch from being passed through to the pin. This is equivalent to putting the port in the input mode. Note also that the data can be written to the Output Latch even though the Output Buffer has been disabled. This enables a port to be initialized with a value prior to enabling the output.

The diagram also shows that the contents of PORT A and PORT B can be read even when the ports are configured as outputs.

TABLE 1. 8755A PROGRAMMING MODULE CROSS REFERENCE

MODULE NAME	USE WITH
UPP 955	UPP(4)
UPP UP2(2)	UPP 855
PROMPT 975	PROMPT 80/85(3)
PROMPT 475	PROMPT 48(1)

NOTES:
1. Described on p. 13-34 of 1978 Data Catalog.
2. Special adaptor socket.
3. Described on p. 13-39 of 1978 Data Catalog.
4. Described on p. 13-71 of 1978 Data Catalog.

ERASURE CHARACTERISTICS

The erasure characteristics of the 8755A are such that erasure begins to occur when exposed to light with wavelengths shorter than approximately 4000 Angstroms (Å). It should be noted that sunlight and certain types of fluorescent lamps have wavelengths in the 3000-4000Å range. Data show that constant exposure to room level fluorescent lighting could erase the typical 8755A in approximately 3 years while it would take approximately 1 week to cause erasure when exposed to direct sunlight. If the 8755A is to be exposed to these types of lighting conditions for extended periods of time, opaque labels are available from Intel which should be placed over the 8755 window to prevent unintentional erasure.

The recommended erasure procedure for the 8755A is exposure to shortwave ultraviolet light which has a wavelength of 2537 Angstroms (Å). The integrated dose (i.e., UV intensity X exposure time) for erasure should be a minimum of 15W-sec/cm². The erasure time with this dosage is approximately 15 to 20 minutes using an ultraviolet lamp with a $12000\mu W/cm^2$ power rating. The 8755A should be placed within one inch from the lamp tubes during erasure. Some lamps have a filter on their tubes and this filter should be removed before erasure.

PROGRAMMING

Initially, and after each erasure, all bits of the EPROM portions of the 8755A are in the "1" state. Information is introduced by selectively programming "0" into the desired bit locations. A programmed "0" can only be changed to a "1" by UV erasure.

The 8755A can be programmed on the Intel® Universal PROM Programmer (UPP), and the PROMPT™ 80/85 and PROMPT-48™ design aids. The appropriate programming modules and adapters for use in programming both 8755A's and 8755's are shown in Table 1.

The program mode itself consists of programming a single address at a time, giving a single 50 msec pulse for every address. Generally, it is desirable to have a verify cycle after a program cycle for the same address as shown in the attached timing diagram. In the verify cycle (i.e., normal memory read cycle) 'V_DD' should be at +5V.

Preliminary timing diagrams and parameter values pertaining to the 8755A programming operation are contained in Figure 7.

SYSTEM APPLICATIONS

System Interface with 8085A and 8088

A system using the 8755A can use either one of the two I/O Interface techniques:

- Standard I/O
- Memory Mapped I/O

If a standard I/O technique is used, the system can use the feature of both CE_3 and $\overline{CE}_1$. By using a combination of unused address lines A_{11-15} and the Chip Enable inputs, the 8085A system can use up to 5 each 8755A's without requiring a CE decoder. See Figure 2a and 2b.

If a memory mapped I/O approach is used the 8755A will be selected by the combination of both the Chip Enables and $IO/\overline{M}$ using the AD_{8-15} address lines. See Figure 1.

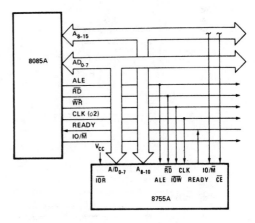

Figure 1. 8755A in 8085A System (Memory-Mapped I/O)

TTL
MSI

TYPES SN54LS373, SN54LS374, SN54S373, SN54S374, SN74LS373, SN74LS374, SN74S373, SN74S374 OCTAL D-TYPE TRANSPARENT LATCHES AND EDGE-TRIGGERED FLIP-FLOPS

BULLETIN NO. DL-S 12350, OCTOBER 1975 – REVISED JUNE 1979

- **Choice of 8 Latches or 8 D-Type Flip-Flops In a Single Package**
- **3-State Bus-Driving Outputs**
- **Full Parallel-Access for Loading**
- **Buffered Control Inputs**
- **Clock/Enable Input Has Hysteresis to Improve Noise Rejection**
- **P-N-P Inputs Reduce D-C Loading on Data Lines ('S373 and 'S374)**
- **SN54LS363 and SN74LS364 Are Similar But Have Higher V_{OH} For MOS Interface**

SN54LS373, SN54S373 . . . J PACKAGE
SN74LS373, SN74S373 . . . J OR N PACKAGE
(TOP VIEW)

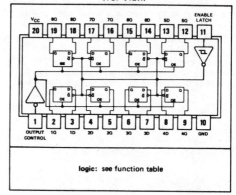

logic: see function table

'LS373, 'S373 FUNCTION TABLE

OUTPUT ENABLE	ENABLE LATCH	D	OUTPUT
L	H	H	H
L	H	L	L
L	L	X	Q_0
H	X	X	Z

SN54LS374, SN54S374 . . . J PACKAGE
SN74LS374, SN74S374 . . . J OR N PACKAGE
(TOP VIEW)

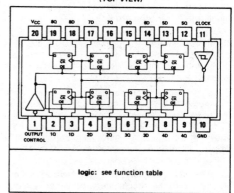

logic: see function table

'LS374, 'S374 FUNCTION TABLE

OUTPUT ENABLE	CLOCK	D	OUTPUT
L	↑	H	H
L	↑	L	L
L	L	X	Q_0
H	X	X	Z

See explanation of function tables on page 1-13.

description

These 8-bit registers feature totem-pole three-state outputs designed specifically for driving highly-capacitive or relatively low-impedance loads. The high-impedance third state and increased high-logic-level drive provide these registers with the capability of being connected directly to and driving the bus lines in a bus-organized system without need for interface or pull-up components. They are particularly attractive for implementing buffer registers, I/O ports, bidirectional bus drivers, and working registers.

The eight latches of the 'LS373 and 'S373 are transparent D-type latches meaning that while the enable (G) is high the Q outputs will follow the data (D) inputs. When the enable is taken low the output will be latched at the level of the data that was set up.

TEXAS INSTRUMENTS
INCORPORATED

TYPES SN54LS373, SN54LS374, SN54S373, SN54S374, SN74LS373, SN74LS374, SN74S373, SN74S374
OCTAL D-TYPE TRANSPARENT LATCHES AND
EDGE-TRIGGERED FLIP-FLOPS

description (continued)

The eight flip-flops of the 'LS374 and 'S374 are edge-triggered D-type flip-flops. On the positive transition of the clock, the Q outputs will be set to the logic states that were setup at the D inputs.

Schmitt-trigger buffered inputs at the enable/clock lines simplify system design as ac and dc noise rejection is improved by typically 400 mV due to the input hysteresis. A buffered output control input can be used to place the eight outputs in either a normal logic state (high or low logic levels) or a high-impedance state. In the high-impedance state the outputs neither load nor drive the bus lines significantly.

The output control does not affect the internal operation of the latches or flip-flops. That is, the old data can be retained or new data can be entered even while the outputs are off.

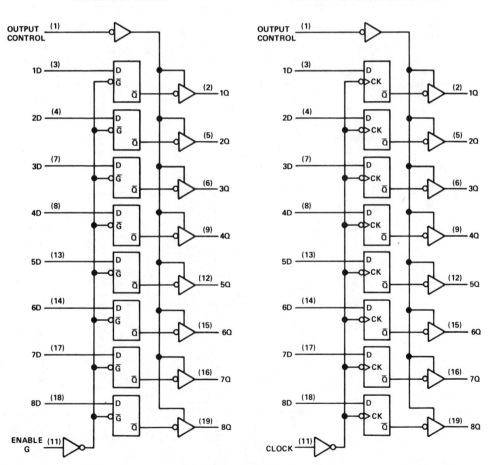

'LS373, 'S373
TRANSPARENT LATCHES

'LS374, 'S374
POSITIVE-EDGE-TRIGGERED FLIP-FLOPS

TEXAS INSTRUMENTS
INCORPORATED

**Versatile
Interface Adapter
(VIA)**

**SY6522
SY6522A**

**MICROPROCESSOR
PRODUCTS**

Preliminary

- Two 8-Bit Bidirectional I/O Ports
- Two 16-Bit Programmable Timer/Counters
- Serial Data Port
- Single +5V Power Supply
- TTL Compatible
- CMOS Compatible Peripheral Control Lines

- Expanded "Handshake" Capability Allows Positive Control of Data Transfers Between Processor and Peripheral Devices
- Latched Output and Input Registers
- 1 MHz and 2 MHz Operation

The SY6522 Versatile Interface Adapter (VIA) is a very flexible I/O control device. In addition, this device contains a pair of very powerful 16-bit interval timers, a serial-to-parallel/parallel-to-serial shift register and input data latching on the peripheral ports. Expanded handshaking capability allows control of bi-directional data transfers between VIA's in multiple processor systems.

Control of peripheral devices is handled primarily through two 8-bit bi-directional ports. Each line can

be programmed as either an input or an output. Several peripheral I/O lines can be controlled directly from the interval timers for generating programmable frequency square waves or for counting externally generated pulses. To facilitate control of the many powerful features of this chip, an interrupt flag register, an interrupt enable register and a pair of function control registers are provided.

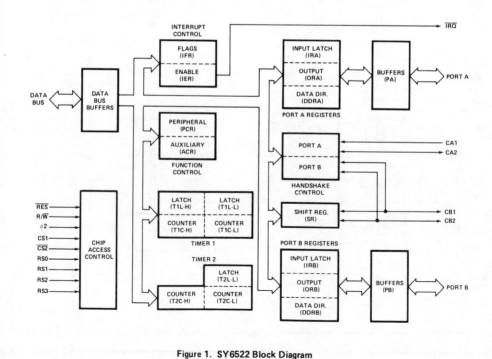

Figure 1. SY6522 Block Diagram

ABSOLUTE MAXIMUM RATINGS

Rating	Symbol	Value	Unit
Supply Voltage	V_{CC}	-0.3 to +7.0	V
Input Voltage	V_{IN}	-0.3 to +7.0	V
Operating Temperature Range	T_A	0 to +70	°C
Storage Temperature Range	T_{stg}	-55 to +150	°C

This device contains circuitry to protect the inputs against damage due to high static voltages. However, it is advised that normal precautions be taken to avoid application of any voltage higher than maximum rated voltages.

ELECTRICAL CHARACTERISTICS (V_{CC} = 5.0V ± 5%, T_A = 0-70°C unless otherwise noted)

Symbol	Characteristic	Min.	Max.	Unit
V_{IH}	Input High Voltage (all except $\phi2$)	2.4	V_{CC}	V
V_{CH}	Clock High Voltage	2.4	V_{CC}	V
V_{IL}	Input Low Voltage	-0.3	0.4	V
I_{IN}	Input Leakage Current — V_{IN} = 0 to 5 Vdc R/$\overline{W}$, $\overline{RES}$, RS0, RS1, RS2, RS3, CS1, $\overline{CS2}$, CA1, $\Phi2$	—	±2.5	μA
I_{TSI}	Off-state Input Current — V_{IN} = .4 to 2.4V V_{CC} = Max, D0 to D7	—	±10	μA
I_{IH}	Input High Current — V_{IH} = 2.4V PA0-PA7, CA2, PB0-PB7, CB1, CB2	-100	—	μA
I_{IL}	Input Low Current — V_{IL} = 0.4 Vdc PA0-PA7, CA2, PB0-PB7, CB1, CB2	—	-1.6	mA
V_{OH}	Output High Voltage V_{CC} = min, I_{load} = -100 μAdc PA0-PA7, CA2, PB0-PB7, CB1, CB2	2.4	—	V
V_{OL}	Output Low Voltage V_{CC} = min, I_{load} = 1.6 mAdc	—	0.4	V
I_{OH}	Output High Current (Sourcing) V_{OH} = 2.4V V_{OH} = 1.5V (PB0-PB7)	-100 -1.0	— —	μA mA
I_{OL}	Output Low Current (Sinking) V_{OL} = 0.4 Vdc	1.6	—	mA
I_{OFF}	Output Leakage Current (Off state) $\overline{IRQ}$	—	10	μA
C_{IN}	Input Capacitance — T_A = 25°C, f = 1 MHz (R/$\overline{W}$, $\overline{RES}$, RS0, RS1, RS2, RS3, CS1, $\overline{CS2}$, D0-D7, PA0-PA7, CA1, CA2, PB0-PB7)	—	7.0	pF
	(CB1, CB2)	—	10	pF
	($\Phi2$ Input)	—	20	pF
C_{OUT}	Output Capacitance — T_A = 25°C, f = 1 MHz	—	10	pF
P_D	Power Dissipation	—	700	mW

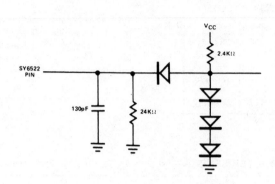

Figure 2. Test Load (for all Dynamic Parameters)

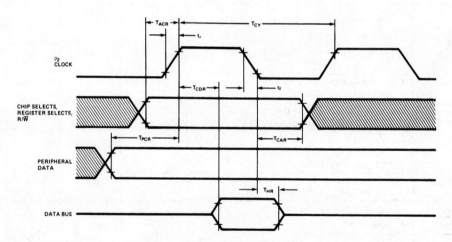

Figure 3. Read Timing Characteristics

READ TIMING CHARACTERISTICS (FIGURE 3)

Symbol	Parameter	SY6522		SY6522A		Unit
		Min.	Max.	Min.	Max.	
T_{CY}	Cycle Time	1	50	0.5	50	μs
T_{ACR}	Address Set-Up Time	180	—	90	—	ns
T_{CAR}	Address Hold Time	0	—	0	—	ns
T_{PCR}	Peripheral Data Set-Up Time	300	—	300	—	ns
T_{CDR}	Data Bus Delay Time	—	395	—	200	ns
T_{HR}	Data Bus Hold Time	10	—	10	—	ns

NOTE: tr, tf = 10 to 30ns.

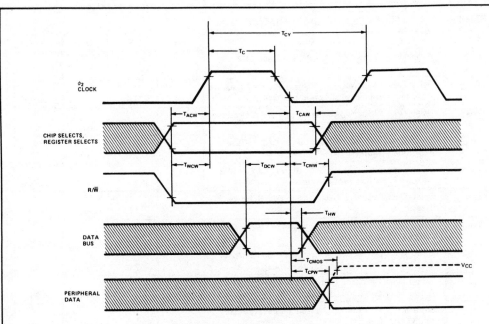

Figure 4. Write Timing Characteristics

WRITE TIMING CHARACTERISTICS (FIGURE 4)

Symbol	Parameter	SY6522		SY6522A		Unit
		Min.	Max.	Min.	Max.	
T_{CY}	Cycle Time	1	50	0.50	50	μs
T_C	$\phi 2$ Pulse Width	0.47	25	0.25	25	μs
T_{ACW}	Address Set-Up Time	180	—	90	—	ns
T_{CAW}	Address Hold Time	0	—	0	—	ns
T_{WCW}	R/$\overline{W}$ Set-Up Time	180	—	90	—	ns
T_{CWW}	R/$\overline{W}$ Hold Time	0	—	0	—	ns
T_{DCW}	Data Bus Set-Up Time	300	—	150	—	ns
T_{HW}	Data Bus Hold Time	10	—	10	—	ns
T_{CPW}	Peripheral Data Delay Time	—	1.0	—	1.0	μs
T_{CMOS}	Peripheral Data Delay Time to CMOS Levels	—	2.0	—	2.0	μs

NOTE: tr, tf = 10 to 30ns.

PERIPHERAL INTERFACE CHARACTERISTICS

Symbol	Characteristic	Min.	Max.	Unit	Figure
t_r, t_f	Rise and Fall Time for CA1, CB1, CA2, and CB2 Input Signals	–	1.0	μs	–
T_{CA2}	Delay Time, Clock Negative Transition to CA2 Negative Transition (read handshake or pulse mode)	–	1.0	μs	5a, 5b
T_{RS1}	Delay Time, Clock Negative Transition to CA2 Positive Transition (pulse mode)	–	1.0	μs	5a
T_{RS2}	Delay Time, CA1 Active Transition to CA2 Positive Transition (handshake mode)	–	2.0	μs	5b
T_{WHS}	Delay Time, Clock Positive Transition to CA2 or CB2 Negative Transition (write handshake)	–	1.0	μs	5c, 5d
T_{DS}	Delay Time, Peripheral Data Valid to CB2 Negative Transition	0	1.5	μs	5c, 5d
T_{RS3}	Delay Time, Clock Positive Transition to CA2 or CB2 Positive Transition (pulse mode)	–	1.0	μs	5c
T_{RS4}	Delay Time, CA1 or CB1 Active Transition to CA2 or CB2 Positive Transition (handshake mode)	–	2.0	μs	5d
T_{IL}	Set-up Time, Peripheral Data Valid to CA1 or CB1 Active Transition (input latching)	300	–	ns	5e
T_{SR1}	Shift-Out Delay Time — Time from ϕ_2 Falling Edge to CB2 Data Out	–	300	ns	5f
T_{SR2}	Shift-In Setup Time — Time from CB2 Data In to ϕ_2 Rising Edge	300	–	ns	5g
T_{IPW}	Pulse Width — PB6 Input Pulse	2	–	μs	5i
T_{ICW}	Pulse Width — CB1 Input Clock	2	–	μs	5h
I_{IPS}	Pulse Spacing — PB6 Input Pulse	2	–	μs	5i
I_{ICS}	Pulse Spacing — CB1 Input Pulse	2	–	μs	5h

Peripheral Interface Adapter (PIA)

SY6520
SY6520A

MICROPROCESSOR PRODUCTS

- Direct Replacement for MC6820
- Single +5V Power Supply
- Two 8-bit Bi-directional I/O Ports with Individual Data Direction Control
- CMOS–Compatible Peripheral Control Lines

- Automatic "Handshake" Control of Data Transfers
- Programmable Interrupt Capability
- Automatic Initialization on Power Up
- 1 and 2 MHz Versions

The SY6520 Peripheral Interface Adapter (PIA) is designed to provide a broad range of peripheral control to microcomputer systems. Control of peripheral devices is accomplished through two 8-bit bi-directional I/O ports. Each I/O line may be programmed to be either an input or an output. In addition, four peripheral control lines are provided to perform "handshaking" during data transfers.

BASIC SY6520 INTERFACE DIAGRAM

PIN ASSIGNMENTS

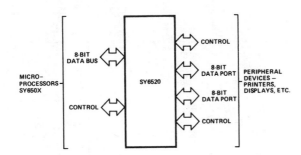

V_{SS}	1		40	CA_1
PA_0	2		39	CA_2
PA_1	3		38	$\overline{IRQA}$
PA_2	4		37	$\overline{IRQB}$
PA_3	5		36	RS_0
PA_4	6		35	RS_1
PA_5	7		34	$\overline{RES}$
PA_6	8		33	D_0
PA_7	9		32	D_1
PB_0	10	SY6520	31	D_2
PB_1	11		30	D_3
PB_2	12		29	D_4
PB_3	13		28	D_5
PB_4	14		27	D_6
PB_5	15		26	D_7
PB_6	16		25	$\phi2$
PB_7	17		24	CS_1
CB_1	18		23	$\overline{CS_2}$
CB_2	19		22	CS_0
V_{CC}	20		21	$R/\overline{W}$

ORDERING INFORMATION

Part Number	Package	Speed
SYC6520	Ceramic	1 MHz
SYP6520	Plastic	1 MHz
SYC6520A	Ceramic	2 MHz
SYP6520A	Plastic	2 MHz

MAXIMUM RATINGS

Rating	Symbol	Value	Unit
Supply Voltage	V_{CC}	-0.3 to +7.0	V
Input Voltage	V_{in}	-0.3 to +7.0	V
Operating Temperature Range	T_A	0 to +70	°C
Storage Temperature Range	T_{stg}	-55 to +150	°C

This device contains circuitry to protect the inputs against damage due to high static voltages, however, it is advised that normal precautions be taken to avoid application of any voltage higher than maximum rated voltages to this circuit.

D.C. CHARACTERISTICS (V_{CC} = 5.0V ± 5%, V_{SS} = 0, T_A = 0–70°C unless otherwise noted)

Characteristic	Symbol	Min.	Max.	Unit
Input High Voltage	V_{IH}	+2.0	V_{CC}	V
Input Low Voltage	V_{IL}	-0.3	+0.8	V
Input Leakage Current V_{IN} = 0 to 5.0 V R/$\overline{W}$, $\overline{Reset}$, RS_0, RS_1, CS_0, CS_1, $\overline{CS_2}$, CA_1, CB_1, φ_2	I_{IN}	—	±2.5	μA
Three-State (Off State Input Current) (V_{IN} = 0.4 to 2.4 V, V_{CC} = max), D_0-D_7, PB_0-PB_7, CB_2	I_{TSI}	—	±10	μA
Input High Current (V_{IH} = 2.4 V), PA_0-PA_7, CA_2	I_{IH}	100	—	μA
Input Low Current (V_{IL} = 0.4 V), PA_0-PA_7, CA_2	I_{IL}	—	-1.6	mA
Output High Voltage (V_{CC} = min, I_{OH} = -100 μA)	V_{OH}	2.4	—	V
Output Low Voltage (V_{CC} = min, I_{OL} - 1.6mA)	V_{OL}	—	+0.4	V
Output High Current (Sourcing) (V_{OH} = 2.4 V) (V_O = 1.5 V, the current for driving other than TTL, e.g., Darlington Base), PB_0-PB_7, CB_2	I_{OH}	-100 -1.0	— -10	μA mA
Output Low Current (Sinking) (V_{OL} = 0.4 V)	I_{OL}	1.6	—	mA
Output Leakage Current (Off-State), $\overline{IRQA}$, $\overline{IRQB}$	I_{OFF}	—	10	μA
Power Dissipation	P_D	—	500	mW
Input Capacitance (V_{IN} – 0, T_A = 25°C, f = 1.0 MHz) D_0-D_7, PA_0-PA_7, PB_0-PB_7, CA_2, CB_2 R/W, $\overline{Reset}$, RS_0, RS_1, CS_0, CS_1, CS_2, CA_1, CB_1, ϕ_2	C_{IN}	— — —	10 7.0 20	pF
Output Capacitance (V_{IN} – 0, T_A = 25°C, f = 1.0 MHz)	C_{OUT}	—	10	pF

Note: Negative sign indicates outward current flow, positive indicates inward flow.

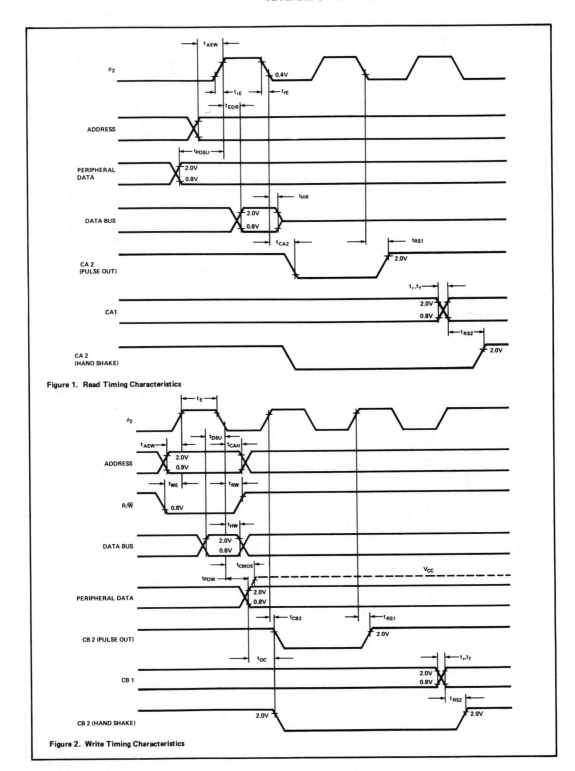

Figure 1. Read Timing Characteristics

Figure 2. Write Timing Characteristics

SWITCHING CHARACTERISTICS (V_{CC} = +5V ± 5%, T_A = 0–70°C, unless otherwise noted)

Characteristic	Symbol	SY6520 (1 MHz) Min.	SY6520 (1 MHz) Max.	SY6520A (2 MHz) Min.	SY6520A (2 MHz) Max.	Unit
READ TIMING CHARACTERISTICS						
Delay Time, Address Valid to ϕ_2 Positive Transition	T_{AEW}	180	—	90	—	ns
Delay Time, ϕ_2 Positive Transition to Data Valid on Bus	T_{EDR}	—	395	—	190	ns
Peripheral Data Setup Time	T_{PDSU}	300	—	150	—	ns
Data Bus Hold Time	T_{HR}	10	—	10	—	ns
Delay Time, ϕ_2 Negative Transition to CA2 Negative Transition	T_{CA2}	—	1.0	—	0.5	μs
Delay Time, ϕ_2 Negative Transition to CA2 Positive Transition	T_{RS1}	—	1.0	—	0.5	μs
Rise and Fall Time for CA1 and CA2 Input Signals	t_r, t_f	—	1.0	—	0.5	μs
Delay Time from CA1 Active Transition to CA2 Positive Transition	T_{RS2}	—	2.0	—	1.0	μs
Rise and Fall Time for ϕ_2 Input	t_{rE}, t_{fE}	—	25	—	25	ns
WRITE TIMING CHARACTERISTICS						
ϕ_2 Pulse Width	T_E	0.470	25	0.235	25	μs
Delay Time, Address Valid to ϕ_2 Positive Transition	T_{AEW}	180	—	90	—	ns
Delay Time, Data Valid to ϕ_2 Negative Transition	T_{DSU}	300	—	150	—	ns
Delay Time, Read/Write Negative Transition to ϕ_2 Positive Transition	T_{WE}	130	—	65	—	ns
Data Bus Hold Time	T_{HW}	10	—	10	—	ns
Delay Time, ϕ_2 Negative Transition to Peripheral Data Valid	T_{PDW}	—	1.0	—	0.5	μs
Delay Time, ϕ_2 Negative Transition to Peripheral Data Valid CMOS (V_{CC} – 30%) PA0–PA7, CA2	T_{CMOS}	—	2.0	—	1.0	μs
Delay Time, ϕ_2 Positive Transition to CB2 Negative Transition	T_{CB2}	—	1.0	—	0.5	μs
Delay Time, Peripheral Data Valid to CB2 Negative Transition	T_{DC}	0	1.5	0	0.75	μs
Delay Time, ϕ_2 Positive Transition CB2 Positive Transition	T_{RS1}	—	1.0	—	0.5	μs
Rise and Fall Time for CB1 and CB2 Input Signals	t_r, t_f	—	1.0	—	0.5	μs
Delay Time, CB1 Active Transition to CB2 Positive Transition	T_{RS2}	—	2.0	—	1.0	μs
Delay Time, ϕ_2 Negative Transition to Read/Write Positive Transition	T_{RW}	50	—	25	—	ns

TEST LOAD

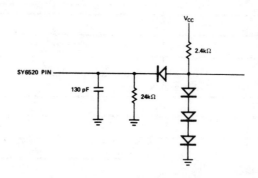

INTERFACE SIGNAL DESCRIPTION

$\overline{RES}$ (Reset)

This signal is used to initialize the PIA. A low signal on the $\overline{RES}$ input causes all internal registers to be cleared.

ϕ_2 (Input Clock)

This input is the system ϕ_2 clock and is used to trigger all data transfers between the microprocessor and the PIA.

R/$\overline{W}$ (Read/Write)

This signal is generated by the microprocessor and is used to control the direction of data transfers. A high on the R/$\overline{W}$ signal permits the processor to read data supplied by the PIA; a low on the R/$\overline{W}$ signal permits the processor to Write into the PIA.

$\overline{IRQA}$, $\overline{IRQB}$ (Interrupt Requests)

$\overline{IRQA}$ and $\overline{IRQB}$ are interrupt lines generated by the PIA for ports A and B respectively. These signals are active low signals and have open-drain outputs, thus allowing multiple IRQ signals from multiple PIA's to be wire-ORed together before connecting to the processor IRQ signal input.

D_0–D_7 (Data Bus)

These eight data bus lines are used to transfer data information between the processor and the PIA. These signals are bi-directional and are normally high-impedance except when selected for a read operation.

CS1, CS2, $\overline{CS3}$ (Chip Selects)

The PIA is selected when CS1 and CS2 are high and $\overline{CS3}$ is low. These three chip select lines are normally connected to the processor address lines either directly or through external decoder circuits.

RS0, RS1 (Register Selects)

These two signals are used to select the various registers inside the PIA.

INTERNAL ARCHITECTURE

The SY6520 is organized into two independent sections referred to as the "A Side" and the "B Side." Each section consists of a Control Register (CRA, CRB), Data Direction Register (DDRA, DDRB), Output Register (ORA, ORB), Interrupt Status Control and the buffers necessary to drive the Peripheral Interface buses. Figure 3 is a block diagram of the SY6520.

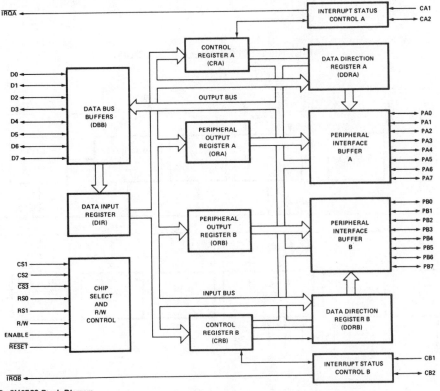

Figure 3. SY6520 Block Diagram

Memory, I/O, Timer Array

Synertek
INCORPORATED

SY6530

MICROPROCESSOR PRODUCTS

- 8 bit bi-directional Data Bus for direct communication with the microprocessor
- 1024 x 8 ROM
- 64 x 8 static RAM
- Two 8 bit bi-directional data ports for interface to peripherals
- Two programmable I/O Peripheral Data Direction Registers

- Programmable Interval Timer
- Programmable Interval Timer Interrupt
- TTL & CMOS compatible peripheral lines
- Peripheral pins with Direct Transistor Drive Capability
- High Impedence Three-State Data Pins
- Allows up to 7K contiguous bytes of ROM with no external decoding

The SY6530 is designed to operate in conjunction with the SY6500 microprocessor Family. It is comprised of a mask programmable 1024 x 8 ROM, a 64 x 8 static RAM, two software controlled 8 bit bi-directional data ports allowing direct interfacing between the microprocessor unit and peripheral devices, and a software programmable interval timer with interrupt, capable of timing in various intervals from 1 to 262,144 clock periods.

FIGURE 1. SY6530 BLOCK DIAGRAM

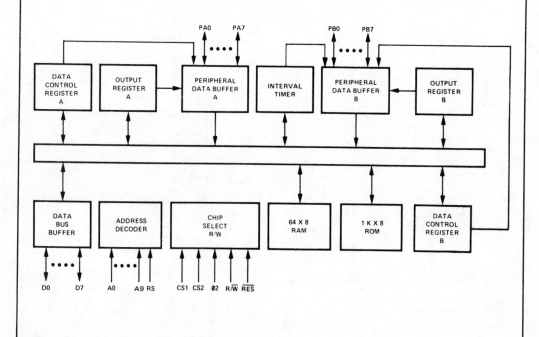

ABSOLUTE MAXIMUM RATINGS

Supply Voltage (V_{CC}) .... $-.3$ to $+7.0$V
Input/Output Voltage (V_{IN}) .... $-.3$ to $+7.0$V
Operating Temperature (T_{OP}) .... 0 to 70°C
Storage Temperature Range (T_{STG})..... -55 to $+150$°C

COMMENT

Stresses above those listed under "Absolute Maximum Ratings" may cause permanent damage to the device. This is a stress rating only and functional operation of the device at these or any other conditions above those indicated in the operational sections of this specification is not implied.

ELECTRICAL CHARACTERISTICS (V_{CC} = 5.0V ±5%, V_{SS} = 0V, T_A = 0°C to 70°C)

	Symbol	Min.	Typ.	Max.	Unit
Input High Voltage	V_{IH}	2.4		V_{CC}	V
Input Low Voltage	V_{IL}	-0.3		0.4	V
Input Leakage Current; V_{IN} = V_{SS} +5V A0-A9, RS, R/W̄, R̄ĒS̄, Ø2, PB6*, PB5*	I_{IN}		1.0	2.5	μA
Input Leakage Current for High Impedence State (Three State); V_{IN} = .4V to 2.4V; D0-D7	I_{TSI}		±1.0	±10.0	μA
Input High Current; V_{IN} = 2.4V PA0-PA7, PB0-PB7	I_{IH}	$-100.$	$-300.$		μA
Low Input Current; V_{IN} = .4V PA0-PA7, PB0-PB7	I_{IL}		-1.0	-1.6	mA
Output High Voltage V_{CC} = MIN, $I_{LOAD} \leqslant -100$μA (PA0-PA7, PB0-PB7, D0-D7) $I_{LOAD} \leqslant -3$mA (PA0, PB0)	V_{OH}	2.4 1.5			V
Output Low Voltage V_{CC} = MIN, $I_{LOAD} \leqslant 1.6$mA	V_{OL}			0.4	V
Output High Current (Sourcing); $V_{OH} \geqslant 2.4$V (PA0-PA7, PB0-PB7, D0-D7) $\geqslant 1.5$V Available for other than TTL (Darlingtons) (PA0, PB0)	I_{OH}	-100 -3.0	-1000 -5.0		μA mA
Output Low Current (Sinking); $V_{OL} \leqslant .4$V	I_{OL}	1.6			mA
Clock Input Capacitance	C_{CLK}			30	pF
Input Capacitance	C_{IN}			10	pF
Output Capacitance	C_{OUT}			10	pF
Power Dissipation	P_D		500	700	mW

*When Programmed as address pins   All values are D.C. readings

WRITE TIMING CHARACTERISTICS

Characteristic	Symbol	Min.	Typ.	Max.	Unit
Clock Period	T_{CYC}	1		10	μs
Rise & Fall Times	T_R, T_F			25	ns
Clock Pulse Width	T_C	470			ns
R/W̄ valid before positive transition of clock	T_{WCW}	180			ns
Address valid before positive transition of clock	T_{ACW}	180			ns
Data bus valid before negative transition of clock	T_{DCW}	300			ns
Data Bus Hold Time	T_{HW}	10			ns
Peripheral data valid after negative transition of clock	T_{CPW}			1	μs
Peripheral data valid after negative transition of clock driving CMOS (Level = V_{CC} -30%)	T_{CMOS}			2	μs
R/W̄ hold time after negative clock transition	T_{CWW}	0			ns
Address hold time	T_{CAH}	0			ns

READ TIMIMG CHARACTERISTICS

Characteristic	Symbol	Min.	Typ.	Max.	Unit
R/$\overline{W}$ valid before positive transition of clock	T$_{WCR}$	180			ns
Address valid before positive transition of clock	T$_{ACR}$	180			ns
Peripheral data valid before positive transition of clock	T$_{PCR}$	300			ns
Data bus valid after positive transition of clock	T$_{CDR}$			395	ns
Data Bus Hold Time	T$_{HR}$	10			ns
$\overline{IRQ}$ (Interval Timer Interrupt) valid before positive transition of clock	T$_{IC}$	200			ns
R/$\overline{W}$ hold time after negative clock transition	T$_{CWR}$	0			ns
Address hold time	T$_{CAH}$	0			ns

Loading = 30 pF + 1 TTL load for PAØ-PA7, PBØ-PB7
       = 130 pF + 1 TTL load for DØ-D7

INTERFACE SIGNAL DESCRIPTION

Reset ($\overline{RES}$)

During system initialization a low ($\leqslant$0.4V) on the $\overline{RES}$ input will cause a zeroing of all four I/O registers. This in turn will cause all I/O buses to act as inputs thus protecting external components from possible damage and erroneous data while the system is being configured under software control. The Data Bus Buffers are put into an OFF-STATE during reset. Interrupt capability is disabled with the $\overline{RES}$ signal. The $\overline{RES}$ signal must be held low for at least one clock period when reset is required.

Input Clock (ϕ_2)

The input clock is a system Phase Two clock which can be either a low level clock (V$_{IL}$ < 0.4, V$_{IH}$ > 2.4 or high level clock V$_{IL}$ < 0.2, V$_{IH}$ = V$_{CC}$ $^{+.3}_{-.2}$).

Read/Write (R/$\overline{W}$)

The R/$\overline{W}$ is supplied by the microprocessor array and is used to control the transfer of data to and from the microprocessor array and the SY6530. A high on the R/$\overline{W}$ pin allows the processor to read (with proper addressing) the data supplied by the SY6530. A low on the R/$\overline{W}$ pin allows a write (with proper addressing) to the SY6530.

Interrupt Request ($\overline{IRQ}$)

The $\overline{IRQ}$ pin is an interrupt pin from the interval timer. This same pin, if not used as an interrupt, can be used as a peripheral I/O pin (PB7). When used as an interrupt, the pin should be set up as an input by the data direction register. The pin will be normally high with a low indicating an interrupt from the SY6530. An external pull-up device is not required; however, if collector-OR'd with other devices, the internal pullup may be omitted with a mask option.

Data Bus (D0-D7)

The SY6530 has eight bi-directional data pins (D0-D7). These pins connect to the system's data lines and allow transfer of data to and from the microprocessor array. The output buffers remain in the off state except when a Read operation occurs.

Peripheral Data Ports (PA0–PA7, PB0–PB7)

The SY6530 has 16 pins available for peripheral I/O operations. Each pin is individually software programmable to act as either an input or an output. The 16 pins are divided into 2 8-bit ports, PA0-PA7 and PB0-PB7. PB5, PB6 and PB7 also have other uses which are discussed in later sections. The pins are set up as an input by writing a "0" into the corresponding bit of the data direction register. A "1" into the data direction register will cause its corresponding bit to be an output. When in the input mode, the peripheral output buffers are in the "1" state and a pull-up device acts as less than one TTL load to the peripheral data lines. On a Read operation, the microprocessor unit reads the peripheral pin. When the peripheral device gets information from the SY6530 it receives data stored in the data register. The microproccessor will read correct information if the peripheral lines are greater than 2.0 volts for a "1" and less than 0.8 volts for a "0" as the peripheral pins are all TTL compatible. Pins PA0 and PB0 are also capable of sourcing 3 ma at 1.5V, thus making them capable of direct transistor drive.

Address Lines (A0-A9)

There are 10 address pins. In addition to these 10, there is the ROM SELECT (RS) pin. The above pins, A0-A9 and ROM SELECT, are always used as addressing pins. There are 2 additional pins which are mask programmable and can be used either individually or together as CHIP SELECTS. They are pins PB5 and PB6. When used as peripheral data pins they cannot be used as chip selects.

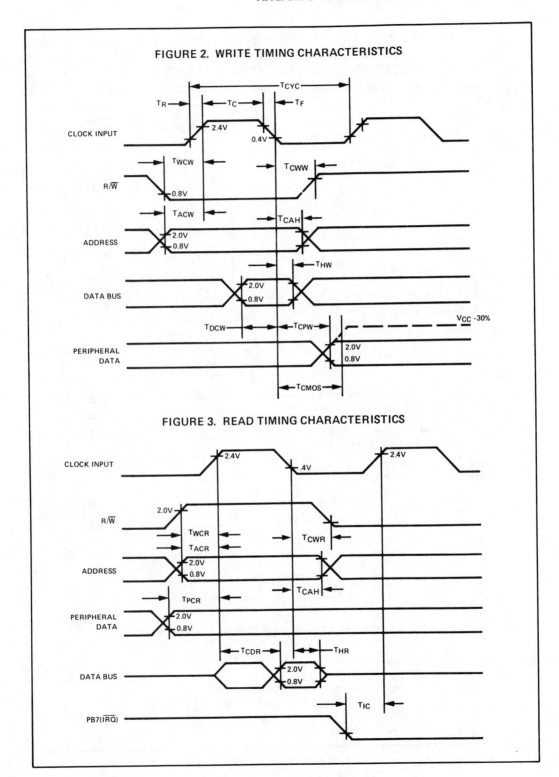

FIGURE 2. WRITE TIMING CHARACTERISTICS

FIGURE 3. READ TIMING CHARACTERISTICS

TYPES SN54157, SN54L157, SN54LS157, SN54LS158, SN54S157, SN54S158, SN74157, SN74L157, SN74LS157, SN74LS158, SN74S157, SN74S158
QUADRUPLE 2-LINE-TO-1-LINE DATA SELECTORS/MULTIPLEXERS

BULLETIN NO. DL-S 7711847, MARCH 1974—REVISED AUGUST 1977

features

- **Buffered Inputs and Outputs**
- **Three Speed/Power Ranges Available**

TYPES	TYPICAL AVERAGE PROPAGATION TIME	TYPICAL POWER DISSIPATION
'157	9 ns	150 mW
'L157	18 ns	75 mW
'LS157	9 ns	49 mW
'S157	5 ns	250 mW
'LS158	7 ns	24 mW
'S158	4 ns	195 mW

applications

- **Expand Any Data Input Point**
- **Multiplex Dual Data Buses**
- **Generate Four Functions of Two Variables (One Variable Is Common)**
- **Source Programmable Counters**

description

These monolithic data selectors/multiplexers contain inverters and drivers to supply full on-chip data selection to the four output gates. A separate strobe input is provided. A 4-bit word is selected from one of two sources and is routed to the four outputs. The '157, 'L157, 'LS157, and 'S157 present true data whereas the 'LS158 and 'S158 present inverted data to minimize propagation delay time.

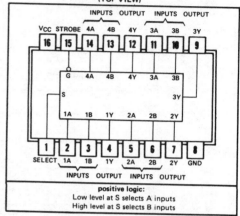

SN54157, SN54LS157, SN54S157 . . . J OR W PACKAGE
SN54L157 . . . J PACKAGE
SN74157, SN74L157, SN74LS157, SN74S157 . . . J OR N PACKAGE
(TOP VIEW)

positive logic:
Low level at S selects A inputs
High level at S selects B inputs

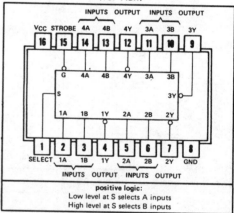

SN54LS158, SN54S158 . . . J OR W PACKAGE
SN74LS158, SN74S158 . . . J OR N PACKAGE
(TOP VIEW)

positive logic:
Low level at S selects A inputs
High level at S selects B inputs

FUNCTION TABLE

INPUTS				OUTPUT Y	
STROBE	SELECT	A	B	'157, 'L157, 'LS157, 'S157	'LS158 'S158
H	X	X	X	L	H
L	L	L	X	L	H
L	L	H	X	H	L
L	H	X	L	L	H
L	H	X	H	H	L

H = high level, L = low level, X = irrelevant

absolute maximum ratings over operating free-air temperature range (unless otherwise noted)

Supply voltage, V_{CC} (see Note 1)	. . . .	7 V
Input voltage: '157, 'L157, 'S158	. . . .	5.5 V
'LS157, 'LS158	. . . .	7 V
Operating free-air temperature range: SN54', SN54L', SN54LS', SN54S' Circuits	. . . .	−55°C to 125°C
SN74', SN74L', SN74LS', SN74S' Circuits	. . . .	0°C to 70°C
Storage temperature range	. . . .	−65°C to 150°C

NOTE 1: Voltage values are with respect to network ground terminal.

TEXAS INSTRUMENTS
INCORPORATED

TYPES SN54157, SN54L157, SN74157, SN74L157, QUADRUPLE 2-LINE-TO-1-LINE DATA SELECTORS/MULTIPLEXERS

functional block diagram

'157, 'L157

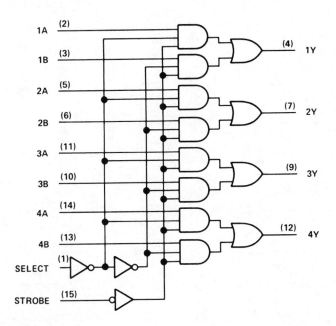

schematics of inputs and outputs

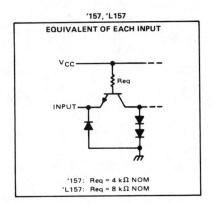

'157, 'L157

EQUIVALENT OF EACH INPUT

'157: Req = 4 kΩ NOM
'L157: Req = 8 kΩ NOM

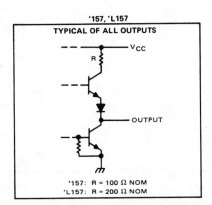

'157, 'L157

TYPICAL OF ALL OUTPUTS

'157: R = 100 Ω NOM
'L157: R = 200 Ω NOM

TEXAS INSTRUMENTS
INCORPORATED

TYPES SN54LS157, SN54LS158, SN54S157, SN54S158, SN74LS157, SN74LS158, SN74S157, SN74S158
QUADRUPLE 2-LINE-TO-1-LINE DATA SELECTORS/MULTIPLEXERS

functional block diagrams

schematics of inputs and outputs

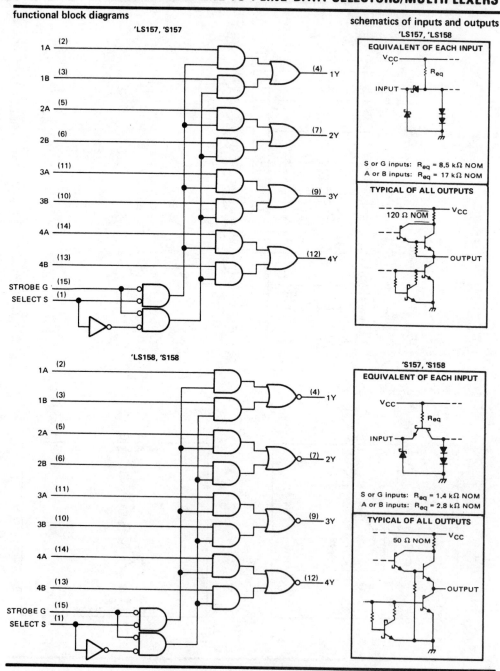

TEXAS INSTRUMENTS
INCORPORATED

TYPES SN54157, SN74157
QUADRUPLE 2-LINE-TO-1-LINE DATA SELECTORS/MULTIPLEXERS

recommended operating conditions

	SN54157 MIN	SN54157 NOM	SN54157 MAX	SN74157 MIN	SN74157 NOM	SN74157 MAX	UNIT
Supply voltage, V_{CC}	4.5	5	5.5	4.75	5	5.25	V
High-level output current, I_{OH}			−800			−800	μA
Low-level output current, I_{OL}			16			16	mA
Operating free-air temperature, T_A	−55		125	0		70	°C

electrical characteristics over recommended operating free-air temperature range (unless otherwise noted)

PARAMETER	TEST CONDITIONS†	SN54157 MIN	SN54157 TYP‡	SN54157 MAX	SN74157 MIN	SN74157 TYP‡	SN74157 MAX	UNIT
V_{IH} High-level input voltage		2			2			V
V_{IL} Low-level input voltage				0.8			0.8	V
V_{IK} Input clamp voltage	V_{CC} = MIN, I_I = −12 mA			−1.5			−1.5	V
V_{OH} High-level output voltage	V_{CC} = MIN, V_{IH} = 2 V, V_{IL} = 0.8 V, I_{OH} = −800 μA	2.4	3.4		2.4	3.4		V
V_{OL} Low-level output voltage	V_{CC} = MIN, V_{IH} = 2 V, V_{IL} = 0.8 V, I_{OL} = 16 mA		0.2	0.4		0.2	0.4	V
I_I Input current at maximum input voltage	V_{CC} = MAX, V_I = 5.5 V			1			1	mA
I_{IH} High-level input current	V_{CC} = MAX, V_I = 2.4 V			40			40	μA
I_{IL} Low-level input current	V_{CC} = MAX, V_I = 0.4 V			−1.6			−1.6	mA
I_{OS} Short-circuit output current §	V_{CC} = MAX	−20		−55	−18		−55	mA
I_{CC} Supply current	V_{CC} = MAX, See Note 2		30	48		30	48	mA

†For conditions shown as MIN or MAX, use the appropriate value specified under recommended operating conditions.
‡All typical values are at V_{CC} = 5 V, T_A = 25°C.
§Not more than one output should be shorted at a time and duration of short-circuit should not exceed one second.
NOTE 2: I_{CC} is measured with 4.5 V applied to all inputs and all outputs open.

switching characteristics, V_{CC} = 5 V, T_A = 25°C

PARAMETER¶	FROM (INPUT)	TEST CONDITIONS	MIN	TYP	MAX	UNIT
t_{PLH}	Data	C_L = 15 pF, R_L = 400 Ω, See Note 3		9	14	ns
t_{PHL}	Data		9	14	ns
t_{PLH}	Strobe		13	20	ns
t_{PHL}	Strobe		14	21	ns
t_{PLH}	Select		15	23	ns
t_{PHL}	Select		18	27	ns

¶t_{PLH} ≡ propagation delay time, low-to-high-level output
t_{PHL} ≡ propagation delay time, high-to-low-level output
NOTE 3: Load circuit and voltage waveforms are shown on page 3-10.

TTL
MSI

TYPES SN54LS348, SN74LS348 (TIM9908)
8-LINE-TO-3-LINE PRIORITY ENCODERS WITH 3-STATE OUTPUTS

BULLETIN NO. DL-S 7712469, OCTOBER 1976—REVISED AUGUST 1977

- **3-State Outputs Drive Bus Lines Directly**
- **Encodes 8 Data Lines to 3-Line Binary (Octal)**
- **Applications Include:**
  N-Bit Encoding
  Code Converters and Generators
- **Typical Data Delay . . . 15 ns**
- **Typical Power Dissipation . . . 60 mW**

description

These TTL encoders feature priority decoding of the inputs to ensure that only the highest-order data line is encoded. The 'LS348 circuits encode eight data lines to three-line (4-2-1) binary (octal). Cascading circuitry (enable input EI and enable output EO) has been provided to allow octal expansion. Outputs A0, A1, and A2 are implemented in three-state logic for easy expansion up to 64 lines without the need for external circuitry. See Typical Application Data.

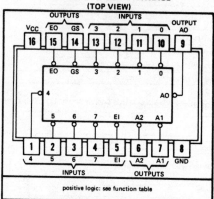

SN54LS348 . . . J OR W PACKAGE
SN74LS348 . . . J OR N PACKAGE
(TOP VIEW)

positive logic: see function table

functional block diagram

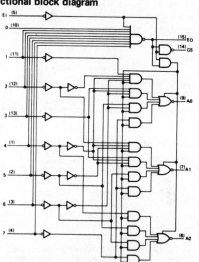

FUNCTION TABLE

INPUTS									OUTPUTS				
EI	0	1	2	3	4	5	6	7	A2	A1	A0	GS	EO
H	X	X	X	X	X	X	X	X	Z	Z	Z	H	H
L	H	H	H	H	H	H	H	H	Z	Z	Z	H	L
L	X	X	X	X	X	X	X	L	L	L	L	L	H
L	X	X	X	X	X	X	L	H	L	L	H	L	H
L	X	X	X	X	X	L	H	H	L	H	L	L	H
L	X	X	X	X	L	H	H	H	L	H	H	L	H
L	X	X	X	L	H	H	H	H	H	L	L	L	H
L	X	X	L	H	H	H	H	H	H	L	H	L	H
L	X	L	H	H	H	H	H	H	H	H	L	L	H
L	L	H	H	H	H	H	H	H	H	H	H	L	H

H = high logic level, L = low logic level, X = irrelevant
Z = high-impedance state

schematic of inputs and outputs

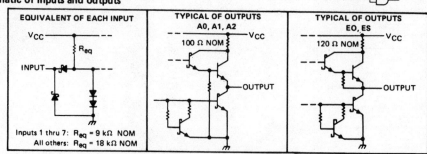

EQUIVALENT OF EACH INPUT	TYPICAL OF OUTPUTS A0, A1, A2	TYPICAL OF OUTPUTS EO, ES

Inputs 1 thru 7: R_{eq} = 9 kΩ NOM
All others: R_{eq} = 18 kΩ NOM

TEXAS INSTRUMENTS
INCORPORATED

TYPES SN54LS348, SN74LS348 (TIM9908)
8-LINE-TO-3-LINE PRIORITY ENCODERS WITH 3-STATE OUTPUTS

REVISED AUGUST 1977

absolute maximum ratings over operating free-air temperature range (unless otherwise noted)

Supply voltage, V_{CC} (see Note 1) . . . . 7 V
Input voltage . . . . 7 V
Operating free-air temperature range: SN54LS348 . . . . −55°C to 125°C
　　　　　　　　　　　　　　　　　SN74LS348 . . . . 0°C to 70°C
Storage temperature range . . . . −65°C to 150°C

NOTE 1: Voltage values are with respect to network ground terminal.

recommended operating conditions

		SN54LS348			SN74LS348			UNIT
		MIN	NOM	MAX	MIN	NOM	MAX	
Supply voltage, V_{CC}		4.5	5	5.5	4.75	5	5.25	V
High-level output current, I_{OH}	A0, A1, A2			−1			−2.6	mA
	EO, GS			−400			−400	μA
Low-level output current, I_{OL}	A0, A1, A2			12			24	mA
	EO, GS			4			8	mA
Operating free-air temperature, T_A		−55		125	0		70	°C

electrical characteristics over recommended operating free-air temperature range (unless otherwise noted)

PARAMETER		TEST CONDITIONS†		SN54LS348			SN74LS348			UNIT
				MIN	TYP‡	MAX	MIN	TYP‡	MAX	
V_{IH}	High-level input voltage			2			2			V
V_{IL}	Low-level input voltage					0.7			0.8	V
V_{IK}	Input clamp voltage	V_{CC} = MIN,	I_I = −18 mA			−1.5			−1.5	V
V_{OH} High-level output voltage	A0, A1, A2	V_{CC} = MIN,	I_{OH} = −1 mA	2.4	3.1					V
		V_{IH} = 2 V,	I_{OH} = −2.6 mA				2.4	3.1		
	EO, GS	V_{IL} = V_{IL}max	I_{OH} = −400 μA	2.5	3.4		2.7	3.4		
V_{OL} Low-level Output voltage	A0, A1, A2	V_{CC} = MIN,	I_{OL} = 12 mA		0.25	0.4		0.25	0.4	V
		V_{IH} = 2 V,	I_{OL} = 24 mA					0.35	0.5	
	EO, GS	V_{IL} = V_{IL}max	I_{OL} = 4 mA		0.25	0.4		0.25	0.4	
			I_{OL} = 8 mA					0.35	0.5	
I_{OZ}	Off-State (high-impedance state) output current	A0, A1, A2	V_{CC} = MAX, V_{IH} = 2 V	V_O = 2.7 V			20			20	μA
				V_O = 0.4 V			−20			−20	
I_I	Input current at maximum input voltage	Inputs 1 thru 7	V_{CC} = MAX,	V_I = 7 V			0.2			0.2	mA
		All other inputs					0.1			0.1	
I_{IH}	High-level input current	Inputs 1 thru 7	V_{CC} = MAX,	V_I = 2.7 V			40			40	μA
		All other inputs					20			20	
I_{IL}	Low-level input current	Inputs 1 thru 7	V_{CC} = MAX,	V_I = 0.4 V			−0.8			−0.8	mA
		All other inputs					−0.4			−0.4	
I_{OS}	Short-circuit output current§	Outputs A0, A1, A2	V_{CC} = MAX		−30		−130	−30		−130	mA
		Outputs EO, GS			−20		−100	−20		−100	
I_{CC}	Supply current	V_{CC} = MAX, See Note 2	Condition 1		13	25		13	25	mA
			Condition 2		12	23		12	23	

NOTE 2: I_{CC} (condition 1) is measured with inputs 7 and EI grounded, other inputs and outputs open. I_{CC} (condition 2) is measured with all inputs and outputs open.
†For conditions shown as MIN or MAX, use the appropriate value specified under recommended operating conditions.
‡All typical values are at V_{CC} = 5 V, T_A = 25°C.
§Not more than one output should be shorted at a time.

TEXAS INSTRUMENTS
INCORPORATED

TYPES SN54LS348, SN74LS348 (TIM9908)
8-LINE-TO-3-LINE PRIORITY ENCODERS WITH 3-STATE OUTPUTS

REVISED JANUARY 1981

switching characteristics, V_{CC} = 5 V, T_A = 25°C

PARAMETER¶	FROM (INPUT)	TO (OUTPUT)	WAVEFORM	TEST CONDITIONS	MIN	TYP	MAX	UNIT
t_{PLH}	1 thru 7	A0, A1, or A2	In-phase output	C_L = 45 pF, R_L = 667 Ω, See Note 3		11	17	ns
t_{PHL}						20	30	
t_{PLH}	1 thru 7	A0, A1, or A2	Out-of-phase output			23	35	ns
t_{PHL}						23	35	
t_{PZH}	EI	A0, A1, or A2				25	39	ns
t_{PZL}						24	41	
t_{PLH}	0 thru 7	EO	Out-of-phase output	C_L = 15 pF, R_L = 2 kΩ, See Note 3		11	18	ns
t_{PHL}						26	40	
t_{PLH}	0 thru 7	GS	In-phase output			38	55	ns
t_{PHL}						9	21	
t_{PLH}	EI	GS	In-phase output			11	17	ns
t_{PHL}						14	36	
t_{PLH}	EI	EO	In-phase output			17	21	ns
t_{PHL}						25	40	
t_{PHZ}	EI	A0, A1, or A2		C_L = 5 pF, R_L = 667 Ω		18	27	ns
t_{PLZ}						23	35	

¶ t_{PLH} = propagation delay time, low-to-high-level output
t_{PHL} = propagation delay time, high-to-low-level output
t_{PZH} = output enable time to high level
t_{PZL} = output enable time to low level
t_{PHZ} = output disable time from high level
t_{PLZ} = output disable time from low level
NOTE 3: Load circuits and waveforms are shown on page 3-11.

TYPICAL APPLICATION DATA

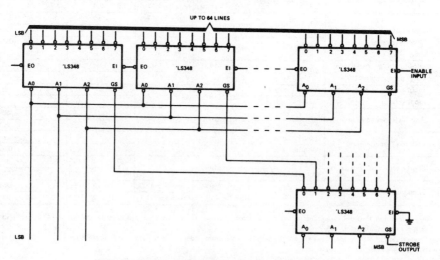

FIGURE 1—PRIORITY ENCODER WITH UP TO 64 INPUTS.

TEXAS INSTRUMENTS
INCORPORATED

Index